PERSPECTIVES ON SOCIETY

PERSPECTIVES ON SOCIETY

An introductory reader in Sociology

Edited by Roland Meighan, Ian Shelton and Tony Marks

Thomas Nelson in association with ATSS

Thomas Nelson and Sons Ltd
Nelson House   Mayfield Road
Walton-on-Thames   Surrey KT12 5PL
P.O. Box 18123   Nairobi   Kenya
Watson Estate   Block A   13 Floor   Watson Road   Causeway Bay   Hong Kong
116-D JTC Factory Building   Lorong 3   Geylang Square   Singapore 14

Thomas Nelson Australia Pty Ltd
19–39 Jeffcott Street   West Melbourne   Victoria 3003

Thomas Nelson and Sons (Canada) Ltd
81 Curlew Drive   Don Mills   Ontario

Thomas Nelson (Nigeria) Ltd
8 Ilupeju Bypass   PMB 21303   Ikeja   Lagos

© R. Meighan, I. Shelton and T. Marks 1979

First published 1979
Reprinted 1979 (twice), 1980

ISBN 0 17 448101 2
NCN 2948 26 3

Printed and bound in Great Britain at
The Camelot Press Ltd, Southampton

CONTENTS

Acknowledgements

The General Editors and publishers acknowledge with gratitude the articles written especially for this book by:

Linda Birbeck, Len Law, R. J. Anderson, Kevin J. Cowen, Stan Meredith, Janice Myerson, Roger Gomm, F. W. Reeves, Sydney Peiris, David Coleman, Janet Harris and Scarlet Friedman, David Neal, M. Chevannes and F. W. Reeves, Helen Reynolds, L. E. Stephenson, Dennis J. O'Keeffe, David Lyne and Christopher Cook.

Acknowledgements are due to the following for permission to reproduce published articles in an abridged or amended form:

Roland Meighan and the Editor of *Educational Review* for 'The Pupils' Point of View' (*Educational Review*, vol. 27, no. 1 (1974)).

Douglas Gibson, Robin Jackson and the Editor of *Educational Review* for 'Some Sociological Perspectives on Mental Retardation' (*Educational Review*, vol. 27, no. 1 (1974)).

Philip Abrams, the Editor of *New Society* and Penguin Books Ltd for 'Age, Generation and Demography' (first published in *New Society*, 1971, and republished in P. Barker (ed.), *A Sociological Portrait* (Penguin Books, 1972).

P. J. Foster and Aldine Publishing Company for 'The Vocational School Fallacy in Development Planning' (from *Education and Economic Development*, C. A. Anderson and M. S. Bowman (eds), Aldine Publishing Co., 1966).

Pauline Marks and Penguin Books Ltd for 'Femininity in the Classroom: An Account of Changing Attitudes' (from *The Rights and Wrongs of Women*, J. Mitchell and A. Oakley (eds), Penguin Books, 1976).

Basil Bernstein and Routledge and Kegan Paul for 'Sociology and the Sociology of Education: A Brief Account' (from *Approaches to Sociology*, J. Rex, Routledge and Kegan Paul, 1974).

Peter Laslett and the Editor of *New Society* for 'In an Ageing World' (first published in *New Society*, 1977).

Anne Howlett, John Ashley and the editor of *New Society* for 'Selective Care' (first published in *New Society*, 1972).

GENERAL INTRODUCTION

Sociology has grown very rapidly in the period following the Second World War, in many countries including the United Kingdom. This has been at the tertiary and the secondary levels of education. In particular, since the mid 1960's there has been a rapid growth of candidates sitting the G.C.E. examinations, especially of the Associated Examining Board. More recently a second generation of G.C.E. examinations have been sponsored by the Cambridge University, Joint Matriculation and London University Examining Boards.[1] All this has taken place at a time when debates about the nature and purpose of sociology have raged as fiercely as at any time in its short history.

The dominant sociological style in Britain when G.C.E. examinations in the subject were being pioneered was of social policy oriented empiricism, frequently couched within a functionalist framework that was implicit or 'taken for granted' more often than explicated. Early syllabuses, examination papers, and recommended booklets re-inforce this impression. The view taken by the authors and editors of this book contrasts with this perspective. Whilst there is no general agreement amongst us about many of the fundamental controversies in sociology, we are concerned to promote alternative theoretical approaches. The diversity of approaches characteristic of higher education should, we feel, be made available elsewhere in the education system.

Our own account is clearly unbalanced, largely ignoring as it does the structural functionalist perspective. We do so because it is easily available elsewhere in the literature. This volume should, therefore, be seen as complementary to several of the existing textbooks. We also believe that sociology is about understanding human societies. The ethnocentricity of much of the reported research and thinking in sociology is something we have also tried to redress.

As teachers and examiners of G.C.E. sociology ourselves we have been aware for a long time that students experience the greatest difficulty in attempting to master the varieties of theory and method in sociology. The tentative nature of our knowledge and the epistemological debate surrounding it has, no doubt, confused many. Compared to many other subjects sociology has much internal disagreement. This may not be entirely fair – sociologists are, perhaps, more honest than some other academics in this respect. Nevertheless, it is clearly a major problem. In part one of this book we have tried to make available this debate,

---

[1] An exposition and criticism of these are available in *Sociology – the choice at 'A' level* edited by G. Whitty and D. Gleeson (Nafferton Books 1976).

especially the less well-aired parts of it, in a form suitable for 'A' level sociology students.

Part two of the book is designed to incorporate unfashionable views of areas routinely treated by one or several, but certainly not all, of the competing paradigms within sociology. We have also, in part three, attempted to introduce to 'A' level students material which has been largely neglected, and which we have reason to believe may become examined, at this level. This is mostly well worked material in the tertiary sector which, for a variety of institutional and other reasons, has yet to percolate down the hierarchy.

Our book is not coherent in the sense that we have a uniform view of the world which we wish to present. We do, however, remain excited by sociology both as it is and as it might become and hope that some of that excitement transfers to the reader.

PART ONE: THE NATURE OF SOCIOLOGICAL UNDERSTANDING

I DESCRIBING AND EXPLAINING

Introduction

In this first section we are interested in how sociologists attempt to make sense of the social world around them. We are all aware of living with, and amongst, other people; we all talk about 'society' in a matter-of-fact way. The task of the sociologist is to describe and analyse the nature of these social groupings and relationships, and to try to explain how and why society is ordered and maintained.

The difficulty is that different sociologists produce very different descriptions and explanations. Within sociology, there is no single set of descriptions and explanations which can be learned; instead, there are varieties of sociology, and often these varieties make sense only when seen alongside each other. There are often major disagreements within the discipline (even to the extent that some sociologists feel a greater affinity with some kinds of psychologists and anthropologists rather than with other sociologists).

In setting out to describe, analyse and explain the social world around them, sociologists make certain *assumptions*. This means that certain notions or ideas are presumed to be 'given' or 'true', and are thus unquestioned. These assumptions relate to the relationship between the individual and society. For example, there are some sociologists who see society as a very strong force acting upon, and constraining, individuals. The papers by Linda Birbeck and Len Law examine society as an external force: both identify the constraint which society imposes upon the individual to whom, in turn, society is seen as an *objective reality*. This simply means that society is perceived as an object or entity which is outside, over and above, the individual. We all probably feel that society is 'bigger than all of us' at some time or other.

Yet even this view of society is interpreted differently by different sociologists. Linda Birbeck discusses a perspective in sociology which assumes that the basis of an orderly, organised society is *shared, agreed values*, that is, deep-rooted notions which are held dear and seen as worthwhile. For example, in our society notions of 'property-ownership' and 'justice' are highly valued. This perspective relates to a *consensus* model of society because of the assumed consensus or agreement on such basic values. Those sociologists who, implicitly or explicitly, adopt this view are frequently also called *structural-functionalists* because of their analysis of the organisation of society. They see society as a structure or framework of parts which are closely linked together. Each of the parts –

called *institutions* – can be identified in terms of its usefulness in keeping society going. Using the term which sociologists use, each part of society, for example a public ceremony such as a marriage, fulfils a *function* for the whole society. Social institutions, then, can be analysed in terms of their consequences for the maintenance of society, and for fulfilling the preconditions or *prerequisites* for society's survival.

Len Law proposes a different view of the structure of society: he does not contest the idea that society constrains individuals and exercises coercive power over them, but he argues that not all groups within society are equally served by existing social arrangements. Society, then, is less characterised by agreed values than by *conflicts of interest* between social groups. Some groups will be trying to preserve their advantageous position regarding both commodities and various forms of power, whilst other groups will be trying to establish an alternative order in which advantages are re-distributed. The structure of society is most appropriately seen as being founded upon *relationships of super- and subordination*. Whilst the various parts of society are still seen as closely linked together, some are seen as having greater importance and influence, and as being in a dominant position with regard to other parts. For example, the economic system is often seen as having that kind of dominance because the satisfaction of basic needs and wants is assumed to be of prior importance. Consequently, it is often argued that individuals in positions of economic advantage are likely to have power in other situations too. In this approach, which we call *conflict-structuralism*, it is still possible to look at the usefulness of parts of society in helping to keep society going, but it is argued that the structural arrangements made will favour some interest groups rather than others.

In reading Len Law's paper you will note that he strongly argues that conflict-structuralism avoids the inherent conservative bias of structural-functionalism. The latter, he suggests, comes about because functionalists seek to show how all parts of society, such as the unequal distribution of power and advantage, help to maintain society: the perspective of functionalism could easily be used by those in positions of power to help maintain those positions. You now have the difficult task of assessing whether functionalism is, or could be, used in this way, and whether this affects its usefulness as an intellectual tool for studying society. In addition, you have the equally difficult task of trying to sort out whether conflict-structuralism as a perspective can also be used by other groups in society for their purposes.

This is no easy exercise upon which to embark, and you might reasonably neglect it for the time being, simply trying to master the ways in which the two perspectives describe, analyse and explain the basic nature of society. Later papers by Roger Gomm and Frank Reeves have been written to help you undertake the exercise more thoroughly, for they show how the work of sociologists, and the analyses they produce, are very much bound up in the society in which they operate.

The first two papers by Linda Birbeck and Len Law are concerned with what have been called the 'prison walls' of society, that is, with the extent to which individuals are held in check by the overriding internal organisation of society. There are some sociologists, however, who assume to a far greater extent that individuals *create* 'society' by their everyday social actions. Social order is an *active* accomplishment of social actors. Rules governing our behaviour, for example, are not externally imposed by an all-powerful, coercive society; rather are they constructed and sustained when individuals interact with each other. The paper by Bob Anderson examines in detail how society is built up through interaction; he assumes that the social world is a meaningful world. The problem of this 'interpretivist' or 'interpretative' sociology is how to describe and analyse the ways in which actors make sense of, and give meaning to, social phenomena. To complicate the problem, however, there are quite differing ways of analysing meaningful social action. Bob Anderson outlines two such ways: *symbolic interactionism* and *ethnomethodology*. Symbolic interactionism offers descriptions of how social identities are built up in face-to-face interaction, and how actors develop and employ strategies and tactics for dealing with other actors in specific social situations. Meaning is often negotiated between actors rather than being imposed upon them.

Just as structuralist sociologists do not explain how they recognise 'social institutions' or 'power relationships', however, so symbolic inter-actionists do not explain how they recognise 'social identities' or 'negotiations'. Although sociologists may list criteria against which to measure the 'real' social world, ultimately, like all members of society, they rely upon their common-sense understanding of the world to recognise and then analyse the phenomena in which they are interested. The problem of recognition is not seen as a problem; 'everyone knows' what the relevant phenomena look like. For the ethnomethodologist (of whom there is no single version) common-sense understandings are the very basis of social order; rather than assuming them, ethnomethodology seeks to study common-sense understandings as 'methods' for accomplishing social order. Social actors can thus be seen as 'practical methodologists', accomplishing social order in the most routine everyday interaction.

Structural-Functionalism
by Linda Birbeck
Stand Grammar School for Girls

Introduction

Structural-functionalism developed, with sociology itself, in Europe during the nineteenth century – very much in response to problems of that time. The eighteenth and early nineteenth centuries had seen the collapse of the Feudal system in Western Europe and enormous changes in social life. The American and French revolutions had suggested ideals of equality, happiness and freedom of the individual. These political changes were paralleled by the complete social and economic transformation of the structure of Western societies brought about by the Industrial Revolution.

Although men had created these changes, they could see that the world was beyond their control. Society seemed to have an existence of its own; it appeared as a dominating force controlling men's behaviour and creating problems which they could not solve. This paradoxical nature of society has been expressed by Gouldner when he states:

> The modern concepts of society and of culture arose in a social world that, following the French revolution, men could believe they themselves had made. They could see that it was through their struggles that kings had been overthrown and an ancient religion disestablished. Yet, at the same time, men could also see that this was a world out of control, not amenable to men's designs. It was therefore a grotesque, contradictory world: a world made by men but, despite this, not *their* world. (Gouldner, 1971, p. 52)

These historical conditions thus gave shape to a kind of sociology which emphasises the power of society and the subordination of men. Society was conceived of as an autonomous and independent 'thing' which forced the individual to conform to certain standardised patterns of behaviour.

In addition, the structural-functionalist perspective has been greatly influenced by a certain view of the nature of man. Some early functionalists (notably Durkheim) would agree with the view of Thomas Hobbes (a seventeenth-century philosopher) that man in a state of nature is a selfish individual, who needs the power of society to restrain and control him if his life is not to be 'solitary, poor, nasty, brutish and short'. The functionalist approach is, then, founded on this basic assumption about the nature of man; it follows that there is a need for society to act as a constraining and controlling force over individuals if social order is to persist.

The works of Comte, Spencer and Durkheim (three major nineteenth-century sociologists) all reflect concern with the need for order and integration in social life if the disorganisation caused by the political, social and economic changes of that time, and the individualism of mankind, are to be overcome and controlled. Thus society came to be seen as a superior force endowed with moral authority to coerce men, and structural-functionalism developed into a concern with how a society holds together and operates as a whole. The implication is that we must examine the structure of a society, and the pressures it generates, if we are to understand the behaviour of any individual or group within that society. The major emphasis is therefore upon the totality of a society rather than upon its constituent parts which are examined only in so far as they contribute to the maintenance of society.

Interrelationship of Parts

This view of society as an integrated system is sustained by the analogy between a biological organism, for example, the human body, and the social organism. Society is seen as a kind of social organism, or system of interrelated parts, all functioning for the good of the whole body. This organic model has been outlined by the anthropologist Radcliffe-Brown (1952), when he states that in each society individuals fit into an identifiable social structure, just as cells are organised in a biological structure. Individual cells may die, but they are replaced and the organism persists unchanged. In the same way, individual human beings may die but they too are replaced and the social structure continues as before. The various parts of society fit together in a definite structure to form an integrated system.

What goes on in one part of society, therefore, has implications for other areas of social life. One can, for example, examine the links between family background and educational achievement or between social class and church attendance. One can also see that changes in one part of the social structure lead to changes in other parts. For example, political change leads to economic change which may lead to educational change and so on.

Moreover, this organic analogy suggests that each part of the structure, each institution or activity, serves important functions for the survival of society. In the same way that the heart, for example, serves vital functions for the continuance of life, elements of social structure such as the family or religious organisations are conceived as important for the survival of the social organism. The function of any institution or activity, then, is the part it plays in maintaining the social structure.

To examine the functions of certain activities enables us to understand the interrelationships between the parts and the whole of a society. For example, a major function of religion is to contribute to the social cohesion of society – by the provision of shared beliefs, basic values and ceremonies which unite the members of a society.

R. K. Merton (1951, p. 50) introduced the distinction between *manifest* and *latent functions*. Manifest functions are those which are intended and recognised by the participants in the situation, whilst latent functions are those which are neither intended nor recognised; for example, the manifest function of a funeral service is to bury the dead, whilst the latent function might be to bring together family members and friends, and foster integration and stability. To consider the latent functions of an activity allows us to look beneath the surface and examine social relationships afresh; we are able to recognise that apparently irrational behaviour may in fact be functional for the group or society involved.

To illustrate this point, let us look at the case (Gluckman, 1955) of the Zulus of South-East Africa who traditionally held a ceremony each year to celebrate the goddess of crop fertility. During this ceremony the women took over the jobs, behaviour and clothes of the men, who remained confined to the huts. The manifest function of this ritual is to please the goddess, thus ensuring a good harvest. However, this ritual may fulfil latent functions in that it acts as a kind of safety-valve for the frustrations of the women, who lead a difficult life with a status greatly inferior to that of the men. This ceremony allows them to reverse roles with the men and express their frustrations. It is therefore valuable in helping to maintain the social order, i.e. it serves a vital function for Zulu society.

Not all behaviour, however, can be said to be contributing to the maintenance of society. There are many conflicts and contradictions in social life which structural-functionalism tends to have difficulty in accounting for and explaining. In an attempt to overcome this problem Merton introduced the notion of *dysfunction* which he defined as 'those observed consequences which lessen the adaptation or adjustment of a given system' (Merton, 1957). This means that the parts of society may in fact obstruct rather than support one another. An activity may create disharmony and disruption in society. It may be dysfunctional for the society as a whole or for any part of that society. In illustration, Merton discusses bureaucracies. He points out that, since bureaucracies stress the need for obedience to a fixed set of rules at all times, they tend to produce a rigid personality and an inability to adapt to change. Thus a bureaucratic method of organisation can be seen as dysfunctional, since it denies the organisation the ability to adapt to new circumstances, and therefore effectively to achieve the aims for which it was originally designed.

Shared Values

The way in which functional activities are carried out in a given society does not occur by chance, but is rooted in the basic values of that society. Structural-functionalists believe that the basis of an orderly society is a shared set of values accepted by all members of that society. This leads to an analysis of society in terms of stability, equilibrium and an underlying moral consensus; for this reason functionalism is often known as 'consensus theory'. The unity of society in this view derives from commonly held beliefs or sentiments. These shared moral values hold society together and, as Durkheim explains, members of society continually reaffirm their belief in such values:

> There can be no society which does not feel the need of upholding and reaffirming at regular intervals the collective sentiments and the collective ideas which make its unity and its personality. Now this moral remaking cannot be achieved except by the means of reunions, assemblies and meetings where the individuals, being closely united to one another, reaffirm in common their common sentiments. (Durkheim, 1915, p. 427)

Shils and Young analysed the Coronation of Queen Elizabeth II in this light, showing that the Coronation was exactly the sort of ceremony in which society reaffirms the moral values which are its foundations. They comment that:

> The Coronation Service itself is a series of ritual affirmations of the moral values necessary to a well-governed and good society. The key to the Coronation Service is the Queen's promise to abide by the moral standards of society. The whole Service reiterates their supremacy above the personality of the sovereign. In her assurance that she will obey the canons of mercy, charity, justice and protective affection, she acknowledges and submits to their power. When she does this, she symbolically proclaims her community with her subjects who . . . commit themselves to obedience within the society constituted by the moral rule which she has agreed to uphold. (Shils and Young, 1953)

Other ceremonies of national importance can be analysed in this way. Recent examples include the Investiture of Prince Charles, Princess Anne's wedding and the Queen's Silver Jubilee celebrations, all of which can be interpreted as fulfilling the function of integration and unification.

Consensus or agreement on such moral values is achieved through the processes of *socialisation* and *social control*. Individuals are socialised into the collective order of society: they learn the culture, that is, norms, values and attitudes, from the various groups (family, school, workmates, etc.) to which they belong. If, despite this process, they deviate from the norms (or rules) of their society, there is a variety of social controls which will restrain them and induce conformity. In this way, the individual is assimilated into the social order. He learns to respect and uphold the basic values on which is founded the whole social system, since these values directly influence the norms, institutions and social structure of which he is a part. Man is thus seen as existing for the collective good. Society is the ultimate point of reference, external to individuals and controlling their behaviour for the good of itself. Shared values are necessary if the society is to continue in order and harmony.

The 'Needs' of the System

Structural-functionalism thus gives an explanation of social behaviour in terms of requirements of the social system, rather than in terms of motives of individuals. If a society is to continue to exist, certain things need to be done to ensure its survival. These are termed (Aberle et al., 1950) the *functional prerequisites* of society. A useful way of illustrating the necessity for these functional prerequisites or imperatives, is to read *Lord of the Flies* by William Golding and to ask yourself the reasons for the breakdown of the society of boys marooned on a desert island. For the moment, the present writer is assuming familiarity with the novel and will use it to illustrate briefly the functional prerequisties of a society.

Lord of the Flies

(a) The children hunt, light a fire and build shelters in order to survive.

(b) The boys elect a leader and allocate other roles to individuals or groups. However, not all the boys are motivated to carry out their tasks and this leads to conflict and chaos.

(c) In *Lord of the Flies* there is a lack of unity and agreement over the aims that should be pursued. For example, being rescued has different meanings for different boys, which leads to unmanageable conflict as the boys pursue different goals.

(d) The boys on the island begin by developing rules and procedures, such as orderly debate regulated by holding the conch. However, these rules break down, which makes an ordered society impossible.

(e) In Golding's novel, the children have been socialised previously for life in modern Britain. This proves inadequate on the island and leads to the use of violence as they come to terms with a new situation for which they were not prepared.

(f) One boy, Jack, is allowed to express his hatred, sadism and lust for power, which has disastrous consequences for the society.

(g) The boys possess no recognised means of handling disruption and

Functional prerequisites

Physical survival of the members must be ensured by adaptation to, and alteration of, the environment.

Tasks have to be shared so that they are carried out competently by able and motivated individuals.

Communication, shared understanding and shared goals must exist among members of a society.

There must be rules, regulations and procedures for all to follow, so that individuals know how to behave to achieve the goals for which they are aiming.

The norms and values of a society must be learned by all its members, who must be socialised into a common culture if they are to understand, communicate and interact with each other effectively, as well as identify with shared values.

In any society certain feelings can be openly expressed whilst others must be suppressed or repressed. Society cannot survive if it allows complete freedom of expression to such potentially disruptive emotions as anger, jealousy or lust.

Every society must possess some means of controlling, when they therefore law and order breaks down. To control one another's behaviour individuals use naked force which signals the end of the society and the existence of the 'war of all against all'.

occur, disruptive forms of behaviour.

Functional prerequisites are met by the different institutions in society. Every society then must have some *economic organisation* to produce food, clothing and shelter for its members, some kind of *family system* to produce new members and socialise them, a *political system* to allocate scarce resources such as power and wealth, and *community and cultural organisations* such as religious and educational institutions which create harmony in society by transmitting shared moral values. However, one prerequisite or societal need can be satisfied by a range of institutions.

Social Facts

The above consideration of functional prerequisites has led us back to the view of society as a social system, where all the parts fit together and work harmoniously to create and maintain a unified whole. The whole is greater than the sum of its parts, which means that we cannot explain society by reducing it to its individual components. We must, instead, look at groups and society as a whole to understand individual elements. Man is subordinated to society; shared language, values, norms, identities and rituals are imposed on the individual by his membership of social groups.

These groups possess various means of controlling our behaviour – from physical violence or imprisonment to ridicule or gossip. Society thus sanctions and prohibits certain kinds of behaviour, and therefore limits greatly the individual's freedom of choice and action. Durkheim developed this notion of society as 'external fact' which coerces the individual and thereby creates a certain degree of uniformity within a society. The common sentiments, morals and patterns of behaviour to which we must conform, he termed '*social facts*'. These are defined as, 'ways of acting, thinking and feeling, external to the individual, and endowed with a power of coercion, by reason of which they control him. . . . This pressure, which is the distinctive property of social facts, is the pressure which the totality exerts on the individual.' (Durkheim, 1950)

'Social facts' originate in society and are thus greater than their individual manifestations, i.e. the behaviour of individual human beings. Society as objective and external entity controls our behaviour and our thoughts. The power of society over the actions of individuals was expounded by Durkheim in his impressive and influential study of suicide (*Le Suicide*, 1897) in which he demonstrated that even something as apparently individual as the taking of one's own life does in fact originate in, and can only be explained with reference to, the society in which the individual is located. Society influences not only our actions but also forces upon us a certain way of looking at reality. For example, we often find the ways of other societies amusing, horrifying or even 'abnormal' and our own behaviour as correct, 'normal' or reasonable. The fact that we take the customs and mores of our own society so much for granted well illustrates the coercive nature of society to which Durkheim referred.

Conclusion

Structural-functionalists have made an important contribution to sociology. By looking at the requirements of the social system, they have enabled us to explain activities, ideas, rituals and institutions in terms of the social structure, and thus understand how everything in the social world is interconnected. They have also demonstrated the extent of society's influence over the behaviour of individuals.

However, there are problems involved with looking at social life in this way, problems which you may already have thought of as you have read this section. These include:

1 The nature and extent of society's control over the individual, and the ability of the individual to control his life and the society to which he belongs.

2 The existence of shared values and normative consensus in a complex society like modern Britain. Many sociologists would question very much whether there are shared values in large-scale industrial societies, even if they accept that they may exist in small scale pre-industrial societies.

3 The conservative bias inherent in this type of theory. Since functionalists examine the various parts of society by looking at the functions they perform in maintaining the social system, they imply that everything which exists has a function and is therefore necessary to that system. This suggests that whatever exists is essential and thus amounts to a defence of the status quo. For example, funcionalists defend inequality because they say it serves vital functions in society (Davis and Moore, 1953).

4 The inadequacy of the functionalist explanation of social change. Because functionalists are concerned with understanding stability and persistence in social systems, they have difficulty in accounting for social change. They have, however, attempted to describe gradual and progressive change, using ideas connected with the biological analogy, and have been particularly concerned with the notion of 'adaptation' to the environment. Social structures are seen to adapt not only to the physical environment, but also to other environmental factors such as technological change or contact with other cultures.

A particular form of change – increased complexity of social systems, or structural differentiation – can be explained in this way. Institutions such as hospitals, factories, schools, old people's homes, have developed in industrial societies in relatively recent times and have taken over functions previously performed by the family. Thus the whole system has become more complex, or differentiated, and, therefore, better adapted to technological change.

The functionalist approach is able, then, to handle gradual, adaptive change but a basic weakness in this perspective is that it cannot easily account for rapid or revolutionary social transformations, which are an important feature of many societies.

These and other criticisms will be developed elsewhere, but the contribution of structural-functionalism to sociology cannot be under-rated.

Conflict—Structuralism
by Len Law
Stockton/Billingham Technical College

We have read in the previous paper that some sociologists find it useful to theorise about society as if it were a system of interrelated parts, somewhat similar to a biological organism, where each part fulfils a *function* for the maintenance of the whole. In this paper it is argued that, although this way of thinking is indeed sometimes useful, it is at other times less than useful and can, in fact, be very dangerous. It is dangerous, not only in that it can lead us to make mistakes in our thinking about how social groups work, but also because it can lead us into making *political* judgements which can be very advantageous to those who control others and very harmful to those who are controlled. It is because of these dangers that the structural-functionalist approach is often called a *conservative* theory. It is conservative in that it can be used by any group in a position of power over others to justify that position and the use of that power.

The major mistake which the functionalists make is called the *fallacy of reification*: that is, the logical error of thinking about non-living things as if they had feelings, wishes, wants, needs and purposes like people do. This fallacy has a long and inglorious history. Indeed, so long have people thought about the world in this way that many are not able to see the stupidity of doing so. For example, when my car, which I call Bessie, goes wrong I often curse and swear at it and have even been known to kick it on the understanding that punishment is deserved. Punishment, perhaps, is deserved but it is not the car that deserves it; it is the men who made it and the person who is responsible for its upkeep, which in this case is me! To take another example, many of us who have been brought up within a religion have been taught to regard the teachings of our faith as coming from some supra-being. Yet it could be argued that these teachings come from other people, frequently clever, wise and devout people, but people just the same.

When the fallacy of reification is used in thinking about the social world, the real dangers can be seen. Over the years, millions of people have been made to give up their lives, or take the lives of others, thinking that by doing so they will further the 'cause' of some *thing* (religion, nation, political creed, football team, etc.) which is thought of as being superior to themselves. Recent examples of this way of thinking include the Russian invasion of Czechoslovakia to defend *socialism* and the war in Vietnam, where the Americans were defending *freedom*. Yet suppose, taking this latter example, we ask the question, 'Freedom for whom?' The answer to this question shows us that the reason used for killing is not clear-cut. Likewise, the easiest way to see through the seemingly very rational thoughts which the functionalists offer us about society is to ask the simple questions: 'Functional for whom?'; 'Who benefits from the social activity described?'; 'Whose social position does the analysis serve?' It is by asking such questions that some of the errors made by the functionalists and their approach can be seen.

If this structural-functionalist approach has these dangers, then what approach can we use to think about the way in which we live with others in groups or societies? The approach which we wish to put forward here is called the *conflict-structuralist* approach. Like the functionalist approach it has a long history in social science; whereas functionalism has been favoured mainly by American and early British sociologists, conflict-structuralism has been favoured mainly by European sociologists and has only latterly found favour in Britain. There are many varieties of this approach and these can be recognised by the prefix or suffix used, though the variety which we favour is often called 'dialectical-structuralism' (Coulson and Riddell, 1970) and is based on the works of Weber and Marx, amongst others (Gerth and Mills, 1948; Marx, 1964; Marx and Engels, 1964).

Like the functionalists, conflict-structuralists believe that society has a definite order, that is, a structure, which to a large degree predetermines what happens at any one moment. We do not, however, see this ordering as a property of the *social organism* itself, for this would be to reify it. We do agree that doing so can be quite useful, as long as the logical and political dangers are borne in mind, but we do not think that it is necessary. Rather, we prefer to see this structure as the result of the past actions of people who have attempted to solve their own problems in their own way and have passed down through the generations certain predefined ways of doing things within which each new generation feels constrained. Over time these predefined ways of doing things, *normative structures*, become outmoded and too constraining, so that they need to be changed if the members of the new generation – or more likely some small section of it – are to solve what they see as their problems. Sometimes these norms change slowly, almost imperceptibly, over time. However, at other times some people gain a great deal from the normative structure of the present and do not wish to see it changed, and in this case *conflict* will arise between those people who want change and those who do not. It is this notion of conflict that most clearly marks the differences between the functionalists and the conflict-structuralists, for though some functionalists have attempted to explain social conflict (Coser, 1954 and 1967; Merton, 1949), they have not been very successful (Coulson and Riddell, 1970). For conflict-structuralists it is this notion of conflict which gives the key to the understanding of human history. It provides a basic tool with which we can analyse what people have done in the past, what they are doing now, and how apparently mystifying patterns of behaviour come together to make that which we call social life.

How then do conflict-structuralists start their explanation of social life? Firstly, we begin with the idea that all people have a set of *needs* and *wants*. All people *need* food, clothing and shelter of a minimum sort; most people *want* more than minimum levels of food, clothing and shelter, and many other things besides. Without these things people cannot live in the way they expect. Further, all people need other people, not just because of the pleasure of being with other people, but because life would not be possible without them. Human infants are physically fairly helpless for the first years of their lives and without other humans they would not survive. Also, it is in this period that human infants learn how to behave in social groups; that is, they are socialised into the normative structure so that they too come to recognise what the previous generation sees as being possible, desirable and necessary in social life. For conflict-structuralists, therefore, social life is primarily to be explained in terms of how it enables people to create the means to satisfy their needs and wants, how they acquire new needs and wants, and how it enables people to create (procreate) other people.

It is because the satisfaction of these needs and wants is so important to people that many conflict-structuralists attach a great importance to the *economic* side of social life. Many forms of social activity are based on the ways in which people seek to solve, either in co-operation or conflict with each other, the problems of their needs and wants. Most of the different types of society are known by the major way in which the people in them seek to overcome these problems. Hence we have the terms 'agricultural society' and 'industrial society', for example. Human history is, according to this approach, an account of the changing ways in which people have created different means of satisfying their needs, the ways in which they have come together in groups to do this, and the ways in which living in groups has itself brought about new needs and wants which in turn require satisfaction.

When conflict-structuralists look at societies like ours they notice that our existence is based on a very complex economic structure. Unlike in 'primitive' societies, in industrialised societies very few people produce everything that they themselves use. Rather, there is a complex division of labour operating in which people play a very small part in the production of one commodity: they buy nearly all the things which they use from others, who in turn buy the things which they themselves do not produce.

Such an economy is called a *market economy*. Life will be relatively pleasant if your *market position* is strong in such a society; that is, if you either have a lot of a commodity which other people want badly, or a lot of whatever it is that people will accept in exchange for commodities (typically money). However, if you do not have some of these things then life may not be so pleasant. Some conflict-structuralists, following Max Weber, call these market positions *class positions*. It is argued that if you have a lot of commodities or money, that is, a strong class position, then you will wish to protect them and even increase them; and it is in the ways in which people attempt to do this that produce other parts of the social structure. (It should be noted that this is but one definition of class: there are others, for example, most structural-functionalists use 'class' to mean 'status', see *Class, Status and Party*, in Gerth and Mills, 1948, pp. 180–95.)

The major part of the social structure which is concerned with the distribution of commodities is called the *political structure*. By this we do not just mean those types of activity which are normally called 'political' (political parties, pressure groups, voting behaviour, etc.); we mean all those social activities which define the *rights* of some people to own commodities and/or tell other people what to do (Worsley, 1964).

The political structure is the distribution of *rights* over things and/or people, that is, the distribution of power within a society. Every facet of human social activity has within it a political structure, and all these 'little' political structures blend together to produce the overall political structure. If the blend is to be relatively stable then all the little political structures must be similar to each other and the whole. If this were not so then people coming from one structure to another might not see the need to do what they are told by their 'social superiors' or might not recognise the rights of others to their property, and this would cause a lot of trouble for everyone, particularly for those who own the property or claim the right to tell others what to do. Such 'trouble' happens quite frequently in most social situations, and it is then that those in 'control' have to 'correct' the behaviour of the 'deviants', ultimately through the use of some form of coercion. It is important to realise though that for most of the time we have been so well socialised that we do not need to be told what to do, we just do it.

Again it is critical to ask, 'Who benefits?' All political structures are bound to benefit some groups of people more than others, and it is going to be in the interests of these groups to maintain the *status quo*, and in the interests of others to change it. So, again, we come to the idea of *conflict* as an integral part of human society. Now we can see how such conflict is often generated between social groups, some trying to maintain their rights and power over people and commodities, others trying to establish a new ordering of rights.

Much of the time such conflict is on a relatively small scale: in a child's insistence on watching a television channel different from the one his father is watching, and the father's defence of his rights to do as he wishes.

Similarly, in the shop-lifter's attempt to 'liberate' a commodity, and in the shop-keeper's use of his or her rights to stop the shop-lifter doing so.

At other times, conflict is on a more organised and larger scale: it is the right of examiners to decide whether a candidate has displayed the *correct* knowledge in the *correct* fashion on an examination script. The candidate is unable to do much about their definition of what is *correct*, except *learn* it. It is the right of an employer to tell an employee most of what to do at work, and the employee can do relatively little about that. It is the employee's right, through a Trade Union, to tell his employer what the latter cannot order him to do; and this has led to 'dispute procedures', industrial tribunals, etc., which have been set up to 'manage' such conflicts. It is the right of a small percentage of our population to own and control the vast majority of personal wealth in our society and to collect most of the income from this wealth, and the inability of successive Governments to do much about that, even when they have actually wanted to. According to J. E. Mead in *Efficiency, Equality and the Ownership of Property* (Allen & Unwin, 1964), 10 per cent of our population own some 83 per cent of personal wealth in our society and receive 99 per cent of unearned income (Blackburn, 1967).

The picture which we get of society when we use this approach is a lot less neat than that which is given to us by the functionalists, for it is often the case that the various parts of the social structure do not fit neatly into position as if they were all parts of one super-organism. Very often the 'fit' is anything but neat. There always seem to be 'hang-overs' from previous times (for example, the wearing of academic gowns and other types of 'uniform' in educational institutions might be described as a cultural hang-over). It must be realised, however, that in many cases these hang-overs can be symbolic of real differences in power and prestige and can have a purpose in modern life. Sometimes, too, we find examples of a new way of ordering things.

So, unlike the 'fit' of the bodily parts of an animal, the parts of the social structure often seem to be in conflict with each other so that the balance of positions at any one time can easily change in ways difficult to predict, for these changes appear to be more the result of the *unintended consequences*, rather than the intended results of some of the actors concerned. For example, the conflict that occurred in Britain between 1970 and 1974 over 'industrial relations' certainly did not end in the way that the Conservative Government had intended. Likewise, the war in Vietnam produced all manner of consequences for which American governments had not bargained. But, given that the picture is not as neat as it might be, we would suggest that it is a little more realistic, a little more accurate, and a lot more useful to our understanding of what makes 'society' tick.

Building Society Through Interaction
by R. J. Anderson
Manchester Polytechnic

Introduction

It is a commonplace to suggest that the important differences between man and the animals, even the higher primates, are that, firstly, man is a language user, and secondly, that he can perceive himself as an object in his own social environment. Now, while this assertion may be common enough, it seems that many of the social sciences have ignored its implications. In this paper, we shall see that it is possible to give accounts of social action which are grounded in these essential characteristics of human beings: our language use and our consciousness. The sociology which attempts to do this is often called *'interpretivist'* or *'verstehende'* sociology. These terms are derived from the methodological writings of Max Weber and in particular the distinction he draws between explanations which are adequate at the level of *causation* and those which are adequate at the level of *meaning* (Weber, 1968). This does not imply that we shall attempt to show how to recover the precise meanings, intentions or purposes of individuals, but rather that we are taking a stance which sees them as acting on the basis of their interpretations of meaning as opposed to seeing them caused or impelled to action by stimuli in their social environment.

The relationships between meaningful and causal accounts are obviously complex. The important implication of the distinction is that we can now see human beings as symbol users, not just in the sense that they communicate with each other in symbols organised into languages, but also that objects, events and actions are imbued with meaning by interactants. They are taken as expressing or symbolising purposes, intentions and meanings, and further action is based on these interpretations. To make sense of the world, men make use of symbols and so discover meanings. Social order is built up out of the meanings that actors attach to social phenomena. The world is not experienced as chaotic but is found to be meaningful. The problem faced by 'interpretivist' sociology is the explanation of how we agree on meanings. It might be argued that such a sociology is based upon individual interpretation and the workings of individual minds. Consequently, such a sociology should be reducible to descriptions of the 'basic' psychological variables. This is, however, a misunderstanding. 'Interpretivist' sociology concerns itself with *the ways* that sense is made collectively and individually, not in the specific meanings, intentions or purposes that are attributed.

If we assume that, for the most part, people do see their world in much the same kinds of ways, then their methods for doing so must be generalisable. Even though you see an approaching Alsatian as a ferocious guard dog and I see it as 'Rover, the family pet', the ways in which we will discover it to be ferocious or friendly are fundamentally similar. It is these similarities that this paper addresses. In order to do this, we shall look at two different modes of analysing meaningful social action: *symbolic interactionism* and *ethnomethodology*. With each in turn, we shall try to set out how they account for social order in terms of the issues sketched out above.

Symbolic Interactionism

Symbolic interactionism is generally regarded as having its origins in the work of George Herbert Mead, although Mead himself never used the term. Mead proposed that the foundation of social life was the ability to distinguish between the 'I', the subject of action, and the 'me', the object acted upon. Consciousness, according to Mead, consists in a process of 'self indications' of objects, events and persons. 'I' indicate to 'myself'. The process of self indication consists in discerning the significance of phenomena. As this is essentially interpretive we can say that objects are imbued with meaning. Consequently, as human beings, we not only set out to achieve our own ends in action but by treating all action as 'meaningful', we are able to discern the ends of others. We can do this simply because we can treat ourselves as 'objects' and so see ourselves as others see us. This is referred to as 'taking the role of the other'.

Weber, although not a symbolic interactionist, stressed that interpretative understanding of social life had to be part of the methodology of social science if it was to grasp the nature of social life. Symbolic interactionism proposes that interpretative understanding is precisely how orderly social life is achieved. Far from being a special method in the social sciences, it is the basis of social life. Our knowledge of our 'self' is built up out of an awareness of our own purposes and an orientation to the interpretation of others; that is, our knowledge of the 'I' and the 'me'. Therefore, identity can be seen as the combination of how I see myself and how others see me. This is itself a product of interpretative understanding and therefore an outcome of a *process* of interaction. Because it is a process, 'final' or 'ultimate' definitions of identity can never be accomplished. Consequently, because identity is used to give meaning to action, understanding can never be finalised either. Both are always potentially revisable. Each new encounter or interaction provides an occasion on which new information designating the 'career' of a particular self may become available. So each new interaction is an opportunity for confirmation or revision of 'who' the 'other' 'really is'.

This process may continue after death when different information or changing attitudes may allow alternative interpretations of what kind of person the deceased was. A striking example of this may be found in the recent promotions and demotions of saints in the Christian calendar. Such movements may be either within or between careers, and are often called 'status passages' (Glaser and Strauss, 1966; Goffman, 1968).

In contrast with the view that a person's identity is largely fixed in early childhood by the ascription of roles such as gender, nationality, class, race and religion, symbolic interactionism suggests that, for each encounter, 'who the other is for this encounter' can be viewed as a product of negotiations over definitions of the situation, identities, careers, etc. A person may be white, middle class and male, but these supposed 'master roles' are only important for interaction when and if they are given significance by the actors themselves. The sharing of significance in any particular context is derived from a conceptual apparatus embedded in a culture. It is here that language becomes especially important, for the meanings we ascribe to events and actions are often carried in the ways that we talk about them.

To a very large extent learning the meaning of things within a given culture will be the same as learning its language. The important point is that whereas other forms of Sociology might talk of the *causes* of particular phenomena, for example, divorce, deviance or falling birth rates, and locate 'role expectations' as one of these causes, symbolic interactionists stress that interpretation provides the *reason* not the cause of social action. The objective variables said to define roles are themselves the product of interpretations. Stating that a rapid rise in standards of living *causes* people to limit their families is very different from stating that a rapid increase in the temperature of water will cause it to evaporate. Decisions to limit family size are based upon particular parents' interpretations of their own personal circumstances. It may be that we can correlate these decisions with some variable or other, but between the cause – the rise in standard of living – and the effect – limitation of family size – lies interpretative understanding and courses of action based upon that understanding.

If symbolic interactionists are not concerned with the 'ultimate' causes of action but with laying bare the parameters of interpretative understanding, it follows that they will not attempt to build causal models which generate causal laws. Most symbolic interactionist work does not try to explain social life in the same manner that the natural sciences explain the physical world. They are simply concerned with describing the processes of social life. As such they offer an ethnography of a particularly precise and detailed kind. In order to give these kinds of descriptions, categories have been abstracted from a number of different settings or analogies. These categories do not exhaustively define the nature of social life. They are simply organising devices for systematic description. They point to interesting areas of exposition and analysis.

Perhaps the most widely known set of categories constitutes the *dramaturgical* model associated with the early work of Erving Goffman (1971). This proposes that social life can be likened to theatre with actors playing to an audience. Dramaturgy suggests that social actors utilise resources in much the same way that performers in the theatre do.

Theatrical performers achieve their success by use of props, scenes, sets and so forth as well as the lines they say. By paying attention to how they present their role, they ensure that its 'reality' is not vitiated. Social actors are seen as providing similar resources which represent or symbolise how they wish to be defined in a given context. They do so in an attempt to ensure a concerted definition of the situation thereby establishing the basis of orderly social interaction. It is important to remember that this is only a description derived from the use of a particular set of categories. We are not saying that people are always deceitful, 'putting on a performance', being manipulative or whatever. The model allows us to describe in fairly precise terms how individuals can 'manage' their roles by providing in each encounter various types of information about the 'self' that is being presented. Furthermore, we can conceive of social interactants orienting to the fact that such information will be provided and so using it to decide exactly what is going on in any situation.

Because of the distinction between the 'I' and the 'me', we can also see the actor as orienting to the fact that others will monitor actions, settings, contexts, clothing and talk for what they can be held to represent. This orientation enables the systematic organisation of resources so that they are consonant with definitions of the situation and the presented 'self'. So, on the one hand, for example, we can see actors utilising knowledge of which people are to be found in surgeries, which people use stethoscopes, which people are normally addressed as 'Doctor' in such places, to find some person who is the 'proper' person to give descriptions of medical symptoms and disorders to. On the other hand, doctors may wear white coats, use consulting rooms, insist on the full use of their title in order to create and sustain their role as doctor so that their patients can produce details of their symptoms and disorders in an unproblematic way.

It is interesting to note that many sociologists have had to manipulate these resources deliberately in order to pass unnoticed in hospitals where they were engaged in research. If they had not done so, their role as observer may well have intruded into the hospital's routine. They would then have been observing responses to their own intrusion rather than to normal hospital life. To prevent this they became just like any other doctor and so an indiscernible part of the hospital's constructed social order.

The concern with routine self presentation explains symbolic interactionists' apparently morbid obsession with deviants such as criminals and the insane. Both categories highlight normal routines: the one, especially those engaged in publicly observable crime like fraud, deliberately manipulates normality to prevent or modify the consequences of discovery; the other is stigmatised as deviant largely on the grounds of the failure to observe normal routines.

Just as the dramaturgical model takes the theatrical performance as its organising principle, so the game model uses the idea of the actor as strategist, operating within a framework of rules to achieve his ends

(Goffman, 1962, 1970; Harre and Secord, 1972). Under this model, social order becomes the negotiated outcome of the strategies actors use. The advantage of the model is that it not only allows us to focus on the ways in which individuals may perform or handle their own and others' strategies, but also how particular strategies are part of a trajectory of action which is itself discerned by seeing strategies and actions as following rules. In this view, then, orderly social conduct is provided by the use of rules to determine what action is or means. Actors are, therefore, seen as *following rules* and not as *governed* by them. A rule, here, does not necessarily mean a prescription, but is a conventional description of that which is ordinarily done, i.e. 'done as a rule'. Clearly, some rules will be held to be definitive of particular kinds of social action. These are seen as definitive or *constitutive* of the game. They define the overall framework of meanings. Other rules are conventionalised preferences for courses of action. So, there is no rule which says how hard to hit a hockey ball or how fast to bowl a cricket ball, but if you pick the ball up and appear to swallow it, whatever else you are doing you are no longer 'playing' hockey or cricket. For your actions to be understandable, those frames must be replaced by others, for example, conjuring or amusing the crowd (Goffman, 1975). Constitutive rules, then, are used to provide the sense of what is going on. To ensure agreement upon the frame, convincing performances, in the sense outlined above, must be given.

Working within the game framework, we can see how actors might use strategies to bargain for the 'promotion' and 'protection' of particular definitions of self and situations by the manipulation of context, scene, talk, clothing and indeed the use of gesture, facial movements and so on. In as much as individuals are able to promote and protect such definitions, then we can see social order, that is, the agreements upon definitions, as created and preserved via the minutiae of face to face interaction. By the utilisation of rules to establish a meaningful order in their daily lives, social actors create and sustain social order. It would follow from this that attention would be paid to the hitherto unnoticed, insignificant, almost ritualised aspects of ordinary life, such as greetings and partings, hand-holding, embarrassment and its management, supportive and remedial interchanges, to enable a satisfactorily detailed account of the ways in which social order is created out of an orientation to rules and rule following (Goffman, 1963; Schenkein and Ryave, 1974).

This particular way of analysing social life has been used extensively to present descriptions of the routines of organisations like hospitals, courts, the Police and schools. (For example, Strauss et al., 1964; Sudnow, 1967; Bittner, 1967; Becker, 1952.) Researchers have shown that the daily life on a hospital ward can be seen in terms of the strategies and negotiations engaged in by staff, patients and visitors. In recommending a patient to be admitted, doctors take into account not only the condition of the patient but also the 'shape' of the ward they are likely to be placed in. This 'shape' is part of a 'conceptual map' of what kinds of patients are generally found on what kinds of wards, what kinds of illnesses they have, what kind of nursing and treatment they get, what the nursing staff requires of them, etc. Patients are allocated where they will fit the 'shape' of the ward. Nurses keep their wards 'in shape' by resisting referrals of potentially disruptive patients, for example, adolescent epileptics on geriatric wards, or by the management of the recalcitrant, negotiation with admissions officers, referring elsewhere, etc. As death is both a routine fact of life in hospitals and also threat to the hospital's credibility, it is managed in ways to make it either unnoticed, as in geriatric wards, or extremely rare, as in paediatric ones. The day-to-day routine that a place like a hospital exhibits is not to be seen as a result of the doctors, nurses and patients conforming to their roles but as a negotiated order constantly undergoing change and having to be preserved in the face of threats of disruption. Within this constructed order, meanings are managed and strategies developed. Instead of freezing the hospital into a still life, symbolic interactionism asks us to view it as a dynamic, human process.

Ethnomethodology

We suggested above that symbolic interactionism is engaged in the kind of detailed descriptions called ethnography. Since much of the work of symbolic interactionists has been concerned with our own culture and their data elicited by participant observation in places which are reasonably familiar to us all, these sociologists have had the advantage of having at their disposal the knowledge and abilities which any competent member of our culture has. In pointing to the symbolic nature of interaction they do not analyse, nor do we expect them to, how it is that they know that 'Excuse me – O.K.' is a remedial interchange, that hospitals are places people are cured in, that this action is part of a particular strategy X and, most importantly, they do not analyse how they know what the frame of the action is so that they can specify the rules that are held to apply.

As a mode of analysis, symbolic interactionism relies upon the commonsense understandings of its practitioners. This is not a criticism of it as being in some way flawed or inadequate. It is founded upon commonsense but takes very little interest in it. Yet commonsense understandings, simply because they are held in common, provide the basis of social order. To propose that agreements on definitions of the situation enable the construction of social order leaves out of account the fact that such agreements have to be reached in the first place. Obviously we could suppose that such agreements were simply lucky contingencies. But to accept that as a characterisation of social life would imply that it is irredeemably precarious, and further, that we know it to be so. A little thought shows that the opposite is the case. We do not live our lives haunted by the spectre of the unpredictability of action. When things do not happen as we expect them to, when people behave oddly or out of character, we can 'normalise' the situation by finding reasons why such behaviour should have happened, for example, the other person is ill, worried, absent-minded, deaf or a foreigner. We assume the continuing predictability of our lives. The fact that we can violate this assumption, thereby showing it to be only an assumption, does not invalidate the claim that we organise our lives in accordance with it. If we did not, what would social life be like? If, on the other hand, we suggest that these understandings, agreements and assumptions are arrived at methodically, then we can account for the routine features of life as described by the symbolic interactionists, as well as being able to specify how, in living their daily lives, ordinary people by their knowledge, and use, of commonsense methods for achieving understanding, accomplish the social order which is definitive of the very routine of their lives. The study of the methodical character of commonsense is called *ethnomethodology*.

It was suggested above that social life was not fraught with indeterminate outcomes. This is because, in our daily lives, we operate with four basic presuppositions concerning what the world is 'naturally' like:

1 The social world is an intersubjective one. The others with whom I interact are conscious beings like myself who make the same assumptions I do.
2 If I were to change places with another and see the world as he does, then I would act in exactly the same way that he does.
3 Although each action that I perform is unique, the world is not random. All actions are, in principle, repeatable.
4 The knowledge which I have of the world is organised into patterns of typicalities. These form 'typifications' which can be used to give sense or meaning to social phenomena.

It will be readily noticed that the first and second assumption provide the framework for interpretative understanding. We have seen that ordinary people do interpretatively understand one another. We are now suggesting that they do so *methodically*. The third and fourth assumptions provide for the patterning, continuity and regularity characterising social life. Knowledge of the possibility of repeatability allows patterns to be drawn up into typifications. Such typifications give us the categories we use to see the world as it is.

If the social world is an intersubjective one, then, the assumptions, typifications, etc., must be shared. This sharing could be brought about because children were born with culture innate. But this is manifestly absurd. Such children would have to learn nothing nor would they show any curiosity about social arrangements. Alternatively, culture could be learned either explicitly or through the routine of daily living. We have shown that meanings are not stipulated in advance but derived from contexts. Consequently, learning a culture either as a young child or as a foreigner must involve acquiring methods for doing so. The ability to discern meaning from context is known as the 'repair of indexicality'. Since meaning cannot be laid down in advance such repairs are achieved in daily life as far as is necessary for the accomplishment of practical purposes – social actors are concerned to live their lives and not to contemplate them.

The methods that are used are grounded in the assumptions set out above and enable actors to accomplish the 'facts' as unarguable 'natural facts of life'. In a famous example, Garfinkel details how he asked his students to write out a part of a conversation that they had had. He then asked them to write a more complete account beside it. One student produced the following:

Husband:

Dana succeeded in putting a penny in a parking meter today without being picked up.	This afternoon as I was bringing Dana, our four-year-old son, from nursery school he succeeded in reaching high enough to put a penny in a parking meter when we parked in a meter zone whereas before he had always had to be picked up to reach that high.

(Garfinkel, 1967, p. 25)

Garfinkel reports that the filling out of the right hand side was much more difficult than the left. It became even more so when he insisted on greater precision and clarity:

> Finally, when I required that they assume I would know what they had actually talked about only from reading literally what they had written literally, they gave up . . . the complaint seemed to consist in this. If, for whatever a student wrote, I was able to persuade him that it was not yet accurate, distinct or clear enough, and if he remained willing to repair the ambiguity . . . then the writing itself developed the conversation as a branching texture of relevant matters.

What Garfinkel is pointing to is how each elaboration generated its own indexical features which required repair. Now, obviously, the participant did not say that he could not understand what was said. The repairs that were accomplished were practical ones for the purposes of understanding what was going on. Similarly, jurors accomplish the facts of 'guilt', 'robbery', 'murder'; coroners decide upon 'suicide', by repairing the indexicality of the evidence. By its very nature evidence cannot show 'conclusively' that the offence or suicide occurred and that the defendant is guilty or that the deceased did commit suicide. Only the recreation of the act in front of the jury or coroner could do that. The jury decides on the basis of such things as 'enough is enough', 'anyone in our place would see it the same way' and so methodically, rationally, commonsensically, they accomplish the 'fact' of guilt, suicide or whatever (Garfinkel, op. cit., chapter 8; Atkinson, 1971).

For the repair of indexicality, actors utilise a number of commonsense methods. These methods are not describable except in the context of their use. This is not a claim that the work is inexpressively difficult or intuitive, but simply that to provide a description of method would require analysis longer than the chapter that was supposed to contain it! Therefore ethnomethodologists insist on the rigorous and detailed examination of data. Their analyses enable demonstrations of precisely how resources are provided and analysed *methodically* by ordinary laymen living their daily lives. Some examples of these methods will be found in a later paper in this volume, *Listening to Conversation* (page 59). In providing these resources for analysis, actors make their actions *accountable* to others. Accountable, here, simply means describable or formulateable. Ordinary people are able to give 'lay sociological' descriptions of their social actions. This accountability must be embedded in the things that they do, for it is not the case that action is accompanied by a running commentary providing explanation. We might do so only in particular circumstances – when giving a demonstration, for example. Imagine buying groceries and, while engaged in buying, giving a running commentary on what you are doing, what your actions mean, etc. Other people must be able to discover what you are doing simply from the actions themselves and then base their own actions on their interpretations. Their methodical analysis is available in the things that they do. All that ethnomethodologists attempt to do is to describe, in a formal way, the methods and procedures by which this commonsense understanding is accomplished. To do that, it treats all social life as a practical accomplishment.

We have suggested that commonsense methods are displayed in ordinary, routine, mundane activities. We have also suggested that the understanding of action is predicated on intersubjectivity. The recognition of a gathering as attendance at a funeral rather than a birthday party is facilitated by the use of typifications as to who is usually present, what they wear, what their demeanour is, and so on. Actions, then, conform to a type or follow a rule. These rules are descriptive and not prescriptive of commonsense knowledge. They are conventional. This conventionality constitutes social order as it is experienced by ordinary people. The 'fact' of social order is then the accomplishment of ordinary people living their daily lives in routine ways. We are not suggesting that these rules are known or that they could be formulated by commonsense actors. Theirs is a 'lay' sociology not a professional one. No one suggests that English speakers should necessarily be able to formulate the rules of English grammar. Yet, when they speak, they follow those rules, for the most part. More impressively, no one suggests that bicycle riders should be able to detail descriptions of metals in tension, centripetal and centrifugal forces, laws of gravity and motion, which enable the riding of a bike.

Ethnomethodology studies the rules and practices of social life which enable those actors to accomplish their lives as the 'normal', 'routine', 'simple' affairs that they are. In doing that in systematic and methodical ways they accomplish the normality, routineness and simplicity that we call social order. Paradoxically, ordinary social life, like bike riding, is both simple and complicated.

II Finding Out

Introduction

These different ways of looking at the social world – sociological perspectives, as we call them – do need, of course, to be checked against the 'real' world. Consequently, a great deal of attention is paid to the methods by which evidence about social phenomena is collected, methods such as questionnaires, interviews, participant observation and experiments. The sociological perspectives discussed the first section of part one have sometimes been linked with particular techniques of investigation, but these relationships are not always strong.

Much traditional sociology of an implicit or explicit structuralist kind assumed that sociologists had at their disposal certain techniques which would enable them to find out 'facts' about society and its constituent groups and institutions. These facts are treated as neutral, that is *objective* in that they are independent of the researcher's own attitudes and beliefs. Formal procedure characterised the conduct of enquiries, involving the formulation of hypotheses, collection of data, organisation, presentation and analysis of data, and acceptance or refutation of the original hypothesis. This research procedure, together with the development of refined statistical measurement instruments, was employed in the search for causal relationships in social phenomena, and reflected an aim to discover the law-like nature of social behaviour.

Clearly this orientation to research mirrored a desire to make sociological techniques as similar as possible to those of the natural sciences. Although it was conventionally recognised that the social and natural sciences could never be identical, nothing was to prevent sociologists from increasing the refinement of sociological techniques so that the scientific ideal could be approached as closely as possible. This 'scientific' approach to methodology is loosely called *positivism*. Although positivistic enquiry has long been critically assessed, it has more recently been put under scrutiny by those sociologists who see society as created or built up by individuals in everyday interaction. They tend to see an essential difference between the world of material objects studied by natural scientists, and the world of active individuals. The latter, it is stressed, interpret situations and give meaning to them. On the one hand, researchers are seen as having to face the problem of trying to find out about processes of interpretation, and about contextual meanings; but on the other hand, sociologists have just realised that research enquiry itself is a social process just like any other everyday event. Sociologists interpret situations and assign meaning in the same way that all social actors do.

The five papers on research methods which follow all display an awareness of these sorts of problems whilst at the same time trying to give the reader a 'feel' for the method.

Kevin Cowen examines the nature and use of *social statistics*; often coming from official or quasi-official sources, they are seen as incontrovertible 'facts' irrespective of who has collected them, and for what purpose the collection has been made. He briefly outlines the historical importance of statistics in developing a 'scientific' sociology, and follows by contrasting the traditional use of such statistics with recent criticisms. In short, we are urged to take an interest not so much in the face conclusions which we can draw from statistics, but rather in the social production of statistics – *how* they are produced. The *production* of a statistic may tell us more about social action than the statistic itself.

Quantified data, in the form of percentages, proportions and averages, are produced by sociologists themselves through their conduct of social surveys. Such surveys usually employ *questionnaire* and/or *interview* techniques. Ian Shelton turns our attention to the questions sociologists ask in these techniques, and to the answers they receive. Presenting questions in written form, as a questionnaire, or orally, that is in interview, is the staple diet of the sociological researcher, and much effort has been addressed to the problem of making the construction and presentation of questions, and the analysis of answers, more refined and sophisticated. Ian Shelton discusses the obvious pitfalls of these techniques, and shows how sociologists try to avoid them. At the same time, he queries the extent to which such techniques can claim, neutrally or objectively, to dicover properties of the social world, and he leaves us to ponder the extent to which the researcher might *create* his data in handling questionnaires and interviews.

Very open, in-depth interviews have been seen as one technique for trying to tap the way people interpret and make sense of the world, but *participant observation* is perhaps the technique most clearly identified with some of the sociological perspectives which assume that society is a subjective rather than an objective reality. Stan Meredith outlines the nature of participant observation – researchers actually joining in the situations which they are studying. He explains how this method is believed to be the most effective way of 'getting the feel' of the situation from the point of view of the participants themselves. The researcher puts him/herself into the position of the other actors to see how the situation looks. In so doing, he may appear to be studying the subjective world of actors, but how does the observer-researcher know that what he sees is evidence of what he is researching?

Some social scientists, like natural scientists, have tried to create very tightly-controlled *experimental situations* in which to observe phenomena. Janice Myerson discusses some of the more traditional forms of experiment which have been employed in sociology, showing how they reflected an attempt to identify, as scientifically as possible, specific factors or *variables* which affect social action. In addition, she describes the more recent use of loosely-constructed experiments which have been used to try to reveal some of the basic rules underpinning social behaviour in everyday situations. These latter experiments try to manipulate situations and actors so that everyday understandings are revealed. Frequently, this 'manipulation' involves challenging actors' definitions of situations; rather than the atypicality of such situations rendering experiments invalid (by criteria of scientific research), however, the researcher would be interested in how actors manage and make sense of such challenges.

The paper by Bob Anderson examines recent work in *conversational analysis*. In so doing he illustrates how some sociologists have turned their attention to everyday talk as both a research procedure and as a topic for research. In the first part of his paper, he examines the status of talk as data, showing how recent conversational analysis tries to avoid the problems inherent in traditional research methods. He argues a return to the retention of the 'specifics of data'; other sociologists should be able to analyse the *same* data rather than similar data collected through replication studies. This re-analysis of the same data means that researchers' management of data is not lost, as it is in coding procedures.

The second part of the paper illustrates how this method of analysis works in practice. Although the space available has not allowed him to do full justice to the complexities of the research involved, Bob Anderson is able to outline three areas of interest: identities and references to persons; beginnings and endings of talk; and turn-taking. More significant than 'conclusions' regarding everyday interaction, however, are the processes by which the analysis is built up. This second part of the paper therefore illustrates a distinctive form of sociological analysis; it is more concerned with the treatment of data than with 'talk' or 'conversation' as new substantive areas in sociology.

Facts and Figures
by Kevin J. Cowen
Kidderminster College of Further Education

Introduction

A glance at the pages of many sociology books will show the considerable part played by social statistics. Graphs, tables and diagrams abound, and in some sociological works there are, for those with little knowledge of the mysteries of mathematics, complicated formulae and equations which demonstrate that the findings are statistically significant, scientifically accurate and seemingly unchallengeable. British sociology in particular has developed a statistical approach to the study of society which has its roots in the origins and evolution of the discipline in this country. In 1901, Seebohm Rowntree published the results of a house-to-house survey of 11,560 working class families in York, entitled *Poverty, a study of Town Life*. He had been influenced by the work of Charles Booth, President of the Royal Statistical Society (1892–4), whose *Life and Labour of the People in London* – a street-by-street study of poverty in the East End, published in 1903 – has been described as the prototype of the modern social survey. Booth's cousin, Beatrice Webb, who in 1909 contributed a Minority Report to the Royal Commission on the Poor Law, continued along with her husband to develop and refine survey technique. By promoting the development of the London School of Economics the Webbs, under the influence of Booth and Rowntree, helped give British sociology a positivist base. Later, as sociologists sought to obtain academic status for their discipline, they stressed its scientific nature by pointing to their data-collection techniques and the statistical presentation of facts. With this in mind it becomes easier to understand why mainstream sociology still retains an emphasis on facts and figures.

Social statistics may be divided into two categories, official and non-official. Official statistics are those collected by government agencies such as the Office of Population Censuses and Surveys, for whom the Registrar General collects details of all births, deaths and marriages, and the Home Office which has responsibility for criminal statistics. In addition the Government operates its own Statistical Service whose function is to collect and disseminate information gathered by the above agencies. This it achieves by such publications as the *Annual Abstract of Statistics* and *Social Trends*. By reference to these publications one can soon discover what proportion of children go to comprehensive school, how many people attend church, the number of deaths caused by suicide and whether or not there has been an increase in offences of violence. Because of the virtually unlimited resources of the Government and its agencies, information can be produced in a form and quantity which would prove too costly for the individual sociologist. Furthermore, sociologists are often denied access to certain kinds of information because it is classified, restricted, or not in the interests of the public! The census is the only compulsory social survey. Consequently sociologists have tended to rely heavily on official statistics, often using them as raw data upon which theories and conceptions of 'problems' are based.

However, the use of official statistics by sociologists is not without its problems. The major disadvantage in using publications such as *Social Trends* is that the information they contain is nearly always produced for purposes different from those of sociologists. Government agencies collect information in order to evaluate existing policies, to provide a basis for new policies, and to monitor any changes within the society. Sociologists wishing to enquire into a particular topic may find themselves relying on data which has been collected for tax or welfare purposes, and not for the purpose of sociological research. For administrative convenience information is classified under headings which often cut across important sociological concepts. The categorisation of social class by the Registrar General, for example, classifies many occupations under a single heading implying a similarity which, for the sociologist, may not be valid.

Non-official statistics are collected by sociologists themselves, usually by means of a social survey. This approach may be used when information of an official nature is unavailable or inappropriate, and when there are sufficient funds to support the research. The data is normally collected, processed and analysed by sociologists and their researchers, and presented as appendices or as illustrations within the actual text to support their conclusions. G. Gorer (1971) lists almost one hundred pages of statistical evidence collected by means of interviews and postal questionnaires. Statistics are certainly a convenient way of presenting information, but how often do we understand what lies behind them? Who collected them and how did they go about it?

Suicide Statistics

1897 saw the publication of a sociological work which has become a classic, and is still quoted as an outstanding example of the application of the techniques of the natural sciences to the study of social phenomena. *Suicide* by Emile Durkheim (1897) helped to establish its author as one of the founding fathers of sociology. By using the data on suicide collected by officials, as well as statistics produced by other researchers, Durkheim was able to compare the number of suicides for different countries. He did this by producing a suicide rate for each country. In the period 1866–70 the suicide rate for England was 67 per million inhabitants, while for France it was 135, and for Saxony 293. (Durkheim, 1897, pp. 47–50.) However, these rates were produced from vastly different totals. During 1866–70 the annual number of suicides averaged 1,459 in England, 5,198 in France, and a mere 741 in Saxony. The size of Saxony's population meant that a relatively small number of suicides became a relatively large suicide rate. Taken to absurd lengths a society of one hundred people with just one suicide each year would have a suicide rate of 10,000 per million inhabitants! Nevertheless, Durkheim compared these different rates and discovered that while different countries had different rates, each country's rate was remarkably consistent, over a period of many years. This consistency also showed itself in the relationship that Durkheim discovered between suicide and male sex, increasing age, single and divorced states, childlessness, residence in towns and the Protestant religion, as well as the inverse relationship with female sex, youth, rural living, war and the Catholic religion. On the basis of these 'social facts' as Durkheim called them, he constructed a threefold typology of suicide – egoistic, altruistic and anomic. Egoistic suicide is related to the degree of social integration within any community. The more integrated a community the less chance there is of a member of that community committing suicide. But, as Douglas (1967) argues, the amount of social integration can itself determine whether or not a death is in fact recorded as a suicide.

> . . . the more integrated the deceased individual is into his local community . . . the more the doctors, coroners, or other officials responsible for deciding what the cause of death is will be favourably influenced by the preferences of the deceased and his significant others. (Douglas, 1967, p. 213)

Accordingly, people who live alone are more likely to have their death recorded as a suicide because they have no family to negotiate with officials on their behalf. Similarly, since suicide is regarded with such abhorrence by Roman Catholics, the activities of families, doctors and coroners can turn a 'suicide' into an 'accident', thereby saving the family from shame, and the deceased from eternal damnation. Douglas criticises Durkheim for his assumption that suicide statistics all measure the same thing. Douglas argues that different definitions are used by officials in determining what constitutes a suicide, and that consequently suicide rates cannot be compared.

Atkinson (1971) shows that not only do coroners use different operational definitions of suicide, but they also use different search procedures to determine whether a death matches up to their definition. When a person dies in ambiguous circumstances, coroners look for particular clues which may suggest a suicide has taken place, and then search for the evidence which will support their initial view. For example, a coroner in a holiday area has been quoted as saying, 'A thing I look for in a drowning is whether or not the clothes are left folded. If they are found neatly folded on the beach, it usually points to a suicide.' (Atkinson, 1971, p. 179.) Following such 'evidence' a coroner will examine the life of the deceased, right up to his death, looking for anything which would make the act of suicide understandable.

According to popular theory, people commit suicide because they are unhappy. So evidence of unhappiness is seen as indicative of suicidal intent. Coroners reach their verdicts by using common-sense notions of what prompts a person to take his own life. The discovery of ill-health, the loss of a loved one, or failure at work are all seen as valid reasons for someone to be unhappy and consequently liable to commit suicide. If a coroner can find something in an individual's past life which might provoke unhappiness this will reinforce his initial judgement and a verdict of suicide will be recorded. The reporting of suicide by the media usually refers to the supposed cause, which in turn helps both coroners and the public to make sense of suicide and provides further support for the unhappiness theory of suicide.

One of the main points which can be gathered from the work of Douglas and Atkinson is that the search for the real suicide rate is pointless since the number of suicides in a given group at a given time is a product of the social processes involved in actually defining and recording suicide. The suicide rate does not exist as an objective fact awaiting measurement – the very process of measurement produces the rate.

Criminal Statistics

An examination of criminal statistics also serves to illustrate this idea that the process of collecting data is a social one, involving individuals making decisions, passing judgements and evaluating information. This is especially important since policies for dealing with offenders are often the result of analysing the known characteristics of convicted criminals. But what if convicted criminals are not typical of all those who commit crime? If the rate-producing process allows only a certain type of individual to become a criminal statistic, then any theory which attempts to explain crime on the basis of official criminal statistics must be suspect.

> The majority of our twenty-one investigations are thus in agreement in showing high rates of 'broken homes' amongst delinquents . . . various British studies place anything from 22 per cent to 57 per cent of their delinquents in this category, whereas control figures when available, range only from 11 per cent to 18 per cent. (Wootton, 1959)

To conclude from such figures that broken homes *cause* delinquency ignores the possibility that coming from a broken home may itself make a youngster more liable to prosecution and committal to institutional care. If parents are on hand when their child gets into trouble they may be able to prevent proceedings being taken. If not, the law will take its course.

Likewise, does the fact that our prisons tend to be filled with working-class men result from the greater tendency of this group to commit crimes, or is it the product of complex processes of interaction which render this group more susceptible to detection and prosecution?

The first problem is that the commission of a crime does not necessarily mean that it will be recorded. Most crimes are brought to the attention of the police by members of the public complaining that they have been robbed or assaulted, or that they have witnessed an offence. If these crimes are not reported, it is unlikely that they will be recorded. In some cases only the person who has committed the offence knows that a crime has occurred. Most shops and stores use a general concept known as stock-shrinkage to refer to goods lost through damage and decay as well as through theft by both customers and employees, and office workers seldom buy their own pens, pencils and envelopes, but 'borrow' those belonging to their employers. Even when there is knowledge that a crime has been committed prosecution does not necessarily follow. Banks are reluctant to prosecute employees who have helped themselves to the bank's money on account of the adverse publicity which would surround a criminal trial. Such an employee would most probably be dismissed or asked to resign but he would not have any criminal record to hinder future employment.

The protection afforded by institutions gives certain groups immunity from prosecution and is most significant in the process by which criminal statistics are produced. This immunity can be seen within the private education system in which the upper middle class child spends so much of his life. For example, a group of children from a private school wrecked a special train on which they were travelling. A spokesman for Southern Region railway explained that the school had been contacted, and as had happened on previous occasions the railways expected to receive sufficient money to cover the cost of the damage (Chapman, 1968, p. 69). Contrast this with the reaction of British Rail towards football vandals! Another example given by Chapman (1968, p. 70) is of a boy of sixteen operated on for a stomach injury resulting from a knife wound. According to the headmaster the boy had been injured in a 'friendly scuffle' and no action would be taken.

Even when the middle class are apprehended the consequences are likely to be much less severe. The contribution of police attitudes and practices to the crime rate can be seen by examining the discretion which the police have available to them. Many criminal statistics originate in an interaction situation between a police officer and a suspect. The police officer may choose to ignore the incident, give a warning, take particulars which will be passed on to senior officers, invite the suspect to the police station to answer a few questions, or he may arrest him. Senior police officers also have wide discretionary powers in deciding whether to prosecute, issue an official caution or take no action whatsoever. The alternative chosen by the policeman on the beat is very often a response to the behaviour and attitude of the suspect. If the suspect exhibits deference and sorrow a ticking-off may be his only punishment, whilst an arrogant and unrepentant attitude may well lead to arrest and prosecution. The behaviour of the policeman depends on the meaning that he gives to the situation in which he finds himself, and part of this is the perceived social status of the suspect. The way individual members of the police force behave in criminal situations depends on how crime and criminals fit into their world view. This view is affected by attitudes within the force and by its organisational practices. With a limited amount of manpower available decisions have to be made as to its allocation. The usual practice is to concentrate on those areas, usually working-class ones, in which, the police believe, most crime is committed. Such policing policies are inevitably self-fulfilling, since any crime which is committed is more likely to be detected and the criminal apprehended. The attitudes of the police towards particular offences may change over time, and from one area to another. This is well illustrated by the following extract quoted by Chapman (1968, p. 107) concerning the Manchester police force and their enforcement of the law concerning homosexuality:

In 1955 there was one prosecution for importuning, in 1956 and 1957 there were none and in 1958 there were two. M. J. A. McKay was appointed Chief Constable at the end of that year, and the number of prosecutions rose to thirty in 1959 and 105 in 1960, to 135 in 1961 to 216 last year (1962).

The role of the police in creating crime can also be seen in the practice of laying traps for potential criminals. In one instance, a police constable, with a colleague, hid in a cul-de-sac to await couples who might make love in motor cars. 'In the eighteen months before April 10th, 1959, he arrested ninety couples. Eighty-nine couples pleaded guilty, and the couple who pleaded not guilty were found guilty' (Chapman, 1968, pp. 119–20). Their offence was outraging public decency.

In addition to the police, other agencies have discretion in the matter of prosecution. The area of white collar crime is one where this discretion is often used to the benefit of the criminal. As defined by Sutherland (1940), this concept refers to 'crimes committed by persons of respectability and high status in the course of their occupations'. An example of this type of crime is income tax evasion which often results in the Inland Revenue merely requiring the tax to be repaid, although a crime has been committed.

What then is the value of criminal statistics? They should not be taken as a measure of the amount of crime, but rather as an indicator of how the police go about their work. Careful study of the statistics shows that convicted criminals are not a cross-section of all those who commit crimes but are those who have been processed through the law enforcement system. Equally, if not more, interesting are the people who commit crimes but fail to become criminal statistics.

Non-Official Statistics

If official statistics are so suspect, then perhaps the solution is for the sociologist to collect his own. But here similar problems may be encountered. Ian Shelton, in the next paper, examines these problems in detail, but one or two examples will serve to suggest that the information obtained by sociologists may be affected by the kind of questions they ask and the situations in which they ask them.

In their inquiry into family life in Bethnal Green, Young and Wilmott (1957, p. 47) state that men see less of their relatives than women. Fifty-five per cent of women had seen their mothers in the previous twenty-four hours, compared with only 31 per cent of men. But, as Jennifer Platt (1971, p. 49) points out, a lot of this information was obtained from the wives alone. Young and Willmott explain that husbands often visited their relatives on their own, and that since husbands and wives tended to lead separate lives, it could easily happen that wives would not know of all the times when their husbands saw relatives.

Katz (1942) has shown how the social class of the interviewer can produce different answers to questions about work and wages. He found that among the subjects interviewed by working class interviewers only 44 per cent spoke out for a law against sit-in strikes, while of those interviewed by middle class interviewers, 59 per cent expressed their support for such a law.

An investigation by Hyman (1954, p. 115) into the effect of an interviewer's sex found that, of 819 women interviewed by women, 49 per cent agreed with the statement that sexual offenders should be publicly flogged, but that the figure rose to 61 per cent for women interviewed by men. The social researcher may be highly trained in the best techniques for gathering information, but he cannot escape the fact that the very process of collecting data is a social event to which both interviewer and interviewee bring their own preconceptions and definitions.

Conclusion

Finally, are statistics of any value at all to the sociologist? Their use is widespread partly for the reasons already examined, and partly because they provide convenient ways of presenting information. However, their use must always be treated with suspicion, not because they might be biased, but because the process of collecting them is always 'social' no matter how 'scientific' it may appear. Their value may lie in the proposition that just as a job reference reveals more about the referee than the applicant, so statistics can give valuable insights into the values, definitions and organisational practices of those involved in the production of statistics. In using social statistics care must be taken not to concentrate on the 'statistical' whilst ignoring the 'social'.

Questions and Answers
by Ian Shelton
Sale Girls' Grammar School

When sociologists wish to find out something about some aspect of social life, such as the changing nature of family life, or attitudes towards comprehensive schools, they often conduct a *social survey*. The survey is the research procedure which the layman usually associates with sociology. The planning and implementation of a survey is very complex, and takes a great deal of time.

One of the major problems when conducting a survey is to decide which members of the public are to be approached for information. If the research project is trying, for example, to find out how marital roles are changing in contemporary families, there are a vast number of families which could potentially provide evidence. Even if the research is more limited in coverage, such as studying the rehabilitation problems of long-sentence prisoners, there are far more prospective 'informants' than the sociologist has time, energy and money to contact. Consequently contact is made with only a selection of the total (in the above cases – of families or prisoners). Such a selection is called a *sample*. Determining the sample is not straightforward because there are different principles and methods of sampling the population in question.

We are more concerned here, however, with the ways in which information is collected from people in the sample. The two main techniques used are *questionnaires* and *interviews*. They are similar in that they both involve the asking of questions; in questionnaires the questions are in written form and are to be completed by people unaccompanied by the researcher, whereas in interviews the questions are asked personally by the researcher or by a paid interviewer.

Questionnaires

Questionnaires are documents containing a number of questions which relate to the research topic (although some questions may relate to more general characteristics). The person who is given the questionnaire is called a *respondent*, that is, one who is asked to respond to the request for information. Since the respondent completes the questionnaire unsupervised, the latter must be clear and unambiguous for there is no opportunity to ask, 'What do you mean by. . . ?' It is also important to make it clear which questions are to be answered by whom. Some questions, for example, are only to be answered by those who have answered 'Yes' to a previous question:

> Q17) Would you bring back the death penalty for murder? Yes/No
>
> Q18) If 'yes' to Q17, would you make any exceptions to the rule? . . .

The overall presentation may be significant; a questionnaire which is unattractive and complex in format may yield a poor *response rate*. This means that few people within the sample actually fill it in. It is a temptation for researchers to collect a vast range of information in the hope that it might turn out to be useful. Researchers yielding to such a temptation are likely to be those who have failed thoroughly to plan their project. An overlong, and thus intimidating, questionnaire is likely to produce a low response rate.

Interviews

Interviews are face-to-face situations in which one person, an interviewer, asks various questions of the respondent. The extent to which this meeting is pre-planned and structured in advance by the interviewer will vary considerably. In *formal* interviewing, set questions are printed on a *schedule* (which is almost identical to a questionnaire in appearance); these questions are presented by the interviewer in a pre-determined sequence, and answers are recorded on the schedule. In *informal* interviewing, however, an interviewer may only have a brief written outline of the topics to be covered, so that the sequence and actual wording of questions are at the discretion of the interviewer. Some forms of informal interview simply require the interviewer to encourage the respondent to talk about the research topic within no set framework of questions. In practice, many interviews will fall at some point between the two 'pure' types of 'formal' and 'informal'.

The purpose of interviews is to try to elicit information in depth whilst trying to minimise the influence of the respondent; less structured, informal interviews, however, have built-in problems because interviewers are left more to their own devices and can therefore influence the respondent. Consequently interviewers are usually subjected to a training programme designed to minimise their personal influence whilst at the same time developing their conversational skills and their sensitivity to the relevance of issues raised by respondents.

Devising Questions

Questions usually elicit fact or opinion. A *factual* question produces an answer which is easily verified: for example, 'How many children under 16 years of age do you have?' Because of their factual nature, interviewers may be given some freedom to reword the questions to ensure clarity and ensure that the questions are understood. Such flexibility is less frequently accorded to *opinion* questions which try to elicit from respondents values, attitudes, and beliefs which are not verifiable: for example, 'Do you approve or disapprove of corporal punishment in school?' Opinion questions are more likely to touch upon sensitive and/or deeply held views, and the phrasing of questions is then more significant. The same is true of questions which ask respondents to give *reasons* for actions: for example, 'Why did you decide to have only one child?'

Researchers have always been aware that they can never be sure that responses are 'true' indications of respondents' feelings and attitudes. Irrespective of whether respondents intentionally or unintentionally mislead the interviewer, opinions are very complex. For example, some opinions may be to the forefront of respondents' minds, whereas others are more deeply rooted and need time and effort before they re-appear! Opinions are rarely cut-and-dried; rather do they have pros and cons attached to them so that the respondent feels that, 'it all depends . . .'. Some opinions are held more strongly than others; consequently the question, 'Do you approve or disapprove of X?' will produce a response that might mean 'Very much' or 'a little'.

It might appear from the foregoing that it is only opinion questions which create problems, but even factual questions can raise difficulties.

Researchers need to be sure that respondents are likely to possess the information required. This is doubtful with a question such as, 'How many times have you been to the cinema in the last two years?' On some issues, such as whether a husband and wife know how much their partner earns, ignorance might well be concealed, and an answer given either to please the interviewer or to maintain a favourable self-image. Researchers are aware, too, that although respondents are often willing to chat, in so doing they might be tempted to temper their responses towards a 'respectable' or 'acceptable' line perceived as being wanted by the interviewer. Consequently they under- or over-state their views.

These reservations about the difficulties inherent in devising questions apply both to questionnaires completed privately and to interviews, although it is in the latter that it is most likely that respondents will develop a conception of the interviewer and take that into account in deciding what to say. It is manifestly impossible to deter respondents from defining interview situations, interviewers and research projects in particular ways, for such definitions are 'normal' social activity. All researchers can do is to try to ensure that the questions themselves create few problems for respondents.

Question wording is highly significant – it affects whether a response is made at all, and, if so, the nature of that response. The main pitfalls are:

1 Questions which are not sufficiently specific. A question such as, 'Are you happy at school?' might produce a generalised 'Yes' or 'No' response; of course, 'happiness' may depend upon which aspect of school life is being considered.

2 Leading questions. 'Do you not think that smaller schools are better than larger ones?' prods the respondent towards an affirmative answer. Similarly, 'a lot of people now think that sex before marriage is reasonable. What do you think?'

3 Presuming questions – where the respondent is assumed to do or to think something. For example, 'How long is it since you last had a cigarette?' presumes a 'Yes' answer to an unasked question, 'Do you smoke?'

4 Double questions. To the question, 'Do you think that Labour has made a mess of government during the past three years, and that the Conservatives should be given a chance?', the respondent might want to say 'Yes' to the first part, and 'No' to the second, or vice versa. A double question prohibits such a distinction.

5 Causal and coincidental links. An ambiguity or uncertainty, similar to 4 above, occurs when a causal relationship is attributed to something: for example, 'Do you think that educational standards have declined since the introduction of comprehensive schools?' It may be that a respondent would want to argue that educational standards have declined, but not necessarily since, or because, comprehensive schools were introduced. Standards might have declined coincidentally alongside the development

of comprehensives. A straight 'yes' might be made, then, falsely implying acceptance of the causal relationship. Similarly, a 'No' response might be made so as to dispute the causal relationship even though the respondent feels that standards have declined. 'Yes' and 'No' answers therefore can mean either the same or different things to different people.

6 Terminology difficulties. Questions using vague words such as 'generally', 'sometimes' or 'seldom' will be interpreted differently by respondents and the resulting responses will not be strictly comparable. Questions using complex vocabularies may create different problems, as when the vocabulary is highly abstract and involves long words, or when it uses technical sociological language: for example, 'To what extent have you been socialised into internalising middle-class traits?'

7 Hypothetical questions. Answers to a question such as 'What would you do if you inherited half-a-million pounds?' might tell us something about escapist ideas, or desired expenditure, or greed. And which one would constitute the 'truth'?

The task of the researcher designing a questionnaire or an interview schedule must be to try to phrase questions in straightforward, everyday language, and to try to avoid ambiguities, leading questions, etc. Often, researchers will carefully try out early versions of questionnaires or schedules on some respondents so as to anticipate any problems in wording or sequence.

Dealing with Answers

Answers depend very much on the questions asked. Typically there are two types of question: open and pre-coded. An open question is one to which the respondent's actual response is transcribed by the interviewer on the schedule in as much detail as possible. The form of the response, its length and the amount of detail, are determined by the respondent. The advantage of such questions is that the respondent's verbatim or summarised response is preserved for later analysis and re-analysis – at least in the form in which it has been noted! The main disadvantage is that of organising a vast variety of responses into some semblance of order. The subtleties of response make later categorisation – *coding* as it is called – difficult, especially when different amounts of response-detail are involved. In short, it is practically difficult to compress written, qualitative responses tightly into categories. The meaning of an answer can often be conveyed by tone of voice, facial expression, gesture and pause, and this part of the response would be missing for office-based coders. Sometimes interviewers are asked to comment upon the manner of the interviewee, for example upon cooperativeness; although this may fill in detail about the interview as a social occasion, office-based analysts are still faced with an interviewer's account of what happened rather than the occasion itself.

Pre-coded questions, on the other hand, involve the determination of codes or categories in advance. On both questionnaires and interview-schedules, there will be a series of answers from which the interviewer can select. For example:

25. What kind of music do you enjoy most?
    1 ☐ rock and roll
    2 ☐ calypso
    3 ☐ other popular music
    4 ☐ jazz
    5 ☐ classical
    6 ☐ country and western

(Coleman, 1957)

This means that data-collection and coding are combined, thus saving a great deal of time. It is arguable too that the interviewers are the best persons to code because they hear answers in full, and therefore have more data at their fingertips than would office-coders. On the other hand, using pre-coded questions requires considerable trust in the qualities of interviewers, for once answers have been coded on the spot, no later checks are possible (unless samples of interviews are recorded).

Pre-coding is more likely to be acceptable if the series of answers are well-tried in pre-tests or pilot surveys, and if the alternatives in the series are exhaustive and mutually exclusive, so that answers are not forced into one category or another. However, it seems impossible to avoid some answers being forced into one category or another; there are inevitably answers which are marginal. In interviews, the interviewer will decide quickly into which category the answer must fall; with questionnaires, the respondent will make that decision . . . perhaps at greather length. The more categories there are, the more marginal answers there are requiring decisions, and the more likely that people will take a middle or less extreme course. The fewer the categories, the less likely that the category reflects the subtleties of emphasis and detail of the actual answer. In sum, it is clear that responses to pre-coded questions are being channelled into particular categories by either respondent or interviewer; and responses to open questions are channelled into categories by office-based researchers.

In both cases, the codes or categories are determined by the research team and, as such, they represent the meanings of team-members. Even if the categories are produced after rigorous pre-testing, those categories embody meanings which are being imposed on other respondents. Consequently, respondents' meanings are being channelled into the expressed meanings of others. Goldthorpe et al., studying the industrial attitudes of affluent manual workers, enquired in interview into the wider social relationships which are based on work:

12. (a) And which of these kinds of people would you be most likely to be put off making friends with? *Hand card*.

People whose work puts them in a different class
People who're a bit common
People from a very different background and outlook
People who live in a way that I'd find it hard to keep up with
People who talk about things I don't understand
(b) Why is that?

(Goldthorpe et al., 1967)

In this case, criteria for choice of friends are presented to the respondent as 'givens'. In more general terms, questions, like codes, must necessarily reflect researchers' meanings (which may have been partly derived from pre-test respondents' meanings); in other words, questions reflect researchers' interpretation and knowledge of the social world. Hence some words are used rather than others in questions; and some topics and issues are raised rather than others. This leads us to the view that the 'findings' of social research are *created* in that they reflect the meanings of data-collectors and analysts, as well as of respondents. What we have to decide is whether this matters: does research – 'give or take a little' or 'within limits' – give us a reasonable picture of the social world? Some of the problems we have outlined are seemingly inescapable, so we might have to adopt a pragmatic stance, accepting findings with a small pinch of salt. And the problem of meaning is acknowledged by researchers. Jackson and Marsden, for example, in their study of working-class grammar school children, comment that, 'not all of them judged "success" by the measure we had applied – total grammar school education' (Jackson and Marsden, 1962).

Interviewing as a Process
Interviewing has always been seen as a complex and skilled activity, usually requiring training. It was suggested earlier that the purpose of structured interviews is to minimise the personal influence of the interviewer, and that the difficulty is primarily with unstructured or open interviews in which the interviewer is left to his own devices. It is important to recognise, however, that both forms of interview are necessarily social occasions involving face-to-face interaction. First, researchers must gain permission to conduct the interview; and gaining the cooperation of the prospective respondent (at home or at work) will require that the interviewer present both self and project in a favourable manner. In other words, the interviewer may have to put on a *performance* designed to impress the respondent with the value, confidentiality, or utility of the interview. Evidence suggests that the interviewer's apparent interest in, and sense of value of, the survey are important in securing a good response rate. Introductions, then, are important in getting cooperation, but they may also be instrumental in fashioning the respondent's perception of the interviewer and the project – information important in developing answers to questions to come. Perceptions of

interviewers' social class, race and sex might all be important in fashioning response.

Second, all social actors communicate by a multiplicity of techniques, and sociologists such as Goffman (1959) have clearly shown that verbal means (words, tone of voice and intonation) are supplemented by varieties of non-verbal means (facial expression, body movement and gesture). Even silence can be communicative. Interviews are no exceptions here, and inevitably formal questionning and answering will be accompanied by complex non-verbal interaction such as smiles and nods of the head, some of which could be interpreted as 'encouraging'. Even the questions themselves can be expressed in different ways – with different inflexions and emphases. Of course, the absence of such non-verbal phenomena might be interpreted as 'strangeness' or 'coldness'; their absence would be noticed.

Third, it is part of standard interview procedure to *probe*. Probing involves the asking of supplementary questions when the answer to the main question is brief or vague. Some probes can be pre-planned in nature and in timing; thus Cicourel and Kitsuse (1964) always follow up a question-and-answer interchange with 'How do you mean?':

> (1) First we'd like to know a little about your work in junior high school.
> (b) (Whatever the response to (a), ask) How do you mean?
> (c) How did your parents feel you did in junior high school?
> (d) (Whatever the response to (c), ask) How do you mean?
> (e) How did your parents feel about the grades you got?
> (f) How do you mean?
> (g) How did you feel about your grades?
> (h) How do you mean?
> (i) How did your friends feel about the grades you got?
> (j) How do you mean?

Other probes might be left to the interviewer. In both circumstances, and particularly the latter, the interviewer is clearly helping the respondent to produce an acceptable response, with criteria for 'acceptability' being in the hands of the interviewer.

Fourth, interviews are not straightforward question-answer sequences as they appear on interview schedules: they are much more elaborately constructed phenomena. By 'construction' we mean that the interview is built-up, maintained and modified through the complex verbal interaction between interviewer and respondent. One of the most obvious illustrations of this is in the incidence of the utterances 'mm' and 'yeah'; thus apparently straightforward statements often turn out to involve complex interaction, with the interviewer skilfully and imperceptibly helping to maintain the interview. In the following example, note how the interviewer's utterances are interspersed throughout single sentences:

Teacher: . . . that's how I see it or that's part of my experience too
Interviewer: Mm
Teacher: I suppose there are other things that they understand that
           they don't have experience of but I don't think that's as easy
           to notice
Interviewer: Mm
Teacher: it's not as immediate that comes out later
Interviewer: Mm
Teacher: perhaps in written work and discussions
Interviewer: Mm
Teacher: later on. . . .   (Shelton, 1977)

We must now question the extent to which the interviewer is encouraging
and rewarding the respondent. We do not know, of course, whether the
teacher being interviewed *interprets* the 'mm' as rewarding a particular
kind of response, or as some kind of general encouragement, that is, part
of 'putting me at ease'. Some 'mm's' may be occasioned by the end of a
clause, but others may come half-way through phrases. It may be that
'mm' allows of, or encourages, a continuation of an answer, rather than
constituting a specific probe. In the following extract, the interviewer's
'mm' is followed by a pause before the respondent continues. Of course,
although the respondent does continue, we do not know for certain that
she felt constrained to do so:

Teacher: and IR would listen a lot more where IP wanted to do all
           the talking and the action themselves
Interviewer: Mm (pause 3·0 seconds)
Teacher: and I felt also that . . .

Yet the complexities of open interview talk are clearly illustrated thus:

Interviewer: By language work this is ⎰ what (   ) adjectives
Teacher: ⎱ I mean formal things
Interviewer: ad ⎰ verbs
Teacher: ⎱ yeah yeah
Interviewer: and so on
Teacher: yeah
Interviewer: Do ⎰ they fa   ⎰ How do they find that
Teacher: ⎱ (   ) structure ⎱ (   )   (Shelton, 1977)

This is a good example of the more sophisticated talk handled in
interviews, embodying (i) interruptions, (ii) overlapping talk (breaking all
conversational 'rules' about one speaker speaking at one time), and (iii)
linking 'yeah's. In the following extracts we can note how respondents
monitor interviewer's talk as part of their process of responding, that is,
they carefully listen to and analyse the interviewer's utterances and use
their analysis as a basis for their own response:

```
Teacher:    Played 'Round the Bend'
Interviewer: (laugh) surprise surprise
Teacher:    Surprise surprise yes
                    *              *              *
Interviewer: what are the consequences of parents telling you
             that on the way  ⌠ that you see kids from then on
Teacher:                      ⌡ yeah on the way you see the kids
             from then onwards                    (Shelton, 1977)
```

In the second extract, we have a long repeat of, 'on the way that you see the kids from then on . . .': the words are identical. The fact that it is identical is all the more interesting because the teacher's repeat commences not only before the interviewer has finished, but does so after only three words of the interviewer's utterance have been expressed. The respondent-teacher is clearly repeating earlier parts of the utterance whilst at the same time monitoring later parts as expressed by the interviewer. This is but one small example; the above cases, however, start to reflect the close cooperation between interviewer and respondent, indicating in turn how the two actors may come to collaboratively build up a version of the social world.

As I mentioned earlier, all this may not matter to you; it is possible to accept the unavoidable limitations of questionnaires and interviews and simply seek to avoid the most obvious pitfalls. Consequently, one would endeavour to present one's research in the most meaningful and attractive manner, trying to produce the clearest, least ambiguous questions possible. On the other hand, you may wish to recognise that social research is a social process, which in turn prompts you to ask whether research 'findings' are necessarily invalidated. Certainly, sociology becomes as much a topic for research as 'the family' or 'schools', for sociology is social activity.

Joining In
by Stan Meredith
City of Liverpool College of Higher Education

Introduction

'Joining in' as a method of social research has traditionally gone by the name of 'participant observation', and in this paper I identify some of the distinguishing features, strengths and difficulties associated with its use.

Of course, all methods of social research involve observation to some extent. What characterises participant observation, however, is the extent to which its advocates insist that their observations and interpretations of a situation or event are informed, as fully as possible, by an understanding of the situation from the point of view of the participants themselves, rather than as it may appear to an outsider. Participant observation constitutes a 'qualitative' approach to research, concerned to try to penetrate the social and normative patterns and meanings of social actors, as a primary basis for explanation.

Research through participant observation has long held a central place in anthropology, and, indeed, it has been applied to a broad range of situations in sociology, among them countless community studies, and studies of factories, hospitals, prisons, asylums, gangs and the police. In all these studies, the researcher has 'become part of a daily round, learning languages and meanings, rules of interpersonal relations . . . and, in short, living the life of the people under study' (Hughes, 1976, p. 118). However, despite the variety of data-source that has been associated with participant observation, its value as a method has been largely overlooked. Undoubtedly, part of the resistance to its fuller use stems from a concern about the capacity of participant observation to meet strict criteria of scientific adequacy. This will be discussed more fully below.

Florence Kluckhohn (1940) defines participant observation as:

> . . . conscious and systematic sharing, in so far as circumstances permit, in the life activities, and, on occasion, in the interests and affects of a group of persons. Its purpose is to obtain data about behaviour through direct contact and in terms of specific situations in which the distortion that results from the investigator's being an outside agent is reduced to a minimum.

Howard Parker (1974, p. 221) interprets this maxim to mean that while the researcher may be watching or taking part, he should not, 'alter the group's direction. One may occasionally alter content, but never form.' In his study of downtown adolescents in Liverpool, for whom theft of 'catseyes' (car radios) was a regular pastime, Parker recalls on one occasion suggesting postponing theft to another evening, because of 'strategic circumstances' only. That is to say, his advice did alter the content of one particular evening in the group's life, but not the form evenings took at that time.

We can see, then, that participant observation ideally requires sharing, without disturbing, the sentiments and experiences of people in social situations. Yet, while Kluckhohn's statement conveys the general tone of participant observation, it fails to hint at the variety of forms such research may assume, and these are numerous. Indeed, there is a certain vagueness about what the method entails, for many writers admit to a strongly personalised element in participant observation. Fletcher (1974, p. 124) notes that, 'a qualitative researcher does his training "in the field"'; Moser (1958, p. 169) comments that, 'participant observation is a highly individual technique'; Patrick (1973, p. 14), in his study of a Glasgow gang, 'expected to have to "play it by ear"'. Recognition of the individualistic and developmental nature of participant observation need not be taken as a drawback, however, but as evidence of its capacity for flexibility within a general strategy conceived by the researcher. Nevertheless, it is possible to recognise recurrent features in the variety of forms this method has assumed, not all of which in fact involve 'joining in'.

Forms of Participant Observation

Raymond Gold (1958) has developed a four-fold classification of research roles.

THE COMPLETE PARTICIPANT

In the complete participant role, the true identity and motives of the researcher are not made known to the people with whom he is participating and whom he is simultaneously observing for research purposes. Such a researcher may, for example, become a worker in an office or factory to learn about the structure and attitudes of work groups, as did Carter (1954) in a factory for four months as part of a wider study of 'Radby'. To answer inquiries about his background, he introduced himself as a student wanting temporary employment, but did not indicate the real purpose of his presence. He endeavoured to become 'regarded as an ordinary workman' (p. 53), and to this end it was 'necessary to establish intimate social relations and not give the impression of disapproval' (p. 50). He sought to overcome barriers arising from his being a 'student' by joining in the customary types of activities and conversations of the men, including laughing at dirty jokes, swearing, 'complaining' with them about wages and working conditions, and going to working men's clubs and cafés.

With the complete participant role there is a large element of pretence, which can pose real dilemmas for the researcher. Such dilemmas are vividly brought to mind by the experiences of the researchers who penetrated a religious cult which believed the end of the world to be imminent. The team, 'had to conduct the entire enquiry covertly, without revealing . . . (their) . . . research purpose, pretending to be merely interested individuals who had been persuaded of the correctness of the belief system' (Festinger et al., 1956, p. 252). They had to sustain their deception yet play a full part in the life of the group, whilst trying, too, to avoid influencing the group's direction. Occasions when one of them would be asked to take on responsibility or initiate action in the group, such as becoming its 'medium' or 'messenger', or even answering the phone, needed extremely delicate handling. Indeed, the researchers do not claim to have succeeded in their goal of complete neutrality and non-influence: they acknowledge that their presence lent support to the convictions and activities of the existing members.

Complete participant roles carry two potential problems. First, that the researcher may become so concerned not to break his cover that he does not perform convincingly in the assumed role; and second, become so involved that he 'goes native': in so doing, he may lose his research perspective and find it difficult to perceive the relationship between his experiences and wider sociological issues.

THE PARTICIPANT-AS-OBSERVER

With the participant-as-observer role, researcher and informant are aware that theirs is a research relationship, and role-pretence is minimised. The researcher's observation activities are not wholly concealed, but are played down while he gets on with participating. This role has been used in many community studies, and was, essentially, the role used by Elliot Liebow (1967) for his study of Negro men on 'Tally's Corner'. He notes that 'the people I was observing knew that I was observing them, yet they allowed me to participate in their activities, and take part in their lives to a degree that continues to surprise me' (p. 253). Sometimes, the researcher may establish and maintain open relationships with certain key individuals in the community he is observing, and their sponsorship may ease his acceptance in the community. Thus, W. F. Whyte's task of entering, living in and studying the social structure of an Italian-American slum, 'Cornerville', in the late 1930's was made easier by the support, over three and a half years, from 'Doc', the leader of the 'Nortons' gang. Whyte came to be known as someone writing a book on Cornerville, but primarily as 'Doc's pal, Bill'. James Patrick, at the time an approved school teacher, found it possible to participate in, and observe, a Glasgow gang on twelve occasions, following an introduction by one of his pupils, Tim, who was a prominent member of the 'Young Team'. Patrick became known as Tim's 'haufer' (that is, his best friend from approved school).

A danger with the participant-as-observer role is that the informants become so identified with the researcher that they themselves become observers. W. F. Whyte noted that Doc became a true 'collaborator in the research' (1943, p. 301). While such assistance can be most profitable, the researcher has to beware inducing changes in the normal behaviour of any of his subjects, or the concealment of their true attitudes. This potential is known as a 'control effect': a change in the behaviour of subjects, unwittingly yet directly, produced by the research process. Indeed, Doc remarked to Whyte that 'you've slowed me up plenty. Now, when I do something, I have to think what Bill Whyte would want to know about it . . . before, I used to do things by instinct' (1943, p. 301).

The danger exists with this role too that the researcher may over-identify and become so involved that he too fully takes the view of his informants and ceases to function as a researcher. As Whyte noted, 'as I became accepted into the community, I found myself becoming almost a non-observing participant' (1943, p. 321). 'Time-out' for reflection or for discussion with a colleague or outside supervisor can sometimes protect against a participant observation researcher 'going native'.

While it is mainly in the above two senses that we use the term 'participant observer', we can note that Gold identifies two other forms.

THE OBSERVER-AS-PARTICIPANT

This role is associated mainly with studies involving one-visit interviews when some formal observation may be possible, but participation is specific and limited. While this position avoids any problems which may arise from longer involvements, it carries the obvious risk of generating only a superficial appreciation.

THE COMPLETE OBSERVER

The fourth observer role is that of the 'complete observer'. In this role, there is no joining in at all by the researcher, as his purpose is to observe people without their knowledge and without interaction. This role is seldom used as a dominant strategy, other than for systematic eavesdropping or gaining an initial grasp of some social setting. Clearly, there is a strong chance with this role, too, that an adequate basis for understanding is not provided.

'Getting in, Staying in, Getting out' (Simey)

With the exception of the fourth type in Gold's framework, participant observation requires the researcher to occupy, and be accepted in, a position in some existing framework of social relationships. This requirement poses practical problems for the researcher. S. Bruyn (1966, p. 18) has recognised that 'the participant observer must be able to find a satisfactory entrée, develop and maintain a role adequate to meet his research needs, and, finally, be able to terminate relationships in a way reasonably consistent with cultural expectations'. The management of these different stages may vary significantly according to the form of participant observation adopted and the personal skills of the reseacher. It is interesting, however, to consider some of the ways researchers have tried to cope with these tasks.

GETTING IN

Participant observers have to conduct themselves, particularly in the early days of their research, in such ways that they may 'become an unobtrusive part of the scene, people whom the participants take for granted and consider to be non-threatening' (Bogdan and Taylor, 1975, p. 41). Many researchers suggest the need to go slowly at first, and spend time 'sizing' the situation, possibly in a manner comparable with that of a detective. It took Liebow, a Jew, about four weeks hanging about on an irregular basis, in the cafés of 'Tally's Corner', making and developing contacts before he effectively penetrated the world of the Negro street-corner men. Significant in his getting in was his preparedness to become an informal legal aide of one of the men, who was on trial. We have indicated already that some researchers have found the problem of entry to be minimised by an introduction from strategically placed individuals or by having some existing contact. Howard Parker, for example, had met some of the

'Roundhouse' boys while working in a holiday centre which catered for youngsters from Liverpool's repressed inner city. He found, on this account, that entry into 'Roundhouse' society was 'easy and rapid' (1974, p. 215).

On some occasions, researchers may have to move quickly because of the exigencies of the research situation or phenomenon – Lane and Roberts (1971), for example, whose presence for intensive research, using a variety of approaches, was not resisted by the leaders of a strike which happened with little warning. Festinger and colleagues (1956) equipped four observers with fake stories or psychic experiences which were instrumental in their rapidly penetrating two groups of an exclusive cult. The ethical considerations of this elaborate disguise were seen as less important than the research task. Others, however, have argued against 'spying' for research. Tom Lupton (1963), for example, in order to circulate freely and avoid suspicion, explained his research purposes to all sides at the onset of his study of work groups. He termed his approach 'open participant observation', which he undertook whilst a 'smearer', then a 'sweeper', in two factories.

Ultimately, it may be the researcher's own personality and style which make possible participant observation in some contexts. Parker (1974, p. 233) accepts that, 'if I hadn't been young, hairy, boozy, etc., etc., willing to keep long hours, accept "permissive standards", the liaison would have failed'. Patrick similarly found that common interests, clothes, even which jacket buttons are fastened, may be taken as symbols of one's acceptability into the social world of a group. These points may indeed be equally relevant to the task of maintaining one's position.

STAYING IN

Elliot Liebow, conscious of being an outsider through race, occupation, education and residence, made himself, no less than his participants, more comfortable on 'Tally's Corner' by adopting their speech and dress – by which he claims to have 'dulled some of the characteristics of . . . (his) . . . background' (1967, p. 255). The participant observer ordinarily has to come to terms with a complex set of norms, relationships and activities, and to try to develop a sense of the meanings these have for the people he is studying. To this end, the researcher's skills in questioning, watching, listening and participating have to be managed effectively without jeopardising his research interests or straining relationships with the subjects. Especially in the early days, the researcher may not be able to ask many direct questions without inviting suspicion, and he may have either to wait for the information to come to him, or to pursue it very sensitively. W. F. Whyte was advised by Doc to lay off asking questions and to 'hang around and you'll learn the answers in the long run without even having to ask the questions' (1943, p. 303). Lest it is thought, however, that the researcher simply receives what the subjects choose to make known to him or selects that which he wants to see and hear, we must remember that the researcher, with continuing contact, is able to gather data by several procedures, in several settings and moods. This variety will allow him to crosscheck his conclusions and retest them repeatedly.

In some cases, researchers have taken on a particular role among their subjects as a useful vantage point for observation. Frankenberg (1957), for example, served on the committee of the Football Club in Glynceiriog; W. F. Whyte accepted the nomination as secretary of the Italian Community Club. The participant observer will anyway find it difficult to resist becoming bound up with the conventions and obligations of the group into whose company he moves. Lupton received 'stick' from his work-mates for not keeping to group norms of working; Liebow found himself and his personal resources (money, car, etc.) caught up in the customary give-and-take of everyday social interaction on 'Tally's Corner'.

When a group's activities border on deviance, this may pose moral dilemmas for the researcher, and his decisions may threaten his relationship with the group. Polsky (1963) has argued that for effective study of law-breaking deviants as they engage in deviance, the researcher has to be prepared in some ways to break the law himself – not necessarily to commit the deviant acts himself, but 'obstruct justice' or become an 'accessory'. This was the line taken by Parker in Liverpool: as with most adults in the neighbourhood, he would receive 'knock-off' and say nothing, even 'keep dixy', but would not actually get his hands dirty. Patrick in Glasgow was 'roundly abused' for his reluctance to join in a gang fight, yet the fact that he shared the frightening experience of being picked up by the police earned him 'a minimal measure of acceptance' (1973, p. 58) from the 'Young Team'.

'Observer fright', it seems, is an aspect of the experience of some participant observers, and most such research has its share of crises, mistakes and embarrassments which have to be managed as they happen. Participant observation can also be very wearying, physically and mentally, and 'observer fatigue' is common. Research tasks such as recording observations, discriptions and comments, and time for reflection and evaluation may be possible only long after the event and/or by ingenious methods (for example, Festinger's team used the bathroom in relays to make notes).

GETTING OUT

Leaving the situation will vary, of course, but typically will be undertaken when the researcher is confident that he has acquired sufficient data to meet his research objectives, in the time available to him. The problem of terminating relationships with research subjects is one that happens whether the research is covert or overt. The management of this task may be harder where the relationships adopted by the researcher have not been understood as existing for research purposes by those he has observed, or where occasional withdrawal during the research has not been possible. Unfortunately, 'exiting' is a neglected feature of research reports. Of the research illustrations used here, Festinger's team, and Lane and Roberts, were able to conclude their research shortly after the conclusion of the event itself; a leaving presentation was arranged for Lupton by his workmates, and a party for W. F. Whyte, who, nevertheless, returned several times. Parker, too, phased his exit very gradually, while Patrick, unable to stomach the gang's violence, left quickly before the occasion of another fight.

Some Further Issues

Participant observation has come under fire from some sociologists on a number of counts. One of these is doubt about the objectivity and reliability of the researcher's observations and interpretations: in short, the extent to which the conclusions reached would be confirmed by another researcher using the same method. We have already noted the possibility of the researcher seeing only those things which agree with his explicit hypotheses or implicit personal tastes and loyalties. Yet, the participant observer may minimise bias by trying to cover all types of events by some kind of sampling device (for example, observing at different times of the day, or days of the week, or varying one's respondents from the group or community), and including a complete account of all events observed in the research report. Further, Becker (1958, p. 27) reminds us that in participant observation, analysis is carried out 'sequentially', important parts of the analysis being made while the researcher is gathering his data. This enables tentative hypotheses to be formulated as the research proceeds, and then be tested by the researcher, deliberately looking for negative cases. Becker also suggests that a record of processes by which conclusions are reached, and of what sorts of evidence are taken as critical at different stages of the research process, is invaluable for others to follow the details of the analysis and to appraise the research.

Another important issue is that of validity, 'the extent to which the collected data reflect naturally occurring social behaviour and processes' (Sanders 1974, p. 7). We have already mentioned the potential 'control effect' in participant observation but ought to note that this is not always the case. Other research methods may also suffer from 'control effect'. Indeed, it is claimed that several features of participant observation make for the construction of more valid accounts than may be possible with other methods. The participant observer typically has the advantages of extended contact to deepen his understanding, and can collect a large number of observations and variety of data, including possibly the opportunity to assess the constraints arising from his own presence. These features are seen to facilitate a faithful portrayal of the subjects' experiences and a firm footing for sociological explanation.

Another doubt concerns whether the findings of participant observation can be generalised to other settings or subjects. It is not necessarily the case, however, that the practitioners of the method do regard their work as a basis for generalisation. Rather, it is viewed as a method which may provide sensitive understanding, 'plausible' explanations, and ideas to guide subsequent research.

Despite the techniques which may be incorporated into participant observation to boost reliability and validity, there remain suspicions that participant observers make unacknowledged inferences and 'subjective' interpretations. However, many of the advocates of participant observation stress the importance of one central notion: that individuals make sense of, and give meaning to, the social world around them in their everyday life through processes of 'interpretation'. Significantly, this is held to be equally true of the researcher engaged in the social act of research: the way in which he makes sense of a social situation is seen to be much the same as the way the participants do – by role-taking and interpretation through interaction. Accordingly, the task of the researcher is to try to capture the process and direction of the interpretations and experiences of the people he studies and to derive an understanding from their point of view. The pursuit of a detached objectivity is seen as a false and forlorn quest. As Blumer (1962, p. 188) advises:

> to try to catch the interpretative process by remaining aloof as a so-called 'objective' observer and refusing to take the role of the acting unit is to risk the worst kind of subjectivism – the objective observer is likely to fill in the process of interpretation with his own surmises in place of catching the process as it occurs in the experience of the acting unit which uses it.

The method of participant observation, critically and carefully applied, is considered to be most suited to this task.

Experiments Without Rats
by Janice Myerson

Have you ever walked into a café and noticed where people sit when they come in? Have you ever tried to see what happens when you try to share a table when there are other ones free? If so, then you have been carrying out an experiment of the sort that has recently become popular within a particular area of sociology. However, this may not correspond with your idea of an experiment. You may suppose that experiments take place in laboratories, are conducted by white-coated scientists and involve the use of apparatus like test tubes and microscopes. This view is not surprising for the experiment has developed with the growth of the natural sciences and is the best method scientists have for testing their hypotheses.

The logic of the scientific method was set out by John Stuart Mill as long ago as 1843 and was named, 'The Method of Difference'. To illustrate what he meant, take two glasses of water which are identical in every respect, for example, in the shape, size and the volume of water that they contain. Introduce a few drops of ink into one of these glasses of water. Immediately the water changes colour. According to Mill's Method of Difference, it is safe to say that the change in the colour of the water is due to the introduction of a new factor or *independent variable*, in this case, the ink. In this way the scientist aims to manipulate those factors or variables which are seen as important in order to observe and measure their effect on the phenomenon under study – the *dependent variable*. The dependent variable is divided into two identical groups, only one of which – the experimental group – is exposed to the independent variable. A highly controlled situation is created in the laboratory to eliminate those factors which are not the subject of the experiment, but which could contaminate it and thus the scientist is able to ensure that changes in the experimental group are the direct result of the introduction of a particular independent variable.

What significance then does the experiment have for the sociologist? Some of the early social scientists believed that social phenomena were no different from natural phenomena. Those methods which were used by natural scientists, and which were seen as being the most accurate way of gaining knowledge, were therefore also held to be appropriate for the social scientist. However, because of the fundamental differences between inanimate objects and human subjects, sociologists have experienced difficulties in trying to use the experiment as a tool of enquiry. Research conducted at the Hawthorne Plant of the Western Electric Company in 1925 provides a useful illustration.

The research at the Hawthorne Plant was inaugurated by the management of the factory in order to ascertain the effect of various changes in working conditions on industrial output. One experiment involved gradually raising the illumination level in three departments of the factory. However, as no direct relationship between the change in lighting and the level of output seemed apparent, they decided to institute a control group. Workers of equal experience were therefore divided into two groups, one of which was exposed to constant illumination, the other to variable illumination. Output rose for both groups. Thinking that the variable of illumination level had not been controlled precisely enough, the researchers then excluded daylight. Again output rose for both groups. Next the researchers took two workers who were told that the level of illumination was being raised when in fact it was not. The workers commented favourably on the increase in illumination and output remained fairly constant.

These results made the researchers realise that the level of illumination itself was not of paramount importance. In order to clarify the significant variables, they decided to study a small group of workers. They asked for volunteers to help ascertain how fatigue and monotony affected output. A repetitive job – the assembly of a telephone relay – was chosen for the experiment. Records were made of the number of relays asssembled by each volunteer and the pace at which they worked. The volunteers were given physical examinations; daily temperature and humidity readings were taken, and records were kept of wage payments which were affected by output. The workers were supported by regular interviews with the researchers. Once the experiment had been established, changes were gradually introduced. For example, rest period times were altered, as was the length of the working day. Results showed that over the two years duration of the experiment, output generally increased, even when working conditions were identical. This lead the researchers to the conclusion that *social* rather than physical factors were of prime importance. By trying to establish an experimental situation in which all factors were controlled, the researchers had in fact introduced into the situation a new factor, the social influence of the researchers themselves. Variation in output was not linked to physical changes but to the amount of attention workers received.

Ethically, too, there are problems for the sociologist which the natural scientist is less likely to meet. For example, if subjects are aware that they are part of an experiment, then they may well alter their behaviour. On the other hand it may be considered morally wrong not to tell them. The use of volunteers also creates difficulties in that they may not be representative of the group under study, by virtue of the fact that they have volunteered. Certain behaviour may also be seen as unjustifiable for the sake of an experiment, for example, depriving people of benefits due to them or removing children from their natural parents in order to test theories of socialisation.

A controversial experiment conducted in 1964 by Rosenthall and Jacobson illustrates some of the difficulties mentioned above. The aim of the experiment was to test the hypothesis that poor children perform badly in school because of teacher expectations and not because they are members of a disadvantaged group. In a school in San Francisco, teachers were therefore asked to administer I.Q. tests to their pupils. Because it was felt to be potentially dangerous to establish expectations that certain pupils might show inferior performance, the teachers were told that the tests were designed to predict intellectual gains in children. The teachers, who were unaware of the experiment, were then informed casually that 20 per cent of the children were expected to show unusual intellectual gains in the year ahead. In fact the 20 per cent had been chosen completely randomly and the difference between them and the undesignated children, who constituted a control group, was entirely in the minds of the teachers. The same tests were then administered to the children on three more occasions over a period of about 18 months. Results indicated strongly that children from whom teachers expected greater intellectual gain did in fact exhibit such gain. Was this experiment fair to those children who were not chosen but who could have benefited similarly from teacher expectations?

Even if these ethical problems can be overcome by the experimenter, practical and theoretical problems still remain. In order to control all the factors except the independent variable, the researcher requires a coherent and undisputed body of theory which will help identify all the important variables involved. It may also be extremely difficult to find experimental and control groups that are alike in every respect, even with the use of sampling techniques such as matching and randomisation. Sherif, writing about his experiments to ascertain how group norms develop and their consequences for the individual, said, 'it took two and a half years to formulate the experimental set-up, although only about six months were needed for the experiments themselves'. In order to solve the theoretical question of when and how norms are constructed Sherif needed to find a situation where subjects would have no ready made rules to follow. He thus chose a dark room which was both sound- and light-proof, and placed a light in it. To a person placed in this room, the light would appear to move, an illusion known as the auto-kinetic effect. A number of students were then taken into the room and asked to judge how far the light moved. Some students were taken in first individually and then in a group, and then individually. Others were taken in as a group first and then individually. As any movement was, in fact, an illusion, Sherif was certain that all perception of movement came solely from the experimental group. All the students set up their own norms of movement, but when a group of students were in the room their judgements of movement converged. Those students who started off with others in the room agreed to a much greater extent than those who first went in alone. When taken in individually after being in a group the students saw the movement in terms of the norm set by the group.

As a result of the difficulties described above, some sociologists have relied on 'natural' experiments such as studying the development of individuals who have been deprived of early socialisation; others have used totally different methods of enquiry, such as participant observation, to test their theories. However, the experiment has not disappeared from the social sciences altogether. Psychologists, notably, have removed some of the problems associated with the use of experiments by using as subjects animals such as rats, although many other species such as baboons and otters have also been used.

This is demonstrated by an experiment by J. Hunt into the effects of infantile experience on adult behaviour. Rats were specifically chosen for this experiment because they have a relatively short span of life compared to other animals. Hunt took two litters of rats, all of whom were weaned at three weeks and put seven animals in an experimental group and used seven as a control. Starting on the twenty-fourth day, he began to feed the experimental group irregularly for fifteen days while the control group had unlimited access to food. The length of time of actual eating and the time between feedings were controlled. At the end of fifteen days, both groups of rats were treated identically and for five months they both had unlimited access to food. Following this, both groups were subjected to food frustration; food was removed from their cages and they were given a subsistence diet for two days and then fed at twenty-four hour intervals for three days. Twenty-three and a half hours after the last feed they were given the opportunity to hoard food pellets and three more hoarding tests were made on successive days during which the animals were allowed unlimited food. Those animals who formed part of the experimental group were found to hoard more than two and a half times as much as their freely fed litter mates, leading Hunt to conclude that infantile experience can affect adult behaviour.

Harlow carried out experiments with monkeys to test the nature of the link between mother and off-spring and to see whether their attachment was only a result of the mother's function of supplying food. He made two mother substitutes, one covered with sponge rubber, one of wire. Both mothers had nipples which could supply milk. He put four monkey babies in one cage and four in another. In the first cage he placed the wire mother with milk and the cloth mother without milk. In the second cage, the cloth mother provided milk and the wire mother was without. He found that with or without milk all baby monkeys preferred the soft cloth mother.

Rats and monkeys thus make more convenient subjects for research as they are easier to control and experiments can be performed on them which would be considered unethical if children were involved.

Recently, however, there has been a revival of interest in the experiment as a valuable tool of enquiry for sociologists. Ethno-methodologists are however not concerned with formalised and artificial experiments such as those illustrated earlier but with experiments of an apparently more impromptu and spontaneous nature. It is argued that these experiments will aid in the search for those rules which are basic to all forms of interaction and in examining the taken-for-granted assumptions that actors make in any particular situation.

In *Method and Measurement in Sociology*, Cicourel describes how, in most experiments, the researcher makes many assumptions about how the participants in the experiments view the world and the researcher takes it for granted that he and all the participants make the same assumptions in a similar way. For example, if an experiment is conducted to investigate how people react in an aggressive situation, Circourel argues that it is first necessary to check that all involved define aggression identically and will experience the situation in the same way. Instead of relying on our common sense knowledge to conceive experiments and analyse our findings, Circourel argues that a much more basic problem must be solved, that is the problem of 'cultural meaning'. Only then will it be possible to conduct a meaningful experiment of the type illustrated earlier.

Garfinkel has attempted to discover some of the basic features of interaction. His strategy is to start with a situation viewed as normal and then systematically to attempt to create chaos. He argues that those methods which create chaos will illuminate the stable elements of social order. For example, in an attempt to demonstrate how shared assumptions and meanings operate, he instructed students to engage in ordinary conversation with a friend and casually insist that the respondent clarified the sense of his remarks. One subject told the experimenter about having had a flat tyre when going to work the previous day:

> *Subject:* I had a flat tyre.
> *Experimenter:* What do you mean, you had a flat tyre?
> *Subject* (appeared momentarily stunned, then answered in a hostile way): What do you mean, 'What do you mean?'? A flat tyre is a flat tyre. That is what I meant. Nothing special. What a crazy question!

In another experiment, students were asked to spend fifteen minutes to an hour acting out the idea that they were boarders in their own homes. Garfinkel told them to act in a polite fashion, to use formal address and to speak only when spoken to. In many cases, 'family members were stupified' and tried to restore the situation to normal. 'Reports were filled with accounts of astonishment, bewilderment, shock, anxiety, embarrassment, and anger, and with charges by various family members that the student was mean, inconsiderate, selfish, nasty or impolite. Family members demanded explanations: 'What's the matter? What's gotten into you? Did you get fired? . . . What are you being so superior about? Are you out of your mind or are you just stupid?' One student acutely embarrassed his mother in front of her friends by asking if she minded if he had a snack from the refrigerator. 'Mind if you have a little snack? You've been eating little snacks around here for years without asking me. What's gotten into you?' One mother, infuriated when her daughter spoke to her only when she was spoken to, began to shriek in angry denunciation of the daughter for her disrespect and insubordination and refused to be calmed by the student's sister' (Garfinkel, 1967). In all cases the situation was restored upon explanation, but for the most part family members were not amused. In one case, a sister replied on behalf of a family, 'Please, no more of these experiments. We're not rats, you know.'

Experiments of a similar kind have been conducted with the object of discovering the way in which people use space to create territories. Complex rules govern every situation; from an intimate meeting to the way we form queues, from who sits where at the dinner table, to the way classrooms and offices are organised. Robert Sommer, a psychologist interested in the influence of architectural design on behaviour, argued that the best way of learning the location of invisible boundaries is 'to keep on walking till somebody complains'.

Robert Sommer used this invasion technique in a series of experiments. In a study area of a college library, observation over a two year period showed that the first occupants of the room usually sat one to a table at end chairs. Mrs Rousso, Sommer's female assistant, chose women who were sitting alone, with at least one book in front of them, and who were surrounded by empty chairs. She then violated library norms by invading their territory – by sitting either directly opposite or next to them. The subjects reacted in different ways – defensive gestures, shifts in posture, attempts to move away. The quickest departures were produced when Mrs. Rousso occupied an adjacent chair and moved it closer to the subject. Other girls sitting in similar positions were left alone but observed so as to act as a control. Sommer also investigated the mechanisms people use to defend their territory under crowded conditions. His experiment was conducted in a heavily used coffee bar at a university. Refreshments were available in a central service area and students could then go outside on the porch or sit in any of eight side rooms. To see how students might defend the side room against invaders, a girl, ostensibly studying, was stationed at a table facing the door in one of the side rooms for twenty-minute periods at various times during the week. She was not able, however, to protect the room from entry by others, although she was successful in defending her own table. Over ten experimental sessions only one student sat down at her table and that during a period of great crowding. The coffee bar was also the scene of another experiment to see whether people in public areas for long periods establish rights of tenure to their space. Students who had been seated for various lengths of time were approached and informed, 'Excuse me, but you are sitting in my seat'. People who had been sitting for only brief periods moved, even when there were vacant tables in the vicinity. However, a fellow who had been sitting there for twenty-five minutes refused, replying, 'Oh, I don't think so'.

Thus, there are a variety of approaches to the use of the experiment within the social sciences. The experiment is a useful aid in the discovery of the basic elements of interaction. However, it is neither a practical nor desirable method of testing hypotheses about complex social relationships. This does not mean that sociological research is inevitably inferior to that of natural scientists, not all of whom can experiment at will. Astronomers, for example, rely on natural experiments to test their theories. Moreover, scientific precision is only a small aspect of research for sociologists. For, as Cicourel observes, 'data' and 'findings' only have validity if the researcher's background expectancies can be examined. It is perhaps ironic that experiments, the essence of scientific method, have been revived by those who have so forcefully demonstrated the problems inherent in positivist enquiry.

Listening to Conversation
by R. J. Anderson
Manchester Polytechnic

The Place of Talk as Data

For a sociologist to spend his time listening to other people's conversations may seem an odd thing to do, but if you think about it you will see that it is precisely how most of us spend a large proportion of our time anyway. We talk, or listen to others talking, nearly all of the time. However, we do not do it with deliberation. We do not sit down on a bus thinking, 'Right, now I'm going to listen to the conductor's talk', nor, when we get home in the evening do we think, 'Now I'll engage in talk with the family'. We talk as part of living our daily lives. But to talk also requires us to listen, to know what to say next and when to say it. Consequently, both talking and listening are a natural part of our daily life.

In an earlier paper (*Building Society Through Interaction*) considerable stress was laid on the study of routine, ordinary activity. One of the points that was made there was that the 'fact' of social order may be seen as a member's accomplishment. Sociologists working in the field of conversation analysis have tried to demonstrate how social order might be produced through the mechanisms of talk. This paper will be concerned with their work into the investigation of conversation as a practical activity.

The interest in talk might appear at first sight to be trivial, or even non-sociological, until it is remembered that the central topic of sociology is social action. One of the ways that we achieve social action is through talk. In an oft-quoted example, the philosopher John Austin (1970, p. 235) makes the point that in the saying of such things as

'I bet you sixpence it will rain tomorrow.'
'I name this ship *Britannia*.'
'I hereby pronounce you man and wife.',

we are performing the actions of betting, naming or pronouncing. The utterances are not descriptions of the activities, they constitute them. Similarly, such things as, 'What's the time?', 'Come here', 'Take the first turning on the right and the hospital is across the road' are not describing, say, a question, a summons or the giving of some instructions. They are those activities. These examples seem to indicate that social action is available for study in talk, for to say something is to do something. There is a further reason why sociologists in particular might become interested in talk. Unlike some of the other social sciences, sociologists' data is derived from the use of talk. Surveys are administered, coding rules defined, questions asked, and observations made, mostly through talk. Yet very little is known about the formal properties of this very important tool of social research. To be sure, philosophers and linguists have discussed the nature of language in the abstract, but little or no attention has been paid to talk as a *social* activity. It is this that conversation analysis sets out to do.

Before going any further it would, perhaps, be just as well if we spent a little time discussing the nature of the data investigated by conversation analysis. When it is said that we are interested in examining social action in talk, we must be clear that we are studying only that which is available to us directly in the talk. That and that alone can provide the data. The most usual and convenient way of handling it is to tape-record conversations and transcribe the recordings. All that can be employed in sustaining the analysis is what is available in the transcription. Obviously, there is always a multitude of alternative possible readings for each transcription. Such alternatives are not a problem to be eradicated but a resource to be explored. Because the data is presented alongside the analysis that it generated, comparisons and improvements by other investigators are easily facilitated. The status of any particular account is, then, tentative. Its strength derives from the plausibility of its description of some features discerned in the transcript. The provision of the data for the reader pre-empts any claim to incontrovertibility or possession of the 'truth' about the data.

This is very different from much of the rest of sociology. Elsewhere it is often necessary for the researcher to fill out his account with explanatory detail, examples or even stories, so that the reader can fully understand the points that are being made. The detail is given to exemplify the argument that the researcher wishes to make. Since it is the researcher who is bringing in and formulating the detail, there is often no means that we, as readers, can check back to verify that the examples given are indeed instances of the points being made. As such, they can hardly constitute 'proof' in any real sense.

To illustrate this point we will look at Huw Benyon's widely read study, *Working For Ford* (1975), where there is an account of the genesis of a strike which is given as an illustration of workers' spontaneous response to the machiavellian tactics of management. Benyon suggests that when the line workers ('the lads') heard that a national agreement had been reached between Ford's management and the various unions which guaranteed a wage increase in exchange for penalty clauses on industrial action, they were so incensed that, through their shop stewards, they demanded an immediate strike. Now, we are not concerned here to doubt Benyon's account of the events. Indeed, we would be very foolish if we did so, for Benyon was a participant in the events and the present writer, at least, was not. The point is that we have no means, in principle, of checking it. This is important for it raises the important issues of 'objectivity', 'bias' and 'rigour' that have already been touched on.

Benyon's work is primarily descriptive and so we might think that it is necessarily open to the kinds of reservations we have expressed. On the other hand, we might feel that 'harder', quantitative data is less so. However, this would be a mistake, for similar problems do arise. As we have already suggested, surveys and interviews use language to elicit answers, even when these answers are pre-coded. Along with the methods for collecting the data, the researcher must specify coding rules for the transformation of verbal answers into the scores of frequency classes. Thus, if we wish to classify responses by social class using the Registrar General's classifications of occupations, we will no doubt operate with 'rules of thumb' for what will count as 'professional and managerial', 'clerical', 'skilled manual', etc. What we will certainly not do is to make these 'rules of thumb' public. Furthermore, we cannot provide, in advance, solutions to all the problems that will arise, for we do not know what all the problems will be. Decisions will be made on an *ad hoc* basis in the light of the general schema of coding rules.

This is not to be seen as a criticism of survey research *per se*. It cannot be, for the procedures are inherent in the method. The point that we are making is simply this. The data (i.e. the original answers) is irrecoverable, buried by coding and transformation rules. All we, as readers, have are the frequencies in the different classes. No doubt most sociologists do attempt to be consistent and systematic in their handling of data. That is not the point. The point is that the nature of the methods prevents us from checking that they are.

The insistence on a return to the specifics of data is probably the only element in conversation analysis that has been borrowed from its supposed progenitor, *phenomenology*, and marks it off from those forms of socio-linguistics and sociology which relate what people say to the wider social structure or sub-cultural variables, for example, race, sex, class. In conversation analysis these variables are treated with analytic indifference, unless, that is, they can be retrieved directly from the data. It may be that talk can be found to express class or power relations (see for example Bernstein [1971] and Labov [1969]) but this can only be achieved by treating what people say as expressive of the variables concerned. In a very real sense, this requires us to read things into the data.

A second and related point may be made here. No reference in transcripts is made to kinesic information or signalling, while the transcription of inflection is somewhat haphazard. Hand and eye movements, facial expression and gesture are often held to be necessary to understanding and to successful communication. However, telephone conversations are managed without their use, so that they cannot, in fact, be *necessary*. They may well be important alternative and supplementary channels which facilitate ease of communication. If they were necessary then it ought to be possible to achieve adequate communication on their basis alone. This does not seem to occur. Instead, where talk is consistently absent, surrogate sign or gesture *languages* are invented. Finally, although such information is clearly available in encounters, and could be video-recorded, it is by no means apparent how it could be transcribed and analysed. This is not to say that it cannot be done, but that, at the moment, no adequate procedures have been worked out. Conversation analysts feel free to treat only the talk itself because either the things that are ignored are of no interest to them (for example, class and race) or they have no way of dealing with them in any rigorous fashion: quite apart from the fact that they do not seem to be of central importance anyway.

In the earlier paper, *Building Society Through Interaction*, it was argued that meanings are not stipulated in advance but discovered from contexts. Meaning can be seen as a practical accomplishment. Consequently, analysts cannot rely solely on grammar or convention to define what utterances do. Such definition can only be brought about by examination of the contexts in which they are produced. Utterances are situated in sequences and their form and function is derived from their sequentiality. Consequently, an utterance such as[1]

*A: Are you coming or not

might well work as a question eliciting an answer, or a demand generating a response, or perhaps even a request making a reply relevant. Exactly what it is can be determined only from the context in which it is produced and treated. This implies that it is not possible to go beyond the data to uncover the meanings *intended* by the participants. Our interest in meanings rests solely at the level of the practices that participants use to make their meanings explicit. Meaning can only be a topic of analysis where it is a feature oriented to by the participants themselves. A concern with meaning, then, is really a concern for the methods members use to resolve the indexicality of all talk. The fact that talk is potentially multifaceted and that sequential implications are not specifiable in advance, is, in itself, a feature that members take into account and have methods for dealing with. Much of the work discussed in this chapter arises from an interest in the ways that sequences of utterances are negotiated.

A recognition that the analyst is not, in any sense, in a privileged position *vis-à-vis* his data, that he does not possess methods for the

---

[1] Because of the very general, and therefore extremely limited, nature of this chapter, it has proved difficult to find suitable illustrative examples. Consequently, many of the examples are contrived and marked * in the conventional manner. I am grateful to Professor Roy Turner of the University of British Columbia for making the data marked 'Coroners' available to me. Data marked 'GTS' are drawn from a corpus that was originally collected by the late Professor Harvey Sacks. Unless otherwise noted, all other data are my own. An explanation of the transcription symbols is given below.

Transcription Symbols

| A ; | speaker notation. | [| two speakers speaking at once. |
| (( )) | transcriber insertion. | // | utterance overlaps at this point. |

uncovering of meaning where members cannot, will prevent us from misconstruing the exercise as a search for the meaning of everything that is said, or from castigating utterances for which we fail to provide meanings, as 'meaningless'. We have to recognise that some things are irrecoverable either because they are not explicitly oriented to in the data we collect (for example, hand and eye movements) or because they are part of a commonly held stock of knowledge shared by the participants and not by the analyst. For example, the following data could be analysed without reference to what and where 'Issy's' is, or whether 'Volkswagen' is the type of car or the place where it was stolen.

> *Coroners*
> A: The car was stolen from um what um in front of Izzy's I think
> B: Yeah um Volkswagen on Georgia

Our interest is in the methods and devices utilised by the participants and not with the excavation of the meanings they share.

Just as there are occasions when meanings are not clear to us as analysts, so there are times when they may be unclear to the participants as well. It is at points like this that we can treat meaning as an analysable feature in that we can look at the methods that are used for resolving the problem. For example, in the following:

> A: He says governments are you know he keeps he talks about governments they sho the thing that they shd do is what's right or wrong
> B: For whom
> A: Well he says // he
> B: // By what standard
> A: That's what that's exactly what I mean.
> (quoted in Schegloff (1972), p. 1)

A is able to use 'By what standard' to recover the meaning of 'For whom'. In this case, the meaning is analysed *retrospectively*. This 'waiting to see what happens next' to discover what has gone before is one of the common methodological devices that members use. It is the formal examination of such methods for the achievement of orderly conversational interaction that conversation analysis is about.

Some Illustrations of this Approach

The rest of this chapter will be given over to the presentation of some work within the ambit of conversation analysis. In order to provide a range of examples much has been compressed or left out. Readers are strongly advised to consult, wherever possible, the originals from which the examples are drawn in order to appreciate the wealth of detail and the degree of sophistication contained in the arguments. The three areas we shall look at are:

1 identities and references to persons
2 beginnings and endings of talk
3 some systematics of turn taking.

1   IDENTITIES AND REFERENCES TO PERSONS

Elsewhere it has been said that commonsense knowledge of the world is not random. Our knowledge of objects, events and persons is organised into a variety of patterns or typifications. Clearly an important place to start investigations might be the delineation of some of the ways that the organisation of our knowledge is displayed in social life, and in particular in conversation. We can begin with the investigation of identity. A demonstration of how this might be done has been given by Harvey Sacks (1972) in his analysis of a story told by a two-year-old child.

> 'The baby cried.
> The mummy picked it up.'

Sacks makes the following observations about the story:

(a) He hears the mummy as the mummy of the baby.
(b) Any other hearer will, on a first hearing, hear that too. This hearing can always be revised, but it is the *first* hearing.
(c) There is a relationship between the actions described. The mummy picked up the baby because it was crying.
(d) We can all make these findings without specific knowledge of the mummy or the baby in question nor of the child who told the story.

The import of this last observation is enormous, for if it is the case that competent users of the English language are able to find the same things from the same fragment of talk, then, the methods that are used to do so must be of the highest order of generality. They must be part of the foundations of our common culture.

In order to set out how such a story can enable the findings made, Sacks utilises the notion of a Membership Categorisation Device (MCD). This is an analytic device consisting of typical members called 'membership categories' organised by virtue of rules of use. The MCD is an elaborated form of typification discussed above. A device may consist of only one member, for example, living Pope, or Olympic high jump champion, or it may have many members for example, householders, car owners. Devices with multiple members may well be organised in a particular way and comprised of a complete set of members. Football teams consist of backs, goal keepers, midfield players and forwards; families of parents and children. An important feature of category use is that one category may be enough for adequate reference to be made. I can talk about a spider without making reference to an eight-legged, hairy, carnivorous, invertebrate arachnid. This adequate reference by the use of one category will turn out to be important with regard to the identification of persons, and comprises the first of our rules of application of categories. It is an *economy rule*: a single category from any one MCD will be referentially adequate.

The second rule is often called a *relevance rule* since it states that if a member of some device is used to categorise some member of a population, that category or another drawn from the same MCD may be used to categorise further members of the same population. So, if 'baby' is drawn from the MCD 'family', another member of that device, for example, 'father' or 'brother', may be relevant. Sacks suggests that as a methodological procedure members operate a maxim, 'if two categories are used to categorise two members of a population and they can be heard as being drawn from the same categorisation device, then, hear them that way.' Now 'mummy' and 'baby' can be heard as being drawn from the device 'family' which, as we said, consists of a 'proper' set of co-members – so much so that we have special categories of 'one-parent families' and 'childless couples'. So, if one member is categorised as belonging to a family, and then another is categorised as belonging to a family, if it is possible, we will hear them as belonging to the same family. In the story, we will hear the 'mummy' as the 'mummy of the baby'.

The third observation that was made was that there is a link between the actions. The 'mummy' picked the 'baby' up because it was crying. To explicate this we can employ another feature of categorisation, namely, that some activities are category-bound to some categories. That is to say that some activities are identified by virtue of their being done by some categories. 'Baby', as we have pointed out, may be a member of the category 'family' or it may be a member of that of 'stage of life'. Crying is something that babies do when they are very young. It is an activity bound to the category in the device 'stage of life' and not that in 'family'. Fifty-one-year-olds may be the 'baby of the family' but we do not expect them to cry, and when they do, that crying is noticeable in a way that the crying of a six-month-old baby is not. Similarly, the activities of being tender and solicitous are tied to the category 'mummy'. We can find that the child was picked up because it was crying since that is what mothers do. This particular set of relationships between categories and category-bound activities demonstrates another hearer's maxim. 'If two actions follow one another and it is possible to see them as sequenced, then do so.' The methodical use of these two maxims enables us to find that the 'mummy' was the 'mummy of the baby' and she picked it up because it was crying. The ties between the utterances were seen as complete in themselves since they were fashioned in accordance with the organisation of our commonsense knowledge.

Further work on membership categorisation has focused on the co-selection of membership categories. When discussing referential adequacy, it was suggested that identification can be provided by use of one category drawn from one device. This has been shown to operate in a particular manner with regard to names (Sacks and Schegloff. No Date).

There seems to be a preference when making reference to persons to start with a name, if possible, and then to relax that preference by adding categories drawn from other devices. If the name should prove inadequate other categories will be provided one at a time. Thus:

> *Coroners*
> *A*: Sparks is the only one I guess
> *B*: Sparks
> *A*: Yeah he was the one that did all
> *B*: Well there's one of them down at the Academy er er Nightingale
> *A*: Oh Oh the other chap on the case

Here the adequacy of a name 'Sparks' is questioned and expanded by the provision of another category which is cut off. With 'Nightingale' the provision of the name and a descriptor both enables and demonstrates successful identification. In the following the same preference is at work but in a more complex manner:

> *C/A/J Methodists*
> *Charlie*: Roughly somewhere near where your friend whatsername
>   used to live
> *Janet*:   Jane
> *Charlie*: No the girl whose father helped us with
>   the ⌈electricity stuff
> *Janet*:   ⌊Oh   Les

'Whatsername' is a pro-term for the name which should have been offered as the identifier of the friend. The failure to place a recognisable identifier at that point provides Janet with the task of offering a name at the next transition point. The name is rejected by Charlie and further descriptors given. Jane, by reviewing the categories offered, 'a friend' whose 'father helped with electricity stuff' is able to offer an alternative identification.

The relaxation of the preference illustrates a procedure of co-selection which operates by following the consistency rule. Each subsequent category is produced to be consistent with those that have gone before. Hearers may well utilise this co-selection to find a category which can tie all of the available descriptors together. They look for a category which, in encompassing all of the given descriptors, might be said to have them as its properties, or to summarise them, as for example in:

> *C/A/J Methodists* (abbreviated)
> *Charlie*: Our Careers Officers is quite a nice young man but he's a
>   little bit disconcerting because um in the middle of a quite
>   ordinary conversation he'll say 'Well I'll have to ask God
>   about that'.
>   ((laughter))
> *Charlie*: It's rather disconcerting he'll be talking quite normally just

er you know like an ordinary person and all of a sudden
he'll bring this sort of ((1 second pause))

Janet: What is he a Plymouth Bretheren.

The descriptor 'Plymouth Bretheren' is offered to provide a category for 'nice', 'ordinary' persons who believe that they have direct access to God.

2 BEGINNINGS AND ENDINGS IN TALK

Later in this chapter, we will try to outline how and why it is that conversation displays two basic properties:

(a) overwhelmingly one party speaks at a time
(b) speaker change recurs.

These two, just because they are obvious, will require some explication. For the moment, however, let us assume that they are a fairly accurate description of our experience of talk. The most important thing about the properties is that they describe a process but not how that process begins or ends. That, in general, one party speaks at a time would seem to indicate that silence can be viewed as *an absence of talk*. That is to say, silences occur in places where there should be talk. Silences are oriented to and noticed by participants, and given significance, even as implying misunderstanding, disbelief or confusion, for example. The analytic importance of silences cannot be exaggerated. Unfortunately we have no space to discuss it here. Nonetheless, we can propose that speakers and hearers routinely face a pair of problems. How can they start a conversation in an orderly manner, and once it is in motion, so to speak, how do they stop it? Now, obviously, simply to suggest that it is always possible to start or stop whenever you please will not do. Our own experience tells us that it isn't that easy. We have all had occasions when someone we wanted to speak to, did not notice us, 'they didn't even say "hello"', and other, equally infuriating times when we could not 'get away' from someone. 'They simply would not stop talking.' Complete freedom just to stop or start might be a bit haphazard and, as we have observed before, social life is far from being haphazard. If people are constantly faced with a particular problem, it does not seem unreasonable to suggest that they may have developed methods for handling the problem, in this case, methods for negotiated entry into and exit from talk. Commonly, conversations start or end in the following ways:

1 *A: Hello
   B: Hello
2 *A: Hi
   B: Hi
3 *A: Goodbye
   B: Goodbye

Given our requirement to notice the detail of social action, rather than dismissing these sequences as conversational 'entry' or 'exit tickets' let us examine how they are organised to see if their organisation provides the method of their use.

All three examples given consist in *pairs* of utterances where the parts of the pair are adjacent. Each part is produced by a different speaker. Further, the parts are differentiated into a first part and a second part, so that if the first part is given, we can expect the second, or return, part of the pair to follow. In displaying these characteristics, greetings and terminators are members of a class of sequences called 'adjacency pairs'. Other members of this class are question/answer, summons/response, request/reply. The adjacency pair comprises a unit pair of actions and so is the building block of conversation. Clearly, this does not mean that people only talk in paired utterances, but that other, more complex, forms are elaborations and extensions of the pair structure. Since the adjacency pair is a discrete unit, it can be employed anywhere in conversation. Two such places where its properties might be useful are at the beginnings and ends of talk. The employment of a pair structure ensures negotiated entry and exit. The exchange of greetings does not mean that conversation will start up, nor, when terminators are introduced, does it automatically stop. Rather, they provide mechanisms which enable starting or stopping should the co-participants wish it. The proffering of a greeting makes its second pair part sequentially relevant. Its failure to appear could indicate that the other is 'not available to talk'. Similarly, the non-production of the second part of a terminal exchange indicates that there is more yet to be said.

The discovery of the adjacency pair form at the beginning and termination of conversations does not have world shattering status. But what it does do, in a very neat manner, is enable us to describe how social actors, by the use of generalisable methods, produce orderly and predictable sequences of actions rather than chaos. The mechanism has the form required for the tasks it does. There is one final point. Although greetings provide a point of entry and terminators a point of exit, their placement immediately adjacent to a major topic may in itself be noticeable.

   1 *A*: Hi
      B: Hi
      A: My Great Aunt Lucy just had twins
   2 *A*: Yeah I really enjoyed that party last night
      B: Goodbye
      A: Goodbye

(The unsatisfactoriness of contrived data is evident here. We can all imagine particular circumstances which could produce these utterances. But the need to imagine *particular* circumstances might indicate that they are somewhat unusual.)

Compare the examples just given with the following protracted entry and termination:

Coroners
A: Coroners Office Corporal Paton
B: Er Pete Friedman in the phone room
A: Yeah
B: Er howrya doing
A: Not sa dusty
B: I tell you Peder ol sport
A: Yus old chum
B: I gotta report in front of me that says Mr MacDonald lost his vehicle.

Coroners
Carl: I think you're ⌈right
Peter: ⌊right
Carl: Well anyways I'll mail the forms out to you
Peter: Fine
Carl: O.K.
Peter: O.K.
Carl: ⌈Bye
Peter: ⌊Bye

It is interesting to note that the protracted negotiations into and out of talk exhibited by these examples utilise the adjacency pair form. The problems involved in this kind of sequential negotiation are discussed in Schegloff and Sacks (1973) and Schegloff (1968).

3   SOME SYSTEMATICS OF TURN TAKING

We can now turn back to the description of conversation given above:

(a) overwhelmingly one speaker speaks at a time
(b) speaker change recurs

and in particular focus on the second element. The fact speaker change recurs must indicate that speakers and hearers have methods for recognising the boundaries of utterances. Given that produced silences are not an endemic feature, it cannot be that hearers wait until a speaker stops and use the silence to discern that he has stopped, before they speak. Most of the time, one speaker follows another without pause and without overlap (Sacks et al., 1974). For this to happen, hearers must be able to recognise what a completion to a present utterance is likely to be as that utterance is being produced. Furthermore, that recognition, or 'reading forward', could only be done through the resources provided by the speaker. Turn transition, therefore, is a *collaborative exercise*.

A supporting argument for the methodical nature of turn transition may be derived from the noticeability of silences. Their indicativeness is to be found in the fact that they are seen as occupying slots or belonging to candidate speakers. This could only be the case if silences were non-normal rather than a permanent feature. The supposition that speakers seek to avoid producing silences has been formulated as a members' predisposition to 'earliest beginnings'. A place where turn transition may occur in an utterance is a 'possible turn transition point'. So, every 'possible turn transition point' is a 'possible utterance completion point'. Speakers provide resources to indicate whether any particular turn transition point should be treated as the turn transition point and completion effected. Hearers monitor these resources to facilitate turn transition. This collaboration enables speaker change with minimal gap and minimal overlap. Obviously, speakers can use a vast array of resources to indicate transition points. We have space for only a few, such as:

(a) the appended question
    A: Would be missionary wouldn't it
(b) the post completor
    1 A: To the cars ((1 second pause)) To our cars
    2 *A: Hold on a minute please
(c) the precompletor
    *A: I just want to say one thing
(d) the standard formula
    *A: Ready, steady, go.

Interestingly, 'story prefaces' work as precompletors by indicating what to look for in the completion of a story. For example.

    GTS 2 mcv 2 0 : 07 : 30
    Ken: I heard a real dirty joke.

Laughter may similarly locate completion, speakers often marking their own 'punch lines' with laughter thereby showing them to be the completion of the joke or story (Schenkein, 1972).

Given the recognisability of transition points, the next issue to be addressed is the methodical character of transition itself. How are next speakers selected? Sacks et al. (1974) suggest that three rules may be in operation:

(a) current speaker selects next
(b) next speaker self selects
(c) current speaker continues.

Sacks suggests that at any possible transition point, all three rules are available for implementation. The ordering of the rules is such that if (a) is not invoked then (b) can be, and if (b) is not, then (c) will be. If (c) is used, the whole rule set is again available at the next possible transition point. Where there are only two participants, if another is to speak there is no real selectional problem. In multi-party conversations, selection may be achieved by the obvious method of a name or pro-term.

> *GTS 2 mcv 2 00 : 00 : 30*
> *A1* : Hey lemme have one Roger
> *C/A/J Xmas*
> *A*: Have you been round to Andrew's to-day

In both cases the use of the first part of an adjacency pair selects the next action. Speaker selection proceeds on the basis of a name or pro-term. A variant on this is the use of topic to select next speaker:

> *C/A/J Xmas*
> *A*: We wanted to know if they wanted to come for Christmas
> *B*: They wanted to come
> *A*: Have they ever wanted to come here for Christmas
> *C*: No I don't think so.
>
> *GTS mcv 2 0 : 02 : 30*
> *Ken*: Hey putcher shoes back on c'mon I can smell you all the way over here.

In these examples speaker change is effected by the use of the topic to select a next speaker, i.e. someone who knows the plans for Christmas or the person who has removed his shoes.

The third element in the rule set was possible continuation by the present speaker. This may be produced either where selectional mechanisms are not utilised or where the present speaker provides resources to the effect that the next possible transition point should not be taken as the transition point. There are many mechanisms which achieve this, such as slot holding devices:

> *C/A/J Methodists*
> *Charlie:*   No he's a Methodist this deeply sort of religious side of things into it *and er* its a bit disconcerting

or prefaces that indicate that an utterance will span several transition points as in the case of the 'story preface' already cited. Alternatively, speakers may continue after a possible transition point because transition has not been effected, the silence *between* utterances being turned into one *within* an utterance.

> *Coroners*
> *Carl*: You could claim your damages from Mrs Pepperleck and me seeing that Mrs Pepperleck was the cause of the accident ((2 second pause)) accorse you don't have to do that.

This paper has been able to do little more than sketch out some of the research interests of conversation analysts. Work is currently being carried out in areas such as the methods for repairing silences and overlaps, sequential timing, and multi-utterance structures. All of this illustrates that detailed and careful analysis of even the most obvious of social activities can reveal the complex structures underlying surface simplicity. The examination of the minutiae of talk shows it to be ordered and orderly. This order is the product of its methodical character. It is in such things as the predictability and routiness of talk that the fact of social order is realised. Conversation analysis is not in any sense peripheral but centrally concerned with the reality of social action.

III SOCIOLOGISTS ARE ONLY HUMAN

Introduction

In the first two sections of part one: the nature of sociological understanding, we have examined some of the sociological perspectives which we can use to describe and analyse the social world, and we have assessed some of the practical techniques through which information can be collected. The two broad approaches we have mentioned are rooted in one or other of the following assumptions: that,

(i) society is an objective reality
or (ii) society is a subjective reality.

However, we noted above the alternatives *within* each of these two basic approaches; we should also acknowledge that individual sociologists might not easily fit into one camp or the other. Our approach has been to treat sociological perspectives as intellectual tools or devices for studying the social world: they are alternative ways of looking at the world, and we cannot say that any one perspective reflects the 'real' world more than any other perspective. Perhaps one perspective is more useful than another to explain a specific problem or issue; perhaps you can use all of them in different ways at different times.

But all sociologists are necessarily born into, and live in, various societies. The intellectual tools they produce and use, and the topics and issues they study, can hardly be separated from the historical and social context in which they live, however much sociologists might like to pretend that their work is 'objective'. In this third section, Roger Gomm analyses the social and political nature of sociological theory and research. He challenges any pretensions that sociology might have to being value-free: he does so, not to highlight the inadequacy of research procedures, but rather to emphasise that sociologists cannot under any circumstances transcend their social nature. This applies to 'independent' university sociologists as well as to sociologists working for governmental agencies or for industry.

Roger Gomm makes his own sociological standpoint clear: he sees society as characterised by 'conflicts of interest between social groups, some of whom are more powerful than others'. This leads him to develop one of the major strands in Len Law's paper, namely that sociology can serve as an important support to the existing social order. You should bear in mind, however, that this analysis is but one; others could take a different view of the place of sociology in social and political context.

Frank Reeves argues that sociology is in fact one set of ideas and beliefs which justifies and influences social behaviour. It therefore has the qualities of any other set of ideas and beliefs in society: it is an *ideology*. Different sociological perspectives, with their varying assumptions about the nature of society, and about the relationship between the individual and society, serve as different ideologies for different social groups which either exercise control or experience the limitations of that control. Sociology as a discipline therefore bears a close relationship to the possession or non-possession of power in society.

Not only does Frank Reeves' paper locate sociology (as an ideology) in society, but his analysis is one which views society as comprising competing interest-groups with differential power. You are now left with the teasing thought that this analysis of sociology-as-ideology might itself be one ideology amongst many . . .

Neutrality and Commitment in Sociology
by Roger Gomm
Stevenage College of Further Education

Introduction

In this paper I will argue that a value-free sociology is impossible and that the very idea is unsociological. My starting points are the observations that sociology is itself a social activity, carried out by real people in a real world and that this real world is one characterised by conflicts of interest between social groups, some of whom are much more powerful than others. (This is to take a view similar to that expressed in the paper 'Conflict-Structuralism', on page 11.) By starting thus I mean to indicate to the reader that the preoccupations of sociologists arise out of their social and historical position and are hence shot through with issues of value.

Problems for Research

The questions asked by sociologists can be understood as their reactions to the flux of political, economic and social events which impinge on them as members of society. For example, one of the best known pieces of sociological research in post-war Britain is that which resulted in 'Affluent Worker' studies (Goldthorpe et al., 1968 a & b, 1969). The historical circumstances which gave rise to these studies were as follows: the heavy investment in industries such as car assembly, engineering and petro-chemicals which, in reducing labour inputs, allowed for high wages for a smaller work force; the post-war labour scarcity in Britain which enabled the bidding up of manual worker wages and the organisation of such industries themselves which gave unions, or indeed quite small groups of workers, considerable bargaining power. All of these factors worked towards wage rates for some manual workers which were comparable to the salaries of some white collar workers. At the same time the increasing scale of enterprises in which white collar workers were employed produced a situation in which their jobs became more like those of manual workers in pay and conditions (Lockwood, 1958).

The phenomenon of the 'Affluent Worker' was widely interpreted as evidence of much more widely spread prosperity with a promise that such was merely the prelude to an even more egalitarian, even 'classless', society in the future. Such thinking was organised by such themes as 'the affluent society' (Galbraith, 1958), 'post-industrial society' (Bell, 1975) and 'the personal service society' (Halmos, 1970) which were academically held versions of ideas widely propagated in the popular press and on the radio. Briefly, such theorising held that modern technology was creating a new social order in which class distinctions were disappearing, in which social class was an irrelevant dimension of politics, and in which decisions concerning human welfare were being taken on rational scientific grounds after democratic consultation – 'the end of ideology' (Bell, 1961). The fact that the Labour Party lost three elections running while a conservative prime minister proclaimed that 'We are all middle class now' seemed to provide proof for these ideas (Crossland, 1960). The phenomenon of the 'affluent worker' plus the 'welfare state' and universal secondary education were seen to mark the end of class conflict in Britain and thus political action by workers on the basis of class interests could appear inappropriate, irrational and old fashioned. Note here how a particular description of social reality generates moral prescriptions, in this case as an attack on the morality and rationality of organised labour. We see this most clearly in newspaper attacks on strikes in the sixties, describing them, not for the first time, as 'anachronistic'.

The Affluent Worker studies were conceived and conducted as a reaction to this climate of opinion. The data was collected and mobilised to present a picture of the affluent worker as essentially still a man who sells his labour power for a wage and whose interests are at important junctures opposed to those of managers and owners. These studies, together with Lockwood's study of the proletarianisation of clerical workers (1958), present a picture of social reality very different from that which appears with the idea of embourgeoisement, and it is a picture of social reality in terms of which working class politics and industrial conflict appear rational and legitimate.

What is a current political, economic or social *issue* at a particular point in time is the result of differential power to describe what is happening, what ought to happen and to define what is important and hence worthy of research. In the example above, we can see sociologists reacting to a climate of opinion of their time. The fact that their findings ran counter to dominant ideas does not alter the fact that the agenda for research was set in a struggle to define the reality of class inequality in the fifties and sixties.

Sometimes the linkage between sociological and powerful sectional interests is very apparent as when research is commissioned by bodies who thus determine the direction of sociological attention. Consider for instance the very large corpus of sociological literature which has been produced in attempts to boost worker productivity without increasing the workers' share of the output. (For a useful summary of this literature see Lupton, 1971.)

While, on the one hand, the determination of topics for sociological enquiry can be seen as emerging from a struggle to define social reality and to gain real world advantages, on the other hand the opportunities for doing sociological work and the social consequences of that work when it is done are also determined by the power structure.

A simple example will perhaps make this more concrete. Recently a housing authority commissioned a study of the geographical origin of its tenants. The survey was duly completed by a sociologist. As a result, two maps were produced from the raw data. One was a map of the residences of black people, the other was a map identifying the residences of people from Eire and Ulster.

Without labouring this example, it can be seen that the opportunity for doing sociology (a salary, a career step) here emerged from the power of the housing authority to commission research, and (in view of the product) presumably from the definition by officials of the housing authority, of minority ethnic groups as 'a problem'. At present it is not clear as to what the consequences of producing these maps will be, but the consequences will be determined by the groups who have the power to use such information. Perhaps the housing authority will use it in a programme to break up concentrations of ethnic minorities. Perhaps the police will use the Irish map as a useful guide in searches for bomb factories. The Irish or the black community might use the maps in a campaign to discredit the authority or a white residents' group might use the information in a campaign against the provision of new houses for black people.

Throughout this example you will discern moral and political issues: about what should be public information; about what confidential information should be available to public corporations and in what form; about whether tenants should be identifiable by ethnic origin, about whether concentrations of ethnic minorities are a good thing or a bad thing; about the rights and wrongs of the politics of Ulster, and about whether some groups should have the financial and legal power to commission sociological research while such services remain unavailable to others.

Denying the Political Nature of Sociology

It is worth commenting here on the way in which so many sociologists have denied the social and political nature of sociology. It is indeed a paradox that sociologists who would explain the activities of any other occupational group in terms of its social and historical circumstances should avoid a similar consideration of sociological work. Instead, those sociologists who have been most concerned to represent sociology as a 'science' have come to believe that social scientists alone among human beings can transcend their social nature and historical position. For instance, homilies such as the one below appear early in most sociology text books:

> The social scientist deals with *highly complex raw material*, namely *human beings*. As an individual he has his own *social attitudes, ethical codes, values* and perhaps *prejudices* and *biases*. If therefore social research is to be *scientific* the individual must divorce his private attitudes from his professional work.
>
> (Sergeant, 1971, p. 21)

In this sort of statement the sociologist is depicted first as an 'individual' with his mind sullied by 'social attitudes' and so on, and then is transformed into an *asocial* being – a social *scientist* without such impediments to discerning the truth. What is glossed over is the fact that sociology is *socially organised knowledge* characterised by collective 'social attitudes, ethical codes, values and perhaps prejudices and biases'.

Divorcing 'private attitudes' from 'professional work' would merely shift the individual from his own idiosyncratic beliefs about society to the equally problematic *shared beliefs* of sociologists as an occupational group. In the example above, for instance, such a divorce would enable the sociologist to put aside his personal scruples about producing maps of black residence in order to do the 'correct' sociological thing.

The idea that the route to the truth lies in transcending one's own individual private circumstances, misses the point that sociologists do sociological work in social situations, at particular points in time, and that their beliefs and activities must be understood in terms of these circumstances if they are to be understood *sociologically*.

What is the effect of claiming that sociologists can transcend the social circumstances of their occupation? The effect is obviously a claim that sociologists have a superior grasp of the truth, which is achieved through putting aside personal biases. This idea may be summarised in the formula 'objectivity through neutrality'. Drawing on Sergeant again, objectivity is defined as: 'the ability to see and accept facts as they are, not as the investigator might wish them to be (Sergeant, 1971, p. 22). This then is not only a claim to a superior grasp of the truth but to trust-worthiness. It says, 'you can trust social scientists to tell the truth because they have no personal axe to grind'.

Note also the way in which 'the facts' are elevated to a supreme position, beyond question. This not only fails to recognise that 'facts' are the products of the procedures used to constitute facts, or the question of whose procedures they are, and whose interests these 'facts' serve, but it grants the truth a 'neutral status'. The truth will be the truth whether you like it or not. This is not an assumption that sociological truth is advantageous to all equally, but it is a licence (if not an obligation) for the sociologist to tell what he considers to be the truth regardless of the consequences for groups this may disadvantage, or advantage.

This notion of 'the truth' as existing 'out there' merely waiting to be discovered and described, is one which is characteristic of positivistic sociology and is based on notions about the nature of social reality which can be questioned. Thus while it may be true that black people are living in those houses, whether we draw a map or not, the map transforms the social significance of their residence. In the social world description transforms what is described and gives it new meanings and potentialities. Moreover much of what counts as 'data' in sociology is itself a redescription by the sociologist of other people's descriptions of the world and its events.

From the set of assumptions that go with the idea of 'objectivity through neutrality', widely held as items of faith by sociologists, the sociologist emerges as a very superior being indeed: a fearless seeker after truth, a teller of the truth regardless of the consequences, and a finder of the truth because his heart is pure. This grandiose *occupational ideology* fades a little when we recognise some of its most famous American subscribers, in their professional capacity as sociologists, as supporters of private profitability, American democracy and the superiority of white anglo-saxon protestant culture over that of other ethnic groups (who must be assimilated as rapidly as possible); as anti-communist, as anti-union and as involved in research programmes to prevent democratic revolutions in Latin America, to de-stabilise Castro's Cuba, and to increase the kill-rate in Vietnam. For a description of the active political involvement of American, value-free sociologists and their associations with the Pentagon and the C.I.A., the reader is directed to *The Rise and Fall of Project Camelot* (Horowitz, 1967).

Why is it that, until very recently, the notion of the unsocial and apolitical nature of sociology was part of sociological orthodoxy? And how was it that sociologists were able to combine activities such as those listed above with the value of value freedom?

The idea of a value-free sociology is most closely associated with the name of the great German sociologist, Max Weber (work published 1949). We should be clear what Weber meant by 'value-freedom'. Weber's methodology for the study of society was to construct 'ideal types' (mental models if you like) of social phenomena such as 'bureaucracy' or forms of life such as 'capitalism'. These were idealised conceptual models of the phenomenon for study which displayed what Weber thought were their essential features. John Lewis writing about Weber's ideal-typical 'capitalism' says:

> Weber derives it from his observation of our commercial attitude to everything, the fact, in his own words that 'all our motives are

pecuniary'. It is in fact veritably a language *game* – 'the money game' 'beggar my neighbour', buy cheap and sell dear, the gamble on the stock exchange, financial take-overs, profitable investment. This is the game operating not only as the mechanism of the business world and the industrial system, but pervading the consciousness of our acquisitive society, and of all classes in that society. . . .

The game then has its own values and is constructed and organised to secure them. It is therefore besides the point to introduce standards or rules from another game, such as the moral principles and ideas which are so often grounds for criticism of the working of capitalism. Weber declares that such principles, often regarded as moral absolutes, are really no more than our subjective or class preferences. The capitalist system itself, he argues, is built on just such preferences, those of the bourgeois class, his own. It is foolish to interpose complaints about inhumanity, injustice and hardship, just as it would be foolish to criticise the play on a football field from the point of view of values of behaviour off the field – to complain that the centre forward has taken the ball away from his opponent quite roughly and had taken it up the field and planted it in the net, very much against the wishes of the other side. Nor may you criticise the economic system for pursuing its own ends, those of the business world, by bringing in the rules of a quite different game for the purpose. (Lewis, 1975, pp. 57–9)

Weber's value-freedom is then a non-judgemental analysis of society in 'its own terms'. Thus, for Weber, a bureaucracy working well is a bureaucracy working to achieve the goals set for it by those at its apex, whether this bureaucracy is a charitable organisation or the C.I.A. Naturally this mode of analysis rules out any critical appraisal of the power structure, for to study a society 'in its own terms' is to accept without question the projects of the most powerful and to banish any speculation that there might be better societies. It is worth noting that, after Weber's death and throughout the Nazi regime in Germany, Max Weber's value-free sociology was the sociology taught in German universities. This is an indication of the way in which this type of sociology can shake down with any political regime. (For an account of the social circumstances giving rise to Weber's own ideas see Gouldner 1973, pp. 3–26.)

The idea of a value-free sociology has been extremely popular among professional sociologists since the war. Two major influences (themselves interlinked) may be detected. Firstly there is the immense prestige of 'science', and the attempts by professional sociologists to construct a sociology modelled on the natural sciences. Secondly there is the incorporation of sociologists into government and business enterprise as researchers and advisers. These two tendencies have been very much stronger in the U.S.A. than in Europe, but until very recently it was the functionalist and empiricist sociology of North America that set the pattern for English and European sociology – so much so that the A.E.B. 'A' level syllabus is still listed under headings ultimately derived from American functionalism, although today this syllabus allows for many perspectives.

In advanced industrial societies, scientific knowledge has become an important means of production. Scientific discoveries are often transformed into profitable commodities or administrative systems. There are clear links between science and the profitability of business; consider for instance the importance of chemical research for the drugs industry or petro-chemicals, or the revolutionary impact of electronic data systems upon commercial enterprises. In so far as the political stability of modern states depends on continual economic growth, it is not surprising that education and research in the natural sciences should be heavily funded by government and big business. Nor is it surprising that, at the same time, sociologists should represent sociology as 'science' capable of yielding answers to 'human problems' in the same way as the natural sciences produce answers to technological ones. What better strategy could be devised for ensuring a share of university resources, research funds, adviser positions or time on school time-tables as well as jobs, careers, and status for sociologists? In the U.S.A. especially, this has been a very successful career strategy. From the early practical application of sociology to boosting worker productivity, carried out by Elton Mayo and his colleagues in the 1920's (Hampdon-Turner, 1970, pp. 215–21), commissioned social research has grown into a multi-million dollar business, and educational provision in sociology has followed accordingly. Of course only some people are in a position to engage sociologists to solve their problems. For instance, Horowitz writes of the Institute for Social Research at Michigan:

> In a list of sponsors of this institute, which is typical of similar institutes elsewhere, we are presented with a veritable 'Who's Who' of the business world. Especially well represented are chemicals, oil and refining, communications, public utilities, banking and investment, philanthropic foundations, food and drugs manu-facturers, auto, steel, aircraft, insurance corporations and last but by no means least, either in numbers or significance, leading federal agencies. Interestingly enough the list does not contain a single labour union. (Horowitz, 1963, p. 133)

One of the central points of the orthodox ideology of the natural sciences is the notion that 'knowledge' can be separated from the circumstances of its production and from its application. This ideological position allows for scientists to divest themselves of responsibility for the way in which their research is used and is presumably what the term 'pure' means in 'pure science'. The neutrality of scientists (which is what scientists mean when they talk about the neutrality of scientific knowledge) is achieved simply by refusing to take responsibility for the political, economic and social circumstances of their actions. Those sociologists who have attempted to model sociology on the natural sciences have taken this ideological position. (For an account of ideology in the natural sciences see Ross, 1976.)

Yet it is still contradictory that the representation of sociology as 'useful knowledge' (saleable knowledge) should be combined with the idea of value freedom, for surely values are entailed in deciding to apply sociology in social engineering. However, value-free sociologists have clouded this issue for themselves in two main ways. Firstly they have made sure that someone else is seen to be making the moral decisions:

> (Social) science can only tell us how to achieve goals; it can never tell us what goals ought to be sought. (Goode and Hatt, 1952, p. 27)

This is of course a somewhat unsuccessful evasion of responsibility. Social scientists describing *how* strikes and wage-demands might be diminished have already taken a moral decision to make this information available to employers.

Passing the buck also partly explains the otherwise curious occupational distinction between sociology and social policy. These are taught as separate academic subjects and despite the fact that people with sociology degrees move from one field to the other, a clear occupational distinction is made which mirrors that between pure and applied science. One of the main distinguishing features of social policy as an academic discipline is the way in which it seeks to grapple with values and clarify those which might form the basis of a fair and equitable society; see for instance Rein (1971). The exponent of social policy is expected to be committed explicitly to a value position.

The separation between social policy and sociology as academic disciplines in England and America occurs historically as sociologists commit themselves to value freedom. You should remember, however, that most of the founding fathers of sociology were desperately concerned to use their sociology for the production of a better society.

The result of this separation has been a corpus of knowledge called 'social policy' which uses 'sociological' techniques to gather data, but which draws very little on sociological theory (Pinker, 1971). The theoretical basis of social policy has been derived either from mainstream economics (which produces somewhat 'right wing' versions) or from the political theory and moral philosophy (which has been exorcised from sociology). It is only recently, with a renewed interest in Marxist political economy, that strong links between sociology and social policy have been re-created. In the separation, however, we can see again a shifting of moral responsibility and accountability by sociologists to another occupational group.

Secondly, for functionalist sociologists the *consensual fallacy* obscures the moral and political implications of applied research in the social sciences. Functionalists operate with a model of society as a functioning system in which each part gears neatly with the next, in configurations which are designed (by the system itself) for the advantage of all; rich and poor, weak and powerful. The system works because it is based on a widespread consensus of opinion by members about what is right and what is wrong, fair and unfair, desirable and undesirable. Since the system is seen to promote the most able people to the most important positions, all the sociologist needs to do in order to establish what is good for society is to ask the most powerful people.

> What is good for General Motors is good for America, and what is good for America is good for the world. (Charles Wilson: Secretary of Defence in Eisenhower's Administration and formerly of General Motors)

There is thus no inconsistency between the use of sociology by powerful groups and 'the public interest': for the 'system' itself is seen to serve the public interest, to make powerful those who will serve the public interest best, and presumably to give them sociologists as helpers.

Alternatively 'scientific sociology' can be used to establish what is good for 'society' by using public opinion poll techniques.

> The fact that there are differences of opinion in a large society as to what these values are (mainstream values) itself represents an unnecessary social lag. For in such recent developments as scientific public opinion polling, the values of a population and the unanimity and relative intensity with which they are held can be determined. (Lundberg et al., 1958, pp. 722–3)

It is argued that, on the basis of majority views, what is good for society can be scientifically determined. This view not only gives short shrift to the values and desires of less powerful minorities – who appear as deviants lagging behind – but neglects the power that dominant minorities have in forming the 'public opinion' of the majority (Parkin, 1970).

The confusion between the views of powerful groups or numerical majorities and something called 'the norms and values of society' has frequently been mirrored by a similar confusion about 'the facts'. A brief look at much of the research conducted in the fifties and sixties shows that all too often what count as 'the facts' are the opinions or preferences of powerful groups or individuals. For instance, rates of educational failure which are produced by the calculations of teachers and examiners have usually been considered as the personal shortcomings of pupils or their families; doctors' diagnoses have been mistaken for the health of the nation, and crime rates, which are the product of laws determining what is illegal and of discretionary decisions to report, investigate, arrest and convict have been treated almost solely as the production of those who have been officially labelled as criminal.

Such sociological research tends to have the effect of underwriting views of social reality which are held by, and convenient to, those who have the power to produce 'facts' for subsequent analysis by sociologists. For instance, if sociological researchers tell teachers that the facts show that working class children are less likely to succeed at school (which is what teachers thought all along) this scarcely improves the chances of working class children succeeding in a social organisation where teachers' expectations and decisions are crucial in determining success or failure. Or if sociological researchers tell magistrates that children from low income families are more likely to embark on a life-time of crime (which is what magistrates 'knew' all along), then this strengthens the magistrates' confidence in using low income as one cue to sift the serious from the less serious cases before him.

There have been times when sociological work has underwritten the common-sense of the establishment on a massive scale. A particularly good example is the massive literature on 'cultural deprivation', especially that which was spawned by the American 'Project Headstart'. This has been very well described by Baratz and Baratz (1970), but here briefly let us say that hundreds of thousands of books, articles and memoranda were written on the educational problems of black and Puerto Rican American children, all starting from the assumption that their poor educational performance stemmed from some *deficiency* in their home life. Descriptions of family life, language use, mothering and so on were then written to 'prove' the *inferiority* of black and Puerto Rican family life. Not surprisingly, since this was assumed from the start, the result was a literature depicting such people as little short of depraved. The point is of course that their family life and their use of language *is different* from that of white anglo-saxon protestant Americans, but that this difference only becomes an inferiority when such children are pro-cessed through schools that pre-suppose a white anglo-saxon protestant upbringing.

The American literature of cultural deprivation then mystifies the fact that dominant groups in the U.S.A. have established school systems which encode their own culture and which work to the advantage of their children, and to the disadvantage of children from other cultural groups. Sociology and psychology here merely provides 'the evidence' to consolidate and support the dominant class and race interests in American education. In the English literature the classic texts which may be read from this critical perspective are Spinley's *The Deprived and the Privileged* (1953), Klein's *Samples from English Culture* especially the chapter on 'Branch Street' (1965), National Children's Bureau *Born to Fail* (1975), and the findings of the Plowden Report (1967).

What is perhaps more important than what sociologists *do* investigate is what they *do not*. For example, a study of homelessness which concentrates on discovering the early circumstances of adults who are now homeless, ignores the workings of the property market which ensures that there are insufficient homes for people to live in. Similarly, studies of the home background of children who fail at school in an attempt to explain school failure misses the point that the educational system is designed to fail the majority (if it did not, the idea of 'educational success' would be nonsensical). The short-sighted nature of so much empirical sociological research is probably a much more important prop to the status quo than the more active support described earlier. It is so because it mystifies the political and economic structures which determine the pattern of life in our society. It is the combination of short-sighted, fact-oriented, atheoretical empirical research with social policy that leads to ludicrous, but politically safe, ideas such as the idea that homelessness can be cured by social work, or that comprehensive schools can increase the educational chances of all children without altering the structure of the labour market, or devaluing paper qualifications.

Thus in value-freedom one can discern an unwitting commitment to the values of the establishment. As Horowitz says:

> The truth is of course not that values have actually disappeared from the social sciences, rather that the social scientist has become so identified with the going values of the establishment that it seems as if values have disappeared. (Horowitz, 1963, p. 135)

Varieties of Commitment

Of course, many sociologists have not allied themselves with the dominant groups of their society and many have been highly critical of the social order and this becomes increasingly true as the dominance of functionalist and empiricist sociology wanes. Instead, many sociologists see themselves as 'committed' to bringing about social change or even to fostering revolution. Levels of commitment, however, must be distinguished. This is complicated by the different sorts of social changes to which sociologists commit themselves.

Those who believe that the type of society in which we live is capable of remedy with appropriate government legislation and without radical changes can be true to their commitment by collecting statistics of misery, proffering evidence to committees of enquiry and Royal Commissions, and conducting research to highlight 'injustices' and 'anomalies' in the Welfare State. They can also pass on their views to their students. Even so they may find that they have to live with some awkward contradictions. For instance, however 'radically' your sociology teacher may fulminate about the evils of inequality he is engaged in inequality work: facilitating the elevation of a select few to 'A' level passes.

Those who believe they are committed to a radical socialist revolution must take a harder road. For them the separation between individual private life and life as a sociologist is impossible. The man who was divorced from himself in the quotation from Sergeant must be put together again. Personal beliefs must also be professional practice and should be realised in action rather than words. This means considerably more than drawing a substantial salary as a university lecturer and writing 'subversive' (and to most people, incomprehensible) books which make a handsome profit for the owners of publishing companies. It takes us beyond sociology, hopefully towards a world in which it is neither possible, nor necessary, for people to occupy a privileged position on the basis of a claim that they know more about social life than do other competent members of society. (As further reading in 'radical' sociology the reader is directed to Colfax and Roach (1971) and Shaw (1975).)

Sociology: A World of Scarecrows and Supermen
by F. W. Reeves

Ideology: Definition and Examples

In the framework of a discussion between Socrates and Glaucon in *The Republic*, Plato, the Greek philosopher, sets out his plan for an ideal state. Socrates has advocated a society consisting of three groups: rulers to make the law, auxiliaries to execute the law, and farmers/craftsmen to produce the material necessities of life. In order to secure the existence of the state, he goes on to suggest that all its members should be told the following fable:

> . . . that all of you in this land are brothers; but the god who fashioned you mixed gold in the composition of those among you who are fit to rule, so that they are of the most precious quality; and he put silver in the Auxiliaries, and iron and brass in the farmers and craftsmen. Now, since you are all of one stock, although your children will generally be like their parents, sometimes a golden parent may have a silver child or a silver parent a golden one, and so on with all the other combinations. So the first and chief injunction laid by heaven upon the Rulers is that, among all the things of which they must show themselves good guardians, there is none that needs to be so carefully watched as the mixture of metals in the souls of the children. If a child of their own is born with an alloy of iron or brass, they must, without the smallest pity, assign him the station proper to his nature and thrust him out among the craftsmen or the farmers. If, on the contrary, these classes produce a child with gold or silver in his compostion, they will promote him, according to his value, to be a Guardian or an Auxiliary. They will appeal to a prophecy that ruin will come upon the state when it passes into the keeping of a man of iron or brass. (Cornford, 1941, p. 104)

It is thought that acceptance of this story will benefit all members of the ideal society, and Socrates hopes that, in time, even the rulers (or guardians) will come to believe in it. Both Socrates and Glaucon recognise that the story is an invention, but are not particularly worried about its truth. Undoubtedly, a story of this kind might be more convincing if it were true, but its main importance arises from the part it plays in getting people to accept these ideal social arrangements. The fable is not only a description of, and explanation for, a society divided into three groups, but a justification and encouragement for its continued existence.

A set of beliefs that is characteristic of a social group or community and that functions to justify and influence social behaviour in this way, may be called an 'ideology', although the term is often loosely used. An ideology may be true in that the events it describes are empirically verifiable, or it may be false and have no foundation in the external world. More often than not, it is a subtle mixture of both true and false statements, open to alternative interpretations. And the claim that the beliefs have scientific weight – given the high esteem in which we hold the science of the physical world – may in itself persuade us to accept them without due consideration.

The history of the nineteenth and twentieth centuries offers many examples of eminently functional ideas flaunting a scientific status. The 1857 *Chambers's Information for the People*, in the name of the science of ethnology, distinguishes five 'varieties of man'. Of these, we are told that the white Caucasians' 'moral feelings and . . . intellect are of the highest order', while 'in intellectual character, the Mongolians are by no means defective, but they are more distinguished for imitative than inventive genius'. The negro 'variety' of man is described disparagingly as having a 'forehead . . . low and retreating and the lower part of the face projecting like a muzzle'. Such 'scientific facts' and 'objective descriptions' would no doubt have assisted Europeans seeking to explain and justify their imperial rule over much of the world's surface. Over a century later, in trying to justify his claim that black people as a group are genetically inferior in intelligence to whites, Hans Eysenck hypothesises a situation in which natural selection might favour the 'dull':

> If, for instance, the brighter members of the West African tribes which suffered the degradations of the slavers had managed to use their higher intelligence to escape, so that it was mostly the duller ones who got caught, then the gene pool of the slaves brought to America would have been depleted of many high IQ genes.
> (Eysenck, 1971, p. 46)

It is, of course, true that the various claims of science should be formally regarded as hypothetical or tentative, and that the amount of evidence accumulated in support of them can differ considerably. Unfortunately, scientific hypotheses are frequently accepted as absolute truth by less philosophical audiences, anxious to serve and justify the needs and interests of the moment. When such statements are used to justify action, they become ideological. If they were supported by a weight of evidence, and if ensuing decisions benefited all members of society, as Plato had envisaged, there would be little on which to comment.

Throughout history, however, important systems of belief have tended to give a false picture of social reality, and to serve the interests of powerful social groups at the expense of the weak. For example, Plato did not regard slaves as part of his state, and Aristotle talked of them as 'animate articles of property': undoubtedly a convenient assumption for slave-masters, if not for slaves. Far more recently, a speech made by Sir Keith Joseph, a Conservative shadow minister, in October 1974 asserted that the balance of the British population, its 'human stock', was threatened. He claimed that the nation was moving 'towards degeneration' for a number of reasons, one of which was that young mothers from unskilled and semi-skilled social backgrounds were supposedly giving birth to an undue proportion of the nation's children:

> Many of these girls are unmarried, many are deserted or divorced, or soon will be. Some are of low intelligence, most of low educational attainment. They are unlikely to be able to give children the stable emotional background, the consistent combination of love and firmness which are more important than riches. They are producing problem children, the future unmarried mothers, delinquents, denizens of our borstals, subnormal educational establishments, prisons, hostels for drifters. . . .
> (*Observer*, 20 October 1974)

The fears expressed and any possible guide to future action arise from a highly dubious interpretation of social scientific research. The *Sunday Times* (27 October 1974) examined in detail the inadequacy of Sir Keith Joseph's factual information, and pointed out that just under one third of the population of Britain comes from families where the husband is engaged in unskilled or semi-skilled work. But whether true or false, the message is persuasive and would leave many people with the impression that they were in danger of being overwhelmed by a profligate and degenerate human stock. The description is convincing and is given extra force by its apparent social-scientific basis.

Sociology as Ideology

1 NON-SCIENTIFIC AND VALUE-LADEN SOCIOLOGY

It is often claimed that sociology is a science. In addition, the previous discussion must indicate its potential as an ideology. Not only may sociology describe and explain social reality, but it can also justify and encourage social practice of various kinds. Is this of any consequence if, as we have often been told, sociology is 'value-free' and 'objective'? Possibly not, but many writers (for example Gouldner, 1970) have gone further and have argued that sociology provides an inaccurate picture of the social world and one that has often served the interests of dominant groups.

It may be true that sociology *ought* to be 'value-free' and to provide an accurate description and explanation of the social world. The more important question, however, is whether *in fact* it is. What is sociology? On one rendering, it is all the knowledge recorded in symbolic form that goes under the name of sociology, whether this is to be found in school text books or university theses. It is not difficult to discover very dubious statements masquerading as 'sociological facts' in current sociology textbooks. For example, Cotgrove expresses the view that 'the traditional labels of "capitalist" and "socialist" are no longer particularly useful for characterising such economies' (1967, p. 120); Wilkins voices strongly anti-communist and dangerously suggestive racial attitudes (1970, p. 234, p. 335, p. 340); and Musgrave apparently believes that striking teachers are unprofessional (1965, p. 213). Despite the scientific pretensions of the authors, much of the material reflects the common sense view of social processes. What passes for sociology is what is generally believed, irrespective of its truth, because the belief is in the real or apparent interests of certain sections of the population. Apart from the blatant values and factual inaccuracies of sociological texts, there are other ways of producing a distorted and inadequate account of actual social processes.

2   IDEOLOGY AS AN INCOMPLETE ACCOUNT POSING AS COMPLETE

Imagine a blind man and a deaf man describing the world. The blind man will describe a world without colour, the deaf man a world without sound. Both may provide different but accurate descriptions of the world. But suppose they go further and each asserts that his description is complete, exclusive, and fully representative of the world. Their accounts, however, will be different. Perhaps there could be two worlds; perhaps one or other of the accounts is false; perhaps both are false. The other possibility is to recognise that the accounts are incomplete, that they are true descriptions of a part of reality, but false accounts of all of reality. Why then should the two men wish to claim that their accounts are complete? In our fictional illustration, we may suppose that the blind man is at a disadvantage in a world that acknowledges the importance of sight, while the deaf man is lost in a world of sound; therefore, both seek to maintain their accounts intact because it is in their interests to do so. Indeed, if their accounts do not correspond to the world, they may go as far as to invent fictional worlds that do.

3   MARX AND ENGELS ON IDEOLOGY

Now social thought, including sociology, is prone to providing exclusive descriptions and explanations of society. Marx and Engels (1846) distinguish two basic forms of ideology – materialism and idealism – that emerge in societies that are divided into hostile social classes. The so-called 'theoretical perspectives' of sociology might well be identified as sub-categories of them.

Marx identifies two sets of relationship into which human beings enter: those with things, and those between persons. Human beings affect, and are affected by, these relationships. A person can be regarded both as a subject, when he affects his physical and social environment, and as an object, when it affects him. But, in a class-divided society, people have varying experience of exercising control, and of being controlled by others. Like the blind and the deaf, they find themselves in different situations. As a result, according to Marx, two ideologies are thrown up: one expressing the instrumental attitude of the active members of the ruling class in exercising control (crude materialism), and the other reflecting the unrequited aspirations of those experiencing the limitations of that control (idealism). Because the ruling class claims to speak for all of society, both ideologies – the instrumental, and the aspirational – will be produced by different sections of that class. But despite the fact that both ideologies pretend to exclusive coverage, neither can accurately represent the totality of social relationships. It is instructive to make use of Marx's description of the two ideologies in examining the fundamental presuppositions of much modern sociology.

4   AN IDEOLOGY THAT SERVES INSTRUMENTAL NEEDS

Those concerned with action in the real world (for Marx, the capitalists) need a science to enable them to control the forces of production. These forces consist of the objects provided by nature, the instruments of production (tools and machines), and labour power. Application of the methods of natural science has been successful in securing at least partial control over nature and machines and, as labour power is seen merely as an extension of the instruments of production, it is automatically assumed that a similar social science will establish control in the sphere of labour as well. Sociology, economics, and psychology come to fill the need for a science that offers the possibility of social control. Berger (1963, p. 15) thinks that sociology can be recommended 'to anyone whose goals involve the manipulation of men, for whatever purpose and with whatever moral justification'.

The raw materials of the natural world, such as water, coal, and iron, on which the wealth of the industrial capitalists was founded, have natural properties that can be discovered and tamed with the help of scientific and technical knowledge. Without this knowledge, a boiler might burst or a girder collapse. Similarly, sociology is expected to offer us knowledge of the rules by which the human 'clay' can be shaped into profitable labour. The one-sided authority relationship of domination to subordination, in which the human being is treated in Aristotelian terms as 'an animate article of property', increases the plausibility of a 'malleable clay', 'puppet', or 'scarecrow' image of mankind. As an indication of the

subjective feelings that might be experienced as a result of such a
relationship, T. S. Eliot's words seem particularly apt:

> We are the hollow men
> We are the stuffed men
> Leaning together
> Headpiece filled with straw. Alas!
> (1925)

Human beings may have properties, but they are seen as passive,
inanimate, and moulded by an outside force: i.e. the capitalists, acting
'under the name of society'. Control by the ruling class of the docile mass
of humanity becomes conceptualised as an abstract force – society –
'socialising' people into pre-defined 'roles'. Dawe in his article, *The Two
Sociologies*, describes it thus:

> . . . . society must define the social meanings, relationships and
> actions of its members for them. And, because it is thus assigned
> priority over them it must in some sense be self-generating and
> self-maintaining.

> This is precisely the logic which combines, in the familiar schema,
> the concepts of central value system, structure, function,
> equilibrium and structural differentiation. (Dawe, 1970, p. 308)

The social abstraction (society) is not derived from all the social
relationships to be found in capitalist society. As we might expect, it
appears most accurately to accord with the circumscribed life of the
factory. But such an existence does indeed correspond in many respects to
the situation of large numbers of people. Its accompanying ideology,
therefore, arising from the universalisation of these particular social
relations, often goes unchallenged. It is true that the view of a social
system 'separate' and 'above' the individuals that go to make it up, clearly
reflects the appearance of a society in which many people have little actual
control over their own lives. But the features of a group of people in a
particular situation at a given point in history are represented as the
features of mankind as a whole throughout history. The omission of the
active human subject, who can change his own circumstances, results in a
set of beliefs pretending fully to describe reality, but, in effect, providing a
distorted or limited account of that reality and serving only to maintain
the interests of those in power. Inasmuch as the limited instance is
presented as the total picture, the 'society on the outside' view of
sociology acts as a false ideology.

5   AN IDEOLOGY THAT SERVES THE ASPIRATIONS

Sections of the ruling class are aware of the imbalance created by the
denial of the 'active side' of man's two-way relationship with the world.
(Man can be an initiator, or 'subject', as well as a product of

circumstances, or 'object'.) But how can the active, creative, initiating human being be restored to the scene without bringing into question the existing social structure that denies responsibility to large sections of the population? The answer lies in idealism – in belief in a non-material world of mind or spirit. Where human beings are dominated by social forces beyond their control, where action appears futile in changing unpleasant conditions, their activity tends to become confined to the realm of the imagination. In some historical periods, aspirations become situated in a religious after-life. In *Animal Farm*, George Orwell parodies this with a description of the raven's view of the animal heaven:

> The pigs had an even harder struggle to counteract the lies put about by Moses, the tame raven. Moses, who was Mr Jones's especial pet, was a spy and a talebearer, but he was also a clever talker. He claimed to know of the existence of a mysterious country called Sugarcandy Mountain, to which all animals went when they died. It was situated somewhere up in the sky, a little distance beyond the clouds, Moses said. In Sugarcandy Mountain, it was Sunday seven days a week, clover was in season all the year round, and lump sugar and linseed cake grew on the hedges. (Orwell, 1945, p. 17)

But the opportunities for people to take action of some kind are seldom removed in their entirety. Even though freedom of action may be prevented in the economic sphere, it need not, as a consequence, be directly situated in a looking-glass after-life. Rather, the possibilities for action vary in inverse proportion to their proximity to the control of the dominant forces of production. Within the strictly-defined bounds of certain smaller institutions, some freedom of action either may be allowed, or may only be restrained by the ruling groups with considerable difficulty.

How, then, might we expect sociology to deal with freedom of action in a society where large sections of the population have little or no control over their everyday life: where the experience of powerlessness is an everyday occurrence? There may well be a search for those limited areas in which people still feel able to affect an outcome in their lives. The experience of partial or limited freedom is then likely to be generalised to apply to society as a whole. With the generalisation having no empirical warrant, no grounding in a wider experience, the luxury of a non-specific, timeless, and universal freedom worthy of superman himself, comes into being. But the freedom of such social theory will be shown to be sadly lacking as a guide to action, except in areas of little consequence to the existing social structure. From the fact that we are free to decide on the number of sugars in our tea, it does not follow that we are free to decide the size of the Common Market sugar quota.

It seems plausible to suggest that there are many different forms of idealism purporting to describe what is, or ought to be, fundamental to human existence. There is, of course, the religious 'reflex of the real world' (Marx, 1867, I, p. 79) situated in an after-life (for example, heaven). But a secular concept of the actual social relationships found in a relatively 'sheltered corner' of life (for example, family interaction, local community politics) can also be idealistically extended and held to be representative of social relationships generally. Various other partially autonomous social and psychological phenomena or social institutions might serve the same function, and enable us to situate the 'idealist vision' collectively or individually. For example, the world of symbolic action (language) might serve as the location for views of a collective realm of freedom, while the 'stream of consciousness', dreams, values, and the imagination might provide the basis for views of individual freedom. Although these speculative suggestions are not clearly formulated in this context, they may serve to explain the nature of a number of sociological positions.

In emphasising the subject to object relationship and neglecting the reciprocal object to subject relationship, Dawe's description of a 'sociology of social action' (1970, p. 214) seems an exemplary candidate for an idealist ideology. It can convincingly be argued that symbolic interactionist, existentialist, phenomenological, and ethnomethodo-logical sociological literature is replete with idealism. Views of action *solely* concerned with freedom to attribute meanings to things, to give meaning to the 'life world', to 'construct reality' at the level of ideas, abandon the material world with all its stubborn difficulties. The neglect of so-called macro-sociology and emphasis on small-group interaction is another aspect of the pressure on the sociologist not to undermine the existing state of affairs by raising the dreadful spectre of wide-scale human impotence. But false ideology arises only to the extent that such sociologies claim to present a total picture of society in an actual or potential form.

6 CONCLUSION

Sociologists may provide a partial picture of society by insufficiently emphasising the interplay between active human beings and social structure; by focusing on the former or the latter, but not both; and then by pretending that the picture they have presented is complete. Sometimes, they are so fooled by their own image of society that they mistake the image for the actuality and the world gains a population of either scarecrows or supermen. In addition, although sociologists' work has scientific pretensions, its loose word formulations, resulting in vagueness, ambiguity, and opacity, leave many of its findings open to question. The suspicion remains that what emerges in the way of explanation and description is what a particular social group *wants to be the case*, rather than *what is the case*. Of course, sociology may at any time be used for persuasion, justification, or encouragement. So may physical science. Our worry must lie in the assumptions of value we come to make on the basis of a distorted image of society offered to us by a 'science of society'. Sociology can act as ideology. Much of it could be false and contrary to our interests. Despite the scientific pretensions of the subject, we should never cease critically to scrutinise it.

PART TWO: A FRESH LOOK AT SOME OLD THEMES

I EDUCATION

Introduction

The purpose of this small collection of papers is to give examples of some of the alternative perspectives of sociology as applied to education. In existing sociology textbooks where education is dealt with, the *structural-functionalist* approach is frequently used, sometimes explicitly, sometimes implicitly (in the material selected). As suggested in the paper by Roland Meighan, this approach stresses the idea of schools and other institutions serving a whole society and its economy, by allocating roles, occupational chances and stressing one set of values. Therefore, schools are usually presented as organisations that have developed rather set patterns to which individuals adapt to some extent or other. An account using this approach may be found in *The Sociology of the School* (part two) by M. D. Shipman. Since schools are seen as performing functions for a society, this approach earns the name of structural-functionalism.

Another type of structuralist approach is the *conflict* approach where the structure of a society, including the organisations for education, is seen as being made up of groups with competing and conflicting interests. The Marxist version of conflict theory outlines conflicts between the social class groupings of a society. The paper 'Education and the Relations of Production' by Frank Reeves takes this approach.

The structural-functionalist and conflict perspectives both tend to start with a view of societies, cultures, and institutions as rather set patterns of values, rules, and behaviours, with the result that individuals are forced, coerced, persuaded or manipulated into some degree of compliance. The alternative perspectives start with the individual and stress how the structures are dependent on large numbers of individuals constructing their personal realities in a particular way, i.e. in accordance with the existing structures. If this does not happen, conflict, and perhaps change of some kind, may result.

The *interactionist* perspective is one that emphasises the activity of individuals in constructing their reality. The self is seen as a social product, in as much as people develop a consciousness of being a person mostly by reference to how others react to them. They tend to react to themselves as other are perceived as reacting to them. Therefore, the idea of a person as totally independent of others is seen as nonsense. Important concepts here are those of labelling, self-fulfilling prophecies, negotiation, and interaction. The paper by Douglas Gibson and Robin Jackson takes this approach by examining the label of mentally retarded, and discussing the proposition that most 'mentally retarded' children are 'manufactured' by those professionally engaged in the process of educational categorisation.

A *phenomenological* perspective is like the interactionist in some respects, but even heavier stress is laid on the subjective viewpoint of individuals, so that the meaning an individual puts on action is the crucial factor. The paper by Roger Gomm discusses this approach to the sociology of education.

The first paper concentrates on a particular theme familiar to most people reading this book, the pupils' view of schooling. After showing how this theme may be treated using various perspectives, the writer, Roland Meighan, goes on to give particular emphasis to a broadly interactionist approach.

The Pupils' Point of View
by Roland Meighan
University of Birmingham

Introduction

A functionalist view of education tends to stress the activity of schools in training and selecting children so that they fit into some necessary slot in society. This view implies that children are things to be manipulated in some way for somebody else's convenience. The images used by people who take this view stress this. The teacher is said to be like a potter moulding clay, or like a gardner cultivating plants, or a builder, building a house on sound foundations. In each case, pupils are seen as things being processed, and often as having no rights (see Stone, J. and Taylor, F., 1976).

This is often the official view. In 1976, the Prime Minister, James Callaghan, made a speech about education and the Secretary of State for Education, Shirley Williams, followed this by starting a public discussion about education. The people to be consulted included teachers, employers and trade unions. Pupils were not mentioned. This is consistent with a functionalist view: why should you consult the clay about what kind of pot it is to be made into? (See *Society Today*, No. 4, 19 Nov. 1976, p. 14 for an elaboration of this point.)

It might seem that any attempts to establish the pupils' point of view and to take account of it are bound to be using other perspectives than the functionalist. Some head teachers I consulted appeared to think like this (Meighan, 1977a). Here are some of their reactions to a research project on consulting pupils about teaching:

(This paper is a revised version of an article first published in *Educational Review*, Vol. 27, No. 1 (1974).)

It is dangerous to involve children in this kind of comment on their teachers.

Discipline would be adversely affected by this kind of exercise.

It is bad for classroom relationships.

Children are not competent to judge these matters.

The teachers had been provided with a written briefing that summarised previous research where the findings contradicted *all* the above statements. (This is not particularly unusual. People operating with particular views of teaching might often behave like this when first given information that is contrary to their beliefs.)

However, it does not follow that consulting pupils automatically suggests a non-functionalist perspective because there are several approaches to moulding pupils or fitting them into slots. One is based on *confrontation*, where teachers order pupils to behave in certain ways, and rely on fear and punishment to get their way. But other functionalist approaches are based on *persuasion, coaxing* and more subtle forms of control (Meighan, 1974a). Consulting pupils and using some of the responses can become a means of coaxing them into niches of society rather than *ordering* them into them. Nevertheless, many attempts to establish the pupils' point of view do use other perspectives, for example, Marxist, phenomenological, interactionist.

Which Perspective is in Use?

There are often clues to the perspective being used in studies of the pupils' point of view, in the concepts used, the methods of enquiry, and the kind of questions asked. Studies using a Marxist perspective may often use the concept of alienation in schooling. Studies using a functionalist perspective would be likely to involve asking pupils such questions as, 'What are the best teachers you have had like?', rather than, 'If you designed the ideal school, what would it be like?' The first question limits the pupil to the status quo whereas the second question is radical in allowing the pupil to consider alternatives, whether or not that pupil has experienced them. Phenomenological studies would be likely to use spontaneous discussion and conversation with pupils as data rather than involving the administering of a questionnaire (see Woods, 1976).

Studies Available

There are only a limited number of studies of the pupils' point of view on schooling in Britain available. Therefore a first conclusion is that this is a neglected issue in educational research.

In some studies the viewpoint of pupils has been one aspect of a larger study. In his analysis of a boys secondary school, Hargreaves (1967) obtained information from the pupils about how they interpreted some of the features of school life, especially streaming by ability.

In contrast, the study by Blishen (1969) concentrates entirely on the pupils' view of schooling by providing selections from essays, written mostly by secondary schoolchildren on the theme of, 'The school that I'd like'. (This was one of the few books on education that I have found difficult to put down.)

The educational weekly, *Times Educational Supplement* (1969), carried a two-part study entitled, 'Child's eye view of Teacher' and this contained a summary of primary schoolchildren's comments on their teachers.The following year there appeared a study of early school leavers' views of teachers and schools by Maizels (1970) whilst three years later a pair of studies reporting the views of primary and secondary schoolchildren in turn was produced by Blishen (1973).

A comparative viewpoint was available in two educational paperbacks. One by Holt (1970) reported his observations of how pupils reacted to schooling in the U.S.A. whilst the other was written by eight Italian boys protesting about their experience of schooling in Italy (School of Barbiana, 1970). Another writer in the U.S.A. (Jackson, 1971) was writing about a 'hidden' curriculum of influences in school that affected pupils considerably but was hardly recognised by teachers at all.

Findings

These studies appear to raise more questions than they answer and have a tantalising rather than a satisfying effect. The questions involved include the following:

1 How do pupils interpret the experience of schooling? Are they critical? Is there a division of opinion? How do the 'successful' react? How do the 'unsuccessful' react?
2 How reliable and valid are pupils as judges of their school experiences? Do they judge some aspects of schooling accurately and other aspects inaccurately? Are the perceptions of pupils useful as feedback and is consultation welcomed?
3 What do pupils see as ideal in schooling? What is a 'good' teacher as they see it? How do they define a 'bad' teacher?
4 How much are pupils aware of any 'hidden' curriculum? Do they recognise the operation of any labelling processes of a self fulfilling kind? Are some pupils alienated from learning? The pupils' view of school includes their view of fellow pupils and this raises even more questions, for example, how do peer groups operate in schools? What is the influence of such groups? Is there a youth culture opposing a school culture?

How Do Pupils Interpret the Experience of Schooling?

The studies so far suggest some tentative conclusions here. Firstly, primary school pupils do appear to be more satisfied with their experiences than those in secondary schools. Secondly, where dissatisfaction is expressed, it is just as likely to come from 'successful' as 'unsuccessful' pupils.

1 PRIMARY SCHOOL

In response to a request to seven- to eleven-year-old schoolchildren for written portraits of teachers came one thousand, two hundred replies. These were analysed by Makins (1969). She noted how children had watched their teachers with obsessive concern, noting mannerisms, subtle changes in mood, and detailed variations in behaviour; they remark on teachers who talk to lonely, left-out children during playground duty and who are angry with children because they are angry themselves. She concludes that on the whole these pupils love their primary schools: 'It is a sad fate to go home. I would like to stay for more education with the great 5' 10" Mr Henshaw.'

The really popular teachers manage without many sanctions and do not shout at pupils very often. They let children talk, they explain clearly, they encourage, they are interested. Makins comments that the essays contained evidence that what children learn matters much less to them than how they are taught. Teachers who are good at something – music, art, photography, sport, it does not appear to matter what it is – are appreciated and so are student teachers who come prepared with new projects.

'On the evidence of our critics, hundreds of teachers are managing to make school so interesting that there is no time or reason for the old tricks and giggles and avoidance routines. They are also succeeding in establishing a relationship with children which makes the rituals of classroom warfare unthinkable.'

2 SECONDARY SCHOOL

The contrast with pupils' reports of their secondary schools is marked. For example, a study by Maizels (1970) concentrated on a sample of how 330 'unsuccessful' pupils who had recently left school at the earliest possible date, or were just about to leave, rated teachers in their secondary school. Schools and teachers were negatively rated for the most part. On the judgements given, Maizels concludes, few of the schools would get a 'pass' mark. Only a minority of pupils felt that their teachers had encouraged them, listened to what they had to say, praised them when they did well, had been pleasant, kind or sincere, or had kept their promises. Only 34 per cent of boys and girls had felt that their teachers had treated them like human beings.

The response of some of the 'successful' pupils was obtained in an essay competition describing, 'The school that I'd like'. (Only children reasonably fluent and whose parents or teachers read *The Observer*, the organising newspaper, were likely to be in such a sample.) Blishen (1969) comments that the essays amounted to an enormous, remarkably good-humoured, earnest, frequently passionate and, at best, highly intelligent plea for a new order in our schools, to replace what was seen as currently dreary and boring.

What the pupils mean by dreary and boring is diagnosed in some detail: 'Everything learnt is second hand if it comes from the teachers and very often out-of-date and misleading if it comes from books'. 'Far better to replace constipated ways of teaching with more active lessons. . . .' The assessment of their experience of schooling was wide ranging and took in amongst other things, the dullness of building design and drear, unimaginative furniture, examinations and their distorting effect on learning, the role of prefects as peer group policemen, the limiting effect of timetables, bells, the triviality of many school rules, the idea of compulsory worship and religious education as attempted indoctrination. Blishen comments that the image of the prison returned to him again and again as he read the essays.

How Useful Are the Judgements of Pupils About Schooling?

Beliefs about the usefulness of pupils' judgement of schooling are plentiful whereas evidence is not. Previous investigations into the characteristics of pupil perceptions of schooling have taken place in the U.S.A. The most systematic attempts appear to be those of Veldman and Peck (1963). The conclusion they reached was that pupil perception of teaching performance was reliable enough and valid enough in most aspects of classroom technique, to be worth considering as useful feedback to teachers about their performance. The general conclusion from limited research available is that this holds good for samples of English children (Meighan, 1974b, 1977a) although there appear to be a few *technical* aspects of performance, for example, the effective use of questions and the effective use of teaching aids, where the perceptions of pupils are less reliable. 'Usefulness', however, can be interpreted in other ways. Are the perceptions useful as feedback so that performance is improved?

The impression of students who took part in research on pupils' perceptions was that it did make a difference and that they did modify or attempt to modify their classroom technique because of things that children had drawn to their attention (Meighan, 1977a).

Another aspect of usefulness is whether the act of consultation affects relationships. Some headteachers feared that this would lead to a deterioration, but the students reported otherwise. Several reported that they were less tense with the children concerned afterwards and in one case, a 'difficult' group simply ceased to be difficult. Obstruction gave way to cooperation to the surprise of both student and supervising teacher. The pupils appeared to regard someone who consulted them and took their opinion seriously, as on their side (Meighan, 1977a). Werthman (1963) reports some similar responses in his studies of delinquents in schools.

What do Pupils See as Ideal?

There appears to be a high degree of consensus amongst pupils about the ideal teacher. The list of qualities children wish to see in their teachers is extensive:

> They should be understanding, the children say, and patient; should encourage and praise wherever possible; should listen to their pupils and give their pupils a chance to speak; should be willing to have points made against them, be humble, kind, capable of informality, and simply pleasant; should share more activities with their children than they commonly do, and should not expect all children to be always docile. They should have conscience about the captive nature of their audience; should attempt to establish links with parents; should be punctual for lessons, enthusiastic within reason; should not desert a school lightly; should recognise the importance to a child of being allowed to take the initiative in school work; and, above all, should be warm and personal. (p. 131, Blishen, 1969)

Blishen goes on to say how the children saw clearly that these 'new' teachers could not easily operate in the present context of secondary schooling and that widespread changes in the organisation of schools might well be necessary.

The bad teacher, as defined by pupils, uses fear as the means of dominance, is extremely moody, miserable, indifferent and lazy. The study by Maizels (1970) shows a similar picture. The unfavourable references to teachers in her study were over-strictness, having favourites, being sarcastic, being moody, overemphasis on time-keeping. Only a few teachers were remembered as kind, sincere, keeping their promises, reliable, pleasant, full of ideas, efficient and encouraging.

The bad teacher, in the essays written on the theme of, 'The school that I'd like' (Blishen, 1969), is found guilty of remoteness, lack of sympathy, attachment to trivial rules, failure to admit ignorance or uncertainty. Such teachers made schools unhappy places, and denied children the kind of relationship with teachers they were seeking and expressing in their view of the ideal teacher.

Teachers are a central focus in children's comments about schools, but the context in which teachers operate is also of concern. Blishen (1969) reports how children commented on various other aspects of secondary schooling. The overwhelming majority wanted mixed schools and comprehensive schools. The buildings came in for considerable negative comment: children were tired of square rooms, unimaginative decoration, desks and the lack of common rooms for pupils. Examinations were seen as a significant cause of 'constipated' teaching and distance in teachers and alternative forms of assessment were desired. Prefects, homework, bells, religious education, all received considerable scorn and alternatives for some of these were suggested. For example, religious assembly and instruction were interpreted as a form of indoctrination that represented a failure to look at a wide range of religions and philosophies and moralities. It was six years later that a private members bill was drafted to propose a remedy for precisely this failure! (British Humanist Association, 1975).

The comments of the children were surprisingly sober and considered, Blishen comments, and intelligent alternatives to the status quo presented in most cases.

Do Pupils Recognise the 'Hidden' Curriculum?

The hidden curriculum is a term used to refer to those aspects of learning in schools that are unofficial, or unintentional, or undeclared consequences of the way teaching and learning are organised and performed. Jackson (1971) uses the term to describe the unofficial three R's – Rules, Routines and Regulations – that pupils must learn in order to survive comfortably and effectively in schools. Other aspects include the messages learnt from school buildings (Kohl, 1970), the influence of teachers' expectations (Rosenthal, 1968), the knowledge structures implied by teaching techniques (Holt, 1970), the effects of different usages of language (Barnes et al., 1969) and the sex roles projected by an institution (Davies and Meighan, 1975). The idea of a hidden curriculum is closely linked with the notion of labelling processes and self-fulfilling prophecies and one consequence may be the alienation of many pupils from learning.

The response of the children in the various studies is often reminiscent of Goffman's theory of total institutions (see Goffman, 1961) where he analyses in detail the coercive, non-negotiable and non-consultative nature of many contemporary institutions including armies, asylums, monasteries, hospitals, and prisons.

Goffman also talks about depersonalisation and this idea is introduced by a high school pupil in the U.S.A.:

> School is like roulette or something. You can't just ask: 'Well, what's the point of it,' he explained, 'the point of it is to do it, to get through college. But you have to figure the system or you can't win, because the odds are all on the house's side. I guess it's a little like the real world in that way. The main thing is not to take it personal, to understand that it's just a system and it treats you like the same way it treats everybody else, like an engine or a machine or something mechanical. Our names get fed into it – we get fed into it – when we're five years old, and if we catch on and watch our step, it spits us out when we're seventeen or eighteen, ready for college.' (From Silberman, 1971, p. 324)

The effects of 'trading for grades' gradually replacing all other educational activity is described by Becker (1968) and also by the boys in the School of Barbiana:

Social climbers at twelve. But your students' own goal is also a mystery. Maybe it is nonexistent; maybe it is just shoddy. Day in, and day out they study for marks, for reports and diplomas. Languages, sciences, history – everything becomes purely pass marks. Behind those sheets of paper there is only a desire for personal gain. The diploma means money. Nobody mentions this, but give the bag a good squeeze and that's what comes out.

To be a happy student in your schools you have to be a social climber at the age of twelve.

But few are climbers at twelve. It follows that most of your young pupils hate school. Your cheap invitation to them deserves no other reaction. (Letter to a Teacher, 1970, pp. 27–8)

The process of labelling and the consequences of alienation, for some pupils at least, is indicated in the above comments from pupils. They are able to recognise some aspects of the hidden curriculum.

Summary

Although the research on the point of view of the pupils is limited, there emerges a considerable degree of consensus in the general findings:

1 Primary schoolchildren tend to enjoy school, whereas secondary schoolchildren tend to be less happy with their school experiences.
2 Both 'successful' and 'unsuccessful' pupils in secondary schools record dissatisfaction. It is not just a reaction of the 'failures'.
3 The dissatisfaction appears to be marked, and not a minor feature. Only the minority of secondary schools appear to achieve even a pass mark in the eyes of the pupils.
4 The views of the pupils are not merely negative. They are sympathetic to the difficulties of teachers. They are able to offer a wide range of constructive, mostly feasible, alternatives.
5 The perceptions of pupils show high degrees of reliability and validity.
6 The pupils' views about preferred teachers show a high degree of consensus as do their views of 'bad' teachers.
7 Pupils are able to recognise some aspects of the hidden curriculum, some of the labelling processes and record their feelings of alienation that result.

Finally, one serious limitation of the studies to date is the habit of putting boys and girls together and reporting the *pupils'* view of schooling. However, the evidence that school presents a markedly different experience for girls, is beginning to emerge. Schooling appears to be significantly sex-typed (see Davies and Meighan, 1975).

Some Sociological Perspectives on Mental Retardation
by Douglas Gibson; Mackie Academy, Stonehaven and Robin Jackson; Aberdeen College of Education

Problems of Definition

This paper is an attempt to provide some sociological perspectives on mental retardation and to help fill the gap in the literature on this topic, a gap noted for some years now (see I.R.M.R., 1972). Throughout this paper, the terms 'mental retardation' and 'mental handicap' are taken to mean the same thing. The term 'mental retardation' is the one currently employed to designate persons who in times past have been referred to as morons, mental deficients, mental defectives, mental subnormals, or, in more general terms, the feeble-minded. However, the labels which are given to mental retardation are far less variable than the 'causes'. Over one hundred 'causes' of mental retardation have been specified.

Thus it is clear that mental retardation is not a *unitary* disorder in the sense that all persons who are officially categorised share a common condition that is produced by a cause that is identifiable, for the term can include (a) persons whose retardation is marked and results from a disease of the nervous system or genetic variation, (b) persons who suffer a fairly specific but less profoundly disabling genetic disorder (for example, Down's syndrome) and (c) persons who have no obvious physical defect and whose intellectual abilities, although inadequate for some tasks, are perfectly adequate for many others (i.e. mildly mentally retarded). This final category, which constitutes the largest proportion of the mentally retarded population (approximately 85 per cent), is one where it is rarely possible to identify with any degree of certainty the precise cause of their lesser intellectual abilities. Clearly, the term 'mental retardation' covers a wide variety of cases.   A further characteristic of the concept of 'mental retardation' is its variation in actual practice. This can be illustrated by reference to the differences between local authorities in their procedures for identifying, classifying and treating children who may be in need of special educational treatment. For example, children identified and formally categorised as 'mentally handicapped' in one local authority could, if they had lived within the boundaries of a neighbouring authority, have remained undetected and thus unclassified. Local and regional anomalies of this kind can result from (a) ideological differences between authorities, where one favours the integration of such children in normal schools and another favours their segregation in special schools, (b) differences in the actual procedures adopted for the identification and referral of pupils, and (c) differences in financial provision for special

(This paper is a revised version of an article first published in *Educational Review*, Vol. 27, No. 1 (1974).)

education which may be dictated by necessity, conviction or expedience.

An Interactionist Perspective

While it is acknowledged that there are degrees of mental retardation of such severity that a child's intellectual impairment is undoubted, it has been argued that most mentally retarded children are 'manufactured' by those professionally engaged in the process of educational categorisation. The description 'legitimate labellers' has been given to those persons (for example, doctors, psychiatrists, psychologists and educators) who are presumed to have the necessary knowledge and skills to make a diagnosis (Cicourel and Kitsuse, 1963; Szasz, 1971).

As a result of their training and experience, the professional labellers will possess a knowledge of trustworthy 'recipes' (i.e. sets of prescriptions to guide future professional action) and will have a tendency, in their dealings with children referred to them, to think in terms of categories. A cognitive process is thus discernible which becomes ritualised in a habitual routine – 'a recipe for action' (Schutz, 1970).

The appropriate 'recipe for action' for detecting and confirming the presence of mental retardation is through the use of diagnostic tests. However, the very process of measurement is in itself revealing. There is an assumption that what is being examined is amenable to precise measurement. In fact, this is an area in which no precision exists, except in the objectives and intentions of the labellers. The diagnostic category arrived at by the labeller is rarely challenged as it tends to be reinforced by both professional support (i.e. the labeller tends to follow occupational group conceptions) and audience support (i.e. the labeller is presumed by his audience to have the necessary knowledge and skills to make his diagnosis). Spurious objectivity and precision is also frequently attributed to coding schemes, statistical analyses and written observations employed in the diagnostic process which are dependent, in reality, on rumour, gossip, conversations, discrepant information and imperfect biographical stock-taking.

What the labellers, set up as the ultimate experts, are really doing is acting in a broad legal sense and defining, in a technical and modern way, whether behaviour is *socially* acceptable or not. Thus the label 'mentally handicapped' imposes a set of values on to a group and implies that the individuals who comprise the group are unable to perform social roles prescribed by the dominant culture. In fact, there is no evidence that persons who have IQs in the mildly retarded range (i.e. 50–70 IQ) suffer from any degree of organic impairment of the brain or central nervous system. What is evident, however, is that persons who become labelled as 'mentally handicapped' do so not because of the presence of any specific organic impairment but because of some inadequacy in social conduct. Further, the 'diagnosis' of mental retardation is usually made after such social incompetence has been demonstrated through the use of intelligence tests (Edgerton, 1968).

One of the consequences of labelling is the development of a self image as 'mentally handicapped'. Persons who have passed through a degradation ceremony and have been forced to become members of a categorised group, experience a profound and frequently irreversible socialisation process (Becker, 1963; Goffman, 1963). They acquire an inferiority status and, perhaps equally important, they develop a self-image based upon the image of themselves they receive through the actions of others.

The ceremonies which accomplish this change of status, ordinarily, have three related phases. Firstly, they provide a formal confrontation between the subject and representative of his community (for example, as in a psychiatric case conference). Secondly, they announce some judgement about the nature of the 'handicap' (for example, a verdict or diagnosis). Thirdly, they perform an act of social placement assigning the subject to a special role (for example, member of a special school or institution) which redefines the person's position in society.

It is important to stress that the expectations held by others play a crucial part in determining the behaviour of a person and such expectations should be taken into account in any general theory of mental retardation. So once a person becomes defined and firmly entrenched as 'mentally handicapped', the expectations of others may make it very difficult to leave this definition.

An Interpretive or Phenomenological Perspective

This approach involves an attempt to enter the world of the people in question and to see the world as they see it. It entails the study of actual behaviour in the child's encounters, typical problems and typical ways of handling them. To do this one would have to use a variety of techniques for getting at 'real life' through participant observation, tape-recordings, etc. This interpretive perspective follows from a recognition that the child interprets the meaning of his situations and directs his own and others' purposes, which are subject to reformulation on subsequent occasions. As Goffman emphasizes, actors are usually unaware of how they do things: they take their routine performance for granted. A central part of Goffman's work is concerned with face-to-face interaction, small group behaviours, the 'presentation of self' (i.e. the performance that 'ego' must 'put on'), and the impression management and information control necessary for 'alter' to interpret his actions correctly.

While Goffman regards social encounters as basically orderly and patterned by co-operative social endeavours, encounters can be fragile affairs, for persons are 'ritually delicate objects' and every competent actor must possess a range of tactics to ensure proper identity-maintenance and to carry out ritual repair work. He must know how to display both the proper respect to others' identities (deference); how to display the appropriate avoidance and presentation rituals and the proper respect for his own identity; how to make requests and denials without causing undue offence; how to apologise and how to accept apologies gracefully (interchange). It is only the use of such skills that enables the maintenance of everyday encounters and one is only granted the status of a 'normal person' on the basis of their demonstrated possession.

Adult interaction with 'mentally handicapped' children, who lack such skills, is markedly different. On such occasions, the child is continuously threatened by aggressive 'face-work' – snubs, sarcasm, gossip and misrepresentation. In the presence of stigmatised persons special regard to 'face-work' is normally paid, since the possibility of incidents is increased. On meeting a stigmatised stranger, one may seek to avoid the presence of 'odd' features, or we may attempt to redefine 'oddness' as something normal and expected.

Davis (1961) found that handicapped people reported that social encounters with unfamiliar actors were characterised by familiar signs of discomfort and 'stickiness'. Methods of attempting to bridge the breaks in smooth interaction included guarded references, common everyday words suddenly made taboo, the fixed stare, artificial levity and awkward solemnity. The handicapped social actor attempts to rectify the position by (a) deviance disavowal and (b) breaking through or 'passing'. 'Passing' involves laying a claim to a better face and having that claim accepted.

Children thus have to learn that how an act is presented shapes the response that it receives and that different audiences and situations require different modes of presentation (i.e. that one varies lines of action according to the particular encounter). A child's inability to focus on, to spell out, what is relevant or his tendency to be too readily distracted or too single-minded may lead to the label 'mentally handicapped' being attached to him. Such children have not yet learned the skill of turning their attention to the right thing at the right time. The teaching of these skills and 'recipes' is therefore of crucial importance. Learning these 'recipes' is a central part of the socialisation process, though one does not consciously have to use them everyday and therefore one rarely notices their use. It is only under special circumstances that one becomes aware of the use of tactics, for example, when one finds oneself in new or ambiguous situations or when the stakes involved are high.

Summary

We set out to explore the usefulness of some sociological concepts regarding mental retardation:

1 A key issue is that of definition. The term mental retardation is used to cover a large range of different behaviours. Perhaps in only 15 per cent of the cases can the precise cause of lesser intellectual abilitites be clearly identified.

2 Most mentally retarded chidren, perhaps 80 per cent or more, may therefore be 'manufactured' by the labellers, for example by doctors, psychiatrists, psychologists, who are presumed to have the necessary skills and knowledge to make a diagnosis. The sociological perspectives outlined suggest that the objectivity and precision of these skills is open to considerable doubt. What is being judged may often be social competency.

3 If many children are labelled mentally handicapped because of social inadequacy, one form of remedial action is for such children to learn the tactical skills or recipes necessary to demonstrate social competency.

4 Future sociological research should therefore focus on the stock of 'recipes' available to the child, their origins and the manner of their embodiment into our social structure. It is also necessary to examine how children acquire such skills and to examine the child's awareness of his situation. Although such a model is so far little developed it would seem central to an analysis of the socialisation of the mentally handicapped child. Goffman would seem to provide us with a conceptual framework and an empirical guide for more detailed and concrete analysis.

Education and the Relations of Production
by F. W. Reeves

Explaining an Expression

The French Marxist philosopher, Althusser (1971, pp. 144 ff) has argued that education serves to reproduce the relations of production. In order to grasp the significance of this claim, it is important to understand (a) the meaning of the expressions 'forces of production' and 'relations of production', and (b) why such relations need to be reproduced.

The forces of production consist of three parts:

1 human labour power
2 the instruments of labour (tools and machinery)
3 the objects of labour (the resources supplied by nature – animals, plants, minerals)

Put simply, human beings work on nature with the help of tools or machines. In our society, factories with their labour force (office staff, as well as factory-floor workers), machines and raw materials serve as an example of the forces of production. Without production, human beings could not satisfy their biological needs and social wants, for there would be nothing to consume.

Generally, human beings relate to each other in the productive process. The relations into which human beings enter in order to produce, the ways in which they organise themselves, are known as the relations of production. In the course of history the relations of production have taken a number of basic forms. In our society, for example, the chief form may be described as capitalist, implying a relationship between two groups: capitalists and workers, in which the capitalists are dominant. Capitalists are the small group of people who own and control the machinery and natural resources, for example, factories and farms.

Working people who do not usually have any productive property of their own must sell their labour power to the capitalists in return for a wage. The goods that the workers produce are sold for more than the amount paid out in wages and replacement costs, and the extra (or surplus labour, if it is measured in terms of the amount of extra time the worker spent working for it) is taken by the capitalist in the form of private profit. This method of extracting profit from the worker is known as capitalist exploitation.

The more the capitalist takes in profit, the less remains to be paid as wages. Marxists believe, therefore, that the interests of the capitalist and worker are incompatible and antagonistic, and that it is only by introducing a socialist society, in which productive property is no longer run privately for the benefit of the minority of capitalists but owned and controlled by working people in the interests of everyone, that this fundamental conflict can be resolved. The capitalists, however, make strenuous efforts to maintain the position of power and influence they have built up as a result of their control of the means of production (the factories and raw materials). But as the workers become conscious that their interests are different from those of the capitalist, they begin to campaign for improvements in their wages and living standards (economic struggle), for laws and decisions to be made in their favour (political struggle), and for a socialist, as opposed to a capitalist, form of society (ideological struggle).

Capitalist relations of production, therefore, cannot be taken for granted. If they are to survive, society must be organised in such a way that every new generation of human beings is forced to accept life as worker or capitalist and to view such social arrangements as inevitable. In Althusser's words, 'submission to the rules of the established order' (1971, p. 127) must be ensured. This involves:

> a reproduction of submission to the ruling ideology for the workers, and a reproduction of the ability to manipulate the ruling ideology correctly for the agents of exploitation and repression, so that they, too, will provide for the domination of the ruling class 'in words'. (Althusser, 1971, p. 128)

Althusser believes that the education system (which he calls an 'ideological State apparatus', is the most important means of actively maintaining ('reproducing') capitalist relations of production.

Explaining a Process

Why does the population continue to accept the exploitative relations of capitalist production? Over the years, many different answers have been provided. In the limited context of the education system, two general but closely related approaches may be identified:

1 the influence of ideas
2 the influence of institutions

The influential ideas approach concentrates on the more obvious substantive aspects of the school curriculum, while the institutional is concerned with more deep-seated structural arrangements involved in the relationship between school and work. Both may be regarded as providing partial and not wholly satisfactory accounts of the way the education system serves to reproduce the capitalist relations of production.

The Influential Ideas Approach

The influential ideas approach stresses the need of the capitalists to impose their way of understanding social relations upon the population as a whole, or in the words of Gramsci (Hoare and Nowell-Smith, 1971), to establish 'ideological hegemony', or the 'leadership' of certain ideas – their ideas. People must come to accept the correctness of the beliefs and social conventions that support the economically dominant group of capitalists. Recognition that there may be other ways of organising social life is prevented from occurring. For the majority of people it seems only 'common sense' that things turn out to be the way they are. Because the workers accept as inevitable their exploited condition, the capitalists need not maintain their privileged position by brutal physical force alone. This is why 'thought control' is so important.

Although the concept of ideological hegemony covers the whole range of ideas predominating in the different social institutions, our account is primarily concerned with the education process. In this section, the contribution to the establishment of 'ideological hegemony' of views commonly imparted by the educational curriculum is examined, while in the next, more deep-seated procedural conventions are dealt with.

Formal education can claim to be apolitical in the sense of not being blatantly party-political. But the apolitical stance is primarily maintained as a result of the dissemination of prevailing social and political values – the imparting of beliefs that are so well established among some groups at least, that their political implications go unnoticed. In addition, the widely accepted doctrine of 'balance' in which ideas 'for' and 'against' a controversial viewpoint are presented, is used as defence against the accusation of political indoctrination. Critics of this value-free position argue that the balance may only be illusory, for the teacher cannot hope to present ideas to which he is hostile as consistently, convincingly, and enduringly, as those ideas with which he sympathises. Furthermore, such a stance may lead to 'a plague on both their houses' attitude in which considered and objective assessment of the facts is confused with a position of non-commitment: precisely what is required to preserve things as they are. Althusser (1971, p. 148) writes of an essential ruling capitalist ideology 'which represents the school as a neutral environment purged of ideology. . . .'

The selection by inclusion or omission of material for the school curriculum undoubtedly results in the presentation by teachers, and assimilation by students, of a particular set of cultural and political values. For large numbers of young people, for example, the startling ideas of great nineteenth and twentieth century thinkers such as Darwin, Marx, or Freud are omitted altogether, or handled gingerly, and usually with hostility, only in the sixth form. Miliband (1969, pp. 239–45) draws attention to the ethnocentricity (emphasis on the superiority of one's own people), nationalism, and the assumption of consensual values of much curricular material.

You might wish to assess these claims against your own experience: whether and in what manner, for example, you were taught about republicanism, humanism, existentialism, atheism, or communism. And what do you think are your teachers' attitudes towards the School Student Union, the feminist movement, euthanasia, abortion on demand, pre-marital sexual intercourse, or gay liberation? It is also worth considering whether the publication of an article such as this in a sociology text book supports or undermines the claim that the curriculum contributes to the maintenance of the status quo. In any case, is it not mistaken to suppose that the study of ideas necessarily results in a commitment to act upon them? And why should some ideas be more persuasive and powerful than others?

Of course a great deal more is learnt at school than the official subject matter of the school syllabus. The education process has many unofficial, undeclared, and unintentional consequences. Waller (1932, p. 24) remarks that, 'the intelligence which the schools reward most highly is not of the highest type – it is a matter of incomplete but docile assimilation and glib repetition rather than of fertile and rebellious creation'. Among other points, Postman and Weingartner (1971, pp. 31 f) claim that, 'Passive acceptance is a more desirable response to ideas than active criticism' and that 'The voice of authority is to be trusted and valued more than independent judgement.' It is undoubtedly plausible to regard acquiescence to the existing state of affairs as the dominant effect of formal education.

The Institutional Approach

In the past, the family into which you were born, or apprenticeship at an early age, served to ensure you ended up in your designated social position and received your just, or unjust, reward. In the twentieth century, the formal education system does the same job and questions of its relationship to social reward are likewise raised.

In very broad terms, education processes you, grades you, convinces you, and then turns you out onto the labour market where the quality of the labour power you have to sell is likely to be judged, at least initially, on your educational qualifications. Expressed in more traditional structural-functionalist language, education is recognised to be about role-learning, role-allocation and role-acceptance (after Parsons, 1959). (The more naïve functionalist, however, is likely to assume that role-allocation and 'integration' into existing society is beneficial to all, and to ignore the question of whether there is an irreconcilable conflict of interests between capitalists and workers. He fails to see that the reproduction of the existing state of affairs may only benefit the capitalist minority which represents 'its interests as the common interest of all the members of society. . . .' [Marx and Engels, 1845–6, p. 52].) The way the education system serves to reproduce the forces and relations of production is examined below.

1   EDUCATIONAL DIFFERENTIATION AND RANKING

Education helps to raise the population to a minimal cultural standard of literacy, numeracy, general knowledge, and 'functional morality'. It facilitates a general social performance in a relatively complex industrial society. But after this has been achieved (usually on completion of primary education), education is likely to offer widely differing and unequal facilities to young people. Within the education system, young people are divided into groups based largely on their social class origin. They have varying amounts of money spent on them, are subject to different kinds of discipline and teacher behaviour, and are taught different subjects to different standards. After the age of eleven, for example, some groups spend twice as long as others in the education system. Rather than creating equal opportunity for children from different family backgrounds, the actual overall effect of education seems to be that of reinforcing the cultural differences between them. Miliband (1969, p. 241) describes the function of schools for the vast majority of working-class children as that of *confirming* class destiny and status. Schools do this 'by virtue of the starved education which they provide'.

Many critics of the education system argue that the school fails actively to encourage, hinders, or possibly actively destroys, the potential abilities of children from unskilled family background, develops mostly specialist technical skills (and severely curtails others) among children from skilled manual or clerical family background, and develops social and theoretical skills among children from professional and managerial family background, so that there is continuity between the destiny of parents and children. This need not be seen as an inevitable outcome but as a result favoured by current educational arrangements. It is undoubtedly the case, however, that, by the age of sixteen, school students show major differences in the levels of valued technical and social skills, and major variations in performance that would take a great deal of painstaking effort to reduce or eradicate. Some young people will leave school barely able to read and write, while others will be producing copious articles for the school magazine.

In addition to helping to create differences among young people in duration of study and social and technical performance, the education system ranks those differences in a hierarchical manner: some students must do better than others. A grading system is built into the education system in such a way that it would be impossible, for example, for all sociology students, however well they performed, to gain B grades in a G.C.E. 'A' level examination. Most examinations are 'norm-referenced', which means that examiners expect ability to be distributed across a range in accordance with a normal distribution curve. Indeed, they design examinations to ensure this result. It may, of course, be necessary to assess an individual's performance in order to develop his ability. For example, he could be told that his work was better than it had been before, or that it conformed to what the teacher regarded as the desirable standard. But formal education is wedded to a system that compares one individual's performance with another's, and uses the grades as an assessment not only of academic, but of occupational worth. The grading is made public by the provision (or worse, the non-provision) of an educational certificate.

2   WORK ALLOCATION

Employers make use of educational qualifications in the allocation of young people to occupations. Generally speaking, the better the qualifications, the greater the choice of occupation and the more satisfying and remunerative the work, especially in the long term. Those school-leavers without educational qualifications, particularly when the labour market is contracting, will generally be confined to the ranks of the unskilled, semi-skilled, or unemployed. At these times, a certificate has an additional advantage to employers in that, unlike the use value (the actual skills) that it theoretically represents, it may be devalued (rather like a pound note) when the labour commodity is over-plentiful. A certificate's intrinsic merit (as a symbol of the quality of labour power and social suitability of the individual that bears it) is subject to extrinsic market factors (supply and demand – a necessary accompaniment of the capitalist way of producing). For example, if jobs are scarce and school leavers are many, employers will raise the educational standard (for example, the number of C.S.E.s or G.C.E.s) deemed necessary for the work in question.

3   JUSTIFICATION FOR WORK ALLOCATION

In Elizabethan times, noble birth entitled a person to certain privileges. Nowadays, teachers, parents, employers, and students themselves, all seem to be convinced of the justice of a system in which the achievement of educational grades carries with it the right to occupy a particular occupational stratum with its attendant social rewards. One way of justifying this belief would be to show a close correspondence between educational achievement and work performance.

In an American study, however, Berg (1969) found that workers with less education but more experience performed better and earned more. He concluded that when industrial productivity is taken into account, the more educated are not always the most productive. His implication is that educational level and the needs of industry should be brought more closely into step, either by promoting the highly educated to posts more suited to their ability or by directing 'educational investments' away from higher education for the few to improve primary and secondary provision for the many. No doubt, Berg is right in drawing attention to the lack of fit between education and work, but he overemphasises the importance of productivity in industry and the contribution that education makes to this, and neglects the general part education plays in justifying people's allocation to jobs that carry with them different rewards.

Although the productive capacity of capitalist society is enormous, it can never satisfy demand. As supplies become more plentiful, prices will fall and the driving force of profit must decline. Capitalist society must, therefore, function on the basis of continuing scarcity and the assumption that human beings are 'insatiable' (Gouldner, p. 430). If material and cultural 'goods' are in short supply, then some principle must be devised for sharing them out. The pattern of consumption, as well as of production, must be justified.

It is widely held, for example, that the capitalist's possession of productive property is his own private affair and, in any case, is just reward for the effort he has invested or the capital he has risked. But to further support his claim to privileged command over resources, the capitalist will often be in possession of an education that has probably extended his abilities, or at least, is universally believed to be of a high quality (for example, public school education, a degree from Oxford or Cambridge) and of use to the 'economy' or 'quality of life', whatever these expressions might mean.

For those whose chief means of livelihood is gained from the sale of their labour power, education comes more fully into its own as an important justification for the unequal distribution of resources. Underlying assumptions exist that people should be rewarded for the use they make of their socially valuable skills – skills that, for some inexplicable reason, perpetually remain in short supply. Education is regarded as the indicator of a person's potential skill, and of his suitability for the most highly rewarded work. The worth of labour power is frequently estimated in terms of educational achievement, but educational success is carefully rationed. Although the presumption may be made that very high and very low academic achievement is indeed related in some way to work performances, whether in fact such a relationship exists in the middle range of the academic spectrum (if, indeed, there is any 'spectrum') is a most contentious issue. Braverman (1974, p. 424) strongly questions, for example, the claim that capitalist society requires an increasing amount of skilled manpower for industrial and office work, 'the thesis of upgrading'. But there is no need for a *real* relation to exist between educational and work performance. All that is needed is for differences of an educational kind to be made apparent and for the *belief* to exist that they are related to work performance.

It is conveniently assumed (although these assumptions are rarely made explicit) that:

1 abilities are differentially distributed in the population,
2 schools allow or encourage abilities to develop fully,
3 schools are equal in the opportunities that they offer,
4 abilities are not specific to a situation but are universally applicable in education, occupation, and social life,
5 schools' assessment of ability is more or less accurate,
6 the population should be rewarded with the good things of life on the basis of the achievement of educational qualifications, and
7 as the differential treatment is an immutable fact of life, resulting from one's own educational effort or lack of it, it should be accepted as fair and just.

As Miliband (1969, p. 241) puts it, 'The educational system thus conspires to create the impression not least among its victims, that social disadvantages are really a matter of personal, innate, God-given and insurmountable incapacity.'

How many of these points do you believe, and why?

There are a number of reasons why the education system excellently serves to justify young persons' allocation to particular occupations. It has the appearance of autonomy (in the case of the state system, it is public, non-profit-making, and 'free') and has the professed aim of developing a child's abilities to the full. Furthermore, at the lower levels, the school undoubtedly appears to be developing the ability of young people (to the acceptable minimal cultural level). It is therefore convenient to assume that it continues to do this at a higher level. After all, it is probably those who benefit from the education system who tend to write about its advantages. But Parkin (1971, p. 63) claims that, 'so far as the secondary modern school or its equivalent is concerned, one of its main socialising effects is to lower the ambitions of those who pass through it to accord with the opportunities of the labour market'. After a while, the young person comes to accept the justice of the school's estimation of his worth.

Conclusion

The dominant and general effect of education is to perpetuate capitalist social relations. But capitalism is not monolithic or crisis-free. The fact that everything is organised for the benefit of the capitalists means that the workers' interests suffer and economic and social problems are solved at their expense (although always in the name of an abstract national interest, for example the price of school meals is increased for the benefit of the hard-pressed 'economy').

The claims of capitalism do not always fit in with our own observations, particularly when we are confronted with an unjust situation, for example, in which a worker has been sacked for organising a trade union or a student reprimanded for putting a political poster on the notice board. As a result opposition arises, at first spontaneously, and then in an organised manner. The institutions of society, particularly those central to the economy, become arenas of struggle. Even within the education system, for example, there are conflicts over the kinds of school that ought to exist (for example, fee-paying public schools versus state comprehensive schools), the manner in which they are to be organised (for example, streamed versus unstreamed), their staff–student ratio, the syllabuses they must follow, and the forms of assessment they are to use, to name but a few. Although it is not always clear how the struggle between capitalist and worker is related to the conflicts within the education system (this requires a great deal of careful analysis), it is worth trying to assess the effects of all education policies, major and minor. Whose interests do you think they serve? And are they implemented in the general interest of humanity?

A Phenomenological Approach to Education by Roger Gomm
Stevenage College of Further Education

Introduction

A short paper such as this obviously cannot do justice to phenomenological sociology or to the philosophy which underlies it. To make matters worse there is no one phenomenological sociology. What follows is inevitably oversimplified and the reader will have to look elsewhere for a deeper and more comprehensive account. For a full introduction the reader is directed to Filmer et al. (1972).

To put matters very simply, the starting point for a phenomenological sociology is the idea that the social world is socially constructed. That is to say that what sociologists observe as 'society' is the result of people making sense of other people's actions and acting themselves on the sense they make, thus providing others with evidence of what is going on.

Looked at in this way, what seems to require further investigation by the sociologist is the question of *how* people make *sense*. I place an emphasis on '*how*' because phenomenologists tend to produce detailed descriptions ('ethnography'), rather than explanations. I place the emphasis on '*sense*' because the central issue for phenomenologists is 'meaning' and how the world is made meaningful to and by its inhabitants through their interpretations.

1   INTER-SUBJECTIVITY

Common experience tells us that at some level or other people 'understand' each other, which suggests that the meanings they attribute to social actions are to some extent shared and are hence *social products* which are a proper topic for the sociologist. In phenomenological sociology shared meanings are spoken of as *inter-subjective* to indicate that although the attribution of meaning is a subjective event that happens inside somebody's head, this is not solely an idiosyncratic affair but involves using rules for making sense. These rules are shared. How far meanings are shared and how far they are peculiar to one group (say pupils) rather than another (say teachers) and how far they are personal and idiosyncratic is an open question which needs to be decided by further investigation.

I will extend this brief introduction by indicating the meanings of two other terms which are used by phenomenological sociologists. The first is *bracketing*, the second is *constitution*.

2   BRACKETING

In attempting to produce detailed descriptions of the way in which the social world is produced, the phenomenologist tries to detach himself from his beliefs and preconceptions about the phenomenon he is studying. This does not mean simply searching his heart for biases and prejudices but something much more fundamental. It means a wilful refusal to know what he knows as an ordinary member of society. This is especially important in what are fairly familiar circumstances such as classrooms or assembly halls. Here a phenomenologist would not be content to use his everyday knowledge of (say) the differences between pupils and teachers – but would try to see with fresh eyes the 'pupilness' of pupils and the 'teacherness' of teachers.

Such an exercise is one you might like to try for yourself. In a school or classroom setting, try placing yourself in the situation of a complete stranger from another culture with no knowledge of schools, and describe what he or she would observe to be going on.

If you do this exercise I think you will agree with the following points. Firstly, you will probably say that 'The stranger wouldn't be able to make much sense of the situation', meaning that since he or she did not share the same knowledge as participants he/she would not be able to make sense of things in the same way as they did, or to understand the relationship between *their* interpretations and their actions. This should alert you to the fact that most sociological studies, even those produced by phenomenologists, actually draw very heavily on what the sociologist knows as a layman. It is a very important task for the phenomenologist to clarify what common-sense knowledge he/she brings into use in sociological work.

Secondly, you will realise that this piece of social action you have been observing is only possible because the participants know how to produce it. They know how to *do* a maths lesson (even if they don't know how to do sums!).

Thirdly, as a stranger, you will notice things which the participants do not notice, or take for granted, or regard as irrelevant. You may notice for instance that this is a situation where one adult confronts a larger number of juveniles; where the adult appears to move freely about the room, whereas the juveniles seem to be restricted to a seated position behind desks, or that the adult appears to control verbal communication, or some other feature so 'ordinary' that participants would not regard it as worthy of comment.

The object of bracketing is not to turn the intelligent layman into an idiot sociologist, but to place him or her in such a position as to be able to see clearly how situations are produced by those who produce them by regarding as important all those things which participants take for granted, for it is these taken-for-granted features which provide the background in terms of which participants interpret and act upon a social situation.

Bracketing is never complete however. As noted, the phenomenologist still has to rely on his common-sense methods of making sense. The task is to make that knowledge explicit. In addition, the phenomenologist may adopt certain working assumptions to guide observation and interpretation; assumptions such as: 'all the people in this situation have projects they wish to achieve' or 'all the people in this situation are busy trying to define for each other what is "really" going on', or that, 'the action in this situation is produced by people following rules'.

3   CONSTITUTION

This term refers to the processes by which people generate information about themselves and their actions and recognise the meaning of other people's actions. Phenomenologists try to describe how social phenomena are constituted by members of society. Consider the following by way of an example:

> From time to time I may be observed walking purposefully away from my office, only to pause, raise one finger in the air, regard it with raised eye-brows, mutter 'Oh', turn on my heel and walk equally purposefully back to my office.

If I act out this little drama to my students, they say, 'Oh, that's easy, you realise you've forgotten something and go back to get it' – which is indeed what I intended them to understand.

Two things are interesting about this. Firstly, it is interesting that I do this at all. That I do, speaks to the fact that most of us, most of the time, conduct ourselves so as to make sure that people understand our actions as we intend them to be understood. We 'present' ourselves as Goffman would say (1969), or as I would prefer to say, as we act we give an account of our actions. In this example what is important is not that I wish people to know that I have forgotten something but that I wish them not to interpret my actions otherwise – as trying to avoid someone, or as wandering about aimlessly.

Secondly, it is interesting that the actions described above as 'doing-having-forgotten-something' are recognisable to others in the way intended. Thus to do 'having-forgotten-something' I draw on my social knowledge of how to do it and rely on observers having similar knowledge to interpret what I do. This action works for me and for observers only in so far as it is constituted according to the rules for constituting 'doing-having-forgotten-something'. By acting in accordance with those rules I produce a piece of social action which can be decoded by others to discover the rules I used to produce it, and hence to 'know what it means'. Thus we might say that the way in which the social world is produced as meaningful to its inhabitants is through their rule-based action, and through their assumptions that the actions of others are rule based.

Having said this, I should point out that the scope for misunderstanding is large. For instance, one who observed me returning to my office might assume that I 'really' wished to avoid her, but 'pretended' to have forgotten something. In this case she would be drawing on what she would count as her knowledge about me, our relationship and so on, to interpret my action. In order to familiarise yourself with the way in which social phenomena are produced and recognised I would suggest that you rehearse some familiar activities (say, doing 'being-busy-in-class', or doing 'having-misunderstood-an-instruction') and consider the various ways in which these performances might be interpreted under different conditions, by different people drawing on different 'knowledge' about you.

Understandably, phenomenologists are at pains to discover and describe the rules through which meaningful social action is produced and recognised (constituted), in much the same way as linguists attempt to discover and describe the rules of language. Indeed phenomenologists are very interested in conversational analysis (see page 59). Note, however, that the analogy between phenomenological sociology and linguistics can be misleading if it is forgotten that phenomenologists are always interested in language or action *in context*, for it is only within a particular context that language or action has meaning for members.

Deviance in Classrooms

As an example of a phenomenological approach to education I will draw upon the work of Hargreaves, Hestor and Mellor, published as *Deviance in Classrooms* (1976). One of the major concerns of this study was the question of how breaches of classroom rules were recognised by teachers, pupils and researchers. This was not an easy task since the teacher's rules for pupil behaviour against which deviance was judged were frequently unclear and differed from classroom to classroom and from minute to minute. A preliminary stage for the researchers was to discover how lessons were moved from phase to phase by the teacher, and hence how the teacher rules-in-play changed from time to time, and how they could be known to be in play. The researchers distinguished five principal phases which they found were common to virtually all lessons:

1 The 'entry' phase
2 The 'settling down' phase
3 The 'lesson proper' phase
4 The 'clearing up- phase
5 The 'exit' phase

Each phase had its own temporal sequence and sub-phases and each was characterised by having different teacher rules for pupil behaviour. Hargreaves et al. found that each phase tended to be ushered in by the teacher's use of what they called 'switch signals'. Sometimes such switch signals were relatively explicit such as, 'Right, get out your books and do the first three exercises on page thirteen'; sometimes switch signals consisted of phrases like, 'That's enough now'. In using a switch signal the teacher brings into play a very complicated set of rules in a way that makes it possible for the teacher to judge pupils' behaviour as conforming to, or deviating from, such rules. The teacher assumes that pupils share a knowledge of the rules, which rules are in play, and how to comply with them by, for instance, knowing which 'books' to get out, how to lay out the exercises and how to do them (sitting down quietly without talking to a neighbour, etc.).

From time to time teachers charged pupils with deviance; with doing the wrong thing. The verbal formulae used by teachers to impute deviance were often indistinguishable from other verbalisations, unless the hearer knew the rules in play. Thus 'Pay attention!' might be heard as a switch signal, when its context was a phase of the lesson when the class had been working at their books individually, or as an imputation of deviance when the phase of the lesson involved teacher lecturing from the blackboard. The researchers, observing classrooms, found that they could only distinguish between instructions and imputations of deviance in the same way as pupils – by following the same rule of interpretation relating the teacher's verbalisations to the context formed by the rules in play.

It not only takes a great deal of interpretive work by the pupil to avoid charges of deviance, but Hargreaves et al. found that the recognition of deviance by teachers was also a complicated matter.

> *Interviewer:* How would you recognise that a pupil was not paying attention?
> *Teacher:* Well, it's hard sometimes, because it may look as though, I mean it's really hard to tell even if they are behaving perfectly quietly whether they are listening. The only way is if you get feedback from them, which you can. As I say, in class discussion, we always discuss a piece of writing before we do it, and there are some boys that you can't drag – I say 'Well what do you think about that?' and they shrug their shoulders and mostly when you get the written work, you can tell whether they have been listening, most of the class, but a slipshod piece of work might not prove they haven't listened, it's just that they are too lazy to do a better piece. (Hargreaves et al., 1976)

Teachers thus employ strategies to detect deviance and use interpretive devices to piece together the 'evidence'; i.e. to constitute a particular piece of behaviour as deviance and as deviance of a particular type. Thus a 'slipshod' piece of work (however that is judged) might be evidence of 'not paying attention'. And then again it might not.

In reaching a verdict the teacher habitually draws upon his 'knowledge' of particular pupils, knowledge which relies on a theory of pupil types. The teacher 'knows' that there are certain types of pupils with characteristic behaviour patterns. Thus a 'slipshod' piece of work from one type, when put together with other evidence might mean to the teacher that a pupil is 'lazy', for another it might confirm that they are 'dull', and for another type that they are 'psychologically disturbed'. By using detective strategies, piecing together the evidence, the pupil is constituted by the teacher as of a particular type and his or her behaviour is thus 'understood' and reacted to. Such is the stuff that school reports are made of.

Alternative Realities

The example above focused on the rules imposed on the class by teachers, in terms of which pupils are judged as 'good' or 'bad' and with the teacher's interpretations of what is and what ought to be going on. It needs to be said of course that in imposing rules on a class, teachers do not have a free hand. Not only are they constrained by the law, by superiors, other teachers and parents, but classroom routines have to be negotiated with the class and pupils have considerable power to thwart, subvert, or facilitate the teacher's projects.

While pupil behaviour which teachers see as breaching teacher's rules is often simply dismissed as 'naughtiness', 'laziness', 'immaturity' and so on, it remains true that pupils also have objectives they wish to achieve in the classroom (a good reason for thumping the person in front) and pupil groups have rules for behaviour against which not only other pupils, but teachers, can be judged as good, bad or indifferent. In a study by Rob Walker, Ivor Goodson and Clem Adelman (1973) the authors claim that teachers are judged as good or bad largely in terms of whether, 'you can have a laugh with them'.

The discrepancy between the pupils' perception of what is going on and that of the teacher is often acute, as shown below.

> *Teacher:* The lesson illustrates the magnetising effect of electricity and introduces them to the idea of make/break circuiting. It normally goes all right.
>
> ───────────
>
> *Pupil:* Science, me and Phil had to make this thing, but I didn't understand it so I just went off and left it to Phil.
> *Interviewer:* What was it? What thing?
> *Pupil:* I dunno. You had to make this thing with wire and wood and magnets and plugged it up to a box and you put the plug on 8, it started to spin around or something. I didn't get it.
> *Interviewer:* What was the idea?
> *Pupil:* Dunno, I didn't bother to read it.
> *Interviewer:* What did they give you, a worksheet?
> *Pupil:* They give you a big tray of equipment with a bit of paper in it telling you what to do. The teachers were there to tell you if it went wrong or something but . . .
> *Interviewer:* So what was the problem then?
> *Pupil:* I didn't want to do it, wasn't interested in it.
> *Interviewer:* Why? Did anybody tell you how to do it?
> *Pupil:* No.
> *Interviewer:* Didn't they? Did Phil do it?
> *Pupil:* He did it but he didn't make it go. (Goodson, 1976)

Alternate schemes for interpreting reality, and alternative rules for behaviour frequently become issues for conflict in school. I will leave the reader to consider the following situation and its likely outcomes:

> Madeline, sitting in the science lab., notices a book on the shelf below her table. She picks it up and opens it below the level of the desk. The teacher notices this:
> *Teacher:* Madeline, come up to the front and bring that book you were reading under the desk.
> *Madeline:* I wasn't reading it. I just picked it up to see who it belonged to.
> *Teacher:* Don't lie, I saw you reading it. Come up to the front.
> *Madeline:* I'm not lying. I wasn't reading it.
> *Teacher:* Don't argue, do as you are told.

The Strengths and Shortcomings of a Phenomenological Approach to Education

It will be fairly clear to the reader by now that a phenomenological approach to education makes such topics as 'educational success' or 'educational failure' very problematic indeed. Naïve sociological researchers who take correlations between 'poor school performance' and 'low socio-economic status' as self-evident proof that low socio-economic status will give rise to pupils of a type who cannot by their *nature* perform well at school, may be merely restating part of teachers' common-sense knowledge about types of pupils. If this is part of the teacher's common-sense knowledge of pupils, it is part of the teacher's equipment for distinguishing between those pupils who are performing badly 'because of their home background' and cannot be expected to do any better, and those who are 'really bright but lazy' and whose performance can be remedied. This is indeed what several sociological studies of schools have suggested; Cicourel (1963), Goodacre (1971), Nash (1973), Sharpe and Green (1975). If this is the case then *teachers' assessments* of home background may be as important for educational success as are the objective circumstances of a child's home life.

To take another example, a statistic which was widely quoted in the quality press in 1972 was that 17 per cent of the school population of a typical inner urban borough was 'psychologically maladjusted'. At first sight this may seem a convenient explanation of the poor performance and discipline problems which are said to characterise inner urban schools. The statistic was derived from the use of the Rutter maladjustment scale (1970); a three-part instrument for providing 'objective measures of maladjustment'. One part of the scale is completed by teachers. It consists of twenty-five statements which the teacher ticks or leaves blank: the more ticks, the higher the chance of a 'maladjustment' diagnosis. The statements below are typical of the scale:

Squirmy, fidgety child.
Frequently fights with other children.
Is often disobedient.
Tends to be absent from school for trivial reasons.
Often tells lies.
Has stolen things.
Fussy, over-particular child.
Has twitches, mannerisms or tics of the face or body.
Irritable, quick to fly off the handle.

No questions are asked as to how it is that a teacher recognises pupil behaviour as 'fussy' or an absence from school as 'for trivial reasons' or about how frequent 'disobedience' has to be to be 'often'. The resulting maladjustment score is taken to measure something about the *nature* of children rather than something about the interpretive procedures of teachers, the rules teachers make for pupil behaviour, and the relationships they make with them (Fitton, B., 1972).

In such a context then the value of a phenomenological approach is to restore the 'hard facts' of education to the phenomena they are. Examination results are the product of the evaluation done by examiners; position in a stream or class is the result of assessments made by teachers; 'maladjustment' is the product of teachers' interpretive work; and 'bad behaviour' follows from the rules teachers make for good behaviour and their methods for recognising breaches of rules and their significance. Of course pupils also have a part to play in their educational careers, but it is interesting that conventional approaches to education have depicted pupils (or their parents or their home backgrounds) as solely responsible for their performance at school.

The strength of phenomenological sociology lies in producing detailed descriptions of the ways in which the social world is produced from the interpretive work of its members. It comes far closer to the nature of social reality than do positivistic approaches which have previously characterised the sociology of education and which tend to reproduce teachers' common sense in the guise of sociology. To illustrate this point you might like to read Nell Keddie (1973) on the concept of 'cultural deprivation'; a teacher's idea transformed into a 'sociological' concept.

On the other hand, there lies in phenomenological sociology a danger that the task of sociological explanation may become buried under a wealth of fascinating detail. It is obviously important (say) to produce detailed accounts of exactly *how* a teacher accomplishes a 'bad report' for a pupil, but it is also very important to stand back from the classroom to ask *why* it is that the educational system is such that the majority of pupils *must* be defined as achieving relatively poor results. This is a question which relates to the political economy of our society and the role of the educational system in reproducing the class structure at each generation. It is not a question to which phenomenological sociology can yield answers. For an alternative see Bowles and Gintis (1976) and the previous paper by Frank Reeves.

II THE FAMILY

Introduction

One theme running throughout this book is that different sociologists, using different perspectives, produce varying descriptions and explanations. Sociologists researching and writing about the family are no exception.

The writings based on perspectives *other* than the structural-functionalist can have a disturbing, if not exciting, effect. The reasons may be partly to do with the sheer familiarity of the idea. We all, or most of us, belong to a family for long periods of our life, therefore any attempt to free ourselves from the powerful, personal emotional experiences of living in a family and to look at the institution in a cooler, more reflective, and more detached way, is potentially disturbing. Yet this is what sociologists try to do.

The reasons for this disturbing and yet fascinating effect may also lie within the alternative perspectives themselves. They tend to question the taken-for-granted ideas of the family in several ways. One is by looking at the family from a member's point of view, when a different picture may emerge from that gained when looking from a society's point of view. The paper by Janet Harris and Scarlet Friedman analysing a woman's view using a phenomenological approach, is of this type.

Many of the writings on the family have used a structural-functionist approach. (Books by Titmuss, MacGregor, and Fletcher come to mind, and a useful summary can be found in Chapter 5 of P. Berger's *Sociology: A Biographical Approach*, Penguin Books, 1976.) The underlying assumption of this approach is that the family is a cornerstone of society and of most, if not all, societies. It follows that everything should be done to preserve the family since no society appears conceivable without it. The possibility that the various functions described by these writers, for example, the regulation of sexual activity, the procreation of children and their primary socialisation, could be organised within structures quite different from those at present available, is excluded. The most that is likely to emerge is the identification of a number of dysfunctions, for example, the isolation of the nuclear family from other institutions such as work, particularly in the case of mothers and children. The implication here is that any dysfunction needs to be 'managed' in some way: the awareness of alternatives to the familiar structure is denied. This is therefore a conservative, status quo approach, rather than a radical review.

The Marxist perspective almost reverses the equation: the possibility, indeed the desirability, of change is seen as a central concern. The paper by Sydney Peiris explores this approach. Change may imply experiment and diversity: 'Possible new patterns are many and varied, and we are concerned to create a situation in which a diversity of family patterns is practised, rather than to promote any particular new pattern' (C. Kensit and R. Buchanan in *Marriage and the Family*, 1969). If this does not sound all that subversive, you may reflect that Bertrand Russell was excluded from teaching at a university in the U.S.A. and branded as an immoral and corrupt person for advocating something similar in his book *Marriage and Morals* (Unwin Books, first published in 1929).

The article by David Coleman takes one kind of interactionist approach to marriage – a territorial analysis. Here the situations in which interactions take place are the subject of inquiry rather than the interaction itself, and the central questions are about where the partners meet, what choice exists and how far afield people 'search'. Our princes and princesses of the romantic mythology turn out to live conveniently within five miles of us, and only rarely over fifty miles away – more likely to come our way by bus than by ship or aeroplane.

One approach not represented in this collection is the *comparative* – where accounts of family types in various societies are compared and contrasted. The disturbing effect of this approach lies in the possibility that an account of other family systems in other cultures may suggest that the ways of others may be preferable to the familiar one. Like readers of the magazine *Which?*, we may have drawn to our attention a potential 'Best Buy'. But if the record player you already own is the worst buy, you are likely to be a bit upset. How much more so if the family arrangements you know, and that your revered parents implemented, now appear to be a worst buy! Perhaps the appeal of *non*-radical approaches is that one is not exposed to intellectual risks of this kind?

The Family: A Marxist View
by Sydney Peiris

The Family in Early Human Society

A sociology of the family tries to show the connections between the social structures within which we live and the psychological experiences we undergo in our families, and in our emotional and sexual relationships. A Marxist sociology looks at the conflicts and contradictions in particular.

Before we discuss the modern family let us have a brief glance at the family in the early stages of human society. In hunting society it would seem there was common ownership of economic resources. Since society was not yet divided into 'haves' and 'have-nots', there was no State in existence to maintain the social order and safeguard the property of the 'haves'.

Prolonged child care typically prevented women from participating in the most socially valued work – hunting. This resulted in women's lesser status compared to men, the hunters. It was on this sexual division of labour that the human family was founded, although today the preconditions for abolishing this division of labour exist in the advanced industrial societies.

In hunting societies, though subordinate to men, the women enjoyed greater freedom and power compared to what was to come. '. . . marriage and sexual restrictions are practical arrangements among the hunters,' writes Kathleen Gough, '. . . mainly to serve economic and survival needs. . . . For the rest, where the economic and survival bonds of marriage are not at stake, people can afford to be freely companionate and tolerant. Hence pre-marital sexual freedom, seasonal group-licence, and a pragmatic approach to adultery.'

The egalitarian quality of social relationships between men and women, as well as between men and men were changed with the rise of inherited private property, in the first stages in the form of herds. Engels described this as the 'world historic defeat of the female sex'. Private property gives rise to the necessity to establish the paternity of those who will inherit a man's possessions. The result is the strict regulation of women's sexuality, in contrast to the earlier relationships which allowed much greater sexual freedom. The new economic dependence of women makes them more controllable by men, both socially and sexually. Women are gradually ousted from activity in society, ending up in confinement to activities in the home.

This historical account does not imply that relationships between men and women developed in the same manner everywhere. In different societies and areas differences in economic and environmental factors accounted for the varying degrees of inequality that came to prevail.

Capitalism and the Family

When we look at the family in England before capitalist industrialisation we see a situation quite different from that which succeeded it.

In the seventeenth century, the production of goods by the family for its own use was integrated with a system of 'family industry', involving the production of goods for sale. Home and work place coincided.

The social respect accorded to women stemmed from the fact that they were engaged in *socially valued* work. Women worked as pawnbrokers, millers, butchers, shipping agents, glassmakers, bakers, innkeepers, etc. 'In pre-industrial Britain,' writes Ann Oakley, '. . . a woman's role in adult life was always the role of productive worker, in the home or outside it. Women were not called upon to choose between work and domesticity as alternative vocations.'

The creation of the factory system led to a separation of home from work, and posed the problem of caring for children. The transition to an industrial society led to the restriction of women to the home.

Ideologies are social belief systems for justifying or encouraging social practices. Ann Oakley points out that no clear ideology of female domesticity existed up to about 1840. The threat of competition from women for jobs promoted such an ideology. It began to spread among the working classes by the second half of the nineteenth century.

The consequences of the Industrial Revolution were more than economic. As Ann Oakley writes, 'The separation of the family from the economy resulted in . . . the idea of a home as a private place – a refuge from the public world of work.'

The social position that women occupy today cannot adequately be explained in psychological terms such as abilities, drives or sentiments. There is a material basis for women's inferior status. 'In a society in which money determines value,' writes Margaret Benston, 'women are a group who work outside the money economy. Their work (*household production*) is not worth money, is therefore valueless, is therefore not even real work. And women themselves, who do this valueless work, can hardly be expected to be worth as much as men, who work for money.'

Political Socialisation and the Family

In societies where the wealth produced is unequally distributed we find human beings segregated into social classes. The State in such societies does not appear to be neutral, but an active agent in sustaining wealth differentials. The State becomes a weapon in the hands of the privileged classes, to be used for maintaining their social advantages in the face of demands from the underprivileged groups.

Marxism is both an instrument of social analysis and a philosophy of human liberation, and its relevance for modern times is not necessarily diminished by the political practices of those countries that describe themselves as 'communist'.

Marxists suggest that for the first time in human history we have reached a stage where the material needs of people in advanced capitalist societies can be fully met as a consequence of the tremendous advances in science and technology. But the transition to a society based on the satisfaction of human needs rather than profit is prevented because of the power of the ruling classes to resist change.

What maintains a capitalist society such as ours is not simply the power wielded by the dominant groups. The aim of the socialisation processes in capitalist society is the creation of psychological structures within individuals such that there is a match between these and the existing social structures. The result is the stabilisation and perpetuation of these social arrangements.

The dominant ideas of our society are the ideas emanating from the dominant class. Through the control of the educational system and the mass media, this class is able to socialise other classes to accept its ideology in varying degrees, although such ideological submission is not in the material interests of the disadvantaged groups.

A primary agent of socialisation is the family. Even when located in the underprivileged groups, the family absorbs and transmits some of the fundamental political norms promoted by the dominant class. Erich Fromm points out that parents, '. . . in their own personalities . . . represent the social character of their society or class. They transmit to the child what we may call the psychological atmosphere or the spirit of a society just by being as they are – namely representatives of this very spirit. *The family thus may be considered to be the psychological agent of society.*'

An important function of the family is political socialisation. 'A political system,' writes David Easton and Robert D. Hess, '. . . to maintain its integrity as a system . . . must be able to mobilise support on its own behalf continuously, or at the very least keep the members of the system in a state of indifference.' The family discourages an interest in politics while simultaneously seeking to socialise the young to accept the political and economic system to which it has accommodated itself. The end product of the socialisation process, which the family shares with the school, is to outlaw from the consciousness of its members *alternative* political and economic possibilities that transcend the existing socio-economic structures.

The Split in Modern Industrial Society

Life in modern society is marked by a split between a public sphere and a private sphere. The public sphere comprises vast, bureaucratic institutions which regulate the individual's economic, political and cultural life. 'The public institutions,' writes Peter Berger, 'now confront the individual as an immensely powerful and alien world, incomprehensible in its inner workings, anonymous in its human character.' In the mirror of society, individuals cannot recognise themselves, for what is called 'society' is not experienced by individuals as the joint creation of themselves and their fellow human beings. Despite the boasts about freedom and democracy, in capitalist society individuals are dwarfed and rendered powerless in the face of institutions they can neither understand nor control. Thus alienated from society they attempt to locate 'real life' in the private sphere – family, friendship networks, religious organisations, leisure activities, etc. – where they feel themselves in a world that is their own and amenable to their influences.

'Marriage . . . is incontestably a form of exclusive private property' (Karl Marx)

Marriage assumes increased importance in a stressful industrial society in that it comes to be felt as a sanctuary for retreat from a public sphere that offers very little possibility for a creative and fulfilling life. The family is the haven where people seek to repair their bruised selves, recover a sense of their human worth, and prepare daily for commuting to that cold, harsh arena called 'society'.

The incessant moral advertising of monogamous marriage in our society is not matched by an equally ubiquitous analysis of the underlying ideology, and a critical scrutiny of the claims made on behalf of the institution. In a critique of monogamy, John McMurtry writes, 'The ground of our marriage institution . . . is this: The maintenance by one man or woman of the effective right to exclude indefinitely all others from erotic access to the conjugal partner . . . (the) restrictions of our form of monogamous marriage together constitute a state-regulated, indefinite and exclusive ownership by two individuals of one another's sexual powers. Marriage is simply a form of private property.'

Although monogamous marriage antedates capitalism as an institution, it cannot but be influenced by the societal context in which it is embedded. 'Of course, it would be remarkable if marriage in our society was not a relationship akin to private property,' McMurtry continues. 'In our socio-economic system we relate to virtually everything of value by individual ownership: by, that is, the effective right to exclude others from the thing concerned. That we do so as well with perhaps the most highly valued thing of all – the sexual partner's sexuality – is only to be expected. Indeed, it would probably be an intolerable strain on our entire social structure if we did otherwise.'

We also need to criticise the idealised images of marriage where there is a failure to show the husband-wife relationship as one of power. John Scanzoni situates the power relationship between the sexes in the context of differential access to economic resources. He points out that, 'Power rests on resources. Husbands, because of their unique relationship to the opportunity structure, tend to have more resources (material, status), hence more power than wives.'

The material basis for the subordination of women lies in their exclusion from economic production. It is not the use of physical force that reproduces this exclusion, generation after generation, but the socialisation processes that women undergo, resulting in the installation of psychological structures of passivity and dependency within their personalities. Woman's *nature*, often presented as puzzling, contradictory and irrational, is the result of *nurture* in a masculine society.

Social Structure and the Meanings of Love

From a Marxist point of view, our social system has succeeded in getting certain myths widely accepted. In the political sphere, one of these is that we have democracy. In the moral sphere, the fiction is maintained that almost anyone is capable of love, and that such a human capacity is *independent of the consequences of societal relationships* into which people enter.

The moral questions that a culture does *not* raise reveal a great deal about itself. The deafening celebration of love in our society is not paralleled by a morally honest attempt to distinguish love from the counterfeit manifestations of emotional insecurity. *The absence of such distinctions in society's everyday vocabulary is functional for maintaining the commonly concocted illusions about love.* The poem by Phylis McGinley gives an example of the inability to make this distinction:

> Stay near me; Speak my name. Oh do not wander
> By thought's span, heart's impulse, from the light
> We kindle here. You are my sole defender
> (As I am yours) in this precipitous night
> Which over earth, till common landmarks alter
> Is falling, without stars, and bitter cold . . .
> Stay near me. Spirit perishable as bone,
> In no such winter can survive alone.

The need for security, in a brutal society hostile to human happiness, is misnamed as love.

In woman's situation, where opportunities for earning her self-esteem in socially recognised ways are blocked, and consequently sustaining a sense of self-value becomes precarious, love acquires supreme importance. So, as Simone de Beauvoir says, for women, 'Love becomes a religion.' Love becomes, very often, the only way out.

The primary source of self-value and emotional security for the woman is her lover or husband. For a large number it is the only source. In relating to him, her socialisation for psychic dependency leads her to abandon the struggle for an autonomous existence. This self-abnegation called love has been well described by Simone de Beauvoir:

> The supreme goal of human love . . . is identification with the loved one. . . . The woman in love tries to see with his eyes, she reads the books he reads, prefers the pictures and the music he prefers; she is interested only in the landscapes she sees with him, in the ideas that come from him; she adopts his friendships, his enmities, his opinions.

Since everything is subordinated to so-called love, 'Small matter to her to have only second place if she has *her* place, for ever, in a most wonderfully ordered world.' But an authentic love, Simone de Beauvoir points out, 'would not pretend to be a mode of salvation. . . .' The price of this salvation is high. For beneath the world of her love lurks an anxious, ceaseless watchfulness. An incident so trivial as the visual attention paid by her lover to another woman, in a pub or café, can sometimes set off tremors of insecurity within her. Simone de Beauvoir writes:

> Her entire destiny is involved in each glance her lover casts at another woman, since she has identified her whole being with him. Thus she is annoyed if his eyes are turned for an instant towards a stranger. . . . And so she is always on watch. . . . She has received all from love, she can lose all in losing it. . . .

Love, on a large social scale, can hardly be possible as long as the present economic, psychological, and sexual power structures between men and women prevail. Until they are destroyed we are likely to delude ourselves about the nature of love, in an attempt to keep the fears that haunt our lives at bay. Let Simone de Beauvoir speak once more:

> On the day when it will be possible for woman to love not in her weakness but in her strength, not to escape herself but to find herself, not to abase herself but assert herself – on that day love will become for her, as for man, a source of life and not of mortal danger.

Sex and Social Impotency

'There seems to be a relationship between rapid capital accumulation and a puritan moral norm system,' write Joachim Israel and Rosmari Eliasson. In the early phase of industrialisation, a capital accumulating society propagates the values of thrift, hard work, and the postponement of need satisfaction. The norm is, 'everything which does not serve the basic processes of production should be repressed. Sexuality therefore becomes acceptable only as far as it functions in the service of reproduction.' But with the arrival of a consumption society, as a result of capitalist development, there arises a necessity for rapid selling of the goods produced. The norm now is on spending, recreation and immediate satisfaction of needs. The new attitudes begin to spill over into the area of sexuality. Sex too becomes an object of consumption, aided by the separation of sexuality from procreation as a result of effective contraception.

The current obsessive preoccupation with sex needs to be understood in the context of our social existence, and not in terms of 'unrepressed instincts' or 'basic human nature'. 'The retreat to purely personal satisfactions . . . is one of the main themes of the seventies,' writes Christopher Lasch. 'Having no hope of improving their lives in any of the ways that matter, people have convinced themselves that what matters is psychic self-improvement: getting in touch with their feelings, eating health food, taking lessons in ballet or belly dancing, immersing themselves in the wisdom of the East, jogging, learning how to "relate", overcoming the "fear of pleasure".'

The excessive preoccupation with purely personal concerns is an expression of *social impotency*. Work organised to a very large extent for the purpose of private profit, provides little scope for human satisfaction. Politics is not seen by the great majority of people as an instrument for the transformation of society. The lack of gratifications in the social sphere is compensated for by what Lasch calls a 'non-stop celebration of the self'. The preoccupation with sexuality is, to a considerable extent, part of this syndrome. For men, the denial of opportunities for excellence under capitalism leads, among other things, to a search for power and self-esteem in the sexual arena. For example, the incidence of rape, which is not simply a sexual act but also an occasion for humiliating and degrading the victim in a show of male physical and sexual power, according to some studies is relatively high in the lower socio-economic groups. These are the groups among whom the feeling of social impotency is likely to be greatest.

The search for a sense of potency as self-affirming persons through the consumption of sex must be exposed in all its sterility. The focus of concern should be on the social structures which, by depriving people of scope for the full exercise of their human capacities, compulsively leads them to over-invest themselves in the sexual sphere. Having made such criticisms, we must assert the need for subjecting traditional emotional and sexual relationships to a radical reassessment. Juliet Mitchell rightly points out that, 'Any society will require some institutionalised and social recognition of personal relationships. But there is absolutely no reason why there should be only one legitimised form – and a multitude of unlegitimised experience.'

On the question of freedom from repressive sexual norms, most Marxist organisations and individuals have been less than revolutionary. They tended to avoid the implications of their own revolutionary philosophy. But it is refreshing to hear the views of two Hungarian Marxists, Mihaly Vadja and Agnes Heller. With regard to sexual relationships, in the context of a discussion on the commune as a possible alternative to the nuclear family, they assert, '. . . that both life-long relations of couples and promiscuity are possible within the confines of the commune'. They also add, 'The commune does not make promiscuity obligatory.' It must be pointed out that by 'promiscuity' they do not mean indiscriminate sexuality, but morally responsible, non-exclusive sexual relationships.

Conclusion

Marxism does not prescribe any particular form of family organisation as suitable for all. As Juliet Mitchell states, what is needed is, '. . . a range of institutions which match the free invention and variety of men and women'. In the short run, creating such a situation demands integration of women into the economy, establishing non-sexist socialisation patterns, and encouraging similar educational aspirations in both sexes. In the long run, political action is needed for replacing the capitalist system with democratic socialism where production is totally subordinated to social welfare, and technology is used as an instrument of human liberation.

In the perspective of Marxism, it is only in the soil of such optimum social conditions that human relationships can truly flourish. In such a society, platonic, as well as sexual, relationships will begin to resemble the beauty and the dignity described by Ronald Tamplin in his poem, *To Deny Possession*:

> Two trees could stand
> Straight and to their tops
> Within the circle of each other's ground.
> Their trunks would rise apart, each tree so much
> Itself that it could stand alone in such
> Completion as to need no more around
> It. But they grow together their leaves fanned
> And closing with the winds. Yet neither stops
> The other's growth or takes the rain that drops
> To feed it. In their height unfringed and
> Free, in some way crowned,
> Some leaves will touch.

(This essay is dedicated to Sue and David Rabkin.)

A Territorial Approach to Marriage
by David Coleman
Lecturer in Physical Anthropology, University
College London

Introduction

Almost everyone is interested in sex. Some are interested in marriage, which indeed comes to almost all of us eventually. On present trends, more than 90 per cent of young men and women in Britain today will marry at least once in their lives; some will make quite a habit of it. Statistically commonplace though it may be, marriage is an exceptionally important event, not just for the happy couple, but also for the sociologists and biologists who study them. This paper is an attempt to show why marriage and the choice of mate is studied academically, and to describe some of the findings of the researches.

Marriage and the Choice of Partners

My academic interest in marriages concerns the choice of partners, and how partners differ in their geographical and social origins. There are several ways of looking at this. At one level – the most titillating and romantic level – we could ask why a particular man and a particular woman chose to marry each other rather than one of the five or fifty other suitable partners they have met in their life. (No one really knows how wide the numerical choice is, and I will return later to the question of how we might define a 'suitable partner'.) 'Love' may be the standard answer to this question, but it is not a very useful answer. We know that couples who marry are more likely to be of similar social class, similar age, similar religious affiliation than a pair chosen at random. This tendency for like to marry like is known as *assortative mating* (and is dealt with in more detail in another article of mine [Coleman, 1977]).

Partners are also more alike than expected in their level of measured intelligence ('IQ') and in other psychometric characters. But psychologists cannot agree whether couples tend to be alike for all psychological characters or, instead, whether they may be attracted to each other because of the support which their different, complementary, personalities provide (Wilson and Nias, 1976). These psychological approaches may take us nearer to an understanding of 'love' and its role in mate selection. Other important reasons for particular couples getting married include chance, inertia and a reluctance to be left out, or put back, 'in the cold'. Although an individual may be attracted to large numbers of women who he sees or meets casually, it seems likely that the number of girl or boy friends before marriage is, in most cases, rather limited. Of these, surveys both in France and in Britain have shown that only one or two may be considered as possible marriage partners. It may be that each successive girl or boy friend in adult or subadult life, when marriage is a real possibility and the norm of age at marriage approaches, is progressively more likely to be married. Severing a friendship is a positive, painful act which most people find difficult. If there is not other partner in sight (and long-continued relationships may diminish the field as the alternatives are themselves married off) then ending the relationship may seem to be a dangerously isolating act, writing off emotional investment and leading to deprivation of sexual consolations for an unpredictable length of time. If the choice is indeed rather small, then the way in which young people meet, move about and organise their social lives may have considerable bearing on the likely origins of their future spouse, and on the breadth of choice which they will enjoy.

Biological and Sociological Reasons for Studying Marriage

Biologists like myself are very interested in the scope of choice, the social and geographical origins of the partners and the size of the marriage market (Coleman, 1973). There are many reasons for this interest. The relative frequency of different genes is known to vary by geographical area and also possibly by social class (Roberts and Sunderland (eds), 1973). These regional and other genetic differences will persist for as long as men find their wives in their own local communities. But if partners have remote origins, then intermarriage will eliminate these differences in time.

Similar considerations apply to cultural elements which are transmitted culturally between generations. Social classes, religions, towns, countryside, the different geographical regions of the nation can all be considered as communities in one sense or another: their members tend to have tastes and attitudes in common and consider themselves distinct from other groups. Marriage between these groups will tend to disrupt their cohesion just as remote marriages erode genetical differentiation. A more homogeneous society will follow, and perhaps a more rootless one, whose members have weak loyalties and little feeling of identification with anything in it.

In this way differences within and between cultures in the habits of choosing a mate, and their change in time, can have radical consequences for the way the society, and its pattern of gene distribution, are structured.

Open and Closed Marriage Systems

Marriages are most informative in this respect when the choice of partner is unrestrained by formal rules or prescriptions. Such rules are common in 'simple' societies. In many cases marriages must be endogamous to the tribe and may be further restricted to particular sections of the tribe. In the case of the Australian Kariera aborigines a man may have the choice of marrying one of as few as a dozen women if the rules are to be kept. Even in large populations, strict endogamy rules may lead to high levels of inbreeding, especially if cousin marriages are preferred. This has happened among the caste Hindus of Bombay, where geographically neighbouring subcastes have become more genetically dissimilar than are blacks and whites in the United States. In other places, notably Japan, marriages may be traditionally arranged by 'go-betweens' which ensures a high level of social and financial similarity between the couples – or rather their parents – without, perhaps, too much similarity in other respects.

In Britain, these customs do not obtain except among recent immigrants. It is possible to think of mate selection more as a process of 'molecular sociology'; a marriage following from the eventual selection of a partner from a series of almost random social collisions between individuals brought together in the course of the mobility which is part of their daily lives. The likelihood of any two individuals meeting in this way is affected by the way in which people are distributed in discrete populations, the way they move around geographically and their habits in frequenting places where others also gather.

The Place of Meeting

In an open society, then, marriages may be to a large extent a by-product of everyday life. If this is so, then the spatial distribution of an individual's daily life, and the sorts of people who frequent the places where he spends his time, will assume great importance in determining whether he will encounter potential mates of similar or different social and geographical origins from his own. Different places and occasions where people meet may attract and mix different elements of society. It is particularly interesting that many modern marriages arise from meetings in places or circumstances whose main function is not usually regarded as specifically social or sexual; work, for example.

A nationwide survey of married couples carried out in 1959–60 by the Population Investigation Committee at the L.S.E. (Pierce, 1963) provides some data for these speculations. Table 1 gives a breakdown of answers given by the survey couples when asked where they had first met each other. A more recent survey, organised by myself, of couples married in the Reading area between 1972 and 1973 showed a similar pattern. In these Reading marriages, 41 per cent met while going about their daily lives; 30 per cent met in quite casual social circumstances ('meeting friends') while 29 per cent met in more defined social circumstances, at parties or dances. As sources of wives, holidays and 'the girl next door' are statistically quite negligible.

Table 1: Selected places of first meeting of husband and wife from P.I.C. sample, marriage cohort 1920–1960 (N = 2,316)

Place of meeting	N	%
Café, public house, etc.	86	3·7
Street, public place	275	11·9
'Always known' or 'same area'	50	2·1
Husband's or wife's home	575	20·5
Work	316	13·6
Church	91	3·9
Holiday	85	3·7
Dance	459	19·8

Marital Mobility

Different places have 'catchment areas' of different sizes. This is shown by the fact that the mean distance separating the homes of couples varies between different places. Table 2 shows this, with data from Reading. The

Table 2: Mean marriage distance for first marriages by place of meeting, Reading area, marriage cohort 1972–1973

Place of meeting	Mean marriage distance	
	Kilometres	N
Dance hall	13·2	109
Place of work	13·7	111
Home	17·6	95
School, college	7·8	63
Clubs	14·7	114
Public house, café, etc.	9·3	84
Street, park, public place	5·6	37
'Same area'	2·3	26
Other	33·2	22
Total	13·0	661

[The standard error in each case, starting with Dance hall, is: ± 2·2, ± 3·5, ± 4·2, ± 2·9, ± 3·3, ± 1·9, ± 1·2, ± 0·9 and 'Other' ± 23·9. Total + 1·4]

distance separating partners' homes at meeting is commonly called *marriage distance*.

There are many attributes known to affect the distribution of marriage distance. With increasing age, for example, people move about more and tend to find partners living further away, although the effect is not very strong. More significant changes are made by social class differences, and by no means just because the upper social classes tend to marry later. In the Reading area, for example, as Table 3 shows, the mean marriage distance for couples where the husband was in social class 1 was 17·1 km, while for those in social class 5 it was only 4·4 km. These differences are associated with those observed according to place of meeting; people from working class backgrounds are more likely to meet in (local) pubs or cafés or in the street, those of more middle class background are more likely to meet at work, and therefore to have more remote geographical origins.

Table 3: Mean marriage distance for first marriages by social class of husband, Reading area, marriage cohort 1972–1973

Husband's class* at marriage	Mean marriage distance Kilometres	N
(Students)	17·1	20
1	17·1	43
2	15·7	121
3 Non-manual	13·5	94
3 Manual	12·0	288
4	11·6	67
5	4·4	30
Total	13·0	663

* Based on Registrar General's classification
[The standard error in each case, starting with students, is: ±8·6, ±4·4, ±4·8, ±3·2, ±1·9, ±3·5 and ±0·9, Total + 1·4]

In many ways the geographical scope of marital mobility is still very restricted. The marriages from Reading, for example, show that 25 per cent of husbands living in Reading married a wife living within 1·5 km, 50 per cent within 4·1 km and 75 per cent within 9·3 km. We also know the distance between each partner's home and the place where they actually met. Fifty per cent of the Reading husbands met their wives within 3·2 km of their homes, 50 per cent of the wives met their husbands within 2·6 km of theirs. If it is true that the geographical pattern of marriage reflects the spatial pattern of an individual's life, then these data may give us some notion of the geographical range of social life – a kind of 'radius of social action'.

The territorial aspects of marriage may be used in other ways to investigate human social life. The proportion of residents of a particular 'community' who marry within its boundaries is often called the 'endogamy rate' of that community. It indicates how reproductively self-sufficient the group may be and, by extension, different endogamy rates in groups of the same size may indicate different levels of social cohesion. In Reading, for example, we find that 82 per cent of men living in the town marry women also living there and if Reading is divided up into 7 different areas the endogamy rates for each average 50 per cent; not the 14 per cent expected from random mating. Clearly marriage still tends to be geographically localised within the town, but it is not clear whether the cause is simply the decline of mobility with distance, or to some neighbourhood sense of identity.

Rosser and Harris (1964) found in Swansea that communities with many local organisations, whose inhabitants felt that they 'belonged', had many more endogamous marriages – up to 45 per cent more than less well 'organised' areas, particularly council estates, where the figure was only about 17 per cent.

However, figures of 'endogamy' may mean little unless they are related to the size of the place concerned. Table 4 shows that the bigger the place in which you live, the more likely you are to marry someone living there.

Table 4: The rate of endogamy, and average marriage distance, in relation to the population size of the home towns of husbands P.I.C. Marriage Survey 1959–60

| | Men | | | |
| Population | Per cent endogamous | | Mean marriage distance (miles) | |
	%	N	miles	N
100–500	40·3	154	26·7	86
500–1000	36·7	60	10·8	35
1001–5000	42·9	184	16·3	101
5001–10,000	51·4	72	36·9	35
10,001–50,000	59·6	381	30·7	152
50,001–100,000	77·2	206	55·6	45
100,001–1 million	78·5	266	55·7	67
Conurbations	98·1	826	126·5	13
Total	74·8	2,222	34·0	534

N.B. Mean marriage distance is calculated for exogamous marriages only

If a partner is not found within the same hometown then he or she is likely to come from near at hand. Fifty per cent of 'exogamous' marriages link couples living not more than 5 miles apart, 69 per cent live within 10 miles, 78 per cent within 15 miles and 81 per cent within 20. But some couples manage to meet and marry despite great distances between their homes: 13 per cent claimed to have been living more than 50 miles apart. Among these marriages, unions between relatives are disproportionately represented, as are meetings on holiday and those cases where one of the partners was in the armed forces. With bigger towns, fewer people marry outside; those who do seem to marry more remote partners than do those who marry out of smaller places, as Table 4 shows. This rather interesting pattern leads us to a general theory relating mobility to the distribution of population.

Central Place Theory and Marital Mobility

A general explanation for the statistical distribution of marital mobility which has been outlined above may be found in the combination of notions of G. K. Zipf (1949) and of the various ideas described as 'central place theory' which originated with the German geographer Christaller. Zipf's viewpoint of 'psychological economy', may be interpreted and extended to suggest that people will travel no further in search of a mate (or any other benefit) than the bare minimum; that travel is a cost in time and in money which, like other costs, the individual wants to minimise as much as possible. Acquaintanceship hence becomes less worthwhile renewing at long range. Central place theories are a contribution to locational analysis. They hypothesise that the size of a settlement is related to the surrounding area and population with which it has economic contacts. Larger areas will need, and can support, a wide variety of specialist services and amenities in health services, jobs, education, justice, entertainments and dance halls which tend to be concentrated in 'central places'. These draw their client populations from surrounding urban and rural areas in a hierarchical fashion. Communications between large towns are better than from a large town to a small one at the same distance, because the occasions for travelling between them are more numerous. Residents of large towns have little need to travel to other places to satisfy their needs – one reason for their high endogamy rates – but if they have to, then they are likely to go to a place of equivalent or greater size which may be further away but which is easier to reach than a closer, smaller place.

Changes with Time

Patterns of marital mobility have changed with time in an interesting way. Parish registers in Dorset, Oxfordshire, Hertfordshire and Northumberland show that before 1870, marriages in rural areas were quite localised. After that, the proportion of endogamous marriages declined from about 75 per cent to about 50 per cent by the turn of the century and marriage distance increased accordingly. Some writers have attributed these changes to the introduction of the bicycle, for with it country people need no longer confine their attention to potential spouses living within walking distance. Even in towns of this period, mobility was overwhelmingly pedestrian. A similar increase in the 1930s has been attributed to the introduction of rural bus services. But the P.I.C. data reveal no significant increases in marital mobility, except in smaller towns, since that date. This seems surprising in view of the advances (until recently) of public transport and the extraordinary growth of car ownership from 20,000 in 1920 to 7 million today. Individuals in 1968 travelled an average of 11·9 miles per day compared to 6·3 miles per day in 1953. However, much of this increase in individual mobility may have passed by the young people in whose meetings we are interested. It is often when they are married that they move into the suburbs and acquire their cars. There must obviously be a limit to the effort which will be expended in keeping in touch with any particular girlfriend or boyfriend.

Summary

An average person living in the average town will still marry someone from the same place, as their parents did. But, unlike the heroes of popular fiction, they will neither marry the person next door, nor a person remote from them in social status or geographical distance. They will meet, very likely at a dance hall or at work, without any previous contact between their families. We still lack an understanding of the way that men and women meet, choose their friends and ultimately their spouses, and the pressures which influence their choice. Nor do we know how many 'choices' a man or a woman may have. I hope that social scientists will direct their talents to investigating this most interesting of social phenomena, beyond the statistical level where geographers and biologists have taken it.

Women in the Women's Movement and the Family: A Phenomenological View
by Janet Harris
Abraham Moss Centre, Manchester
and Scarlet Friedman
University of Warwick

Introduction

According to a phenomenological perspective, people explain their experiences of the world in accordance with their interests arising from their behaviours within their biographically determined situation. Consequently, when analysing women and the family, it is necessary to describe how women interpret their own situation, rather than impose an analysis 'from the outside' as structuralists such as Engels and Talcott Parsons have attempted.

Women who identify with the Women's Liberation Movement, some of whom we interviewed, are evolving new projects, i.e. choosing and creating new ways of living together. These women articulate a rejection of the 'common sense' explanations of their behaviours which in the past they had taken for granted, in favour of a new 'common sense' that serves the new projects they are developing. This paper is an attempt to explore the 'thinking as usual' of many women in the movement.

A phenomenological examination of the meanings articulated by women *outside* the movement is beyond the scope of this paper, and such a study might well yield rather different meaning systems to those reported here.

The Problem of Evidence

Some evidence has been taken from public statements such as motions passed at national women's liberation conferences and from the publications of the women's press, i.e. writing by women for a movement readership often published by a women's publishing collective. However, most of our evidence has been derived from conversations, in-depth unstructured interviews and notes of the many and regular small group discussions held since the late 1960's in the context of consciousness raising groups, self development groups, for example, the Women's Song Writing Group, and campaign oriented groups, for example, Women and Education. Most of the ideas expressed below come from women who have been involved in the movement for several years and who have subjected their entire lives to retrospective reinterpretation. Their thinking may be characterised by the phrase, 'then I thought, now I know'. We cannot avoid acknowledging the methodological problems inherent in trying to examine the meanings held by any group of people, not least one whose members have explicitly changed their perceptions over time, or are in the process of so changing. Perceptions and meanings are therefore being changed during the process of collecting data, and perhaps, because of it. Consequently, it is conceivable that those of our data collection techniques which involved face-to-face interaction have failed to reflect our subjects' 'thinking as usual', even though that was our target. The wider problems of unstructured interviews are dealt with in an earlier paper in this volume – 'Questions and Answers' by Shelton (page 35) and need not be developed further here. We should note, however, our intention that every one of our sources of evidence involved the use of language. The data we were investigating were the typical interpretations of the family as it affects women made by women in the movement. As Harré and Secord (1972) note, to study people who are not only agents, but watchers, commentators and critics of their own and others' actions, it is essential to use a research method involving language. It is through our linguistic powers that we mediate our experience, selecting our observations according to the system of meaning we operate. At the same time, we acknowledge that language is a fundamental mechanism by which the social world is created (see the earlier paper, 'Listening to Conversation' by Anderson [page 59]) and that social meanings can be created during the act of social research (see the paper 'Questions and Answers' by Shelton [page 35]).

Unfocused, in-depth interviews are one of the most useful ways of tapping women's interpretations, though these too carried two major sources of error. Firstly the subject might misinterpret the questions and the interviewer, the responses. Secondly, the interview might fail to reflect the subject's 'thinking-as-usual'.

The confusion arising out of the first problem was, we feel, reduced by the possibility of interchange between interviewer and respondent, since it was clear to both that the interviewer was a member of the same social world as the respondent, operating the same labels and logic, and therefore capable of empathy. Normal thinking is characterised by gaps or contradictions. When interviewed in depth, these became clear to the speaker, who then tried to impose consistency upon her thinking. This was very noticeable when we interviewed women who had decided to marry since becoming involved in the movement.

The second problem, common to all interviewing, is that of the respondent displaying *impression-management* (Goffman, 1959) and this may have been exacerbated by the interviewers' open identification with the women's movement. An attempt was made to reduce this by control of paralinguistic responses (facial expression, tone of voice) and consistent expression of support and sympathy or *unconditional positive regard* as Rogers (1951) puts it. Questions were kept as brief and open-ended as possible; many prompts comprising a non-verbal enquiring grunt. In this way it was hoped subjects would articulate their own thinking rather than distort it to fit the imputed expectations of the interviewer. How far the views expressed were affected by the interview situation is impossible to judge. Results must therefore be regarded as tentative.

It is important that the views expressed below are not regarded as representative of the Women's Liberation Movement. This term implies a monolithic organisation, which it is not. Women in the movement hold differing views about what aspects of society need changing and what methods they use to effect that change.

Some 'Findings'

'EVERY WOMAN GETS MARRIED, IF SHE CAN'

Getting married, living in family units, is commonly portrayed as the 'normal', 'acceptable' and 'proper' way to live. Learning how to fit in and be accepted in this society is learning that, as a woman, one's fulfilment is achieved through marriage and children. To be 'feminine' is to be concerned primarily with the home and 'good homemaking'. A woman who takes an interest in the world outside the home is considered to be rejecting her inherent femininity or just waiting until the right man comes along to guide her back to her proper place: the home. Germaine Greer (1971) sums up the theme of many conversations we had: 'If intellect impedes feminisation, intellect must go' (p. 94). Women who do not accept marriage and family as their only option are usually derided and almost inevitably subject to such labels as 'spinster', 'old maid', 'frigid', and so on.

> If a woman doesn't marry she's considered an old maid or spinster – not exciting and independent but a pitiful failure. Because we are taught that the only place we can be satisfied is in the home, we find it hard to believe a woman would choose not to marry. We assume she wanted to marry but no one wanted her – her independence and freedom are seen as her failure. (Angela Rose, 'We are women', 1973)

'HAD THE WEDDING PLANNED FOR YEARS. I WAS JUST WAITING FOR THE RIGHT MAN TO COME ALONG'

Having accepted that marriage is the goal, a woman assumes that it is a natural progression from love to marriage. Each man she meets is viewed with an eye to marriage. A proposal of marriage is seen as proof of a man's love.

> I always knew as a child that I was going to grow up and go to college and then get married and that's as far as a girl has to think. After that, your husband determines and fills your life. (Friedan, 1968, p. 64)

Women in the groups often thought that in getting married not only does a women fulfil her own expectations but those of her parents. Most parents see their daughter's marriage as the continuation of the family ideals they have stressed to her throughout her life.

The marriage ceremony is symbolic of this continuation of a woman's life being defined in terms of her dependence on a man. Her father 'gives her away' to a man whom she usually promises to 'love, honour and obey', while the vicar pronounces them, not 'husband and wife', not 'man and woman', but 'man and wife' (Comer, 1974, p. 55).

Once married, a woman has not yet satisfied all the expectations of her family. The couple are now pressured to 'settle down', set up a 'nice' home and start *their* family. The many interviews conducted by Friedman for her research, indicate that even women following post-graduate degree courses regard the decision to have children as automatic rather than problematic.

'I WANTED A HOME AND FAMILY OF MY OWN'

Women we talked to had regarded being married as giving a woman the status of having achieved one rung on the ladder of social respectability. Whether it is introducing one's partner to an employer or attending a contraceptive or antenatal clinic, we found that there had been a relief at being able to refer to him as 'my husband' as opposed to 'my friend'.

To be seen as married may relieve a woman from constantly being bothered by men in a social world where even at 13 and 14, 'the girl is a sex object – for experimentation in the healthy development of boys' (*Spare Rib*, No. 58).

> . . . he gives you a week. If you haven't performed by then, he throws you over. If you have, he still does, but he gives your telephone number to all his friends. (Jill, aged 14)

By being regarded as another man's woman, she can choose to avoid or refuse sexual advances with less offence being taken. In any case, the sexual advances may diminish as she is no longer officially available.

However, in return for this 'protection' she is now expected to provide her husband with all the sexual, emotional and homemaking services he requires. Once again the 'normal' woman, now a 'wife' is usually expected to adjust her own sexual and emotional needs to those of her husband. She has been led to believe that she must ensure this 'compatibility' if she expects to 'keep her man'.

The relationship is usually expected to be monogamous. The ideology of monogamy is that sexual possession of another person brings security. Through the gradual development of his dependence on her, a woman may, to some extent, control her husband's involvement in other relationships, whether sexual or platonic. Yet limiting the other person's involvement in relationships, though, necessarily limits one's own. Women we interviewed had found it was very demanding on their resources to try to meet all of each other's needs. Are these demands conducive to the sort of security that is intended or more to jealousy, deception and righteousness in feeling wronged? The discussions often came to the latter conclusion.

Getting married is mostly seen by the woman as securing her a partner in providing and caring for children in a long-term way. Yet many jobs require the provider to be away from the children during most of their waking hours. The marriage provides shelter and basic income, but not necessarily emotional support. The alternative of bringing children up alone seemed harder to some women because of dependence on the state for Social Security payments and accompanied by feelings of guilt.

Women in the group often concluded that most women are attracted to the appearance of control in their own home; they frequently see housework as less alienating than being a small cog in a vast factory or business firm. They had usually found, however, that such control is limited to cooking, cleaning, furnishing, and to some control over one man and their children. Should the location of the husband's job change, the wife was expected to move with him, thereby often losing a carefully built up support system of friends, neighbours and relations.

'I THINK I'LL PACK IN WORKING AND GET MARRIED. IT CAN'T BE ANY WORSE'

Although marriage is seen as an alternative to work, most married women do in fact work outside the home as well as in it. Despite the Equal Pay and Sex Discrimination Acts, most of the jobs open to women are low-paid with poor working conditions. 'Well over half the female work-force in this country is employed in semi-skilled and unskilled labour . . . women work at jobs which are direct extensions of their traditional servicing role' (Comer, 1974, p. 44).

In most cases a wife's economic status is still primarily dependent upon her husband's job and wage while she is considered to be working only for 'pin money'.

> To the men in the office you're a mother, a wife or a daughter and sometimes, a possible mistress. If you're a mother, they depend on you for everything, moral support, food (coffee) and lying for them on the telephone. If you're a wife they also depend on you for the same things, but you can also get yelled at or pecked on the cheek. If you're a daughter you can get a pat on the head for being a good girl or else a verbal slap. But never are you just another human being deserved of respect and possibly as talented and ambitious as they are. (Secretary in a publishing office)

'. . . THERE'S NOT A MINUTE OF THE DAY WHEN I CAN HAVE ANY THOUGHTS TO MYSELF'

Literature is scattered with descriptions and analyses of marriage from the inside. Some interesting ones are to be found in Allen et al. (1974, pp. 193 and 194):

> . . . since every woman's loyalty was primarily to her husband, none of us could really be honest with each other. For one of us to explode at the impossibility of the situation would have been too threatening for the others; we were all vulnerable to being thought failures.
>
> What actually happens is that you go mad. But nobody notices, not even you. I use the word 'mad' to describe a state of dislocation in which you don't know where or who you are. You are a kind of bewildered prize in the tug of war between children and husband. Your life should be heaven but it feels like punishment and prison. There is no time or space to worry about yourself; you are constantly at the mercy of those around you. No women can emerge

from this situation totally undamaged, and many women are damaged severely.

'SISTERHOOD IS POWERFUL'

Group members often argued that unless they can talk about something it tends to remain beyond their understanding and control. Without words to define an experience and their attitude to it, they tend to remain objects in the grip of circumstances, rather than subjects monitoring their own experiences and directing their responses according to their own values. Hence the crucial relevance of consciousness-raising groups.

Through regular and reciprocal confidence-sharing within small groups, they found that they were learning about themselves, their needs, and establishing an identity chosen by themselves, not conferred by other interested parties. The aspirations of such groups and of the action-based collectives that may emerge from them are epitomised in names such as 'Women are People' and 'Jam Today' (women's rock band); while the deprecation of patriarchal attitudes is shown in the title of the magazine *Spare Rib*.

In the late 1960's in England, many women in the Women's Liberation Movement thought that the main focus should be on the following specific demands which became motions passed at National Conferences:

1 Equal pay
2 Equal education and job opportunities
3 Twenty-four-hour nurseries
4 Free contraception and abortion on demand
In the 1970's two more demands were adopted:
5 Legal and finanacial independence
6 The right to a self-defined sexuality and an end to the discrimination against lesbians.

Although these demands are useful in drawing people's attention to issues or campaigns, many women we talked to have since come to the conclusion that as sexism penetrates the whole fabric of society, including ourselves, the changes to be worked for are far more fundamental than these six demands would suggest. This feeling is expressed by the Lawrence textile strikers in 'Bread and Roses', sung by the orginators in 1912 and by the Women's Movement in the 1970's.

> As we come marching, marching,
>   unnumbered women dead
> Go crying through our singing their ancient
>   cry for bread.
> Small art and love and beauty their drudging
>   spirits knew.
> Yes, it is bread we fight for – but we fight
>   for roses, too.

For example, our conversations led us to conclude that creating alternatives to the burdens of responsibility and guilt which are fostered in the family requires that we think more about how we relate to each other and our children, and that we decide collectively how to share responsibilities. As Abbott and Love (1972, pp. 147–8) write:

> The concept of bond between women is key if women are going to work together in a steady and organised fashion to reshape society, but emotional 'sisterhood' alone – awareness of common suffering – is not sufficient, based as it is on a recognition of common powerlessness and may reinforce powerlessness.
>
> The female bond is more than women suffering together. It is more than working together on simple tasks as women have done for years. It goes further, to involve a basic trust and reliance, a feeling that women can be powerful and effective, and it requires that a woman takes herself and her life seriously. Once this bond has been firmly established, a sense of common commitment makes possible projects of increasing importance and complexity, involving planning over years and across geographical and socio-economic distances. The importance of a female commonality cannot be underestimated in the light of the history of all male solidarity with reference to women, in all aspects of community life.

Yet women we spoke to had grown up with the idea that the three roles of daughter, wife and mother would provide them with security and protection.

A particular view of security is taken here. It is defined as a role position within a family and regarded as unproblematical. An alternative analysis would stress that to experience security women need to control their own lives for example, what they produce and consume, through the making of collective decisions. According to this latter analysis, protection implies a situation in which women's feelings, ideas and attempts to construct a way of life are respected and valued. Such protection is seen to derive from women relating to each other in an equalitarian and co-operative way.

There was general consensus about the latter view of security and protection; though some women we talked with had experienced the former 'role-security' too. Many women spoke warmly of their mothers who had continued to provide emotional support even when the daughters had rejected the family role to which their mothers had devoted their lives. ' . . . I feel this amazing feeling for the fact that she gave up her life for me.'

Such feeling expresses the bond forged through 'common powerlessness' and 'emotional sisterhood' (Abbott and Love, 1972).

A feminist group in America (Hoffman et al., 1970) summed up the situation as follows:

By virtue of having been brought up in a male society, we have internalised the male definition of ourselves. That definition views us as relative beings who exist not for ourselves, but for servicing, maintenance and comfort of men. That definition consigns us to sexual and family functions, and exclusion from defining and shaping the terms of our lives. In exchange for psychic servicing and for performing society's non-profit making functions, the man confers on us just one thing: the slave status that makes us legitimate in the eyes of the society in which we live. This is called 'femininity' or being a 'real woman' in our cultural lingo. We are authentic, legitimate, real to the extent that we are the property of some man whose name we bear. To be a woman who belongs to no man is to be invisible, pathetic, inauthentic, unreal. He confirms this image to us – of what we have to be in order to be acceptable by him – but not of our real selves; he confirms our womanhood – as he defines it, in relation to him – but cannot confirm our personhood, our own selves as absolutes. As long as we are dependent on the male culture for this definition, for this approval, we cannot go free!

Summary

To summarise, this paper has attempted to look at the family through a phenomenological perspective. It has tried to articulate the typical interpretations operated by some women who identify themselves with the Women's Liberation Movement. They (and ourselves) may well be 'typical' (in Schutz's sense) members of the movement. The only statement we can make with confidence is that none of us would wish to be regarded as spokeswomen representing the entire movement. Nevertheless, this small study suggests and illustrates some of the 'thinking-as-usual' operated by some groups of women now.

It also demonstrates a methodology which was essentially linguistic, in order to tap the social construction of reality; evidence being derived from open-ended interviews, small group discussions, writings produced and read by women who identify with the movement and the only national policy statement: the six demands passed at annual national conferences.

III COMMUNITY

Introduction

Readers expecting to find a precise sociological definition of 'community' will be disappointed. The concept involved is a general idea rather than a specific, focused meaning. Community refers to the idea of personal belonging to groups outside the family and personal experience of such groups. It might seem that *location* is the key factor, since people in a particular geographical locality frequently meet face to face, and are often described as a community – a village, a school or a street, for example television's 'Coronation Street'. Location is usually an important, but not an inevitable, feature. Community can refer to a sense of belonging beyond a particular locality and members can have personal contact despite being geographically scattered. An example often quoted is that of the Jews; others are Esperanto speakers, Humanists and, as an example of a 'community of scholars', sociologists.

The vagueness of the concept of community can be seen if we make a list of the various communities to which we personally belong at a given time. Yet the usefulness of the idea is illustrated in the same activity, since this list of apparently rather unrelated communities is shown to have at least one basic, common feature, a *sense of belonging*, a shared interest with others, an involvement.

The length of these lists, and other characteristics such as the presence or absence of a locality factor, may be seen to be linked with, amongst other things, facilities for communication. Access to a car, a telephone or the financial means to travel widely, often helps explain a 'cosmopolitan' list. The absence of these communication facilities might be a key factor in a 'locally orientated' list.

The contrasts between rural and urban communities have been a central concern in sociology. The contrasts between village and city life are a starting point, whilst the study of rural towns and suburban communities is a continuation of this work. In the U.S.A., the Chicago school of sociologists became well known for writings on these themes. A useful short summary of ideas that emerged from the Chicago school is given in P. L. Berger and B. Berger's *Sociology: A Biographical Approach* (chapter six). In cities, the nature of community changes. Traditional rural ways of thinking and acting have little chance of being maintained, for the experience of cities is the experience of face-to-face contacts with people who are strangers. Some cease to be strangers, but most remain so if only for the fact that so many individuals perform the same job. Your postman may become less of a stranger, but bus drivers change routes, schedules and shifts, so that a constant stream of strangers may present themselves.

The study of suburbia was an attempt to describe and explain the changes that occurred when people began to move out of the centre of cities to live on the outskirts, and also in nearby, smaller towns which became known as dormitory towns. The phenomenon of commuting by car, train, or bus was an associated study.

A current concern is with the 'urban crisis' where the city is seen by more and more of its inhabitants as an unattractive place. In place of rural depopulation, when movement from villages and towns to the cities was the dominant trend, the reverse movement of people going from cities to live in rural towns and villages is in evidence. In the U.S.A., the 'collapse' of cities like New York and Washington is now talked about.

The papers in this section try to give different perspectives on the concept of community. The paper by David Neal uses a Marxist approach. Community is often taken as an 'Hurrah' word, i.e. we are largely expected to be in favour of it. Some of the competing interests of groups within communities are outlined in this paper and a less rose-tinted picture emerges.

The paper by Mel Chevannes and Frank Reeves gives an account of a black community view of the white community. This 'seeing yourselves as others see you' is often disturbing and provocative, but it can be seen as part of the sociological imagination and awareness referred to in earlier parts of this book. This particular contribution is not simply an ethnography, nor a case study. Perhaps it is biography with strong sociological elements? Berger, in *Invitation to Sociology* (Penguin, 1963), says that such raw material becomes sociological when the interpretation is broader than the data. The writers discuss this issue in their preface.

The third paper attempts a sociological analysis of a relatively closed community, the Masons, Helen Reynolds uses several perspectives in trying to arrive at as full an understanding as possible of this particular example of community.

Stimulating though the context of community is, its ambiguity remains. One writer, Hillery, in *Definitions of Community* (Rural Sociology 20, 1955), counted ninety-four different definitions. The conclusion was: 'All the definitions deal with people, beyond this common basis there is no agreement.'

The Conflict in 'Community' by David Neal Stevenage College of Further Education

Given the currency of such a word as 'community', the number of articles written upon it, the traditional inclusion of it in sociology text books and the number of journals that use it in their titles, one might expect it to be well grounded, highly meaningful and sophisticated in its usage. Unfortunately, although we have produced numerous 'community studies' (few of which include 'people' in any relevant sense) our understanding still tends to be limited. In large part, sociologists have tried to understand and explain community by associating it with variables like 'locality', 'social activity' and 'social structure' (Clark, 1973). One variable which is usually mentioned but not developed is that of conflict although work by Coleman is an exception to this (Coleman, 1957). In an advanced, industrialised society one could argue that a study of sectional interest and the resulting conflict is the most appropriate way to treat the explanatory potential of 'community'. The fact that we have not done so when the tool for such an analysis, i.e. community of interest, has been with us for some time, is all the more strange.

Conflict

So, what kinds of connections can be established between community and conflict? In one way the strength of conflict might be taken to indicate something about the 'quality' of community relationships. As Gamson says, in his study of New England towns:

> Many of the conventional communities are rather dull and stagnant, while some of the most rancorous ones are among the most vital. Some of the conventional towns not only have an absence of rancorous conflict but a general absence of change; the rancorous towns have the strains that accompany change but some of them also have the advantage of stimulation and growth. The absence of rancorous conflict is no necessary sign of an 'ideal' community. (Gamson, 1966)

With this as a base one can proceed to ask a range of questions. For instance, it is to be expected that individuals engage in such 'rancorous conflict' because the issue is important to them in the ways in which they live out their lives. Thus, one would want to know what sort of issue it takes, and how deeply it is felt, for people to represent themselves in this fashion. In addition: who feels it to be important?; What sort of action do they feel able to take?; Do the groups that emerge survive over time?; What other issues do the various groups rally around?; What other variables (for example, class) help clarify the membership of particular groups?, etc. It is through an examination of these and other variables that one is able to talk about the basic constituents of community life.

Clark puts the same point in a slightly different way when he speaks of a 'sense of significance' (i.e. an individual's assurance of his worth) and a 'sense of solidarity' (i.e. the mutual dependence individuals can feel by having something in common with others) being derived from such group membership (Clark, 1973). Coleman stresses that an analysis like this would enable various community groups to appreciate the ways in which community problems are actually dealt with so that they (the problems) can be ' . . . met in one way rather than another' (Coleman, 1957, p. 1). This is particularly useful because it encourages us to perform analyses to determine the 'dynamics' of community action, i.e. the sorts of alliances which are made between individuals and groups, the processes of negotiation and the rationales of those concerned, and the location of power. The last of those is crucial to remember, for as McNall and Johnson say, 'If behaviour is drama, then who wrote the play, who directs the actors, who buys the tickets, and who is really backstage?' (McNall and Johnson, 1975). In this way one is able to cut through the confusion associated with community in order to see just what aims individuals are *allowed* to achieve through association. Marx makes the point well:

> Only in community . . . is personal freedom possible. In the previous substitutes for the community, in the State, etc., personal freedom has existed only for the individuals who developed within the relationships of the ruling class, and only insofar as they were individuals of this class. The illusory community, in which individuals have up till now combined, always took on an independent existence in relation to them, and was at the same time, since it was the combination of one class over against another, not only a completely illusory community but a new fetter as well. In a real community the individuals obtain their freedom in and through association. (*German Ideology*, p. 83, students' edition, ed. C. J. Arthur, Lawrence and Wishart)

Not only do Marx and Engels highlight those sorts of questions mentioned above but they also remind us that senses of community might still be illusory to the extent that 'small' community skirmishes might cause us to lose sight of wider issues, for example structural inequality, which, paradoxically, those skirmishes themselves probably identify. What I am suggesting is that there is an important relationship between an individual's experience of local community affairs and that individual's sense of 'what society is like'. The one informs the other. Thus, one would be interested to know exactly how individuals do interpret those experiences. For example, is society judged to be caring and beneficent because some people are satisfied to know that the local community conducts successful bingo sessions and because it offers cheap meals to pensioners? Alternatively, can interpretations be less parochial such as those prompted by the Upper Clyde work-in, the establishment of the Meriden Cooperative for Triumph motorcycles and the events surrounding the William Tyndale School? Did such 'local' affairs generate wider questions concerning the need for State investment and control of industry? the true impotence of local councils when it comes to important matters, for example the ravages of an economic system upon local employment and what we use our schools to educate for in society? For some, this wider perspective would be the only way to interpret local events, i.e. to see those events as the result of the way in which a particular economic system is controlled. For others, society is still a nice place because people enjoy their bingo.

Community of Interest

Progress in this type of analysis can be made with the concept 'community of interest'. This recognises that people make associations for particular reasons and not just because they live in a given locality. Thus, one would study, '. . . those groups which gather first and foremost because of shared beliefs, values and concerns rather than because of proximity of residence or because of established patterns of social relationships' (Clark, 1973, p. 411). The idea is not particularly new (see Pons, 1970; Webber, 1964) but if developed, it would allow the sociologist to readily acknowledge the meaning that community has for those concerned rather than just making a particular sociological sense out of a situation.

In Rex's *Sociology of a Zone of Transition* he attempts such an approach (Rex, 1967). Here, implicitly, he is able to indicate the communities of interest generated by a scarcity of housing and accommodation. Thus, slum dwellers, owner occupiers, council tenants, landlords and lodgers, engage in their various struggles around this issue. At the same time, the people who constitute those categories above may also appear in such categories as Jamaican, Irish, Pakistani, British, and so on, but no one such group *totally* constitutes any one of the housing classes. Consequently, at times, a Pakistani landlord's community of interest is with all other landlords. At other times his community of interest might be with other members of his immigrant group in helping to provide them with accommodation. Rex argues that this in turn helps the new immigrant for he can readily identify with his racial peers. Each competing group is a community of interest but not sufficient in itself. Rex uses this pattern of social relationships for groups and across groups to explain the nature of the conflict in such an inner city area as Sparkbrook. The situation is further compounded when one begins to look at the ways in which relevant others, for example, building societies, finance companies, local councils, are able to concentrate some immigrants within certain housing classes. For example, it might be difficult to become a lodging house owner if building societies or finance companies discriminate in any way deleterious to immigrants. Similarly, the local council and private owners might favour children of tenants as new tenants which leaves slum dwellings available for immigrants while allowing the council to avoid the political hazards of leasing any new council property to new arrivals.

The situation is highly unstable, as Rex states, but in a way it is a conflict that is well contained since the competing interest groups were seemingly unable to crystallise the initial problem in such a way as to encourage those groups to combine to radically change their position. One would therefore be very interested to reveal those processes which enable communities of interest to address 'whole' problems rather than aspects of them.

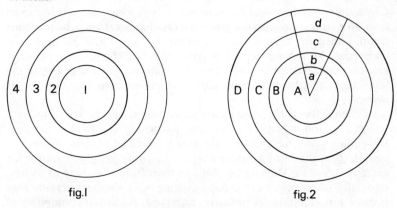

fig.1   fig.2

Key to Figure 1 1 – level of project/shared beliefs/problems, etc.; 2 – local district level; 3 – local administrative level; 4 – societal level.

Key to Figure 2 (a) Tolmers Square Tenants Association, later to become Tolmers Village Association and, later still, groups of local squatters who battled alongside the tenants. (A) Those people who were not interested in the Association or its particular aims, for example, long-standing, working class tenants who 'just wanted to get a new roof over their heads, with running hot and cold water, instead of sharing a sink on a landing' (Wates, 1976, p. 127) and those who advocated new housing.

(b) Neighbouring areas that had already been 'developed', for example, the Euston Centre, which provided something of a bad dream for the tenants' group indicating what could happen to their area. (B) Those areas of the neighbourhood that were not part of the Tolmers Square development proposals and thus bearing little relevance to the group or its aims.

(c) (i) The local council departments that the tenants' group had to deal with, for example, Camden Council's Planning Department, council meetings, particular councillors who gave support, etc. (ii) Those dealings with the firm wishing to develop the property, Stock Conversion. (iii) The alliance forged between the tenants' group and influential journalists like Christopher Booker and Bennie Gray (who lived locally but not near the Square) who were able to give the development a great deal of publicity and eventually put in their own bid to the council along lines approved of by the tenants. (C) All other council business, other non-interested parties.

(d) (i) Other examples of similar developments, for example Southwark (see Ambrose and Colenutt, 1975). (ii) Policies pursued by national government, for example, Office Development Permits which helped to make such developments profitable and the Rent Act of 1957 which raised the permissible maximum rents for private tenants. Also relevant here for the analysis would be those policies which tended to make it worthwhile for companies to invest their money in property; the Community Land Act and the Rent Act of 1974 which encouraged some landlords to leave properties empty rather than let them, which in turn compounded the homelessness situation in general and the neglect of properties like Tolmers Square in particular. (iii) The national publicity given to the development. (D) The vast majority of us who are, at the same time, too busy and too parochial in our own communities of interest.

At the centre of the analysis are those issues, beliefs, concerns, etc., which are the *raison d'être* of any particular community interest. Depending upon the example, the group might be of some concern to people from the local neighbourhood, the wider geographic area, for example London, Manchester, and, perhaps from elsewhere in society, especially where there are groups existing with similar interests. But, because not everybody is similarly concerned, the actual community of interest is better represented by a sector, as in Figure 2. Here, a community of interest might well see it as part of its task to open out the arms of that sector into areas (A), (B), (C), and (D), to gain support for its cause, or at least to know the nature of its opponents. It is in area (C), for example, that one would locate one's analysis of the local council's attitude towards the project, which councillors, for instance, could be relied upon for support, how the council allocated its money to other projects, etc.

A Case Study: Tolmers Square

A reworking of an existent case should make the scheme clear – *The Battle for Tolmers Square* (Wates, 1976). (It must be stressed that what follows is a reworking of the data, not an approach that Wates would necessarily support.) This particular conflagration came about '. . . because of a conflict of interest; a conflict between property developers who wanted to redevelop the area for offices and various sections of the community who would suffer if this kind of redevelopment took place' (p. 21). Characteristically, the inhabitants of such an inner city area (Euston, London) were relatively ignorant of the redevelopment proposals. Students who happened to be studying the area acted as catalysts in prompting a local opposition group, the Tolmers Village Association. This '. . . consisted of an uneasy coalition between small business interests, middle class residents and a few young, working-class tenants. From the start, the long-standing working class community played little active part' (p. 127). This association would be represented by (a) in Figure 2, the non-involvement of others by (A) Wates details the way in which this association was formed, the way in which it was preceded by another, related to the Rent Act, and more briefly, why some in the area never did join in. In addition, he relates the history, largely political and financial, of the local authority, Camden, represented by (c), and that of national government as well (d), which was influencing the local situation, for example, the mechanics of property speculation, the Rent Act, the Community Land Act. At the same time he reveals how those wishing to develop the property form a community of interest, how multifarious its constituent members were and how they related to all four areas, (a), (b), (c) and (d). As a result, what is presented is an integrated community study showing the bases of community association and linking the various groups to their political, economic and social histories. To the extent that Wates also compares a similar project in another part of London (Southwark) we are better equipped to gauge the sorts of unpleasant experiences that can happen to people who live on land that processes of capitalism have made profitable (Ambrose and Colenutt, 1975).

We have few such community studies as yet even though Norman Dennis warned in 1958 just how trivial our data would be if we continued to study what traditional neighbourhood community groups do. As he rightly suggests, what we need to know is the role that community interest groups are allowed to play in our society and upon which sorts of issues, other than just children's playgrounds, amenity spaces and the siting of zebra crossings, they are based. One would also want to know about those world views which discourage some people from getting involved at all.

The Control of Change

One important resource we have here is John Dearlove's paper, *The control of change and the regulation of community action* (1974). This helps to operationalise the sorts of ideas contained in area (c) of Figure 2. Dearlove argues that when it comes to controlling local affairs, especially controlling public resources, most of us occupy the role of subjects, clients, supporters and helpers rather than as masters, customers, demanders and disrupters. Even where people overcome the constraints of a dominant self-help ideology in our society we can all think of unsuccessful and futile campaigns of the past. This apathy, associated with haphazard leadership and organisation, restricts any group's command over events or information. Then, in seeking greater participation through communities of interest, one can be faced with the 'siege mentality' of those who govern, who appear to hope that if they can stall for long enough then interest groups might disappear, change or fight it out among themselves. In time some groups might have some of their lesser demands partially met, which in turn allows the local authorities to claim just how responsive they are to local needs. It is important in the analysis to note which groups receive such support. For example, note the eventual involvement of the authorities in successful community projects like claimants' unions and neighbourhood law centres. Perhaps it is the case that where such groups can be a constant source of public embarrassment to the local council financial support is forthcoming to buy off any critical function those groups might have possessed. This in turn helps to bolster the illusion that 'reasonable discussion' in such situations pays off. More usually, the community of interest having discovered that consensual approaches to action reap no more than the authorities are prepared to give, are criticised for adopting conflict strategies. This serves to damage the group's credibility among the non-informed and diverts attention away from the initial demands. It is all the easier, seemingly, if there are 'outsiders', 'agitators', 'extremists', 'students', or any other degradating label to point at. In this way one can begin to identify what sort of community of interest the authorities themselves are representing and just how this is linked, in their rationale of their duties, to others' definitions about action towards the 'common good'.

One other tactic Dearlove mentions is that of co-option. In many ways one can identify the same sorts of constraints being placed upon local authority community workers, i.e. if community has anything to do with greater freedom then how are community workers allowed to perform their roles when employed by a set of paymasters who also control community change? Cheetham and Hill introduce the problem like this:

> The dilemma for the community worker is immediately clear. Does he give equal support in terms of advice and encouragement to every group or does he, explicitly or implicitly, discourage some and throw in his lot with the others? Assuming he possesses such Machavellian skills, can or should he be neutral, perhaps with the intention, often only idealistic, of helping the different groups achieve a relatively equal balance of power as a context for a fair fight in which the 'best man' may win? (Cheetham and Hill, 1973)

Given the context of their employment we ought to know more than we do about community workers: who they feel they can support, what action it would be politic to take, which needs are decided upon as being in any way immediate, what community work has to do with the management of change in society or whether community work is really only something that goes on inside the bingo sessions of community centres.

The framework that I have outlined above is not limited to the socio-historical analysis of the usual elements of community studies. The framework could equally well be applied to any group with a sufficiently important, to them, common base. Indeed, an easy extension would be into Becker's work on the genesis of student culture (Becker, 1968) or other adolescent cultures (Hall and Jefferson, 1976). It should at least be clear that if we as sociologists are going to use the term community it must be treated as a critical concept, not a gloss.

Footprint in the Sand: Black Exploration of the White Community – an Autobiographical Approach by M. Chevannes and F. W. Reeves

Preface

The title 'Footprint in the Sand' refers to the occasion when, after many years of isolation, Robinson Crusoe comes to a realisation that there are other human beings on the island, and begins to react to them in what he regards as an appropriate way.

In this article, the authors present a first-person account of a black young woman's vivid impressions of a country which is to become her new home. The story is told in hindsight by a woman who has now learnt to mistrust the ignorance and hasty generalisation of her own experience and to recognise that her previous views had certain characteristics in common with white colour prejudice. An important difference does, however, lie in the separate social positions in which white and black exist, and the distinct uses to which their respective sets of beliefs about the other are put.

The paper serves a useful purpose in offering us an insight into the dangers of making any kind of disparaging judgement about another group's customs, and into the amazing way ethnocentric white views on hygiene, morals, etc., are closely paralleled by contradictory black views on the same subjects.

The question may be raised about the sociological value of the article. Is it, in fact, sociology? A mistake may lie in thinking that all valuable 'socially orientated' discourse must invariably fall under discipline headings such as sociology or literature. This is only likely to be true if it has been purposely written with the conventions of a particular discipline in mind.

'Footprint in the Sand' is a little like a traveller's tale except that it is written with the intention of exposing the misunderstanding of traveller and native alike. It describes social behaviour and the various ways it is interpreted and evaluated against group norms. But the objective occurrence of the behaviour and the subjective response it kindles are not clearly distinguished. This separation is not always possible. Indeed, the young black woman remarks that she was not able to act as a detached observer because of 'powerful feelings and protective strategies'. She contrasts her behaviour with that of the anthropologist. Perhaps, then, the article consists of the 'raw material' upon which sociology must draw. But the account already shows an appreciation of sociological and social psychological interests in the incidents described and in the concepts and theories that are used to analyse them. There is even the hint of a Marxist analysis in the conclusion.

Overall, the account is of interaction between two communities and of each's interpretation of the other's behaviour. But the article does not fall into the main stream of interactionist sociology. It is biographical, and the observer doubles as actor.

Life and Attrition in England

I came to England because my parents sent for me. I did not want to come as I had a good job as a telephone operator.

The impressions I gained in Jamaica of life in England were limited and naïve. The frightening prospect of a country in which the sun might shine and the temperature remain cold had stuck in my mind from a distant geography lesson. And in England, they had to wear heavy clothes as a protection against the weather. I think we had all been given the impression of a land of remarkably intelligent white people from the fact that Englishmen had written most of our school text books. In addition, we had been taught that England was our mother-country and we tended to imagine a mother as a source of warmth and understanding. Nevertheless, to me, Jamaica was a 'developing' country, dependent on the skills of her people, and I felt a little guilty in abandoning it for England.

As the plane came in to land at Heathrow airport, I caught my first glimpse of England. From above, I saw nothing but little factories. I later came to realise that what I had seen from the air were not factories after all. They were rows of barrack-like terraced houses, each with its own chimney. In Jamaica there is no need of artificial fires to increase the heat from the sun: the need is to reduce the temperature. When at last I entered one of these ugly buildings, I recognised the interior comfort of a home.

Another initial source of amazement was the sight of white men sweeping roads and cleaning windows, jobs I could never have imagined were performed by white people.

My parents lived in a small, rented house in Sparkbrook, Birmingham. My mother worked as a hospital seamstress while my father was a car worker at Longbridge.

Two rows of terraced houses faced each other across a road crowded with fast-moving traffic. There were no trees, no green spaces – only a labyrinth of bricks and asphalt.

I arrived in Birmingham on a Sunday and on Monday began work as a nursing auxiliary at the hospital which had obtained the work voucher for me. (My mother, who worked in the sewing room, knew the matron.)

During my stay at the hospital, I performed various chores on a female ward. On one occasion I was giving a bed-bath to a patient who had one leg in plaster, when she kicked me with her one good leg and uttered abusive remarks about my colour. This was my first personal experience of colour prejudice and I burst into tears.

On my way home from work one evening, not long afterwards, two little boys met me in the street and shouted 'blacky'. When I reached home I was most upset. My mother warned me that I would have to start standing up for myself. She had long since become hardened to this commonplace hostility but, coming straight from Jamaica, I had not been prepared for it.

While I was at the hospital, I soon realised that I was not after all being trained to become a nurse. If I wanted to be a State Registered Nurse, I had to undertake a three-year training. I began to write to various hospitals for application forms, and was eventually accepted by one nursing school after I had taken the entrance test. At interview, the person in charge of the school of nursing tried to convince me that State Enrolled Nurse training (two years) was of equal status to S.R.N., but fortunately I insisted I wanted the three-year training. When I started the S.R.N. course, I found out that there were a number of English student nurses who had neither taken an entrance test nor passed any G.C.E. 'O' levels. As I was in possession of a number of Associated Examining Board G.C.E. 'O' levels (I had taken British examination board G.C.E. exams in Jamaica), I remember feeling aggrieved at this apparent unfairness in the selection process.

While working in the hospital, I noticed the frequency with which black nurses were given menial tasks and were not permitted to take on the level of responsibility commensurate with the stage of training. If, for example, a black and a white nurse were both working on a ward, the white nurse would be put in charge, be given custody of the keys, and be expected to see visitors, to talk to the nursing officer, and to write the ward report. Without these opportunities to assume responsibility, it was difficult for the black nurse to demonstrate her abilities and to perform well in the examination and upon qualification.

I recall one occasion when a woman, to whom I was giving a bed-bath, ordered me to remove my 'black hands' from her body. Such incidents occurred regularly. Because black nurses never received moral support from the ward sister and, in the end, never expected any, they usually resorted to seeking out other black nurses, regardless of their country of origin, to share their experiences. But there were few answers to the white world apart from 'grinning and bearing it', pretending a lack of understanding of what was going on, and remaining calm, detached, passive, and unemotional.

After my general training and work as a staff nurse, I took a midwifery course. At that time, although there were a large number of black midwives, I cannot recall seeing one in the position of ward sister. Nevertheless, I had an enjoyable training in that I did not experience any overt racial hostility. Covertly, however, it still showed itself in the differential allocation of ward placements and periods on night duty, in gestures and facial expressions in wards and classrooms, in the deliberate avoidance by whites of contact with blacks, and in the selection of whites for one tea or lunch break and of blacks for another.

Once, when I happened to win a nursing prize, I was told by a perturbed matron that it was most unusual for girls like me to be given prizes. This same matron later reprimanded me for using my employer's name as a referee on so many occasions. As I was making application for health visitor training, she had to write references, and because of the difficulties others associated with my colour, I was forced to make numerous applications.

The health authorities were obviously taking up my references, but I was not being called for interview. In the end, my perseverance paid off. At the first interview I was pointedly told that health visiting was for 'our girls' and that I should consider working instead as a domiciliary midwife. They wished me luck, but they thought my aspirations were unrealistic. (I should point out that these experiences occurred with the health authorities from which I was requesting sponsorship and not at the educational establishments where health visitor courses are based.) Finally, however, I *was* offered a place at a health visitor training school. A sympathetic interviewing panel asked me directly about the number of applications I had made and the reasons for it. There *were* fair-minded people in England.

Forming an Impression of the English

From the time I discovered their country, I realised I had a great deal to learn about English people and their ways. If only I could have acted as an anthropologist who seeks to understand, from every-day observations, a complex and confusing situation. Every anthropologist finds himself allocated to some position in the society which he is studying. My position was that of a young black Jamaican woman – an immigrant. I was not able to act as a detached observer, maintaining a value-free stance, and with emotions under strict surveillance. English behaviour was often unusual, and sometimes decidedly hostile, and I reacted to it with powerful feelings and protective strategies. It was not easy at first to distinguish the unpredictable and harmless from the really unpleasant. I had little understanding of the dangers of making generalisations from single experiences of the heterogeneous English society, and when I met an unusual situation I turned to my relatives and friends for help. Their advice, although not necessarily well-informed, gave me the support I so often needed in making sense of my experiences.

My resulting ethnocentric views about the English are interesting more for the way they often duplicate English sentiments about Jamaicans than for their grounding in reality. I generalised from one or two incidents and assessed the trait against Jamaican norms, instead of accepting the possibility of the existence of different patterns of behaviour and different ways of assessing it. The English revealed themselves as unhygienic, morally lax, irreligious, unfriendly, hypocritical, untrustworthy, insincere, and colour prejudiced. They neglected children and old people and were inhibited about most things – even about death and bereavement. Although I later realised the danger of making such sweeping judgements, it is worth describing how I arrived at these conclusions.

ARE THE ENGLISH UNHYGIENIC?

I remember my cousin's account of a domestic science lesson in which the teacher, Mrs X, had set out to give the mainly West Indian class of girls a lesson in basic hygiene, no doubt, from her point of view, much needed. She had pointed out the importance of regularly washing underwear and, to reinforce the point, had added that she herself washed out her 'pants' in the kitchen sink every night before going to bed. My cousin and her West Indian friends howled with derision. In the West Indies, the cooking of food and the washing of clothes are kept strictly apart, and separate utensils are always used. The idea of 'polluting' one's sink with dirty underwear shocked the girls deeply.

Once, when I was invited to an English home for lunch, I was asked to enter the kitchen while the family were washing up. Plates were placed on the draining board with soap flakes and pieces of food still adhering to them. No rinsing took place. Instead the soap and food were wiped around with a tea towel. We Jamaicans always rinse our dishes.

While I was working in hospital, I was surprised how infrequently English women patients changed their nightdresses. Many of them would wear the same nightdress for three or even four days at a time. I had always believed that a clean nightdress should be worn every day and that it was unhygienic not to do so. I also had the idea that the nurses would have more respect for those patients who changed their nightdresses on a daily basis.

DO THE ENGLISH LOVE ANIMALS MORE THAN CHILDREN?

On another occasion when I visited an English home, I observed that the family dog was treated in the same way as a human being. The animal was fed from the husband's plate during and after the meal. Later the same plate was returned to the table to be washed along with the other crockery. A little later, the dog was allocated a prominent position on the settee. I learnt that on many occasions the dog slept in the wife's bed.

In recounting this story to Jamaican friends I received a sympathetic ear. It was widely known, they said, that the English care more for their dogs than for their children. After all, a *royal* society existed for the prevention of cruelty to animals, but there was only a *national* society for the prevention of cruelty to children. Their views seemed to be confirmed by the daily newspaper reports of babies abandoned in lavatories, shops, and streets. Although I am no longer willing to assume Jamaican superiority in the care of children, I still feel that dogs should be treated in a normal, that is, Jamaican way, for example, fed from a special container, kept out of doors and out of beds.

ARE THE ENGLISH INHIBITED ABOUT DEATH?

Among the English, death is treated as a private family affair and members of the family behave as if they are unaffected by it. At least, the way they avoid all mention of the subject to the extent of remaining totally silent about any grief they do possess gives that impression. I noticed that few people attended a funeral and when it had taken place, the dead person's name just dropped out of conversation. I have always felt that the bereaved should be encouraged to give public vent to their grief. This would enable feelings to be shared and would be comforting and supportive to all concerned. When we lose a relative, people come and talk with us, make offers of help, and stay for a while after the funeral. Everybody meets in the house in which the deceased lived. The actual funeral becomes not only a family, but a community affair, involving anyone who cares to participate. The process comes to a climax on the ninth night after the person has died. Family, friends, neighbours, and the entire community gather inside and outside of the house and sing, eat and drink, until morning. Dreaming about the dead person is not discouraged, and people show interest in the dreams. Such interest is thought to demonstrate care and affection for the deceased.

ARE THE ENGLISH MORALLY LAX AND IRRELIGIOUS?

Jamaican common-law unions have sometimes been criticised by the English as unstable and promiscuous. But the majority of common-law unions (a sexual relationship between a man and a woman, often with children) are stable and long-lasting. Although legal marriage is generally regarded as the ideal among all Jamaicans, common-law unions among the less formally educated are not despised but regarded as a stage in a relationship, sometimes, but not inevitably, leading to marriage. In England, I have known many married men and women to have had sexual relationships outside of their legal union. And, nearly always, they disguised the fact from their marriage partner. Because of this practice, I felt that Jamaicans treated marriage with more reverence and respect than the English. In addition, the English as a whole have a far less severe attitude to divorce than Jamaicans, who sometimes socially ostracise divorcees.

In other respects, too, I saw English people as morally lax, as 'not knowing how to behave'. Couples kissed in the streets and lay together in parks and public places. Many English people did not go to church and never mentioned religion except disparagingly. To the Jamaican, who saw religion as part and parcel of a whole way of life, they were sacrilegious and unchristian.

ARE THE ENGLISH UNFRIENDLY, HYPOCRITICAL, UNTRUSTWORTHY, INSINCERE, AND COLOUR PREJUDICED?

Sometimes at the hospital, I would work closely, and in a friendly manner, for three months with a particular English girl, but when she saw me after work at a bus stop, she would turn her head away. Or she might pass me on the street, as if she had never seen me before. Others at least would acknowledge me with a 'plastic' grin – but without ever stopping to speak. In the wider world, people, often with parcels, would stand on a crowded bus, rather than sit beside me in the only vacant seat.

When I had to move to a new town to do my health visitor training, I needed to find somewhere to live. I looked quite naturally in the local paper for rented accommodation. Often I was offered accommodation when I telephoned the address, but when I went round to view the place a few minutes later, I was informed by the landlady that it had just been taken. I soon became tired of wasting my time and began to mention my colour on the telephone. The conversations sometimes went like this:

> 'I understand you've got a bed-sitter to let.'
> 'Yes, that's right.'
> 'I'm Jamaican. Do you mind?'
> 'You mean you're coloured?'
> 'I'm black.'
> 'Oh no! I don't think the other tenants would like that.'

> 'I saw in the paper that you've got a flat to let.'
> 'Are you Welsh?'
> 'No, I'm Jamaican.'
> 'My God, that's even worse!'

Eventually, when I was so desperate I did not know what to do next, I managed to get temporary accommodation by stopping a black man in the street and asking him if he could help. He took me to his brother who let me a room until, with the help of a sympathetic white health visitor, I eventually found a bed-sitter. She approached the estate agents on my behalf without telling them about my colour.

In 1975, I tried to buy a house. I discussed all the details of the property on the phone with the agent and arranged to meet him half an hour later at his office. When I arrived he told me the house had temporarily been taken off the market, and without eliciting any further details from me, declared he had no other suitable property. Six months later the *for sale* sign was still standing in front of the house in question.

These, and other similar experiences of what I took to be blatant discrimination, supported my view that the English were prejudiced. But it was no use telling them this. Even sympathetic whites would attempt a defence of discriminatory practice:

> Yes it's wrong but you can understand it. They're just worried about their house prices falling.

If house prices did fall as a result of my living next door, didn't that confirm that the English were prejudiced? But aren't Jamaicans (particularly those who produce a set of beliefs like those above) equally prejudiced?

The Nature of Prejudice

The word 'prejudice' is often loosely used and it is important to distinguish between fallacious belief (ignorance), faulty reasoning from which it might result (hasty generalisation), preference, and prejudice. For a variety of reasons it is possible to be mistaken about others' conduct. I know now I was wrong in thinking the English did not *feel* grief. I interpreted their behaviour wrongly. In other examples given, I may have considered only exceptional cases of English behaviour and generalised to the group as a whole. The wide variety of social practice among English people (and, for that matter, in most societies) increases the likelihood of the fallacy of *hasty generalisation* occurring. But whether or not our beliefs about people are factually correct, we often go further and evaluate the social behaviour of others against our own personal, moral, aesthetic, and technical standards. When we like one thing better than another we talk of having a *preference* for it. In other words we have a pro-attitude towards it. Now social psychologists have tried to isolate one particular type of attitude called *prejudice*. They have stipulated that attitudes are prejudices when (i) the facts on which they are founded are false, (ii) they are particularly resistant to revision, (iii) they are hostile, and (iv) they are directed towards all members of a group who are looked upon as being alike. As for the last point, I had become used to expressions such as:

> You're not as black as all that.

(This meant: as she has unexpectedly turned out to be civilised, it can't be possible for her to be black as well, although it does seem to look that way.)

> You're ever so nice.

(This meant: she is a remarkable exception to the rule that black people are unpleasant.)

> You're ever so English.

(This meant: she's not really like *them*, at all.)
Franz Fanon (1967) put it this way:

> When people like me, they tell me it is in spite of my colour. When they dislike me they point out that it is not because of my colour. Either way, I am locked into the infernal circle.

The characteristics of prejudice, of course, raise the important questions of why people are prepared to accept false information, to put up stiff resistance to changing their views, and to act upon their prejudices in ways that may create untold suffering. There is indeed a difference between ignorance, preference, and prejudice, as I found out to my cost. It would appear that people cling fast to prejudice because it serves their deep-seated psychological needs. And individuals' needs are generated on a wide scale by the social pressures upon them.

I had been told that English prejudice had been founded on empire. To justify their rule over a third of the world and their accompanying privileges, the English came to believe in their own superiority. Although this might adequately explain how prejudice was originally generated, and why a particular group was selected for victimisation, it does not seem to account for the potency of present-day hostility towards me and my country-folk.

To me, the most simple explanation for prejudice lies in the form in which it is manifested. People have to struggle hard to stay alive and to maintain their living standards. They constantly fear the encroachments of ill-health, dirty conditions, bad housing, physical danger, lawlessness, unemployment, poor education, and shortage of money and the things that money buys. But control over these matters is seldom and never entirely in their hands. The social forces that govern people's lives are mysterious, and frequently have unintended consequences. Yet explanations are still sought for, and defensive action is taken in the face of danger.

Black people, it seems, just happen to be the convenient butt for white frustrations; a distraction from the forces that really threaten people's wellbeing. It is understandable that the rationality of an economic situation that accepts, for example, the inevitability of homelessness existing simultaneously with unemployment in the building industry, is very difficult to grasp. Instead, the insecure seek to blame a readily identifiable and relatively weak minority. Their fears are confirmed in symbolic interaction, and prejudicial norms of speech and action are born.

But being in receipt of the blame is a depressing experience. I have only to open a newspaper to find myself type-cast as a member of a black horde about to overwhelm a green and pleasant land that had been free from all housing, health, and education problems until I arrived. I become anxious about the future every time some politician calls for repatriation. If the English are worried about our numbers, how are we likely to feel about theirs? I know, as a matter of fact, that because of the age composition of the black population (which contains so few people of pensionable age) black people as a whole take less from the social services than the whites. But rather than believe their own officially accepted figures, many English people rely on the statistics of their paranoid imagination. It serves a useful scapegoating function.

If black and white could learn to understand the forces that affect their lives, and to take control of them through political action, there would be no cause for despondency. One role of sociology might lie in helping the individual to escape from prejudice, in order to understand the other person's point of view. But to see through another's eyes does not only require detailed knowledge of his situation and social conventions, but the confident renunciation of one's own insecurity and sectional interest.

The Freemasons: A Closed Community?
by Helen Reynolds
Codsall High School

Introduction: The Concept of Community

Communities can be, and have been, defined in a variety of ways. The central distinction appears to be as follows. Are communities to be recognised by the nature of their atmosphere, feelings of harmony and cooperation and a sense of common interest or are they to be defined by organisational and material criteria? A street may be a community in terms of common residence but, if conflict exists between its inhabitants, the term 'community' may be inappropriate. In general the term also implies a positive value, and developing community is often perceived to be desirable. It is, however, possible for a community to be held together for negative rather than positive reasons.

'Open' and 'closed' are terms used to describe both entire societies and groups existing within the wider social context. The term 'closed' usually refers to a homogeneous group with shared culture, norms, values and beliefs. A community of this kind would operate mainly on the level of primary groupings, i.e. face-to-face contact with common agreement on behaviour and attitudes.

The term 'open' usually refers to societies where there is a plurality of alternative value and belief systems available for organising and understanding experience. Such societies can be interpreted as having communities *within* communities. Completely closed communities are more difficult to sustain as each individual will of necessity be a member of a large number of groupings. Nevertheless, closed communities are said to exist. Examples used are monasteries, boarding schools, ships, hospitals and prisons. Studies of such communities have tended to stress organisational aspects but have suggested that what might appear to be a community to outsiders is in fact a complex set of social relationships often characterised more by conflict than any sense of 'community spirit'.

Goffman (1961) deals with some other issues in *Asylums*, for example, definitions of sanity vary according to one's position in a closed or total community.

By making reference to Freemasonry I intend to examine the concept of a 'closed community' from a variety of perspectives. While the definition of 'closed community' is open to question it is here defined as being exclusive, employing selection and initiation procedures, and pursuing its own norms and values which may be transmitted to the next generation. It also implies a degree of consensus and common interest.

Freemasonry may be interpreted in a number of ways ranging from a functionalist viewpoint requiring an examination of its function or role in modern society to an interactionist approach assessing its contribution to the consciousness of the individual. Alternatively with a conflict perspective, it may be seen both as a source and creator of conflict. At the same time more understanding of its position in society may be gained by studying its objectives, meaning and significance as perceived by its members.

Freemasonry: Background Information

There are at present about one million Freemasons in Britain with approximately 25–30,000 joining each year. People who wish to join must do so of their own choice. To join a candidate must be male, over twenty-one, believe in God and be able to pay fees which may be ten guineas or more a year. It is usual for possible entrants to be encouraged by existing members and it may be to their advantage to do so. The official masonic statement holds that, 'a man who after many years attains high rank in Freemasonry will find that he has made a vast number of friends'.

It is possibly no coincidence that a large number of members of the medical and legal professions are masons. Masonry is increasingly popular with members in the commercial and business fields and a number are to be found in the police force. It is, however, the policy of the masons that the craft should not be used for direct business advantage. Many leading religious figures such as the Archbishop of Canterbury and the Chief Rabbi of the Commonwealth have held high masonic office. The Catholic and Orthodox churches discourage membership of the masons or any 'secret' society. About 15 per cent of Conservative members of Parliament join, but it is rare for a member of the cabinet to be a mason. As a movement, masonry is weaker in the Labour Party. Many masons are drawn from the aristocracy and the royal family. The Duke of Edinburgh has been initiated but apparently takes little active part. Freemasonry has a world membership of over six million and has included most American presidents.

In Britain, total masonic assets could be in excess of twenty million pounds. Apart from full time salaries, expenditure is mainly on charity for distressed masons, the upkeep of the Royal Masonic Hospital which is outside the National Health Service, the Royal Masonic Schools and homes for the elderly. Charitable work is usually an internal affair although occasional donations are made to outside charities. These and other details are given in the account of masonry by Colin Cross (1967).

The extent of Freemasonry as a world wide movement, and its great wealth, require that the concept of communities be extended to mean 'community of interest' since culture and nationality will inevitably affect belief and practice.

The Development of Freemasonry: A Functionalist Analysis

'Truth is the object of their worship and they represent truth as light; they tolerate all forms of faith, profess one philosophy, seek truth only, reach reality and their plan is to lead all human intelligence by gradual steps into the domain of reason' (Levi, 1969). The symbolic end of Free-masonry is the rebuilding of Solomon's Temple. The ideal society will be achieved, for some masons, when the Temple is actually rebuilt. For others, this will be when social unity is restored by an alliance between reason and faith.

The legends of Freemasonry are discussed in *The History of Magic* by Eliphas Levi (1969, p. 283). Emphasis was originally made on work, study, wisdom and the knowledge of nature, science and truth and also the emancipation of women. Freemasonry did not appear in Britain until the seventeenth century and seems to be linked with the European Gilds of Stonemasons. It is from this background that the ritual tools of masonry, for example compasses, level, tracing board, are derived. Freemasons belong to Lodges, of which there are now about seven thousand, and they may, by successive initiation, become Grand Master.

Freemasonry in ancient times, and where it emerged in Britain, seemed to be a vehicle for relatively radical thought, as a system of meaning which extended conventional religious belief to develop concepts of scientific and social progress. Freemasons were frequently attacked by Cromwell in the past, and by Hitler, more recently, as being subversive. Their basic principles of equality and progress might have produced this response but it is more likely that this was due to the excessive secrecy and mystery with which they conducted their affairs. It was often supposed that they provided opportunities for political conspiracy.

Freemasonry survived the Industrial Revolution and the transition from rural to urban life. Indeed it may in its practices and beliefs have contributed, together with Protestantism, to the rise of capitalism in Britain (Weber, 1930). It was unusual as a belief system in its blend of scientific, magical and religious beliefs and practices. It was potentially capable of absorbing scientific and technological advances at a time when religion and science seemed to be in conflict. As a closed community Freemasonry appears to have changed in its orientation and has less commitment to development and social change than formerly. There is, therefore, some conflict between stated beliefs and actual practice.

In the present day, Freemasons are unlikely to be thought of as radical. The movement tends to adopt a more middle class orientation, valuing stability and a belief in tradition. The latter are supported by having high ranking members who are also members of other elite groups. Its activities as a group or community tend to be supportive of the existing social framework.

As a phenomenon, Freemasonry can be defined in terms of its relation with and effect upon the wider society. Equally, it can be examined in the light of the individual's perceptions of it. It cannot, however, be reduced to the sum of individual perceptions as it has real effects at a group and at a cultural level and links with other social processes and groupings.

How Does the Individual Experience Freemasonry? An Interactionist Approach

THE INTRODUCTION

In everyday life some individuals will probably become aware by hints and allusions that many of their associates are masons. The existing masons will invite the individual and he may well feel honoured to be chosen, at the same time appreciating the numerous benefits which may accrue from membership. Friendship, brotherhood and personal progress may motivate him to join.

THE INITIATION

Initiation is a primary feature of closed groups and communities indicating the boundaries through which an individual must pass to gain acceptance. Many initiations are in the form of ordeals and test the individual's commitment to the community he wishes to join. They serve to reinforce a sense of solidarity as all members will have been initiated in the same way. In the case of the masons, the candidate must not wear metal and is sometimes provided with alternative clothing. His left trouser leg is rolled up and slipper placed on his right foot. His left breast must be exposed, a hangman's noose is placed around his neck and he is blindfolded.

The 'Tyler', an official of the Lodge, stands with drawn sword outside the Lodge door, to repel intruders. After the required ritual of knocks, the candidate is guided into the Lodge and a dagger placed against his chest. He is questioned on his motives for joining which should not be 'mercenary'. He is expected to take an oath on the Bible to keep the secrets of masonry. The oath still refers to 'having my throat cut across, my tongue torn out by the root and buried in the sand off the sea at low water mark'. The blindfold is removed and he is given his apron while he inspects the various masonic tools and emblems and observes the senior members on their thrones. On receiving the apron, these words are spoken:

> I invest you with the distinguishing badge of a mason. It is more ancient than the golden fleece or the Roman eagle, more honourable than the garter or any other order in existence being the lodge of innocence and the bond of friendship.

He is taught the secret word 'Boaz', the signs, handshake and steps by which recognition between masons takes place. He is then asked to donate to charity but having left his money outside he has nothing to give. He is counselled by the Worshipful Master to remember his 'poor and penniless' state on entering the Lodge, when asked for help by a fellow mason.

There then follows a dinner with toasts and the singing of anthems including an extended 'God Save the Queen'. The masonic name for God is the 'Great Architect of the Universe' or the 'Grand Geometrician'. Any believer in God may join but religion is never discussed. A generally held belief is that a good Mason will dwell after death in the GLA or Grand Lodge Above. Freemasons attach great importance to their ritual, and further ceremonies are necessary to reach higher 'degrees', or offices. Promotion depends on seniority, regular attendance, knowledge of rituals and regular donations to charity. To be a Worshipful Master of a Lodge may involve a mason in expenditure of between fifty and one thousand pounds a year.

While ritual is important, it is no longer as secret as in former times and the details may be seen by outsiders. Nevertheless, masons stress secrecy and are reluctant to speak about their experiences. This confirms their position as members of an exclusive group and emphasises the distinction between them and others.

Freemasonry and the Individual

In order to explore this question it is necessary to investigate the perceptions of Freemasons. While it is difficult to obtain information except on an informal level, contact with friends and relatives of masons and ex-masons suggest that a variety of perceptions may be in operation.

Many Freemasons are committed in principle to an ideal of a virtuous life, to the development of the self, to the pursuit of truth and to charitable works. The nature of this 'truth' and 'virtue' is not clear since many Lodges do not engage in study, research or techniques which might lead to this end. In addition, charity tends to be only between fellow masons and their relatives. For them, it does provide a mutual aid system in times of hardship.

An individual's belief and commitment to the rituals and beliefs of masonry will therefore be dependent upon the value he places on these aims. If highly valued, the rituals may well represent a rite of passage from an old life to the new, a rebirth giving meaning and significance to life.

It is also necessary to distinguish between an individual's 'because of' and 'in order to' motives. That is, he may join the masons because of his social or class position, social pressure, occupational orientation, religious upbringing, family connections or from a sense of alienation from everyday life. These motives may be neither expressed nor conscious and it is a problem of sociological method as to what extent they can be inferred. The individual may, on the other hand, have both expressed and hidden 'in order to' motives. He may join in order to pursue self-knowledge, gain friends and the like. He may also join in order to pursue his own economic interests, thus using the movement for instrumental rather than intrinsic purposes.

On the other hand, there are also, many who are described as 'knife and fork' masons who come primarily for the ceremonial dinners, mutual friendship and possible social and economic benefit. For these masons, ritual activities and mystical beliefs would have little intrinsic significance, merely indicating the exclusive and special nature of the 'club' to which they belong.

In between these two positions lie the masons who believe in their charitable role and have a commitment to the upholding of traditions and morality. To these, the ritual and belief would operate in much the same way as church attendance – as a justification and reinforcement of existing behaviour and beliefs. It may also perform similar social functions to those of the golf club. Furthermore, membership of a Lodge provides a 'career' quite distinct from that pursued in everyday life. Consequently, it is possible to acquire status and rank by progressive initiation, thus satisfying the individual's desires for prestige which might otherwise be unfulfilled.

Given that there are at least three main positions from which masons may perceive their activity, it is difficult to arrive at any conclusion as to whether Freemasonry is truly a closed community. While a set of beliefs and practices are common to all, the extent of commitment of each individual is likely to affect the degree of unity and consensus in the group. Wider social and international links make shared values even more unlikely. What is shared appear to be the obligations to and expectations of each other in conditions of hardship or need. To this extent Freemasons are exclusive and closed since help depends on membership.

In addition it is necessary to link perceptions of masonry with the individual's perceptions of his daily life and other groups to which he belongs. For one individual, masonry may simply reinforce and maintain everyday reality rather than making a distinction between them. For another, entry into a Lodge may represent another dimension of reality not experienced in daily life. In this case, the community involvement is closed off from everyday experience.

Similarly, a person's perceived position and status in his social grouping may influence his commitment and belief. A Grand Master may be more committed to masonry as his position depends upon it. A junior member may, on the other hand, express more commitment than he really feels for instrumental reasons, for example, he wishes to gain acceptance and the benefits of membership.

It is clearly impossible to define a closed community purely on the basis of apparently shared belief and practice. Other dimensions must be taken into consideration. A 'community of interest' cannot necessarily be assumed.

Freemasonry in an Open Society

Having examined masonry from the individual's point of view it is necessary to look at the role of masonry in the wider society. Its actual effects may not be deliberate or consciously determined but are partly brought about by existing social patterns and what people believe Freemasonry to be. For example, the Lodges in Northern Ireland have become heavily involved in political and religious conflict.

Closed Communities may either be described as functional in themselves, or functional for society, depending on the perceptions of those involved. A closed or total institution, such as many psychiatric hospitals, may be perceived as having a positive role in maintaining definitions of sanity and protecting the community. As Goffman has shown, however, in his study *Asylums* (1961), the existence of such an institution indicates the inability of a society to deal with certain conflicts and problems, actually contributing to the formation of some deviant groups. Within the hospital community the aims of inmates and staff conflict; they perceive and define their shared situation in different ways. An example is described by David Sudnow in *Dead on Arrival* (p. 7, 1976), and the film *One Flew Over the Cuckoo's Nest* explores a similar theme.

It can be argued that Freemasonry does, to a certain extent, maintain the existing social framework on the level of manifest functions. Freemasonry's involvement with charitable work, its upholding of traditional moral and social values and its great wealth clearly contribute to the maintenance of certain parts of the social system.

At a latent level it provides a network of relationship and influence, together with selection techniques, which may promote a career, provide credit guarantees, and give sponsorship of social activities and financial discounts. The latter may be obtained by the giving of correct signs and allusions. As such it performs a similar role to that of the public school background and 'the old boy network'. On both levels, manifest and latent, it has moved away from the original aims and principles of social unity and equality.

It has, in addition, a number of consequences for both the individual and the society. It is discriminatory on sex and class dimensions. Women are not initiated and are only barely tolerated on the occasional ladies' nights, often held only once a year. Membership of Lodges has been known to cause distress and conflict in family life as wives and children are not allowed to share in masonic activities even though they may receive certain benefits.

A similar analysis has been made of witchcraft covens in British society where membership is characterised by a variety of individual perceptions and responses to his or her situation. While membership may have emotional, social and economic functions for the individual it may preserve, perpetuate and even create conflict in the wider community of which it is a part. This has also been found to be so amongst certain ritual societies where witchcraft accusations are the main method of solving conflicts. They do not, however, remove the social conditions from which these conflicts emerge.

The masons' attachment to often apparently obsolete ritual practice and belief, its secrecy and exclusivity frequently cause envy, suspicion and hostility, so dividing both smaller and larger groupings. While it may provide meaning and significance in individual terms its wider social effects cannot be ignored. In theory its original aims were for unity; in practice it functions to preserve inequalities and divisions. The actual content of masonic activity may not be responsible for this but the fact that it is a relatively closed and exclusive group may well be the reason for its effects on the wider society, the members of which may well perceive it in this way.

It is also possible to analyse and examine Freemasonry in the same way as traditional religion. On the one hand, its organisation, political and economic power and social functions may be observed. On the other hand, this does not provide an adequate explanation for the understanding of religious belief. It is also possible that an analysis of the development from radical sect to a more conformist church type organisation might facilitate understanding of Freemasonry. This process might explain that whereas in the past a genuine closed community existed, now merely the framework remains as a vehicle for the promotion of certain groups in society, dominated more by self interest than shared values and objectives of social unity.

Organisation, Belief System, or Closed Community?

Freemasonry may be understood by reference to all these categories but, in each case, analysis depends upon the definitions in use. These may centre on objective criteria such as membership, wealth, content of belief and official statements of shared values. Alternatively a more subjective approach may be undertaken where the perceptions and experiences of the individuals concerned are seen as of primary importance.

Freemasonry must also be seen as an ideology in terms of its relationship to the maintenance of social divisions. Its relatively closed nature and the wealth and influence of its members associate it with other elite groups where it may well reinforce existing power structures.

Since Freemasonry draws much of its influence from members who have status and power in other spheres, its effects on society and the individual may be better understood by reference to categories other than that of the 'closed community'. If we use 'closed community' as an ideal type, the masons are a *relatively* closed rather than *totally* closed community.

IV DEMOGRAPHY

Introduction

The interactionist, phenomenological and other approaches that start with individuals, and stress how social structures depend on large numbers of people constructing their realities in a particular way, often treat statistics with some scepticism. It can be argued that this is a continuation of the critique of C. Wright Mills in his book *The Sociological Imagination* (1959) where he suggests that the quest for statistical information can easily bypass issues that are of more central significance and of more sociological concern. Such an approach lacked 'sociological imagination'. Mills also offered an explanation: that this statistical approach was essentially more of an administrative method than a sociological one. It both depended on, and perpetuated, a narrow view of humanity, an administratively convenient view of people with a concern to predict their behaviour and then control their lives by planning programmes for them.

Demography, which may be defined as the study of population statistics, is a significant example of an activity that has great administrative value, for no administrator can function very effectively without information about populations, migrations, age groupings and sex groupings. Indeed, the origins of demography appear to be partly in the need for this kind of information to facilitate political decisions such as the size of voting constituencies, and even earlier, for tax gathering purposes.

The two papers in this section are attempts to take a fresh look at demography, not in order to dismiss it as a field of study, but to establish clearly that there is only so much that can be done with this kind of information. Beyond this point lies distortion and error. The first paper by Philip Abrams is concerned with the use that can be made of demographic data generally, and of data on age in particular, in understanding the social meaning and organisation of the life cycle. It is argued that the reliability of demographic projections is limited by the increasing freedom of individuals to determine their own family patterns. For example, attempts to predict teacher supply based on birth rate projections have not been conspicuously successful. Moreover, survey data correlating age with other variables are seldom self explanatory. Age, and in particular the idea of youth, continue to be meaningful bases of social experience which can be understood more effectively through longitudinal studies and through a theory of generations.

The paper by L. Stephenson concentrates on some limitations and some distortions arising from the population statistics concerning black people in the U.K. The message of both writers is somewhat similar: in the case of demographic information, handle with great care. In the hands of the unsophisticated, or the unscrupulous, this information can be very misleading!

Age, Generation and Demography[1]
by Philip Abrams
University of Durham

Demographic data, that is, basic information about rates of birth, marriage, death and migration, is commonly treated as one of the 'hardest' types of data available to the social scientist. At the same time it is well known that demographic predictions and projections are, of all the types of social prediction, the ones most likely to go wrong. The fact that in the late 1970's Britain is experiencing a so-called 'crisis of teacher-training' – that is to say, the fact that we are training far more teachers than government is willing to pay to teach – is a direct result of the official belief that the marriage and birth rates of the early 1960's were themselves social facts which could be treated as a given and continuing basis for social policy. The belief that information about fertility in 1960 could provide a basis for knowing what sort of families people would have in 1970 is the immediate cause of teacher unemployment in 1977. Yet there is a sense in which demographers never learn. In the early 1960's we were told with complete confidence that the population of the United Kingdom would increase towards a figure of 66 million by the end of the century. Today, in the 1976 edition of *Social Trends* (HMSO, 1976, p. 62), we are told that the probable population of the United Kingdom in the year 2001 is a mere 59 million. About seven million people have been demographically written off. Yet the basic datum on which both projections are based is the same: it is the number of women of child-bearing age already or prospectively in the population. Given this information the demographer assumes that the child-bearing behaviour of tomorrow's adults can be extrapolated in a law-like manner from his knowledge of the child-bearing behaviour of the adults of the immediate past.

Demography, especially as used in official statistics and policy, is, in other words, the most grossly Durkheimian form of sociology. The belief that rates of behaviour constitute social facts is here given a rigidity which Durkheim himself would never have proposed. As a result the

---

[1] This paper is a revised version of an article first published in *New Society*, 1971 and republished in P. Barker (ed.), *A Sociological Portrait* (Penguin Books, London, 1972).

demographer is constantly having to revise his projections; constantly having to note that women of child-bearing age in today's population are not behaving in the same way as women of that age in yesterday's population and that the projected increase in population as a whole is not therefore going to occur. But instead of abandoning the whole business of demographic projection and recognising that family size, and family relationships, are too susceptible to changing social pressure and personal choices to be treated as social facts in this way, the tendency of the demographer is simply to produce a new projection offered with all the spurious authority of the one that has just been discredited.

To some extent this odd behaviour can be explained as a matter of history. Demography was one of the earliest social sciences. It established itself in the setting of an essentially pre-industrial social order between 1660 and 1720 in England. Its assumptions still tend to reflect the social realities of such social orders – realities in which marriage, fertility and mortality were relatively fixed from generation to generation and in which trends in any of these types of behaviour matured slowly over long periods and in a more or less invariant manner. Plagues, wars and famines apart, demographic data did look like social facts in pre-industrial societies. In the more 'ideal-typical' versions of such societies biological age was also a cardinal principle of social organisation, status and hierarchy. In some pre-industrial societies, to know a man's age was to know almost everything about him. The 'natural' phases of the life cycle provided a stable basis for the social division of labour, privilege and identity. By contrast, the extent to which age indicates or controls an individual's social role and status in advanced industrial societies is remarkably slight. Of course people are still assigned to childhood, adolescence and retirement in relatively inflexible ways; the social organisation of the life cycle is still an important dimension of social organisation as a whole. But for all the recent concern about 'youth culture' and the 'generation gap', the striking feature of industrial societies is how little, in comparative terms, age matters.

But not only age; the law-like constraints of the life cycle as experienced in pre-industrial societies have been relaxed in other ways too. The technologies of birth control and the politics of divorce and women's liberation have freed people from subjection to the social facts of marriage rates and fertility rates. Medicine, institutional and social care are progressively making even the facts of mortality variable. Death was, of course, the beginning of demography. It was the predictability of the incidence of death by gender, age, occupation and medical history that permitted the formation and profitability of life-insurance organisations. And it was from that basis that demography as a predictive, statistical social science sprang. By collapsing the certainties on which demography was constructed, advanced industrialism makes the understanding of the life cycle sociologically problematic in a way it has not been for a long time.

As it happens, information about age in survey research occurs more frequently and systematically than about any other single variable. A study of surveys carried out in Britain, Europe and the United States in 1965 found that age was the background variable on which information was most regularly collected in all three areas. The institutions sampled included government departments, academic research institutes and market research organisations. In Britain alone there were then 82 agencies conducting about 2 million interviews a year; and at least one question on ages was included in every case. So what is information about age supposed to indicate?

The age-profiles of whole populations – that is, the proportions falling into a series of given age-brackets – can be determined with great ease through research of this kind, and they provide suggestive materials for describing society if not for explaining it. Such descriptions in turn can plausibly be held to indicate the current, if not the prospective, incidence of certain sorts of social problems. As a matter of commonsense, age indicates the point a person has reached in the process of *biological* maturation and development; age-profiles of a population are accordingly an easy way of mapping both the human resources and the social problems of different populations. The United Kingdom, for example, is steadily acquiring a larger and larger proportion of older persons who, as a result of successive political decisions, have to be regarded as non-productive and dependent on others. The qualification is important; it is not a biological fact that people under the age of 16 or over the age of 60 or 65 do not work and must be supported by the work of others; rather, it is a product of our political history. Nevertheless, Britain is becoming an older society. In 1900 the median age of our population was 24; today it is 34; by the end of the century we are told it will be 38; and of all demographic projections those involving mortality are the least unreliable since the tendency of medicine to extend life and the unwillingness of most people to choose death as an alternative to life are both fairly invariant. To put it more directly: given a falling birth rate since the early 1960's and greater longevity among the old, the proportion of retired and dependent persons in the population as a whole has to increase. Whereas there were 2·4 million people over the age of retirement (65 for men, 60 for women) in 1901, there were 7·1 million in 1971, and the projection for 2001 is 8·5 million. In other words, in quite dramatic terms Britain is an ageing society; with a population growth since 1900 of 45 per cent, the number of people in the population over the age of retirement has increased by 196 per cent. At the same time, although the number of people under the age of 16 in the population has fractionally increased in *absolute* terms, it has declined as a *proportion* of the whole population. So while the overall 'dependency ratio' – the proportion of the population that will on grounds of age have to be supported by others – may be said not to have changed very much in the first three-quarters of this century (from 35 per cent to 38 per cent) its *constitution* has changed remarkably and in a way that gives us a new and acute social problem. At least it does for so long as we choose to treat men over 65 and women over 60 as 'economically inactive'; but again, that is a political not a demographic fact.

Unreliable as projections based on fertility rates and marriage rates are now recognised to be, the implications of our survival rate taken in conjunction with current levels of fertility are impressive. At the moment, women are marrying younger (the average age of first marriage is now 23 as compared with 26 in 1900) as are men (25 now as compared with 27 in 1900); and both men and women are getting divorced and remarrying more frequently (remarriages now account for 28 per cent of all marriages as compared to 13 per cent in 1900). With the exception of the professional middle classes all married couples are having fewer children. Generally, the increasing popularity of marriage seems to be negatively related to family size. As marriage and parenthood both become increasingly matters of choice it seems that marriage is being chosen more frequently and parenthood less frequently. The current birth rate of 12.4 live births per 1,000 of the population is the lowest the country has had this century and compares with a figure of 18 in 1961 and 29 in 1901. We do not, of course, know whether these trends will continue. It is difficult, for example, to know what allowance to make for the possible effects of future economic changes on people's attitudes to the 'value' of children. But for the moment we plainly have a population profile with a bulging forehead (of the elderly) and a receding chin (of the young) – a profile which, however sceptical one is about the reliability of demographic projections, already has a serious message for policy-makers.

Serious it is, but unfortunately not unambiguous. Data of this sort have always been taken seriously in the formation of social policy; and they have almost always been found to be both impressive and controversial. One of the first people to realise the social relevance of simple age-profile data was Joseph Rowntree. In 1890, in the face of vigorous advocacy of universal old age pensions as a panacea for poverty, Rowntree showed, in the final chapter of his *Poverty: a Study of Town Life* (1910), that the contribution of old age pensions to eliminating poverty would, at that time, have been depressingly slight. The age distribution of the population of the poor revealed, only too brutally, that the problem of poverty in 1890 was at the other end of the dependency-ratio. It was a problem of *child* poverty: 44 per cent of the poor were below the age of fifteen. By contrast, the age-distribution of the population today, and still more of that projected for the end of the century, points to a situation in which the primary association of dependency (if not of poverty) with old age will, at last, be justified. Accordingly, as Brian Abel Smith has pointed out, services for the old will increasingly demand 'the major part of social security expenditure'.

Rowntree's work was an early and clear example of the way in which

Telephone Message

TIME RECEIVED _____ DATE 1/10/91

FROM _____

Mrs, Thornhill College
phoned to confirm that
Thurs, 10th Oct at 2.30pm.
is fine

RECEIVED BY ____ Maria

Liam Worby

age data gain a social as distinct from a biological meaning. Perhaps the most cogent part of his work is where he demonstrates how the *social* organisation of the life cycle (the exclusion of children from employment) compounds the problem of poverty which is induced through directly *biological* dependence (children have to be reared). His discovery was a dramatic step beyond the use of age data common at that time in demographic research, and it had dramatic implications for policy. Anyone looking at Rowntree's chart, in which he expresses the life cycle as a series of age-specific waves of poverty and affluence, can see that the periodic reductions of well-being are a consequence not only of biological facts but equally of the labour market and the kinship system. He showed that in important respects the life cycle is a social artefact. Free universal nursery provision, communal living, major reform of family relationships could all change the social meaning of age. Demographic data for their part tell us something about the scale of our social problems; they cannot on their own tell us why those problems exist or what should be done about them.

The type of understanding of the social meaning of age achieved by Rowntree has effectively been put to use in market research as well as in social policy. The relationship of age to income and thence to consumer behaviour is one of the most reliable bases for creating and exploiting new markets. Just as there are age-specific phases of the life cycle when income is relatively diminished in relation to needs so there are periods when people whose income is at other times tightly committed find they have money to spend. The most exploitable of these periods – perhaps because it is not overshadowed by the memory of earlier periods when personal income was under pressure – is late adolescence and early adulthood, between starting work and having children, i.e. the age group from 15 to 29.

We may never be able to show conclusively just how far the explosion of youth culture in Britain in the 1950's and after was a direct result of commercial opportunism responding to this discovery of the teenage consumer. But many organisations involved in marketing clothes and music in particular have admitted frankly how important the demonstration of this reserve of disposable income in a particular age category was in revolutionising their strategies of production and marketing during the past twenty years. In any case the sociologically significant thing about this aspect of youth culture is not that survey research helped reveal the existence of disposable income in the hands of the young, but rather that the young were persuaded to dispose of this income in certain ways by deliberately exploiting the idea that spending in those ways was somehow itself associated with the idea of being young. Age was here given a special social meaning.

What the original research had revealed was an enigmatic correlation. People in this age-category not only had disposable income above their immediately felt needs, but also could be induced to respond in a uniquely sensitive way to the appeals of fashion. For this age-category, the idea of newness could be given very positive appeal. The *explanation* of this relationship is not something which research of this type is likely to bring to light. It involves a deeper look at the social organisation of age than one needs in order to make successful decisions about the marketing of a new magazine or a new singer. Predictability, not understanding, is all that that type of research requires or produces.

The 1971 campaign against cigarette smoking was centred on the idea that smoking was out of date, peculiarly associated with being middle-aged. It was a shrewdly calculated campaign. But I doubt whether its sponsors could point to any survey research that explains *why* it was likely to work. Yet Simmel argued that the force of the idea of fashion lies in the way it combines innovation with imitation. It permits individuals to distinguish themselves from others, not as isolated or eccentric individuals, but as members of an admired and safely-daring, fashion-leading group. In a society where people are already predisposed to identify themselves in terms of age, the association of the idea of fashion with that of youth could become a powerful source of real social change.

Political sociology gets a bit closer to explaining the social meaning of age than either demographic or market research have normally done. This is not so much as a result of the theoretical interests of political sociologists but rather because, for commercial polling agencies, age is a standard variable. A very high proportion of research in political sociology is carried out for academics by commercial polling agencies. So researchers found themselves confronted with large numbers of tabulations relating age to voting behaviour. The problem is what the tables mean.

To begin with, the tables were allowed to speak for themselves; and what they said was, for the most part, pretty trivial. In *How People Vote*, the authors, Benney, Pear and Gray (1956) found that age made little difference to interest in politics, though there did appear to be some truth in the old adage about being radical in youth and conservative in old age. Using a single age-break – 21–49 on the one side, 50 and over on the other – they found that in Britain, in all social classes, the old were measurably more likely to vote Conservative than the young.

The old adage still has wide currency in political research, as has the commonest explanation of it – that it is the biological and psychological process of ageing that itself produces the growing conservatism. Thus, in *The American Voter*, one of the best of the voting studies, Campbell et al. (1965) say: 'There is, furthermore, a substantial tendency for conservatism to increase with age, as we might expect on commonsense grounds.' Elsewhere, however, these same authors are properly sceptical about commonsense expectations. Studied more carefully, the data complicate the issue. There is, for example, the problem of the differential mortality rates of different social classes; the old are dispro-portionately middle class. The data begin to produce puzzles and contraditions which cannot be accepted at face value. There is the finding that the young are more likely to change party allegiance in any given election campaign than the old, and the finding that the older you are in electoral experience the more likely you are to have changed allegiance. To make sense of the data, the idea of the 'political generation' was invoked. Crucial here is not how old you are, but *when you were young*.

The classical version of this strategy was adopted by Berelson, et al. in their *Voting* (1954). They say: 'The younger generation raised in the New Deal era showed a high tendency to vote along the socio-economic class lines associated with the Roosevelt elections.' They develop this into an elaborate theory: 'A whole political generation may have been developing, for whom the socio-economic problems of their youth served as bases for permanent political norms – a semi-permanent generation that would later bulge the ranks of the Democrats in certain age groups. Presumably an age-generation can be transformed by political events and social conditions into a political generation . . . a generation that retains its allegiances and norms while succeeding generations are moving in another direction.'

This strikes me as a good explanation. But it is entirely unsupported by the survey research. The same line of explanation has, nevertheless, been developed in more recent studies – most conspicuously by Butler and Stokes in their *Political Change in Britain* (1969). This study reveals, I think, more clearly than any other single work just how far survey research can take us in understanding the social meaning and organisation of age; and where it almost necessarily breaks down.

The importance of the work of Butler and Stokes (not only for political sociology) is that the authors appreciate that the problem of generations lies in linking personal time (the life cycle) with social time (history). They suggest four ages in the life of political man. First, there is a time of infant innocence, devoid of meaningful political information, but in which a good deal of very salient emotional colouring for later political learning is absorbed from one's immediate family environment. Then, there is the period of childhood, adolescence and young adulthood, in which politics is first directly perceived, and in which relationships to politics are worked out in a way which is partly calculating, and partly shaped by the persuasive influences of close emotional attachments to family and friends. After this phase of relative plasticity and political experiment, there comes the phase of adult life proper, in which commitments harden and settle, and interest in politics tends to increase. Finally, in the phase of old age, political allegiances are typically strong though interest in politics, other than in issues specifically related to the situation of the elderly, declines.

All of this is well supported by a large body of research over and above that of Butler and Stokes themselves. It is the next step that is critical, and far less secure. They seize on the fact that the second phase of the political life-cycle is the one in which people are most susceptible to change, most capable of responding in new ways to events: most in the market, as it were, for a political identity. They then suggest that British history since 1880 reveals four great, and very distinct, phases of political history. People who were in the second phase of their political life-cycle during each of these distinct historical eras have, it is argued, developed distinctive patterns of orientation to politics, which have in important ways stayed with them ever since. This is not accompanied by any serious attempt to find evidence to support these authors' assumptions, justified though they may be. To pin down the social meaning of age we need both a different sort of evidence and, more importantly, a different sort of theory from that which is normally found in political sociology. One place where these do sometimes turn up is in the mass of sociological and psychological writing published since 1960 on 'the problem of youth', or more specifically, on 'youth and dissent'. Here the issue of generations as social structures and hence of the social significance of age is addressed much more directly.

What survey research offers us here is, in the first place, a number of seeming paradoxes. In industrial and industralising societies, age-stratification – that is, the distributions of power and inequality derived from and legitimated by differences in age – diminishes. At the same time generational conflict – that is, the appeal to age as a proper basis for social differentiation and for demands for equality – increases. Youth in particular becomes an ideological symbol and a categorising label of great force, for both old and young, in just those societies where the fact of being young is least likely to be treated as a sufficient and decisive determinant of a person's status or destiny. In societies where the movement from being a child to being an adult takes a single day and is marked by highly ritualised ceremonies of passage and recognition this phase of the life-cycle, the phase of transition, cannot become problematic in the way it is when the same passage is an unstructured, open-ended experiment lasting for an indeterminate number of years. The studies of protest tell us *both* that age data alone will not serve to identify the protest-prone *and* that those actively engaged in protest movements are concentrated in particular age categories. In particular there is some evidence that in industrialising societies they are likely, whatever their actual age, to feel themselves young (see Abrams on the conflict of generations, 1970).

In practice, what we are faced with is a situation of relative deprivation. Age stratification is diminished but not eliminated – the young are after all still 'treated like children'. And because age is increasingly discredited as a legitimate or effective basis of inequality – respecting your elders is less an automatic or absolute matter – those age-linked inequalities that remain are seen as a legitimate focus of discontent. Yet discontent is not voiced by whole age-categories but only by particular groups or groupings within age-categories that are experiencing some predicament of the category as a whole in a particularly acute way.

It is always youth-related-to-something-else that locates the sources of protest, not just youth in itself; age, plus family background, plus educational experience, plus race, plus class. We do not find many social phenomena which are universal to any given age category. But we find many phenomena for the occurrence of which membership of a particular category, for example, youth, is a necessary condition. In the case of youth, most of these are phenomena of change: cultural innovation, migration, revolution, fashion.

However, the picture is not totally obscure. One means of getting more informative data is the longitudinal, as opposed to the simple cross-sectional, survey. In *College Generations and their Politics*, Seymour Martin Lipset and Everett Carll Ladd showed how effective even approximation to this technique can be. Lipset and Ladd used a succession of single cross-sectional surveys to create a quasi-longitudinal study, in order to investigate the relationship between age and political attitudes over a 40-year period. They found that there has been a 'historical slope' towards the left in the attitudes of successive generations of college-educated Americans, but that this has been offset by what could be called a 'biographical slope' towards the right within the life-cycle of each particular generation. The *net* move to the left over the whole period, and for the foreseeable future, is thus much less than cross-sectional studies of the young on their own would suggest (Lipset and Ladd, 1971).

When we turn to longitudinal studies proper – to that body of research which, having selected a population on the basis of chronological age, then studies that population at frequent and regular intervals over long periods of time – we find a rich body of information. Some of the best of this work has been done in Britain, for example by the Medical Research Council team headed by J. W. Douglas, and in the National Child Development Study directed by Professor N. R. Butler. Though studies of this type use chronological age as an initial basis of sampling, their focus is not on age as such but on tracing sequences of development, and on establishing correlations between these sequences and a wide range of variables which are also treated longitudinally.

The pay-off in terms of firm data has already been enormous. Research of this kind gives us a means of isolating the significance of age, as distinct from, say, the phasing of experience in an individual's life. This is a very important distinction. The longitudinal studies cast doubt on the notion, derived from earlier clinical psychology, of *critical ages* in personality development. They substitute for it the much more flexible idea of an *optimal phasing* of processes of development.

This raises again the problem of self-definition. Many studies have shown that individuals may identify themselves as being 'of' a particular generation in ways which can be startlingly unrelated to their actual biological age. The most interesting versions of this are the people who manage to be 'young after their time' (the 40-year-old hippy). More familiar are people who are 'old before their time' – who seem to have been over-socialised into the roles and responsibilities of middle age, when most of their contemporaries are still sowing wild oats. The 'too old' self-definition seems to be especially common in people born to older parents. The 'too young' self-definition seems associated with an unfulfilled quest for satisfactory intimate personal relationships of the kind usually formed in late adolescence.

But the real research on this remains to be done. My own guess is that analysis of the phasing of critical personal experiences and critical historical events would give us the answer.

Demography and race: Some limitations and some distortions
by L. E. Stephenson

Introduction

Demography may be defined as the study of population statistics. These statistics include the total number of people and their characteristics such as age and sex distribution, rates of mortality and fertility and rates of migration. A knowledge of the characteristics of a population is essential to policy makers in terms of planning, such as providing resources for education.

At a superficial level, demography is quite an easy subject for the layman to grasp, in that, numbers can be counted and most of the factors involved are within the experience of the average person. The analysis of population statistics, on the other hand, is more difficult and is generally beyound the capacity of people without the necessary statistical training. With the required training, analysis of population statistics can be straightforward.

The most difficult aspect of demography is the attempt to explain the causes of change in population statistics over any given time period and the projection of population characteristics into the future. Population projections are invariably wrong for the simple reason that the factors governing the characteristics of a population do not remain constant over time and our understanding of these factors is very inadequate. This is the area where a lot of misplaced quantification and spurious precision is being made. Admittedly, demographers mention the assumptions on which their projections are made, but unfortunately, some of the people who use these statistics, politicians and the press in particular, tend to ignore the assumptions on which the projections are made.

This paper is about the limitations and distortions of population statistics concerning black people in the United Kingdom. The term 'black' includes people of Afro-Caribbean and Asian ethnic groups. The writer accepts the proposition that statistics are necessary for policy formulation. However, unrepresentative statistics used in policy-making may lead to a worse situation than that which the policy makers were trying to improve. The view that statistics about the black population in Britain are biased and unrepresentative will be presented in the rest of this paper. This view can best be developed by examining the path demographers follow in order to understand populations and the sources of their information.

The Demographer's Approach

The first step in demography is to understand the current situation in terms of four major features:

1 The size of the population
2 The age and sex distribution of the population
3 Fertility and mortality rates, i.e. birth and death statistics
4 The movement of the population in and out of the country, i.e. immigration and emigration

For the United Kingdom, information on these topics are obtained from the following sources:

1 The census
2 The Registrar General's Returns
3 General Household Survey of the Office of Population Censuses and Surveys
4 Home Office migration statistics

Other information on the black population is obtained from:

1 The Department of Education and Science statistics on the numbers of immigrant pupils
2 The Department of Employment count of unemployed people

The Census Material

The total size of the population of the United Kingdom can be estimated from the census, but it is extremely difficult to estimate the size of the *black* population from current census methods. The last full census was in 1971 and it did not collect any information directly concerned with the black population. All the information available is based on the individual's own birth place and the birthplace of his parents. Inferences about the black population can be drawn from the birthplace data but with varying and uncertain degrees of reliability. Many white people were born in India, Pakistan and the West Indies, and, from the census figures, it is very difficult to isolate such people who enter Britain from the black ones. One estimate from the census put the proportion of white immigrants from the 'New Commonwealth' at 25 per cent of the total in the age group above 15, and that a large proportion of the parents of that 25 per cent were born in the New Commonwealth countries. The situation becomes even more difficult to assess when it is realised that over 40 per cent of the 'people from the New Commonwealth' were born in this country and could be black or white. It is very difficult to separate the white children born to people from the New Commonwealth from white British children, and even more difficult to separate children born to black 'immigrants' from those born to white 'immigrants'. It follows that any figures about the total size of the black population should be looked on with considerable scepticism.

The above discussion should indicate the difficulty of using 'country of birth' or even the 'parents' country of birth' statistics to provide estimates of the size of the black population. Third generation black people are in fact included in the white population, the census provides no way of isolating them. The census method, of course, has serious implications for future censuses. Future censuses will be obliged, for the sake of consistency, to gather information on the birthplace of grandparents, then great grandparents, ad infinitum. These censuses will still not provide the necessary information on the size of the black population, the main concern of those requiring migration figures.

Other Sources of Information

Another source of information that deals with black people of school age is the Department of Education and Science statistics on the numbers of immigrant pupils. Since 1966, the D.E.S. has required schools to keep statistics of immigrant children, defined by the department as:

1 Children born outside the British Isles to parents whose countries of origin are abroad, and
2 Children born in the British Isles whose parents have lived in Britain for less than 10 years.

Like the 1971 census, the D.E.S. definition of immigrant pupils does not reveal the number of black school children. This, of course, is the least important objection. For what use are such statistics? What are the policy implications? The figures collected can be criticised on the following grounds:

1 The statistics will not show the number of black children in schools
2 They will not necessarily reflect the needs of immigrant pupils in schools
3 They will not distinguish between immigrants of many years residence in this country and those newly arrived unless details of arrivals were also available.
4 Children with no educational problems will not be distinguished from those who need special treatment.

The methods used to estimate the black population are very limited and the limitations have invariably led to distortions both about the total black population and about the black school population. Generally, the distortions show a much larger black population because of the association between 'black' and immigrant, black being used as synomymous to immigrant! Hence the 'immigrant' or 'black' school population includes white children from foreign countries or children whose parents were born in foreign countries as well as black and white 'New Commonwealth' children born abroad and in this country. Similarly, the total 'black' population includes white people born in the New Commonwealth and their children born in this country. Therefore, in the hands of the unsophisticated or unscrupulous, these figures can be very misleading.

Predicting the Future?

The discussion so far has been centred on the limitations of the methods used to estimate the current total black population and the black school population in the United Kingdom. Far more serious is the readiness to *estimate future changes* in the black population based on this inadequate information about past and present black population. It is in this area that the most serious distortions are made. In order to estimate the total black population of the United Kingdom, say for the year 2000, one would need a lot of information such as:

1 The total population at two given time periods, say 1960 and 1977
2 The rate of change of the population over that time period through:
a. Fertility
b. Mortality
c. Migration
3 The reasons for the rate of change of fertility, mortality and migration.

Information from these could be used to show the population trend between 1960 and 1977 and the trend line extrapolated to the year 2000 to give an estimated black population on the assumption that the factors which caused the change between those years would remain at the same rate. This is the crudest of methods for projecting future populations. The method could perhaps be refined by including, for example, possible changes in fertility. Fertility changes could be refined by discovering the number of women in the childbearing age range and determining their intentions concerning having children! Perhaps a refined mortality rate could be arrived at with the aid of medical records and fatal accidents records.

PROBLEMS WITH THE MIGRATION RATE

The rate of migration is influenced by too many economic and political variables to make sensible projection possible. These variables may themselves change over a given period of time. The main factor which encourages the movement of black people to Britain is economic – the same factor which encouraged millions of British people to migrate to the

Americas, Africa and Oceania. Black people came to Britain in order to improve their living standards. Over 80 per cent of adults from the New Commonwealth came in the 1950's and before 1968. This was a period when Britain had severe labour shortage and this produced bottlenecks in the economy. People from the New Commonwealth were positively encouraged to come to Britain to work. Workers from Asia and the West Indies were recruited in their home countries by leading British companies, by London Transport and other public sector employers.

The conditions of the 1950's and the 1960's, however, have changed and these have affected the flow of people from the New Commonwealth into Britain. The economic conditions in Britain have changed from one of labour shortage to one of labour surplus, even though there are still labour bottlenecks in certain sectors of the economy due to shortage of skills or to the attitude of the indigenous population to doing certain types of work. The changed economic fortunes of Britain, however, can only partly explain the reduction in the flow of black people to Britain. It seems that the main explanation of the reduction in black immigration to Britain is one of changed political attitudes to black people. Since the late 1960's the governments of the United Kingdom, both Labour and Conservative, have introduced laws which strictly control black immigration. Black people coming to Britain today are mainly United Kingdom citizens from East Africa and dependants of people already here. Even the flow of dependants is strictly controlled and applications are considered over a long time period before approval for entry is given.

Black people find it extremely difficult to get work permits today and those who do so are the well qualified. For example, in 1974 less than 2,000 people from the New Commonwealth received 12-month work permits compared with about 8,000 from non-E.E.C. countries. Some people will infer that the 2,000 immigrants from the New Commonwealth means that 2,000 blacks have entered the country. Others might imply that the total figure of 10,000 was due entirely to black immigration. The migration figures also tend to obscure the outflow of black people from the United Kingdom. For example, the emigration of West Indians from the United Kingdom seems to be greater than their immigration into the country. Figures for 1973 show that 2,000 people from the West Indies, mainly dependants, came to settle in Britain but over 4,000 went back to the West Indies in that year.

It seems very evident, therefore, that current or past migration flows cannot be used to predict or even help to estimate the number and characteristics of the future black population. In the first place, our knowledge of the current situation is very limited and imperfect and in the second place the factors which govern population movement may change. The economic situation in the black countries could improve alongside a decline in the economic fortunes of the United Kingdom; in which case black workers, particularly those with marketable skills, could be attracted away from Britain. On the other hand, Britain's economic performance could be improved to the extent that further growth can only be possible with more labour, some of which may have to be recruited from the New Commonwealth. The black population could therefore be lower or higher in the future.

PROBLEMS WITH THE FERTILITY RATE

A complete pattern of both fertility and mortality is required in order to assess fully the trend in the black population. This pattern is extremely complicated and therefore it has been simplified by using a simple measure. The best known is the *Net Reproduction Rate*. This rate is the average number of daughters who will be born to a girl who is now a baby, if current fertility and mortality rates remained unchanged. Under these conditions, the black population will exactly replace itself when the Net Reproduction Rate is 1·00. The Net Reproduction Rate is of no value if the assumptions on which it is based are ignored. One may even go further and suggest that the Net Reproduction Rate is meaningless because the factors on which it is based will not remain constant but will vary a great deal over time and that the rates of variation cannot be predicted.

It is currently the case that the fertility rate of the black population is greater than that of the white British population. However, is it greater than those of the Irish immigrants or immigrants from Europe and the Old Commonwealth? The fertility rates are higher among immigrants because generally they are of a younger age group than the indigenous population. This does not mean, as has often been implied, that the black population is having more babies at a constant or at an increasing rate. In 1970, for example, people from the New Commonwealth, including whites, had 46,000 babies compared with 39,000 in 1975. This was a fall of over 13 per cent in a five-year period amongst a relatively young population. It is reasonable to expect the fertility rate of the black population to fall as the population gets older.

The factors which govern fertility rates can vary from time to time. These factors are not fully understood. Some workers point to the correlation between fertility rates and the knowledge and availability of contraception and the availability of social activities outside the home, the levels of education and living standards. The general feeling is that, as conditions improve, fertility tends to fall. If this is true then one could expect a fall in the fertility of the black population. If the government is concerned about the future size of the black population, their policy should be to improve conditions for that population.

The conclusion, here, is that it is very difficult to predict the future of the black population based on current fertility rates, given the mortality and migration rates. The factors on which predictions are made may change. The Registrar General's projection of population growth usually states very carefully the assumption used, but generally, the figures are used without referring to these assumptions.

Summary

Official statistics on the black population of Britain are limited in many respects:

1 They are limited as far as the total is concerned. It is very difficult to isolate the white fraction of the immigrant population from the New Commonwealth.
2 They are limited as far as births are concerned. Many of the births attributed to the black population are births to white people from the New Commonwealth.
3 They are limited as far as projections are concerned. Current assumptions of fertility and migration are unlikely to hold in the future.
4 They are limited in so far as they treat the black population as a homogeneous group. For example, although the birth rate for the black population is higher than that for whites, that for West Indians is similar to that for whites.

The study of population is a very interesting discipline which combines the skills of many other disciplines such as statistics, sociology and geography. A knowledge of the total population and its characteristics are vitally important for policy formulations. It seems, however, that there is no official policy concerning the black population but one of immigration control; in reality this is, black immigration control. Figures concerning the total black population have no policy implication and this may account for the general weakness in their collection. The same can be said about the figures collected by the Department of Education and Science. To allay fears and improve race relations, it is necessary to improve the demographic material about race. The current limitations and distortions need to be understood, and the difficult task of removing them attempted.

PART THREE: SOME 'NEW' THEMES

Introduction

In part three of the volume we intend to illustrate some of the more recent developments in sociology. In sociology, as in many activities, there are fashions, and it would be proper to refer to some of the areas we have chosen as areas of revived interest rather than supposing that they are entirely new. In any event they are selected from areas of sociological research which have made considerable advances in the recent past. There are five sections each containing an overview of a particular specialism and then a piece which is representative of, at any rate, some tendencies within the field. It is by no means an exhaustive list. We could, for example, have examined the growing interest in the sociology of sport but have, of necessity, been obliged to limit the areas chosen. They are all provoking considerable interest in tertiary education (and often elsewhere) but as yet are relatively neglected in secondary and further education. In part this section is an attempt to encourage teaching in these areas in schools and colleges.

Dennis O'Keeffe's paper on the sociology of development and the accompanying extract from Foster are an attempt to explore the complexities of the gross international inequalities of wealth. This is clearly a complex issue and requires a knowledge at least of economics in addition to sociology. Like much else in social thought in the West, yesterday's assumptions are being challenged and considerable confusion and disarray are demonstrated in the literature. Foster's piece challenges one of the most sacred of the development cows, the supposed utility of technical education provision. The import of Foster's article may well have been underestimated in Britain in the period following the 'great debate'.

David Lyne examines the social significance of age. In particular he explores the possibility of serious schism in society between different age sets. A point which emerges here is the socially constructed nature of age groups. The particular significance of this and other factors with respect to 'old age' is pursued in the essay by Laslett.

Christopher Cook tackles the fundamental issues raised by the sociology of knowledge. There is a long tradition and a recent revival within sociology of examining the social roots of what counts as knowledge and how such knowledge is distributed between and within societies. The accompanying piece by Bernstein, though not directly representative of a 'new sociology of knowledge', nonetheless applies several concepts derived from the perspective of the sociology of knowledge in the analysis of that socially significant branch of sociology concerned with education. For better or worse, that has clearly had social policy implications in Britain and elsewhere.

Roger Gomm's description of the sociology of medicine is timely in view of the interest shown by British sociologists in this area, an interest which was, no doubt, stimulated by the British Sociological Association's annual conference on that theme in Manchester in 1976. The B.S.A.'s largest study group is devoted to this sub-discipline and the tendency of British sociology increasingly to have an applied flavour is demonstrated here. This does not mean, as Roger Gomm shows, that sociologists working in the field are wholly or even primarily concerned with solving administrators' problems. The accompanying piece, by Howlett and Ashley, maps some aspects of the inequality of health provision, as provided by the N.H.S., in Britain. Such issues are at the forefront of much debate in medical and political circles in the late 1970's.

Finally, Tony Marks' paper attempts to describe the substantial growth in interest, by sociologists and others, in the social construction and distribution of gender roles. In large part promoted by the 'Women's Movements' in many societies, a new substantive area of enquiry is now established in many Universities and Polytechnics. It may well be that the B.S.A. conference in Aberdeen in 1974 has again provided a stimulus in developing this new interest. Certainly the volumes deriving from that conference have proved influential (Barker and Allen, 1976). Pauline Marks' essay shows how varying conceptions of femininity affect, among other things, the type of educational careers pursued by girls. In particular the unstated, taken-for-granted assumptions about the nature of the two sexes is seen as highly significant for educational outcomes.

None of our authors would claim that sociologists have a monopoly of truth and even less wisdom on these or other problems raised in this volume. We are all, nevertheless committed to the view that apparently biological categories such as age and sex have as *part* of the truth about them a sociological perspective, and that even truth itself is not the asocial phenomenon which some would have us believe.

I DEVELOPMENT

Some Problems in Development
by Dennis J. O'Keeffe
Polytechnic of North London

What is Development?

'Development' is not easy to define. However, the use of the term in sociology implies social change and growth towards higher forms of organisation. It is important to note immediately the co-existence of positive and normative elements in such a concept. Positive statements are those relating to facts (at least in intention). Normative statements are those relating to values, for example to moral preferences. 'Development' has a built-in normative element, in that it seems to imply desirable as well as factual change. (However, 'normative' in this sense is not to be confused with the sociological term 'norm' which means an expected pattern of behaviour.)

Like many terms in social science, 'development' is borrowed from other sciences, in this case biology. Just as biology studies the maturation and evolution of plants and animals, so social development theory studies the evolution of society. However, sociologists differ widely as to the scientific significance of the concept 'development'. Some authorities believe that there are 'laws' of social development which can be scientifically stated, historical paths which can be charted and predicted. The extreme version of this is that human history is a meaningful process whereby man struggles towards higher, better forms of social life (Marx, K. and Engels, F., 1971). On such a view the possibility, even the inevitability, of higher social forms is contained in previous social forms. The history of progress can be traced through the theoretical scheme devised by Karl Marx, which explains the main factors in man's social development in a comprehensive and scientific way.

The contrary position does not deny the possibility of progress, so much as the possibility of explaining it successfully through a grand theoretical scheme. On this view, history involves a considerable, even a dominating, element of unforeseeable events. This means that the future cannot accurately be predicted in a systematic way. Neither can past events fully be explained. The implication of this is that sociologists and historians can never hope for more than partial theories of development (Aron, R., 1967, pp. 197–202).

There is no disagreement that social change occurs, that societies do alter – sometimes dramatically – and that the process is uneven. A huge social and economic, as well as cultural, gap exists, for instance, between the inhabitants of those cities and the members of stone-age New Guinea tribes. The sociological controversy concerns the processes involved in these differences.

TWO MEANINGS OF DEVELOPMENT

'Development' has two main sociological uses. First it may refer to the development of a society within a certain overall institutional form. For example, one might examine the development of a feudal society, or of British capitalist society in the nineteenth century, or of Indian society since independence. Here the main features of the society being examined remain largely intact, 'development' implying the enlargement, diminution or constancy of those features. For example, in nineteenth-century Britain, much development throughout the century involved the expansion or contraction of features, the tendencies of which were present, in outline, at the beginning. Two good examples are (a) the expanding power of the industrial capitalist class (the factory owners) and (b) the declining influence of the aristocracy.

The second, more dramatic, use of development, is to describe a society changing from one major form to another, for example an agrarian society in the process of becoming an industrial one, as happened in Japan in the twentieth century. Naturally it is at times difficult to distinguish this overall change from the less dramatic one. Small-scale changes can accelerate and become far-reaching in their effects. An example in modern industrial society would be the gradual extension of state power over social and economic life.

Economists sometimes distinguish development from 'progress'. Development merely implies change towards new social and economic forms. Progress implies actual increases in average living standards. It is pointed out that at times of rapid development living standards may actually fall, as was perhaps the case in early nineteenth-century Britain (Ashton, T. S., 1954) or perhaps in India since her independence in 1947, considerable development having been partially swamped by population growth.

There is no universal agreement, either positively or normatively, about development. That is to say that social scientists do not agree on how it occurs or on what form of development is morally desirable. Development is nevertheless a central topic among sociologists. How different sociologists view development depends on how they differ about understanding society generally. Particularly important is the issue of identification. What is the character of the societies we analyse? What are the key characteristics of advanced 'western' societies? Must all other societies pass through a stage similar to the present western one? What sort of further social development are western societies likely to undergo?

There is not even an elementary consensus on these questions. It is variously claimed that advanced western society is, or is not, capitalist (based on an economy dominated by a profit-seeking capitalist, or 'bourgeois', class) and that pre-industrial societies must, or need not, pass through a capitalist stage before they can achieve socialism. The greatest difficulty again is that 'capitalism' and 'socialism' are terms combining positive and normative features. It is often not clear when they are used whether neutral description, or moral approval or disapproval, is intended.

We cannot pursue these issues of identification very far here. Suffice it to say that, in the case of capitalism, the question is whether the continued existence of considerable private ownership of the means of industrial production is sufficient to justify calling a society 'capitalist', whereas in the case of socialism the essential issue is whether the term merely implies the central control of most economic life by the state, or whether it is a rallying cry for those who wish to end human injustice and exploitation. Socialism in the first sense now obtains in a third of the world, and has been influential everywhere. In this positive sense the fascist societies of the first half of the twentieth century were partly socialist also. However, if one insists on a moral notion of socialism, then arguably there is not, nor ever has been, a socialist society anywhere. The importance of identifying what we are discussing is clear. If we do not properly conceptualise the societies we examine, we are not likely to trace their past development very realistically, nor to establish very convincingly what shape their future development is likely to take.

The Process of Development

Despite all these difficulties we can outline some fundamentals of agreement. First it seems clear that once, perhaps 10,000 years ago, all human beings lived in societies somewhat similar to those stone-age cultures which survive in remote parts of the world. Such societies, like their present-day counterparts, had a primitive hunting and food-gathering economy, and a relatively simple social structure. (This is not to deny of course that *all* social life is immensely complex.)

Today even non-industrial societies tend to have economies and social structures which are complex by such stone-age standards, and an increasing proportion of societies are urban and industrial in character. It is evident then that considerable 'development' has taken and is taking place. What is the basis, historically, for such development?

TWO CRUCIAL TECHNOLOGICAL DEVELOPMENTS

Few writers would dispute that technological change is indispensable to development, though precisely how it is initiated must remain problematic. Certainly we can distinguish two great technological developments around which social and economic development materialised, two fundamental discontinuities in human history. The earlier was in relation to man's food supplies and can perhaps itself be divided into two. First, there was the development of pastoral farming, when men learned to flock sheep, and herd cows and horses. This permitted a considerable increase in the possible size of populations, through provision of meat, milk and clothing. Secondly, came the discovery of agrarian or crop farming. This permitted larger, but also sedentary, populations. In combination, these two technological innovations permitted the emergence of the earliest human 'civilisation' in the lands of the fertile crescent in the fourth millennium B.C.[1] Such societies also learned the use of the wheel and the mounted horse, and invented writing. These, however, are not indispensable to agrarian society. Inca society, in Peru, which flourished, roughly, in our late middle ages, was illiterate, ignorant of the wheel, and had no pack of animals save the llama, which cannot be ridden. Inca society nevertheless achieved a sophisticated agrarian economy. It is for *industrial* society that the wheel and literacy appear to be essential conditions.

Both aspects of the farming revolution permitted larger populations. They also generated more complex social structures, permitting the emergence of social class divisions, that is of social ranking in relationship to the ownership or control of the dominant means of production. The pastoral revolution allowed the emergence of class through one social group coming to control the herds; the agrarian breakthrough allowed a class of landowners (or controllers) to dominate society. The latter form has been especially important historically. Most societies in recorded history have been agrarian. Agrarian production has been the basis of the slave societies of antiquity and of pre-Columbian America, of feudal society in Europe, of tribal society in Africa, and of the 'oriental despotic' societies which some allege survive in Asia. Even today a majority of societies are predominantly agrarian.

The second great technological change began in Britain in the latter half of the eighteenth century. This involved the replacement of agricultural production as the central social and economic activity, by machine-based production, in workshops and factories, of a whole new range of goods. The general name given to the process whereby this development occurs, is 'industrialisation', whilst the type of society and economy which the process brings about is called 'industrialism'. Industrialism is associated with enormously increased control by men over their natural environment. Very many social and economic changes are involved. What follows is a brief summary of these.

First industrialism brings a huge increase in the output of the economy. This connects with a second change, namely a dramatic rise, at least eventually, in living standards. Third, industrialism has been associated with a rapid increase in urbanisation and the numbers of people working in non-agrarian employment. Fourth, industrialism greatly increases the

---

[1] The earliest known city, in the vicinity of Jericho, is some 10,000 years old. This implies that the genesis of the agrarian technology we are discussing goes back far beyond the fourth millennium. Nevertheless, it was in that period, in the countries we now call Iraq and Egypt, that these discoveries first blossomed fully.

complexity of social and economic life. Occupations become more specialised, and specialised institutions such as health and education systems develop, along with a much larger and more specialised system of government. Fifth, industrial strata such as the bourgeoisie (capitalists), the middle classes (managers and professionals) and the proletariat (industrial working class) become more significant, whilst agrarian strata such as the aristocracy and the peasants (small landowners) become less important.

We need to qualify the above statements. In modern economies agriculture is itself an industrialised activity, and since development is an uneven process, it is possible for a class of peasant farmers to survive in an industrial society (for example in France). Furthermore, an advanced economy can be mainly agrarian (for example, Denmark and New Zealand). In this last case, however, it is perhaps best to regard the society as having an industrialised agrarian economy.

Perhaps the two most important points to note are these. First that industrialism has two main forms, which may be called the 'western' and the 'socialist'. In the former (countries like Britain and the U.S.A.) considerable private ownership (capitalism) continues. In the latter (for example in U.S.S.R. and Czechoslovakia) capitalism has mainly been eradicated. Secondly, industrialism is an expansionist phenomenon, that is, one which tends to spread. In the nineteenth century, industrialism was confined mainly to north-western and west central Europe and the U.S.A. In the twentieth century it has spread more widely and embraced Russia, Japan and Spain among many others. At present certain other societies appear to be industrialising rapidly, including Brazil, Iran, Hong Kong, East Germany and some other East European countries.

This brief discussion of the process of development has been necessarily descriptive, because no generally agreed theoretical account of the process exists, though Marx, Weber, Durkheim, Gershenkron and Rostow are among a host of writers who have contributed. However, the Marxist version has been the most influential, and there follows an elementary exposition of it.

Early man lived under simple communism. Hunting tools were held in common. When agriculture developed, social classes appeared, as men divided into the minority who owned land and the majority who merely worked it. However, from the sixteenth century in Western Europe agrarian society was increasingly and often violently replaced by industrial society. The capitalists replaced the agrarian rich as a dominant class and the industrial working-class replaced peasants and serfs as the principal exploited class. The future, however, holds out the promise of a return to communism, this time an industrial communism, when the workers will overthrow the capitalists. The working-class are the last historic class.

It is fair to say that most western sociologists and the overwhelming majority of historians and economists rejected this theory. This brief account has been included simply because the theory has been so much more influential than any other.

Development and Government

Social scientists are distressingly ignorant and divided on the relationship between social development and forms of government. There has been a tendency to attribute a secondary status to the machinery of government, seeing this as an adjunct to economic and social life. This view has been influential both within and without the Marxist tradition (for a Marxist view, see Miliband, R., 1969). It has been claimed in particular that the underlying similarity in socio-economic problems has induced a 'convergence' between societies like the U.S.A. and U.S.S.R. at the governmental and administrative level (Kerr, C., 1962). Against this may be advanced the view that socialist societies tend to be very alike governmentally, however different their socio-economic development. Thus, while the U.S.S.R. and China are at very different social developmental stages, they have systems of government which more closely resemble each other than that of any western industrial society.

Empirically it is worth pointing out that most societies, whether industrial or not, have a one-party form of government. This is especially true of non-industrial societies. However, one very large under-developed society, namely India, has a multi-party parliamentary system, recently suppressed, but now apparently revived. The truth may be that there is no determinate relationship between social and economic developmental stages and the form of government which obtains. Max Weber, indeed, argued that such relationships are never more than probable. (For a discussion of this see Aron, R., pp. 204 f.) If we applied Weber's notion to, for example, late twentieth century non-industrial societies, we would predict that probably such societies would be one-party states. We would also, however, admit that India is an important exception.

Finally, we should note that there is great disagreement about the nature and worth of different types of government, and how these connect with development. Rather vague notions like 'freedom' are passionately and exclusively associated with 'capitalism' as opposed to 'socialism' and vice-versa. The reader is advised to tread warily in this contentious area.

Contemporary Developmental Relations Between Countries

It is usual to distinguish three broad stages in international variations in development. These are the 'First World' which includes the advanced societies like U.S.A., Japan and Britain which have highly complex and at least partially capitalist economies; the 'Second (or communist) World', itself spanning wide variations in development; and the countries of the 'Third World' in Africa, Asia and Latin America. These last are also very different in character, and have different problems. Some are rich in resources and have relatively small populations, for example, Brazil. Others have huge populations, such that their main problem may in fact be demographic, such as India.

Variations in the Third World are in fact so considerable that some scholars now identify a 'Fourth World' – countries which are particularly backward or stagnating such as Jordan or Thailand or Haiti. However, one is faced with a choice between manageability and accuracy. Either our classification will be neat, and lose accuracy, or it will be accurate and become unwieldy. What needs to be remembered is that our three or four categories are very general, and one could wrangle for hours over the location of many countries within this typology. Certainly there is no agreed account of social developmental stages, nor of the inter-relations between countries at different stages. There is no agreement as to how Britain, France and the U.S.A. attained their present level of development, nor how they presently relate to countries at earlier developmental stages.

Despite the popularity of Marxism, there is little disagreement outside the communist world that Marx's famous prediction that the advanced societies would be transformed by revolutionary socialism has been invalidated. The communist revolutions have actually occurred in backward societies like Russia, China and Cuba. Such considerations have in recent years given birth to a revised body of Marxist theory which is usually called 'neo-marxism' (Foster-Carter, A., 1974). This body of theory now occupies the centre of one half of the contemporary debate on development. We will now therefore outline what neo-marxism has to say about development, and what positions are espoused by its opponents.

TWO VIEWS OF UNDER-DEVELOPMENT

For neo-marxists, 'under-development' is a specific condition not arising in the spontaneous history of a society but fastened on it by external forces. The general claim is that the advanced capitalist world grew rich in the past through the exploitation of weaker nations, often under conditions of direct imperialism in the eighteenth and nineteenth centuries. This direct imperialism has been replaced in the twentieth century by 'neo-colonialism', where nominal independence in Africa, Asia, and Latin America has been subverted by informal exploitation. Eric Hobsbawm has indeed claimed that informal empire was already widespread in the nineteenth century (Hobsbawm, E., 1968).

Under neo-colonialism the essential economic relations of First and Third World countries remain unchanged. Patterns of trade, of foreign investments and aid (low interest loans and hand-outs) constitute a framework which under-develops the societies caught within it. Their elites are attached to imperial interests, their raw material and food are sold at ruinously low prices, their capital resources – desperately needed for local investment – are sucked into the advanced capital markets of New York, London and Zurich, and their skilled labour attracted away into foreign employment. Their economic development is accordingly retarded. The most famous name associated with these views is that of A. G. Frank (Frank, A. G., 1970). For Frank, the poor world suffers from a vast organisation of exploitation, reaching from the mines and plantations of poor countries, through the modern sectors of those countries, and then to the overseas metropolitan beneficiaries of this system of profit extraction.

Against this position may be advanced a rather loose cluster of views, the central claim of which runs as follows. The wealth of the advanced countries comes from their production and their trade, not from their exploitation of others. The rich countries predominantly invest amongst themselves: the U.S.A. in countries like France and Japan, for example. It is similar in the case of trade. The problem of the less developed countries is not one of too many trade and investment links with the rich world but rather of too few. Economic history is littered with countries whose development involved heavy dependence on economic links with more developed societies, for example the link between the U.S.A. and Britain in the nineteenth century, or France and the U.S.A. since the Second World War. Neither is it in the interests of the advanced world to stifle development in other societies. On the contrary, development provides expanding markets and tends to dampen the enthusiasm for socialism as a developmental alternative. Furthermore, the example of France which has received huge American investment and yet often pursued anti-American foreign policies, shows that heavy investment does not automatically confer power on the lender, a case rendered even stronger by the recent heavy lending by western economies in the communist world (Smith, R., 1976).

It will by now have been realised that in every respect the nature and history of development are controversial. A parallel controversy, or intellectual confusion, obtains in the debate on policies for development, as we shall see in our last section.

Strategies for Development

Here the existence of disagreement has serious consequences. Various beliefs get institutionalised in official international agencies like the United Nations, the World Bank and the International Monetary Fund. However, most authorities believe in development, though they disagree as to what development is. Only President Nyerere of Tanzania has formally repudiated 'western' affluence as a legitimate developmental goal, though it seems likely that many socialist governments have no desire for it.

There is a degree of consensus that in many societies social changes are needed for the greater personal emancipation and welfare of their citizens. The general name for these social changes is 'development'. Official international strategies for this have, however, changed with alarming rapidity. The most usual approach in the last three decades has been to compare developed with less developed societies, and, having isolated the differences, seen as 'deficiencies' in the less developed countries, to pursue policies for overcoming these deficiencies.

For years the notion of a 'vicious circle of poverty' was institutionalised, and most official policies were designed to break this vicious circle. The vicious circle involved low incomes, leading to low savings, leading to low investment, leading to low production, leading to low incomes in a never-ending chain. The notion has been powerfully challenged by some writers, who point to Japan, Spain and many other societies which have successfully industrialised in the twentieth century. However, until recently the vicious circle was the official wisdom (Bauer, P., 1971).

At first, in the 1950's, the emphasis was on industrialisation. The less developed countries were not industrial. They should therefore pursue policies for rapid industrialisation, involving centralised planning, foreign capital injections, and the rapid transfer of resources from agriculture to industry. Such policies were to be combined frequently with the nationalisation of foreign owned assets and the direction of labour on a huge scale. Gradually, however, the failure of this strategy became apparent, as countries like India and Egypt, for example, were not industrialising as rapidly as desired.

A two-fold shift in policies therefore took place in the 1960's. First, the emphasis gradually shifted away from physical capital to human resources (human capital) as scholars became increasingly concerned with the differences in the labour markets of First and Third World countries, such that developmental aid began increasingly to take the form of help and advice in establishing education systems in less developed countries. Simultaneously, however, there was a shift of policy away from the promotion of industry to that of agriculture. Less developed societies were agrarian, it was argued. It was therefore their agricultural development that needed to be pursued. Eventually these two changes coalesced in the policies advocated by writers like Thomas Balogh, in which agrarian-based education was the key-note. The outcomes of all these interventions are today before us. Plans for industrialisation have not usually been fruitful in India or Africa, many Third and Fourth World countries have costly educational and medical systems which nevertheless reach very few of their citizens, and the evidence seems to be that one cannot galvanise agriculture into greater productivity through manipulating the school curriculum (see Foster, P., 1967). Finally, in many cases foreign loans and investment do not seem to trigger off any process of further development.

There is disagreement as to what is happening. Some less developed societies appear to be modernising rapidly, for example, Venezuela, Mexico, Brazil, Iran, Hong Kong, South Korea, Singapore and some of the communist societies. Even India appears to have improved her economic performance in the last two years. In this development, trade may be the modernising dynamic. However, there is indisputably vast poverty and misery in many parts of the world, the continent of Africa being a particularly striking case, since many countries there seem to be retrogressing developmentally.

Clearly, the international developmental strategies cannot be shown to be a significant factor in promoting such changes as are taking place, and in many instances appear misguided. For this reason the neo-marxists advocate the totally different policy of developing countries breaking their major links with the advanced world and by discipline and united effort, raising their national consciousness, and developing from their own resources. Frugality is the price of independence. Poor countries must go it alone. This is the path chosen successfully by Russia (until recently), China, North Korea, Cuba, Vietnam and now Angola. Russia is an exception to this list now because, in company with some of the developmentally most successful communist economies such as East Germany, she has now run up enormous debts in the west.

Conclusion

The reader will have grasped how astonishing the degree of intellectual disagreement is in this area. This has been but a brief guide to an enormous literature. The author hopes his own views have not intruded, and advises the student to tread warily in this confusing but fascinating debate. Clearly, social scientists are disunited as to what development is, what kind of development is desirable and how development is best to be achieved.

The Vocational School Fallacy in Development Planning
by P. J. Foster

In current controversies regarding the relationship between the provision of formal education and the economic growth of underdeveloped areas, few issues have been debated with more vehemence than the question of the desirability of providing technical, vocational, and agricultural instruction within the schools. So far as Africa is concerned, the controversy has been sharpened by the publication of a series of observations by the British economist, Thomas Balogh, on the conclusions of the 1961 Conference of African Ministers of Education at Addis Ababa.[1]

[1] UNESCO, United National Economic Commission for Africa, *Conference of African States on the development of education in Africa*, UNESCO/ED/181, Addis Ababa, 1961. Balogh's observations are to be found in 'Catastrophe in Africa', *Times Educational Supplement*, 5 January 1962, p. 8; and 9 February 1962, p. 241. Also in 'What schools for Africa?', *New Statesman and Nation*, 23 March 1962, p. 412.

Briefly put, Balogh's views may be stated in the following manner: Since between 80 and 95 per cent of Africans are dependent upon agriculture, the essential need in African education is the development of large-scale technical and agricultural programmes within the schools at all levels: 'The school must provide the nucleus of modern agriculture within the villages' and play a central role in the general raising of standards of living within the subsistence sector. Present educational facilities constitute an obstacle to rural progress because people are not trained for agriculture, and academic systems of formal education are the chief determinant of attitudes hostile to the practice of rural agriculture. Schools are regarded as primarily responsible for the flight from the rural areas to the towns. Balogh's views, stated in perhaps more measured terms, are paralleled in a recent United Nations publication in which it is observed that one of the chief educational priorities in economically developing areas is 'the creation of a fully integrated system of agricultural education within the general framework of technical and vocational education'.[1]

Although only two examples of this trend of thought are given here, it is possible to indicate numerous current publications dealing with education and economic development that accord high priority to schemes for agricultural, vocational, and technical education as against the provision of substantially more 'academic' types of instruction. In the following pages I hope to show that these views are generally fallacious and ignore a series of crucial variables that must be taken into account if any realistic proposals for stimulating economic growth are to emerge. In developing the discussion I shall use examples from Ghana, which is not altogether unique among African territories in spite of the relatively high level of *per capita* income that it enjoys.

It should be said at the outset that there is no disagreement with two of Balogh's contentions. First, it seems clear that agricultural development and a rapid rise in rural incomes must definitely be accorded priority in all development schemes. Apart from the probability that such growth must precede even limited industrial development, there is the immediate question of raising the bare subsistence basis upon which many African cultivators are obliged to exist. Second, it is likely that such programmes must depend in part upon the provision of technical and agricultural education as a necessary but by no means sufficient condition of growth.

However, in spite of vague general agreement of the desirability of such programmes, there is a virtual absence of explicit data regarding their nature. For example, what would be an educational scheme adjusted to developmental needs look like? What role would the schools themselves

---

[1] United Nations Committee on Information from Non-Self-Governing Territories, *Special study on educational conditions in non-self-governing territories*, New York, 1960, p. 8.

play in such a programme? At what stage in formal education should specifically vocational subjects be begun, and how would technical and agricultural schools be integrated with the general system? Then there is the problem of the content of studies; frequently vocational curricula are ill-designed to serve the needs of developing economies. Agreeing on the need for agricultural development does not lead us directly to any particular specifications for educational content or organisation. Even assuming that well-validated prescriptions existed, it is equally apparent that these would vary considerably with the degree of effective centralised control exerted by governments. This latter factor seems to be rarely considered by educational planners, yet it is probably the single most crucial variable in determining the effectiveness of an agricultural or a technical programme.

Having entered these caveats, our major disagreement with Balogh lies in the 'strategy' that he proposes and the degree to which he places reliance upon *formal* educational institutions in instituting change. Secondly, Balogh tends to view vocational and general education as substitutes for each other rather than to see them as essentially complementary and hardly substitutable.

There is, perhaps, a general tendency to accord to the schools a 'central' position in strategies designed to facilitate economic development. To some extent this reflects an appreciation of the relative lack of alternative institutions that can be utilised, but it stems partially from the notion that schools are particularly manipulable institutions. It is widely believed that schools can readily be modified to meet new economic needs and, more particularly, to accord with the intentions of social and economic planners. I shall argue, on the contrary, that schools are remarkably clumsy instruments for inducing prompt large-scale changes in underdeveloped areas. To be sure, formal education has had immense impact in Africa, but its consequences have rarely been those anticipated, and the schools have not often functioned in the manner intended by educational planners.

I. The Colonial Experience in Ghana

If there is anything surprising in Balogh's views it lies not in their originality but in the degree to which they reproduce with virtually no modification a series of arguments that were first stated in equally cogent fashion by the Education Committee of the Privy Council in 1847.[1] So far as Ghana, in particular, is concerned, the viewpoint was forcefully advanced in the Appendix to the Report of the Commission on the West Coast of Africa in 1842 and by a succession of colonial governors and educators thereafter.[2] Indeed, stress on the provision of vocational and

[1] The text of this early document is to be found in H. S. Scott, 'The development of the education of the African in relation to Western contact', *The Yearbook of Education*, Evans Bros., 1938, pp. 693–739.
[2] There is considerable literature on this point but a few major examples may

agricultural education was included *without exception* in every major document related to educational development in the Gold Coast up till the grant of independence in 1957.

In spite of this, by 1959 the structure of the Ghanaian educational system was essentially that prevailing in most of British Africa: an expanding base of primary- and middle-school education of a predominantly academic variety capped by a group of highly selective grammar schools and a university college modelled closely upon British prototypes.[1] In that year only about 1 per cent of all persons enrolled in formal educational institutions were receiving instruction in vocational, technical, or agricultural subjects. The paradox in Ghanaian education has been the emphasis placed on vocational and agricultural training in all documentary sources and the relative absence of it within the actual system of education.[2]

A priori, it might be suspected that no serious attempt was ever made to implement schemes for agricultural and vocational training in the schools or that such proposals remained stillborn as the result of disinterest in them by the colonial rulers. In the case of Ghana this argument can be totally dismissed. There is ample documentary evidence throughout the latter half of the nineteenth century and the early twentieth that strenuous efforts were being made by both government and missions to establish agricultural schools, devise special agricultural curricula, and provide technical and vocational education. The development of academic secondary schools upon the British model was regarded with disfavour, as being inappropriate for the economic needs of the Gold Coast. Agricultural education was regarded as the key to economic development in that area. Particularly in the case of the activities of the Basel Mission, a system of schools based on agricultural and technical education was attempted which was probably unrivalled in

---

be cited. See the report of the Commissioner in the Appendix to the 'Report of the Committee on the West Coast of Africa', *Parliamentary Papers*, vol. 11, 1852. Also Gold Coast, *Report of the Committee of Educationalists*, Accra, Government Printer, 1920; Jesse Jones, *Education in Africa: A Study of West, South and Equatorial Africa by the African Education Commission*, New York, Phelps Stokes Fund, 1922; Gold Coast, *Report of the Education Committee*, 1937–41, Accra, Government Printer, 1942. This list cannot present numerous additional statements of this nature and there should be no need to refer the reader to the famous policy statements of the Advisory Committee on Education in the Colonies.

[1] Ghana, Statistical Reports Series I, No. 6, *Education Statistics 1959*, Accra: Office of the Government Statistician, 1959.

[2] The Ghanaian Ministry of Education, like most African Ministries, does not include in its reports technical and vocational training being undertaken in special schools connected with Railways and Harbours, the Public Works Department, etc.

any other territory in Africa.[1] Yet all of these earlier experiments were unsuccessful, and the educational history of the Gold Coast is strewn with the wreckage of schemes corresponding to Balogh's proposals.

In practice, the demand by Africa for western education was and is predominantly oriented toward the provision of more academic-type schools. This preference springs, I contend, from a remarkably realistic appraisal of occupational opportunities generated within the exchange sector of the economy as a result of European overrule. So far as the clientele of the schools was concerned, the primary function of formal education was to enable individuals to move from subsistence activities to occupations within the European-dominated sector. An examination of opportunities within that sector throughout the colonial period reveals that *relatively* there was a greater demand for clerical and commercial employees than for technically trained individuals. Opportunities certainly existed in technical fields and in agriculture, but they were inferior to the other alternatives. Access to most of the highly paid occupations was, therefore, achieved through academic type institutions. Those who criticise the 'irrational' nature of African demand for 'academic' as opposed to 'vocational' education fail to recognise that the strength of academic education has lain precisely in the fact that it is pre-eminently a *vocational* education providing access to those occupations with the most prestige and, most important, the highest pay within the Ghanaian economy. The financial rewards and the employment opportunities for technically trained individuals were never commensurate with opportunities in the clerical field. Since the graduates of the academic school were manifestly more advantageously placed,[2] the pressure for 'academic' education reflected fairly accurately the demands for alternative types of skill within the exchange sector of the economy. One of the major ironies of the situation is that while proponents of technical education were criticising the neglect of technical provision in the schools, the products of such technical institutions as existed were often experiencing difficulties in obtaining employment. Frequently those persons entered occupations unrelated to the training they had undergone.[3]

This form of 'wastage' among trained manpower is endemic in underdeveloped countries.

1. Initially, trained individuals may be produced for whom there is no actual demand so far as the market is concerned. There may be a considerable 'surplus' of these trained men where 'new nations', in their

[1] For a succinct account of the activities of the Basel Mission, see W. J. Rottman, 'The educational work of the Basel Mission', Appendix A.I to *Special reports on educational subjects*, vol. 13, part 2, H.M.S.O., 1905, pp. 307–18.

[2] See also I. M. Wallerstein, *The emergence of two West African nations: Ghana and the Ivory Coast*, Columbia University Press, 1959, p. 241.

[3] See Gold Coast, *Report of the Education Department*, 1935, para. 332; also Gold Coast, *Legislative Council Debates*, 1933, pp. 5, 94; and 1935, p. 5.

desire to emulate more economically developed areas, invest considerable sums in the training of technicians before they can be utilised in the
existing economy.

2. Second, a real demand may exist for trained personnel, but at the
same time scarce personnel are not utilised and skilled workers are
involved in tasks not directly relevant to their professional accomplishments. This would appear to occur more commonly in government
services.

3. Third, skilled personnel may not enter the type of job for which they
have been trained because opportunities seem so much greater in
alternative occupations. Thus, for example, many graduates of the Basel
Mission schools who received agricultural and industrial training entered
clerical employment. Here the most saleable component of their
education experience was literacy, not trade training, and the former was
thus utilised in the job market.[1] Wastage of skills must always be
considered in assessing programmes of vocational training.

To be sure, such wastage has also been characteristic of developed
countries, but in the case of many of the 'new' nations such a
phenomenon is particularly undesirable in view of the limited resources
available.

We do not intend here to underestimate non-economic factors that
contributed to African demand for academic schools though these, in
fact, reinforced the pattern we have described above. The European
colonial élite itself acted as a reference group for African aspirations;
emulation of that élite led to a pressure for 'parity' between metropolitan
and colonial institutions. Since the colonial élite provided only a partial
image of western society and was composed overwhelmingly of
administrators and government servants educated primarily in academic
institutions, African demand for education was understandably oriented
to the acquisition of that kind of education that was perceived to be the
key to European-type occupational roles. In this the Africans were acting
astutely. One of the striking features of most post-colonial economies is
the domination by government agencies of well-paid and high-status
employment opportunities. Since such institutions, through recruiting
primarily upon the basis of 'universalistic' criteria, stress the possession of
an academic formal education, a higher premium is placed upon such
schooling than occurred in early stages of development in most western
societies.

In this context, one of the most striking differences between many of
the new nations and the western world at earlier periods of its
development is their lack of mobility opportunities lying outside the
formal educational structure. Systems of apprenticeship, opportunities to
open small enterprises, etc., all provided institutionalised modes of social
and economic ascent in western society. The relative absence of those
sorts of alternatives to formal education in many new nations sometimes

[1] Rottman, op. cit., p. 300.

produces the paradoxical result, as in Ghana, that educational requirements for obtaining employment are now as high, if not higher, than in the former metropole itself, notwithstanding a very low level of diffusion of formal education in the population as a whole.

Thus when colonial peoples were involved in unequal competition with resident Europeans for a limited number of high-status jobs, it was considered imperative to obtain qualifications virtually identical to those prevalent in the metropole. This was a perfectly rational estimate of the relative advantages of alternative types of education; in the competition for scarce job opportunities nonmetropolitan curricula were by definition inferior.

It is important to note, however, that the termination of colonial overrule has made virtually no difference to the overall structure of occupational opportunities within the exchange sector. To be sure, Ghanaians are less involved in direct competition with Europeans for high-ranking posts within the administration. However, in the nongovernmental sector there has been little change in the premium placed on academic training; indeed, there has been an intensification of certain features apparent in the colonial period. At present, out of a total employed labour force of 2·56 million not more than 13·7 per cent (or 350,000) are employed full-time in the 'modern' sector of the economy. It has been calculated that the rate of growth in wage employment opportunities amounts to just over 4 per cent per annum; though this estimate is probably too low, a rather generous estimate of employment growth would be 20 to 25 thousand per annum.[1] On the other hand, the annual output of the middle schools alone has now risen to over 30 thousand per annum.

Parallel with this, however, has been the fact that government employment has absorbed an increasing proportion of the labour force: 42 per cent in 1951 and 51 per cent in 1957. The progressive enlargement of existing government agencies and the creation of new public corporations has, if anything, tended to favour employment for clerical and administrative workers. Since, relatively speaking, the balance of job opportunities has shifted even more in favour of clerical employment, there is a mounting demand for the academic secondary school education that provides access to such positions.

What is implied here is that although considerable attention has always been paid to the so-called problem of 'white-collar' unemployment in West Africa, there has been little realisation that opportunities for technical employment have been even more limited and certainly more poorly paid. In virtually every African territory there appears to be a current stress upon the need for the provision of technical education

---

[1] These estimates have been computed from the 1960 *Population Census of Ghana*, Advance Reports of vols. 3 and 4; Ghana, *Quarterly Digest of Statistics*, Accra, Office of the Government Statistician, 1959; and Ghana, *Economic Surveys*, 1955–8, Accra, Government Printer, 1959.

upon a massive scale to meet the 'needs' of the economy. Sometimes such demands are based upon the conclusions of manpower surveys, the source of whose projections may not be too clear. Yet a sober inspection of the actual structure of job opportunities within an economy such as that of Ghana gives no reason to suppose that the products of technical schools can be absorbed soon on a large scale. In actuality, we are not faced by the problem of white-collar unemployment at all but by a far more serious form of generalised unemployment.

II AGE

Age Stratification
by David Lyne
Padgate College of Higher Education

'Of all the class struggles in modern society, the most underrated
may prove to be those between age classes, especially those between
youth (in the sense of adolescents and young adults) and adults . . .
there is considerable evidence to indicate that the struggle between
age classes is a distinctive class struggle in its own right and
furthermore is one of the more serious and least tractable.' (Lenski,
1966, p. 246)

Lenski's argument that conflict between age classes can be as significant
as that between economic classes derives from two observations; that the
younger generation is subject to the authority of the older and that it is the
older generation that has a disproportionate share of society's rewards.
Such inequality between the generations, he suggests, can be a major
factor in social change. A prolonged educational experience and subsequent economic dependence on adults creates in youth a sense of class
identity. Their inability to redress these grievances through conventional
political channels inclines them to violent and even revolutionary action.

It will be the argument of this article that Lenski, and other
commentators writing in the late 1960's, were misled by the spectacular
but transient confrontations between students and adult authority; that
they overemphasised the interests held in common by youth and that in
seeing youth as the 'new proletariat', they attributed to the younger
generation a much more significant role in bringing about change than
the facts would warrant. These are reservations which are made with the
benefit of hindsight. In the context of the late 1960's, Lenski's thesis can
be seen as a seductive argument. With young people, particularly
students, involved in radical political confrontations in a number of
industrialised countries, youth indeed might seem to act as a class, with
interests of its own in direct opposition to those of adults. Youth appeared
to challenge adult authority in so many areas. It condemned a much
expanded educational provision – for its alienating effects, for the content
of its courses and for the dominance of the examination. It rejected what
it saw as the continuing exploitation of capitalist production and the
consumer society. It resisted American involvement in Vietnam and was
prominent in the Civil Rights' Movement and the protest against

continuing discrimination. Youth appeared to be involved in a total rejection of adult society, conventional adult values and an oppressive adult authority. Well might Jencks and Riesman talk of the 'war between the generations (Jencks and Riesman, 1967). In colleges and universities, in America and in Europe, a violent rift seemed to separate the generations as never before.

What is more, the members of the emergent class were unified by a powerful ideology that provided a justification for their action, whatever the immediate cause. Lewis Feuer (1969) suggests that the common thread to student protest was an abiding concern with alienation. According to Feuer, the resentment which youth expressed towards the adult world did not derive from economic need. Living affluent, secure, cosseted lives they, the students, could hardly complain of economic exploitation. Their hostility had a moral source; it was directed against the large bureaucratic organisation which denied them the right to a meaningful existence. Ralph Turner, too, sees alienation as 'the main symbol of the new era' (1969, p. 396). Interpreted to mean a loss of one's real self, alienation becomes an expression of outrage at the depersonalising and demoralising effect of modern institutions. Contemporary social movements are pervaded by this concern with alienation. It is in terms of alienation that the young are conscious of injustices and it is from them as an age group and not, as in previous eras, from socio-economic classes, that the pressure for change comes.

Though reaching the same conclusion, John and Margaret Rowntree (1968) reject the prevailing image of the affluent, middle-class student. They argue that the ailing structure of American capitalism is supported by the remarkable expansion of two main sectors, education and defence. These two areas absorb the surplus manpower produced by capitalism, and young people, who contribute disproportionately to these areas, are economically exploited within them. It is with the expansion of these areas that youth becomes a potentially revolutionary force. It is in the student power movement, and the resistance to the draft, that young people gain a growing awareness of their exploitation. It is youth's awareness of its common identity and its sense of ideological purpose that provides the real impetus for change.

In contrast to the heady atmosphere of the sixties, the mid-seventies seem to hold far less promise of that change. Economic recession, graduate unemployment and fewer openings for the ex-radical, seem to have produced students with markedly more materialist and less ambitious aims. Consideration of the above arguments, less than a decade later, raises the question of whether youth does constitute such a significant factor in social change. Do young people, or for that matter adults, have sufficient common interest as a generation to warrant their description as a class? Youth has traditionally been seen as involving problems but can the younger generation be justifiably approached as a class?

The Situation of Youth

Eisenstadt (1962) provides the clearest exposition of why the situation of youth in industrial societies is seen as problematic, why youth should experience a degree of uncertainty and ambivalence towards the adult world. In a rapidly changing world, youth lacks clear role models with which to identify. The technical expertise of youth may well be superior to that of the older generation. Adult values may seem to be irrelevant to the new situations that youth experiences. Youth's status is transitional and uncertain but, with the expansion of the provision of higher education, more people, and for longer periods, have to experience the insecurity it entails. Problems of self-identification can be resolved by involvement with youth organisations. Of these the most dramatic, the revolutionary student movement, offers an escape from a dreary and uncertain present to a future with the promise of self fulfilment and meaningful social change.

The danger of Eisenstadt's argument would appear to be that it explains away the radical criticism of society at the core of student protest. Rather than looking at the content of the criticism, it suggests that involvement in the student movement is merely a way of resolving the psychological tensions associated with youth's problem of identification. It also does not go far enough in examining the consequences of involvement in revolutionary student movements for youth. For if students indeed become committed to ideologies which lead to the rejection of so many aspects of adult conformism, this may well prevent their later incorporation into adult life. Bennett Berger (1963) is one of the few authors to appreciate this, and he explores which adult occupations allow individuals to retain those basic orientations to society which are shaped by their youthful experience.

For the vast majority, however, entry into full-time work will involve an abandonment of the ideologies of youth. Their radical commitment will be difficult to sustain. It is essentially a transitional phenomenon. From this point of view, the effectiveness of youth movements as agencies of change must be questioned. Not only are such movements relatively short lived but they involve only a small proportion of youth taken as a whole.

Descriptions of youth culture indicate that radical concern about society is typical of only a small minority of the young. Youth is characteristically portrayed as hedonistic, irresponsible and impulsive. Whilst recognising that it is difficult to achieve an accurate portrayal of youth culture, it would seem that the vast majority of youth culture can perhaps be understood as a reaction by adolescents to the problems so imminently facing them in adulthood. There seems, however, to be very little basis for the growth of class identity between unskilled youth enjoying independence and short lived temporary prosperity and twenty-year-old students developing a commitment to radical change of society. In fact the life chances of the young are markedly different; they derive in large part from the economic status of their parents. The majority of students have predominantly middle class backgrounds still, and their educational experience and career prospects, though less promising than in the 1960's, distinguish them from the mass of school leavers.

One of the paradoxical aspects of the student movement of the sixties is that it was a revolt of the advantaged. According to Richard Flacks (1967), 'the current group of student activists is predominantly upper middle class and frequently these students are of elite origin'. He tentatively suggests that among the reasons for this are, first, that these students may well have grown up in families with considerable ambivalence about the dominant values in society, and secondly, that economic and occupational incentives towards conformity are likely to be ineffective for individuals who already enjoy affluence and high status by virtue of family origin. To put it simply such young people can afford to be radical. These though are the exception. There seems to be little evidence to suggest that the majority of adolescent school leavers have values markedly different from those of adult society. What is interesting also is that with the prospects of graduate unemployment, cuts in public expenditure, more restricted career opportunities, student radicalism too seems to have diminished. Students seem now to be more concerned with the pressing problems of their own material situation.

Youth as an Exploited Group

Youth does suffer material and social disadvantages as a group in comparison with adult society. As Lenski suggests, young people are invariably subject to adult authority. If working, they receive lower rates of pay than those of adults doing comparable work. There exists legal restrictions on many areas of life – for example, sex, marriage, voting, credit facilities – which emphasise their inferior status. These deprivations indeed are shared but it is surely significant that the restrictions associated with age are of a temporary nature. Every adolescent can anticipate becoming an adult and so does not develop the sense of being trapped in an inferior social status. What is more, whilst these deprivations are held in common, other fundamental aspects of life differ from person to person. Economic status, career prospects and political and social attitudes are so divergent that there is little to give a common consciousness of exploitation.

This internal differentiation within the so-called class of young people, along relatively permanent and significant features makes it difficult to accept the arguments of Lenski and the Rowntrees. Political and economic identities do seem to cut across age categories, limiting identification over common problems and demanding different kinds of reaction in charged political and economic circumstances. It would seem likely that that section of youth which experiences exploitation most severely will also become the exploited adult and eventually the impoverished elderly.

The Situation of the Adult

The student movement is the nearest example to a generation becoming aware of its class identity and acting on that awareness. It is very difficult to conceive of the older generation as a class in itself. Lenski argues that it is the older generation which enjoys the lion's share of the rewards. But, in reality, it is only a section of the adult population which merits this description. Great inequalities of wealth, income and power divide the adult population. It is easier to see interests dividing the adult population than it is to locate those interests that they have in common. Age, for instance, does not appear to be an important factor in explaining the distribution of wealth. If it was, we would expect to see a concentration of wealth ownership in the older generations, and much less inequality of wealth among people of the same age group, than exists in the population as a whole. Wealth, however, is unevenly distributed within the generations as Table 1 shows. What is remarkable here is the consistency of the concentration of wealth in each of the age groups.

Table 1: Inequality of wealth by age of Great Britain 1963–1967

	Male			Female		
Proportion of wealth in that class owned by the top:						
Age	1%	5%	10%	1%	5%	10%
25–34	31	51	64	55	81	93
35–44	28	49	63	44	75	89
45–54	28	53	67	38	66	81
55–64	27	51	66	29	57	72
65–74	28	53	68	27	54	69
75–84	29	57	72	26	54	69
85–	30	60	75	28	57	72
Whole population	32	58	73	32	58	73

(*Source:* A. B. Atkinson, *Unequal Shares*, Table 10, p. 52. [Penguin 1974])

True, there is a slight tendency with respect to males for wealth to increase with age but much more remarkable is the similarity between the age groups in the concentration of wealth.

Age still carries with it certain advantages. The principle of seniority as a basis for promotion is still a widespread feature within many organisations. Members of the Cabinet and senior personnel within the civil service and business generally are over 50 years old. Some pensioners can enjoy relative prosperity having both a state pension and substantial occupational pension. On the other hand, a great number of the elderly are living around the subsistence level. At least half retired men and three-quarters of married women have no occupational pension. The financial situation of the elderly over 80 years of age tends to be much worse than that of the young elderly. In other words, within the older generation there exist social, political and economic differences which make it difficult to conceive this section of the population as possessing any identity of interest. Even when one looks at those over pensionable age the differences within this category would appear so great as to suggest that it is inequalities persisting through one's working life into retirement that are the real divide, as opposed to age itself.

In traditional societies age and seniority constitute basic criteria for allocating social, economic and political roles but in modern industrial societies age by itself loses much of its significance. The very rich and the very powerful tend to be older men, but the aged can suffer economic deprivation and exploitation just as severe, if not greater, than that suffered by youth. Retirement often means not only a sharp reduction in living standards but also a continuing withdrawal from social and political involvements.

The fact that retirement can be experienced as a very painful change of identity by some people and yet be seen by others as an opportunity to develop new talents and interests should alert us to the notion that age definitions vary considerably. This is illustrated by a comparison of the age identities of males and females as these do not correspond with chronological age. People of the same chronological age may be described as either old or middle-aged. What is more, they will differ in the way that they feel about their age. For some, advancing years will bring with it respect for the experience and wisdom which they are deemed to have gained over the years. Others at the same age will be seen, and will see themselves, as old and 'past it'. Their physical strength gone, their experience irrelevant, they will be defined as old as soon as they retire.

Eisenstadt (1962) argues that the characteristics of any one age cannot be fully understood except in relation to other ages. This is undoubtedly true, but just as the experience of these other ages will vary within a society so will entry into, and experience of, old age vary. There is every difference between a retirement willingly anticipated as a culmination of a successful career, entered into after a person has reached the peak of his earning capacity and a retirement following an unskilled job in which opportunities for earning have been substantially reduced as one has got older.

Once again, the subjective experience of the retired will vary considerably. There is little basis amongst the retired for the emergence of a common consciousness, of an awareness of themselves as a class. The political implication of this is that the old rarely pursue their interests together. The old do not use the aged as a primary reference group. They identify more readily with their former occupations, their families and the political party with which they have traditionally aligned themselves. This is not surprising as being old is seen as the most distasteful stage of the life cycle and it is perhaps painful to identify oneself with the aged.

Furthermore, as the most salient issue for the elderly – income – is a convenient political slogan for all parties to adopt, if not necessarily to promote, it is difficult to identify the interests of the elderly with any one political party. This tends to inhibit the development of political groupings made up exclusively of old people. They tend to pursue their interests separately through the existing parties.

Conclusion

It is for these reasons that I reject the argument that age is a significant unit of stratification in industrial society. Internal differences of economic resources and experiences within the generations do not allow of sufficient community of interest. Youth is the category which comes closest to justify being regarded as a class and the student movement of the sixties did seem to suggest that youth could be a significant factor in social change. But the radical character of these movements did not last; the impetus for change did not continue. It would seem that the writers of the sixties ascribed to those spectacular confrontations between university authorities and the student bodies, too great a significance. There has been little evidence of students and other sections of youth developing a common identity, just as there is little evidence of older generations developing a generation consciousness. It is not age but economic power that provides the key to an understanding of stratification within our society.

In an Ageing World
by Peter Laslett

We have to realise how old, how very old, we are. Nations are classified as 'aged' when they have 7 per cent or more of their people aged 65 or above, and by about 1970 every one of the advanced countries had become like this. Of the really ancient societies, with over 13 per cent above 65, all are in north-western Europe. At the beginning of the decade East Germany had 15·6 per cent, Austria, Sweden, West Germany and France had 13·4 per cent or above, and England and Wales 13·3 per cent. Scotland had 12·3 per cent, Northern Ireland 10·8 per cent and the U.S.A. 9·9 per cent. We know that we are getting even older, and that the nearer a society approximates to zero population growth, the older its population is likely to be – at least, for any future that concerns us now.

To these now familiar facts a number of further facts may be added, some of them only recently recognised. There is the apparent paradox that the effective cause of the high proportion of the old is births rather than deaths. There is the economic principle that the dependency ratio – the degree to which those who cannot earn depend for a living on those who can – is more advantageous in older societies like ours than in the younger societies of the developing world, because lots of dependent babies are more of a liability than numbers of the inactive aged. There is the appreciation of the salient historical truth that the ageing of advanced societies has been a sudden, a precipitate change.

If 'revolution' is a rapid resettlement of the social structure, and if the age composition of the society counts as a very important aspect of that social structure, then there has been a social revolution in European and particularly western European society within the lifetime of everyone over 50. Taken together, these things have implications which are only beginning to be acknowledged. These facts and circumstances were well to the fore earlier this year at a world gathering about ageing as a challenge to science and to policy, held at Vichy in France under the lingering, symbolic shadow of the senescent Maréchal Pétain.

There is often resistance to the idea that it is because the birthrate fell earlier in western and north-western Europe than elsewhere, rather than because of any change in the death rate, that we have grown so old. But this is what elementary demography makes clear. Long life is altering our society, of course, but in experiential terms. We have among us a very much greater experience of continued living than any society that has ever preceded us anywhere, and this will continue. But too much of that lengthened experience, even in the wealthy west, will be experience of poverty and neglect, unless we do something about it.

If you are now in your thirties, you ought to be aware that you can expect to live nearly one-third of the rest of your life after the age of 60. The older you are now, of course, the greater this proportion will be, and greater still if you are a woman. Expectation of life is a slippery figure, very easy to get wrong at the highest ages. At Vichy the demographers were telling each other that their estimates of how many old there would be and of how long they will live in countries like England and Wales are due for revision upwards.

They said this in full awareness that nearly all demographic predictions have been wrong in the past, which is where the historian can produce his one claim to superiority. For there can be no doubt whatever of the suddenness with which ageing in the west came about.

The difference in the experience of England and France implies that there is no one story of how nations age. Moreover, it is an error to suppose that the process of ageing necessarily coincides historically with industrialisation. In our country industrialisation had been going on for nearly 150 years before 1911, when the take-off of the over-sixties can be seen to have occurred.

The ageing of the population increases sex differences among the old. There are now no more than 70 Englishmen over 60 for every 100

Englishwomen, and only 46 among the old old, those over 75. The level in pre-industrial times for these two western countries was already high. We can now make estimates as early as the 1500's in the case of England, which seems to have had enough older people for much of her history to qualify as 'mature' that is with 4 per cent over the age of 65. This was especially so in the early eighteenth century, just before industrialisation began.

The one historian present at Vichy was able to report a number of other recent advances in social knowledge bearing upon the position and prospects of the elderly. There were the facts about the structure of the household in the west, which show that among English-speaking peoples the three generational household has always been inconspicuous, well under 10 per cent of all households. In traditional English society, about half of all married couples seem to have lived alone with each other, against two thirds today. As many as 14 per cent of widowers, and 19 per cent of widows, were entirely solitary, as compared with 37 per cent and 48 per cent in the 1960's.

The full figures imply a distinct resemblance between older persons then and now in the matter of independent living. Something like three-quarters of them headed their own households in our pre-industrial past and there is some evidence that the elderly English have always preferred living on their own, with access to the households of their children rather than actually living with them, just as they seem to do today. Widowed mothers quite frequently made themselves useful in the households of their married children, however, especially in Victorian times.

In southern France, on the other hand, in southern and eastern Europe, and in parts of Germany, the elderly, married and widowed, were far more frequently located in extended family groups, and there was much more variation. We ourselves seem to have inherited from our English ancestors a set pattern of how the older citizen shall live, though it is not one which corresponds to the stereotype of the aged patriarch and matriarch surrounded by their children, grandchildren and relatives. Elsewhere on our continent all this may have been very differently arranged, and the nations of the world would do well to disentangle their pasts the one from the other.

The study of ageing and the aged is still dominated by the physiologists and medical scientists and the importance and intellectual fascination of their researches are unmistakable. You can't listen to them talking without marvelling that anyone can continue to smoke cigarettes, or fail to take exercise, though the effects of diet on the ageing process and on the well-being of the old no longer seem so clear as they did until recently. Fatness, as one medical demonstrator showed at Vichy, cannot be simply related to the health of the elderly. Indeed quite fat people last very well, better than the lean: but not, of course, the really obese.

There can be little doubt that the pursuit calling itself gerontology, which came into being a generation ago as the one noticeable response to the ageing of advanced societies, has substantial achievements to its credit

– the insistence, for instance, that ageing must be looked at over the whole life course, and not confined to the final years; that becoming old is nevertheless most emphatically not a matter of calendar years lived; and that a blanket category of the old which fails to distinguish between the young old and the old old, or to recognise the enormous differences between individuals, is entirely inappropriate. The further recognition that the condition of the old is not to be judged from the very small minority who have to be rescued by the welfare services is crucially important too. For this is an error which has led to widespread misapprehension.

Indifference to gerontological advances can be sombre indeed in its consequences. It is in this way that the tyranny of compulsory retirement at a set chronological age has been able to fasten itself on our occupational life. It is this which has made it possible for a social and political regime, evidently baffled by the problem of unemployment, to shift the burden wherever it can from those who happen to be citizens in their twenties and thirties to those who happen to be citizens in their fifties and sixties. The researchers themselves have been equally impressed by the injustice to family feeling and family solidarity implied by the prevalent belief that older persons are neglected by their immediate kin.

Financial exchange between the generations is not extensive, and probably never has been. But the exchange of support and of caring which research has revealed is truly remarkable, and for all we know as great now as ever it was in the past. Those of the old who do have children with whom their relationship is satisfactory also have a family function, even though they do not all live together as a group. They are 'wanted'; yet they maintain their independence while preserving these essential emotional relationships.

Whether this will continue, however, must depend on two things. One is the number of immediate relatives, and especially children, that future old people will have. The other is the effect of divorce on family linkages. Research on both these questions is in progress and results will come in due course. But it is possible to prophesy that with zero population growth and with the divorce rate increasing at its present pace, the younger people of today may have to look forward to a late life without reliable linkages with those more youthful than themselves. Advanced societies may be about to lose their vertical bonds, their structure over time.

In spite of this progress in our knowledge of the aged, it seems that the phase marked by the word gerontology is coming to an end. It is significant how little that word was used even at a world assembly of experts. The confining of such vital social information within the walls of an 'academic discipline', however interdisciplinary it is; the dominance of the research attitude, especially that of medical research; the lingering feeling that age is an 'illness', and as such it should and can be 'cured'; all this seems to disturb the relationship between those who get to know and those who ought to know.

Simultaneously with the sudden growth of the relative number of the aged in the population, and with a pronounced increase in the expectation of life, the scope of the educational system grew enormously. This has meant that the elderly in the late 1970's in Britain and elsewhere are the least instructed part of the population. They lack a consciousness of themselves as well as of the process which has put them into the position which they occupy; they lack leadership as well as effective organisation. The developments we have described have given rise to a considerable literature, but it seems to evade the fundamental issue of justice between the age groups, especially in the matter of resources for education.

Since it is the elderly who lived and worked through the time of educational expansion, it could be said that they have been paying the bill but not sharing the benefits – not as personal enrichment. Justice between age groups and between generations is a thorny problem in political philosophy, and never more so than when inflation wipes out savings and erodes pensions. Equity suggests that persons of all ages should have equal shares in the social fund, but the young, those between the ages of 15 and 25, have had a monopoly in that very considerable part of it which goes to education. This could only be justified if it could be shown that such a monopoly is for the benefit of everyone at every age. In my view, the historical facts we have examined makes such a justification impossible today. The elderly, exploited in the past, are being cheated now by the allocation of educational funds as well as by inflation.

They are compensated to some extent by the disproportionate share of the health fund which goes to the care of the old and infirm. But to say this is to imply once again that ageing and illness are synonymous, and that the old old, who really are heavily dependent on the health service, represent all the elderly. Meanwhile everyone who has attained the age of 50 stands in great and growing need of instruction, enlightenment and education in preparation for retirement, in the use of their lives after retirement, in all that has to do with the arrival of a huge community of those past the stage of working full-time for a living.

The erroneous view that education occurs once and for all early in life is taking a long time to disappear. Untrue for people of all ages – what doctor, what plumber can now be told before his thirtieth birthday all that he has to know to do his job for the rest of his life? – it is entirely irrelevant to those whose working days are over, but who have several decades still to live. In France a token recognition of this has come with the establishment by some universities and for limited purposes of *les universités du troisième âge*. In America, as might be expected, there is a myriad of experimental programmes. Here, though we have the most effective and successful of all distance teaching institutions in the Open University, nothing constructive has so far been done.

There is a certain symmetry between the dilemma presented by the educational needs of the aged and a dilemma within the university system itself. Much of the traditional curriculum is losing its support in institutions whose function is to satisfy the needs of the young, preparing them for 30 years of earning and responsibility. Egyptology, classical Chinese, Greek and Roman literature, are scarcely relevant to these purposes. Are these subjects then to die as resources for maintaining them get relatively scarcer? As we now take stock of our new situation we may find therefore that it is the elderly who should carry responsibility for the continuity of our culture.

But we must not fall victim to the intellectualist fallacy. The mass of the elderly are not intellectuals, and never will be, however much education becomes available and however much its content is changed. A great deal of sympathetic creativity is going to be needed now that we have begun to acquire a sense of historical proportion about the position of the aged in our society.

III KNOWLEDGE

What is Knowledge?
by Christopher Cook
Polytechnic of North London

Introduction

The field of knowledge has been revived as an area ripe for sociological study. Until recently, the study of the nature and validity of knowledge had been largely philosophical. This forms the subject matter of epistemology, which tackles the question of how knowing is possible, and examines the grounds on which we can claim that we know something. What sociologists have attempted is to undertake such enquiries themselves, in order to demonstrate that some of the issues about knowledge are *social* issues. In doing this, sociologists seek to turn certain philosophical questions into sociological ones. Thus, the question, 'How is knowing possible?' is answered by stressing the social context in which knowledge has been developed, and the use to which it is put. This leads us to define the sociology of knowledge as the study of the development and use of knowledge in society. This implies, of course, that the methods and theories of sociology are employed in such an enterprise.

As used in sociology, the term 'knowledge' has come to mean several things. Not only does it refer to that which *is* true by some criteria of certainty, but also to which people *believe* to be true. From this it follows that a sociological definition of knowledge includes facts, theories, skills, methods and beliefs. This broad emphasis has led to what has been termed a 'subversion of absolutism' (see Young, 1971, p. 6), since the sociology of knowledge directs our attention towards the socially derived, sustained and situated character of much (if not all) knowledge. This means two things. Firstly, knowledge is seen as human (or social) in its production and use. Secondly, some knowledge originates from a particular point in the social structure and may be used in the interests of those who produce or possess the knowledge. In this sense, having knowledge is similar to owning a valuable commodity. Patents, trade associations and professional bodies aim to protect this kind of knowledge and restrict its general diffusion.

Sociologists working in the field of knowledge answer the fundamental question of how knowing is possible, by asserting that there is a relationship between social structure and knowledge, although the nature and extent of this link is highly contentious. Some views, particularly those of earlier sociologists, assert that knowledge is fundamentally social in origin, but tend to suggest that knowledge, in the form of ideas and beliefs, exerts an independent force in society. Knowledge and ideas 'pull' in a particular direction to create new social structures. Weber showed that the emergence of a protestant ethic of worldly asceticism in Europe fostered the development of capitalism and caused radical changes in social structure.

Current views, largely deriving from Marx, tend to tie knowledge much more closely to social structure. They see knowledge as the product of specific social structures and stress in particular the man-made and socially situated character of knowledge within that structure. The production, use and nature of knowledge is seen as ideological, in that it comprises a system of persuasive ideas and beliefs that serve to maintain or change the social structure. Thus knowledge may be said to serve the political end of maintaining and recreating the conditions for the existence of a social structure in which rewards, privileges and power are differentially distributed. In this view, a radical change in knowledge (or re-interpretation of existing knowledge) could promote and accompany changes in social structure.

The Views of Marx and his Followers

Marx saw material conditions, the economic structure in particular, as setting limits to intellectual life. His conception of history emphasises 'the formation of ideas from practice' in that the manner in which men organise their material production determines (in the sense of setting limits) such things as social structure, ideologies and ways of thinking. Quite clearly Marx saw knowledge (in the form of ideas and ideology) as limited in both its generation and diffusion. Indeed ideology is seen as one of the means whereby dominance is asserted and maintained. Thus, for Marx, there is a clear link between social and political structures and ideology. In *The German Ideology*, Marx and Engels assert, 'The ideas of the ruling class are in every epoch the ruling ideas, i.e. that which is the ruling *material* force of society is at the same time its ruling intellectual force.'

There are various interpretations of this view. One is to see all knowledge as ideological in the sense that it comprises part of the superstructure which serves to maintain a social structure and in particular to allow a ruling class to maintain its position. An interesting extension of this would be to question the extent to which this view obtains in contemporary capitalist societies, in which there may be a substantial degree of *public* ownership, and certainly substantial governmental concern in promoting economic activity. Does such a view still apply under conditions in which massive international business corporations may be more powerful than national governments? What about the state-controlled economies of the socialist societies, which in certain important ways resemble the bureaucratised industrial economies of the West? In these instances we may not be able to discern a ruling *class* as readily as when Marx and Engels were writing. This does not necessarily refute their position, particularly if we consider the second part of the proposition quoted above. We could ask if Marx and Engels sought to apply their views to a global social structure. Perhaps they did (or at least we should) for there are clearly fundamental differences in the distribution of economic, technological and industrial power, between the industrial nations and the rest of the world. Such power includes the knowledge (and ideologies) which serve to maintain this difference, despite programmes of foreign aid for economic development.

Knowledge and Social Control

RECENT DEVELOPMENTS

A similar case is advanced with respect to the situation within capitalist countries. It is argued by Althusser (Davies, 1976, pp. 100–2), for example, that certain sections of the ruling class have the task of transmitting the ruling ideologies by means of control exercised via 'Ideological State Apparatuses' (for example, the church, education system, mass media), which are supported by 'Repressive State Apparatuses' (for example, the army, police). In this view, the education system has now replaced the church as the most important means of inculcating ideologies, which include not only knowledge useful to production, but also, critically, what are termed the social relations of production. Examples of the latter include the acceptance of hierarchies of many different sorts, including those of knowledge and skills, and the attitudes and values appropriate to the smooth and efficient running of the system of production (for example, punctuality, diligence, the acceptance of authority and subordination). Importantly too, capitalist, or indeed socialist, societies' notions of individual worth and abilities are largely developed within the education system.

Bourdieu analyses the means whereby knowledge is 'extremely concretely reproduced in class interests' (see Davies, 1976, p. 138), in that particular styles of thought and practice are sustained and reproduced in the academic and social processes of the French education system. Bourdieu's essays form part of a well-known, recent book in the sociology of education, *Knowledge and Control* (Young, 1971). In his introduction, Young seeks to shift emphasis in the sociology of education towards a sociology of knowledge and to re-define the study as 'an enquiry into the social organisation of knowledge in educational institutions'. Such an enterprise, he argues, could explore the ways in which the school system works to allow particular dominant social groups to maintain their position by means of their ability to define what counts as appropriate school knowledge and accepted ways of thinking. This is to be achieved by an examination of how and why significant categories (for example, subject disciplines, 'rationality', 'ability') arise and are maintained, together with an account of the relationship between such categories and the social position of those who propagate and accept them.

Such a view then sees knowledge as essentially a social product, with the emphasis on the activities of individuals or groups in the promotion (or suppression) of certain knowledge. In this sense, all knowledge is social and this is an important point. It is quite another matter to assert that one way of seeing things is as good as *any* other, or that truth (or knowledge) is *only* relative. This is a relativist position and will be examined in the next section.

SOCIALLY CONSTRUCTED KNOWLEDGE

If knowledge is seen as a social product, this lays particular stress on the socially *constructed* nature of that knowledge. Bodies of facts, and disciplined ways of thinking and acting (for example, subjects, scientific methods, logic) have been produced by man's collective activity in attempting to comprehend and act upon a pre-existing external world. However, this stress does seem to make knowledge and truth rather arbitrary. Does it suggest that any way of viewing things is as good as any other? Are the distinctions and categories of human thought *merely* conventional? Does this mean that to change something all we need to do is to change our minds about it? To each question we must answer, 'No', for one of the important messages of the sociology of knowledge is that knowledge and truth are not individually optional matters (see Davies, 1976, p. 104). Conventional they must be, in part, for otherwise communications could not take place and, whether we like it or not, there is an external world, physical and social, to which our knowledge must bear relation, and from which it derives. It is quite another point to take the view that we may, logically, be *mistaken* about something we believe to be true. Our knowledge is, indeed, often proved wrong by the test of experience and we are obliged to revise it. New theories and hypotheses are advanced to explain, or predict, that which we may not be able to comprehend by means of existing knowledge and understanding. New knowledge may be said, in this sense, to grow out of the old. The study of the development of scientific knowledge provides us with a number of striking examples, as documented by Kuhn (1970).The discovery that the 'indivisible' atom could be split is one such case. If we admit the logical possibility that our knowledge may be wrong, we are presupposing that there is a correct view, though this may have to remain unattainable. In the last resort, our existing knowledge stands or falls by the test of experience. Our knowledge may represent only the best approximation to the truth as we understand it at any one time (see Pring, 1976, pp. 76–81). We are unlikely to be in a position to assert that our knowledge is perfectly correct, except in the partial sense of working within an agreed set of definitions and distinctions.

SOCIALLY SITUATED KNOWLEDGE

A further problem central to current sociological interest in knowledge is that of the relationship between interests and the social position of those who produce and use knowledge. The contemporary neo-Marxist view links the production and use of knowledge to social structure. It asserts that knowledge is ideological in the sense that it serves to maintain the social structure and that knowledge is produced and used to effect this end. This should not be taken to imply that we can assume causal links or conscious motive in all cases, nor, indeed, that knowledge is 'massively organised "mystification"' (Davies, 1976, p. 112), as some writers seem to suggest. Quite clearly we can show instances of the use of knowledge as serving particular vested interests (or indeed the suppression of knowledge counter to certain interests). New knowledge is constantly sought and used to maintain and further interests on the part of individuals and corporations, or indeed governments. Groups with a common interest (for example, professional bodies, trades unions) may collectively seek to determine the limits of what is appropriate knowledge in a particular field and lay down rules as to its diffusion and use. Although the regulations as to who may practise as a professional may protect the public from charlatans, the development and use of alternatives (especially by lay-people) is also restricted. Examples include the position of 'fringe' medicine and legal or medical self-help. A slightly different case of professional activity is the publication of this book. It is compiled by teachers and examiners actively interested in the diffusion of material suitable for a particular examination.

The sociology of knowledge provides further case studies. Mills (1943) gives an account of the activities of a number of writers in the promotion of a common perspective towards an understanding of social problems. In particular he relates the views to the similar social origins of the writers. The study by Platt (1969) and Kuhn's (1970) book give further instances. The article by Bernstein accompanying this paper outlines the development of the sociology of education and links the terms of the current debate to the interests of the participants. He castigates those who concern themselves solely with the question of the ideological position of the participants, for such a view assumes that *all* activity (including the production and use of knowledge) occurs in response to a belief or interest directly connected to social position (Davies, 1976, p. 99). Bernstein urges us to examine the arguments and evidence of the various writers. We should not limit our concern solely to questions about their social or ideological position. Becker (1967), too, warns of this danger. 'Sociology of knowledge cautions us to distinguish between the truth of a statement and an assessment of the circumstances under which the statement is made; though we trace an argument to its source in the interests of the person who made it, we have still not proved it false.'

Conclusion

In general, we cannot assume that because a sociological explanation of knowledge is possible, we are justified in refuting the content of the knowledge. We *may* be able to show that the development and use of particular ideas and beliefs served to support or indeed create social structures, as Weber did. We *may* be able to demonstrate that knowledge has served the interests of particular groups and indeed reveal something of the exercise of power in our society. The activities of professional bodies would be a case in point. At the very least a sociological understanding of the social and historical circumstances of the development of knowledge should provide us with useful evidence and insights as to the nature and production of knowledge, and thus contribute to an answer to the question posed above; that is, the problematic nature of the relationship between social structure and knowledge.

Sociology and the Sociology of Education: A Brief Account
by Basil Bernstein

It might be instructive to analyse changes in the approaches of sociologists to education in England since the Second World War.

On the whole, our knowledge of schools is almost wholly confined to the surface features of their selective principles. This is partly because such knowledge is relatively easily acquired, partly because of its policy and educational implications, partly because of the interests and training of sociologists and partly because of the relatively low per capita cost of such research. However, it is important to add that because such features are surface, it does not mean to say that they are not of considerable significance. Such research enables us to map the incidence and variation of the problem which these selective principles create. This research does not (neither is such research designed to do this) give us any specific understanding of *how* the selective principles give rise to the behaviour with which they are correlated. It is also true that these studies did not focus upon the knowledge properties of the school in terms of its form, content and manner of transmission. This was because these studies took as their problem stratification features within and between schools. Because the knowledge properties of the school were not treated as problematic, but as an invariant, the research emphasised continuities and discontinuities between the knowledge properties of the home and those of the school. This in turn gave rise to a view of the school as an agency of unsuccessful assimilation, and the view of the family as a primary source of educational pathology.

The debates of the 1950's focused upon the organisational structure of the schools, the social origins of measured intelligence and its relation to attainment, within the wider issues of manpower requirements and social equality. The basic concern was the *demonstration*, not explanation, of institutional sources of inequality in education. The poverty surveys of the early twentieth century were replaced by the surveys of educational 'wastage' in the mid-twentieth century. Apart from London and Leicester, there were few universities of this period which possessed viable departments of sociology. During this period, there were only *two* major sociologists engaged in research or systematic teaching in the sociology of education. The sociology of education in the fifties did not exist as an established examined subject in the Colleges and Departments of Education, nor in undergraduate degrees in sociology. The first taught masters' degree in this area was established at the University of London Institute of Education only in 1964, and the first degrees were awarded in 1966. It is very important for the student to realise that the interest of sociologists in the social basis of symbolic systems, the forms of their legitimation, the interpretative procedures to which they give rise, the manner of their transmission, is of very recent origin.

The first teaching approach or paradigm was developed essentially by Floud and Halsey, who were the two major sociologists active in educational research in the middle fifties or early sixties.

Their research was essentially a development of the enquiry into social mobility carried out by Professor D. Glass of the London School of Economics. The book which reported his extensive investigation contained five chapters on education (Glass, 1954). Jean Floud taught at the London School of Economics before taking up a position at the University of London Institute of Education, and A. H. Halsey obtained his degree at the London School of Economics. Jean Floud was faced with the problem of constructing advanced courses in the sociology of education, and with the supervision of students who wished to read for higher degrees in this area. Both Floud and Halsey were active in creating the sociology of education as a field of study.

One of the major problems in the transformation of a specialised field of research into a subject to be taught, is what is to be selected from the parent subject which can be used to legitimise the specialised field as a *subject*. This is particularly important when the new subject is to be created out of a low status field of research, such as education. In the case of the sociology of education, the legitimising institution might be said to have been the London School of Economics, and the legitimising area was the problems and process of industrialisation. This was partly because this area of sociology at both theoretical and empirical levels was well documented, partly because it reflected the then current L.S.E. interests in stratification and mobility and industrialisation, and partly because it could be fitted into a *weak* structural functional approach in the context of problems of social policy and educational planning. This approach did not call for any major thinking of classical and contemporary sociology in terms of its potential application to a sociology of education. Once the approach was established as a taught course, with the development of a University syllabus, reading lists, examination papers and finally textbooks, it became difficult for some to think outside of what became the legitimate contents. The approach, once institutionalised, reinforced the existing research and defined future problems. The approach bore the hallmarks of British applied sociology; atheoretical, pragmatic, descriptive, and policy focused. Yet if we look back to the mid-1950's, it is not easy to see how there could have been an alternative. There was little work available at theoretical or empirical levels to form the basis for comparative studies of education, studies of organisations were few, and they were limited to industrial, administrative and custodian institutions, studies of professional groups and the professionalising process were in their infancy, there was little interest, either in Britain or in the U.S.A., in the study of cultural transmission, and the major theoretical approach was that of structural-functionalism. It is important to emphasise that the number of active workers in the field of the sociology of education at that time in England could be counted on the fingers of one hand! Indeed, it is amazing that the approach was so successfully institutionalised. It happened, perhaps, because it coincided with the expansion of educational departments in the Colleges of Education at a time when the focus of interest was on the relationships between the home and the school. If educational psychology had not been so preoccupied with the diagnosis and measurement of skills, child development and personality, but instead had developed a social psychology relevant to education, the story might have been different.

From the mid-1960's onwards, there was a massive expansion of sociology in Britain and in the same period sociology became established in the Colleges and Departments and Institutes of Education. The rationale for the establishment of sociology in the education of teachers was given by the first approach. However, during this period, new sociological perspectives were attaining influence in the U.S.A. From different sources, Marxist, phenomenological, symbolic-interactionist and ethnomethodological viewpoints began to assert themselves. Although there are major differences between these approaches, they share certain common features.

1 A view of man as a creator of meanings.
2 An opposition to macro-functional sociology.
3 A focus upon the assumptions underlying social order, together with the treatment of social categories as themselves problematic.
4 A distrust of forms of quantifications and the use of objective categories.
5 A focus upon the *transmission* and *acquisition* of interpretative procedures.

The movement arose in the U.S.A. at a period of political, economic and educational crisis in an overall social context of advanced technological control. During this period, students in the West, particularly in Germany and in the U.S.A., were turning their attention to the authority and knowledge properties of the university. This brought into sharp focus the social organisation of knowledge, the manner of its transmission and the power relationships upon which it rested. Fundamental questions were raised about the existing classification and framing of educational knowledge as to its significance for the structuring of experience and as a repeater of society's hierarchical arrangements. At the same time, the ineffectiveness of U.S.A. schools to educate even in their own terms, Black, Puerto-Rican, Mexican, Indian minority groups gave rise to a tidal wave of educational research. This research was mainly carried out by psychologists and it was based upon a deficit model of the child, family and community, rather than upon a deficit model of the school. The reaction against this definition of the problem, itself associated with the rise of black power, led to a reconsideration of the power relationships between the school and the community it served; it led to a major questioning of the administration of school systems; it led to a major questioning of the organisational forms of education, and in particular to a major questioning of the transmission and contents of school knowledge. The impact of these intellectual movements and of the political context in the U.S.A., upon the sociology of education in England, led to a broadening of its concerns and almost to an identification of the field with the sociology of knowledge.

We should also bear in mind that the belief in the 1950's and 1960's in England that the development of the comprehensive school would reduce educational problems was shown to have an inadequate foundation in the seventies onwards. The Newsom Report raised fundamental questions about the content of education for the 'average' child. The proposal to raise the school leaving age created a 'crisis' of the curriculum. The development of the Schools Council led to an increase of interest in curriculum development. A number of new chairs in Curriculum Studies were established. Research continued to reveal class differences in educational attainment. It would not be too much to say that the emphasis was shifting from the organisational structure of schools to an emphasis upon what was to be taught. It would also not be entirely wrong to suggest that the incentive to change curricula arose out of the difficulties secondary schools were experiencing in the education of the non-élite children. We can thus trace a number of influences in both the U.S.A. and here, which lead to a rather different approach to the sociology of education. We have only to compare the textbooks by Ottaway, Musgrove and Banks and the reader edited by Halsey, Floud and Anderson with Young's collection of essays and the Open University reader *School and Society* to see the impact. We now have a second approach to the sociology of education which is, itself, partly a response of the new generation of sociologists to intellectual movements in sociology and to their personal and political context.

I shall briefly compare the two approaches. Both approaches share a common concern with the interrelationships between class, selection and equality. However, the first approach placed its emphasis upon macrostructural relationships as these controlled the relationships between levels of the educational system, the organisational features of schools and their selective principles, and the interrelationships with the division of labour, social stratification and social mobility. The basic unit of this approach tended to be an element of a structure, for example, a role, or a structure examined in its relation to another structure. The basic unit of the second approach is a situated activity and it focuses upon interactional contexts and their contents. The second approach focuses upon the knowledge properties of schools and is therefore concerned to study the social basis of what is defined as educational knowledge. Whereas the first approach made explicit how social class entered into, maintained and repeated itself in the organisational structure of education, the second approach carries out a similar analysis on the contents of education. As a result, curricula, pedagogy and forms of assessment are brought sharply into focus and their ideological assumptions and forms of legitimation are explored. This switch in focus has enabled the sociology of education to draw upon the sociology of knowledge and to take advantage of the approaches mentioned earlier. Whereas the major technique of enquiry of the first approach was the social survey or enquiries based upon large populations by means of the closed questionnaire the second approach favours case studies of ongoing activities in which participant observation, the tape recorder and video machines play an important role in the construction of close ethnographic descriptions which as yet have not been made in this country.

It is customary to characterise the first approach as structural-functional, but if one reads Floud and Halsey carefully, they specifically point out the limitations of this perspective.

> The structural-functionalist is pre-occupied with social integration based on shared values – that is, with consensus – and he conducts his analysis solely in terms of motivated action of individuals to behave in ways appropriate to maintain society in a state of equilibrium. But this is a difficult notion to apply to developed industrialised societies, even if the notion of equilibrium is interpreted dynamically. They are dominated by social change, and 'consensus' and 'integration' can be only very loosely conceived in regard to them. (Floud and Halsey, 1958)

They did, however, accept the thesis of increasing subordination of the educational system to the economy in advanced industrial societies. They saw the development and structural differentiation of the educational system very much as a response to the needs of the technological society and they saw education as active essentially in its role of creating new knowledge. Their basic view was that education was contained by the rigidities of an out-moded class structure which deeply penetrated its organisational forms. *It is important to realise that Floud and Halsey used a manpower and equality argument as a double-barrelled weapon to bring about change in the procedures of selection and the organisational structure of schools.* They were aware of the need to study the contents of schools and universities and explicitly and repeatedly used a Weberian approach to the issue. Halsey's elaborate analysis, within a Weberian framework, of the British universities, focused on the distinctive role of British university teachers as creators and transmitters of knowledge. But it is now fashionable to belittle the earlier work of Floud and Halsey and to consider that their treatment of education paid little regard to its problematics. This is quite untrue. For them, the existing organisation structure was certainly something not to be taken for granted – nor were the procedures of selection. Halsey wrote a major piece on genetics and social structure. They were both considerably involved in attacking the assumptions underlying the measurement of intelligence. Taylor, a student of Floud, wrote a book showing clearly the dubious assumptions underlying the creation of the secondary modern school.

Whereas the first approach tended to assume a normative system, and the problems of its acquisition, the second approach takes as problematic the normative system and its acquisition, but it, itself, presupposes a complex structural arrangement which provides, at least initially, and often finally, the terms of local situated activities. Negotiated meanings presuppose a structure *of* meanings (and their history) wider than the area of negotiation. Situated activities presuppose a situation; they presuppose relationships between situations; they presuppose sets of situations.

Part of the difficulty arises out of the confusion of the term structure with structural functionalism. Structural relationships do not necessarily imply a static social theory, nor do they imply features which are empirically unchanging. At the level of the individual, they exist in the form of interpretative procedures. For example, the relationships between subjects is a structural relationship, and specific identities are created by the nature of the relationship. Whether these structural relationships are repeated, and how they are repeated, depends upon a range of factors. The structural relationships, implicitly and explicitly, carry the power and control messages *and* shape, in part, the form of the response to them at the level of interaction. Because relationships are structural, it does not mean that the initially received objective reality is without contradiction, or a seamless fabric, nor that there is a uniform shared subjective meaning.

What is of interest is that the new approach is not an approach, but it is made up of a variety of approaches (some of which are in opposition to each other) which have been outlined earlier. As a result, there has been a refreshing increase in the range and type of questions we can ask. Of equal significance, there is now the possibility of a wider connection between sociology and the sociology of education, which in turn provides a much stronger source of legitimation of this field. However, major questions still remain unanswered only at a highly formal level. For example, there is the issue of how we relate macro and micro levels of explanation. Berger (1966) argues that this can be done by relating his phenomenological approach to the sociology of knowledge to symbolic interactionism. This does not show us *how*, it simply indicates a *direction*. Others have suggested relating symbolic interactionism with forms of Marxist analysis. However, this again misses the question of how theories which are based on very *different* assumptions are to be related. There is also the very perplexing issue of what happens when we move from raising questions or writing highly speculative essays to the giving of answers. It is not at all clear how we obtain reliable knowledge, which can be made public and plausible.

Whilst we are told of the sins of empiricism, of the abstracted fictions created by observer's categories and arithmetic, of the importance of close ethnographic study of situated activities, we are not told precisely what are the new criteria by means of which we can both create and judge the accounts of others. We are told and socialised into what to reject, but rarely told how to create.

In the same way as the first approach to the sociology of education defined research problems so the recent approaches carry research directions. It is therefore important to consider where the emphasis is falling in order to ensure that our range of questions is not always coincident with whatever appears to be the approach.

And this takes us to the heart of the matter. In a subject where theories and methods are weak, intellectual shifts are likely to arise out of conflict between *approaches* rather than conflict between explanations, for by definition, most explanations will be weak and often non-comparable, because they are approach-specific. The weakness of the explanation is likely to be attributed to the approach, which is analysed in terms of its ideological stance. Once the ideological stance is exposed, then all the work may be written off. Every new approach becomes a social movement or sect which immediately defines the nature of the subject by redefining what is to be admitted, and what is beyond the pale, so that with every new approach the subject almost starts from scratch. Old bibliographies are scrapped, the new references become more and more contemporary, new legitimations are 'socially constructed' and courses take on a different focus. What may be talked about and how it is to be talked about has changed. Readers typifying and, more importantly, reifying the *concept* of *approach* are published. A power struggle develops over the means of transmission and evaluation. This power struggle takes the form of the rituals of the generation, as the guardians of the old approaches (usually the successfully established) fight a rearguard action against the new. Eventually the new approach becomes institutionalised, and every sociology department has a representative. A new option is created, and the collection which is sociology has expanded to include a few more specialised identities: ethnomethodologist, symbolic interactionist, phenomenologist, structuralist. People begin to say the subject is alive, our range of questions has expanded; the sociological imagination has been revitalised! The dust finally settles and students have a few more approaches to learn, which are then suitably regurgitated in examinations in the form of the dichotomies given in the early part of this article. What is a little remarkable is that our forms of teaching sociology in England do not even give rise to *either* new explanations or even new approaches. We appear to be almost wholly parasitic on the Americans, who provide for some of us a constant source of the emperor's new clothes.[1]

We shall now raise issues of a very general nature, which at first sight may seem far removed from the everyday activities of schools, and yet these everyday activities carry within themselves the processes and practices crucial for the understanding of more general questions. It is a matter of some importance that we develop forms of analysis that can provide a dynamic relationship between 'situated activities of negotiated meanings' and the 'structural' relationships which the former presuppose. Indeed, it is precisely what is taken as given in social approaches which allows the analysis to proceed in the first place. Neither can the relationships between structural and interactional aspects be created by metasociological arguments as in the case of Berger, when he shows how his phenomenological approach can be linked to symbolic interactionism. The levels, if they are to be usefully linked, must be linked at the *substantive* level by an explanation whose conceptual structure directs empirical exploration of the relationship between the levels.[2] In a way, the concepts of classification and frame which I have developed attempt to do this. The concept 'classification' is a structural concept. It points to that which is to be repeated. However, whether it is or not depends upon the strength of 'frames' at the interactional levels. As both concepts have built into them *both* power and control elements, then we can see how different forms of constraint, emerge as the relationship between these concepts changes.

If we are to consider the relationships between schooling and society a crucial question becomes that of accounting for the constraints which limit the style educational knowledge takes for groups of pupils and students. For example, in England until recently the style for élite pupils was specialised. Compare the number of 'A' level subjects offered with the

---

[1] We are often made aware of continental thought through the writings of American sociologists.

[2] It may be unwise to formulate the issue as one of levels. It is more a question of formulating the problem in such a way that one is not denied access to a variety of viewpoints. It is possible that 'approaches' sometimes function as sociological mechanisms of denial.

number of subjects offered by European students. Now this specialised style for élite pupils has a number of consequences. The first is that we cannot possibly understand the form and content of education in England unless we take this into account. It is quite remarkable that no sociologist has concerned himself with this question, neither for that matter have historians. Now in order to come to terms with such a question, we need to consider the relationship between culture and social structure, between power and control from a historical and comparative perspective.

There is also a tendency to view the structuring of knowledge in schools in isolation from other symbolic arrangements of society. We might ask if there were any relationships between the attempts to de-classify and weaken educational frames (particularly for the non-élite children) and the musical forms of a Cage or a Stockhausen. Even within schools, the emphasis upon the stratification of knowledge may promote interest in certain subjects or groupings at the expense of others. Witkin at Exeter and John Hayes at King's College London are almost alone among British sociologists interested in education who are concerned (albeit from different perspectives) to understand the educational shaping of aesthetic experience. (The first group of students in England to protest against the form and content of education were art students.) We have in education also a remarkable opportunity to study changes in the forms of socialisation which control the body as a message system. From this point of view, the transformation, over the past decade or so, of physical training into physical education and movement is of some interest. It might be of interest to examine if there are any relationships between the latter shift and the shift of emphasis in English from the strong framing and classification of aesthetic experience to weak framing and classification of such experience; from the word abstracted from the pupil's experience to the word as a critical realisation of the pupil's experience. Latent in the teaching of English is a crucial sociological history of the class structure and one means of the latter's control. If we are to take shifts in the content of education seriously, then we require histories of these contents, and their relationship to institutions and symbolic arrangements external to the school. We need also to submit the pedagogy of 'spontaneity' to sociological analysis in order to investigate forms of implicit control and the transfer of implicit criteria.

In the same way as we discussed the importance of examining the range, variation and change in what we have called knowledge styles at both the societal and school levels, it is equally as important to consider range, variation and change in what we can call organisational styles.

In England over the past decade, there has developed a variety of secondary school structures and within any one such structure there are often considerable differences in the internal organisation between schools. It is also possible that, cutting across this diversity, there may well be for certain groups of pupils a similarity in how organisational and knowledge features of schools affect the ongoing relationships between teachers, between pupils, between teachers and pupils. To what extent do the controls of higher education and the economy in combination with the focusing of the initial class socialisation of pupils create a context of *plus ça change, plus c'est la même chose?* Finally, we need to ask what are the social controls which monitor and change the range of organisational styles within and between levels of the educational system? And all these questions must be examined from both an historical and a comparative perspective. (We could of course extend the form of this general question to the professional socialisation of the teacher.)[1]

Sociologists are creatures of their time, and the range of approaches to their subject is in part a realisation of the political context and the sociologist's relation to it. As I have attempted to argue, sociologists of education are particularly sensitive to this political context, because the areas of cleavage, dilemma and contradiction in the wider society are particularly transparent, are most visible in the educational arrangements. Thus, there is a resonance between the value positions underlying the various approaches and the problems of educational arrangements, because these problems are the problems of society, which in turn calls out the sociological approaches. Thus, depending upon who is counting, we may have two, three or even four sociologies from which, given time, there will be derived a similar number of sociologies of education, each with their own legitimators, readers, references and special forms of examination questions. The research of one will not be acceptable to the other, because of disputes over the methods of enquiry and/or over disparate ideological assumptions. However, because these approaches attempt to make explicit the assumptions underlying socialisation and their categorial expressions, they temporarily lift the weight of these categories, so that we can see a little how we are, what we are, and in as much as they do this, they restore to us a sense of choice and create a notion that it can be different; whether the 'it' refers to sociology or society, for in the end the two are the same.

Yet it is a matter of doubt as to whether this sense of the possible, that is, the construction and *systematic* analysis of the alternative forms social relationships can take, is developed more by socialisation into an approach, into the sect which is its social basis, or by openness to the variety of social experience. This does not mean that our stance is aesthetic, or one of spurious objectivity, or that we are insensitive to the violations in our political context. Rather, it means we need to explore the ambiguities and contradictions upon which our symbolic arrangements ultimately rest; for in these ambiguities are both the seeds of change and man's creative acts. In order to do this, we must be able to show how the

---

[1] Clearly, these questions about the range and variations in organisational and knowledge styles, their social antecedents and consequences would lead on towards fundamental questions which conceivably might move the sociology of education towards the wider issues of a sociology of culture.

distribution of power and the principles of control shape the structure of these symbolic arrangements, how they enter into our experience as interpretative procedures *and* the conditions of their repetition and change. This may require a widening of the focus of the sociology of education and less an allegiance to an approach and more a dedication to a problem.

IV MEDICINE

Social Science and Medicine
by Roger Gomm
Stevenage College of Further Education

Introduction

A social science perspective on medicine presupposes that the
organisation of health care is *not* simply a rational response to the
problems presented by 'illness' or 'disease', and that 'health', 'illness' and
'disease' are not simply biological matters. In this paper I want to discuss
the contention that illness and disease are social products and in so doing
indicate the types of topic which are interesting to social scientists who
study medicine.

By writing of illness and disease as social products I mean two things:

1 That the conditions which are labelled as 'diseases' occur in patterns
which suggest that the processes that distribute health chances are social
processes;
2 that the definition of 'health', 'illness' and 'disease', the diagnoses of
such conditions and the treatments adopted vary from place to place and
time to time and that medical knowledge and the organisation of medicine
must be understood as the creation of particular sets of social and
historical circumstances. (For a discussion of the definition of 'health',
'illness' and 'disease' see S.S.R.C. 1977, Appendix III.)

The Social Distribution of Health Chances

ILLNESS AND SOCIAL CLASS

As its name suggests the subject of epidemiology (Morris, 1964), which is
now an important sub-discipline of medicine, began its life with the study
of the epidemics which were so common in the nineteenth century.
Almost from the outset it was apparent that epidemic diseases tended to
cause greatest mortality among the very young and the elderly, the lower
working class and the inhabitants of urban slums. The study of epidemics
disclosed the mechanisms through which infectious and contagious
diseases are transmitted and gave an impetus to environmental
engineering projects which resulted in sewage controls and pure water
supply and to attacks on over-crowded slums and unhygienic food
distribution (Hodgkinson, 1973). At the same time, the obvious
association between socio-economic status and epidemic mortality

demonstrated that the risk of illness and death showed a close relationship to a more fundamental underlying pattern of social inequality.

We can see how this pattern persists by looking at the statistics for deaths of children under five years old and at those for adult male premature death (Table 1), both broken down by social class. Child mortality figures show that the risk of dying before reaching the age of five is more than twice as great for a child born into an unskilled manual worker's family than for a child born into a professional or executive home (H.M.S.O., 1976). Looking at the adult figures you will see that the

Table 1: Deaths of all men between 15 and 64, by selected causes and social class. The figures show the extent to which a social class group departs from the average for all men of this age

Cause of death	unskilled	semi-skilled	skilled	managerial	professional
ALL CAUSES	+43	+3	average	−19	−24
Tuberculosis	+85	+8	−4	−46	−60
Stomach cancer	+63	+14	+1	−37	−51
Lung cancer	+48	+4	+7	−28	−37
Coronary disease	+12	−4	+6	−5	−2
Bronchitis	+94	+16	−3	−50	−72
Duodenal ulcer	+73	+7	−4	−25	−52

Sunday Times, 26 September, 1976

risk of death before reaching the age of sixty-five is much greater for unskilled manual workers, and that even diseases popularly associated with 'overworked' executives (for example, heart diseases, ulcers) in fact cause a much higher mortality among unskilled manual workers.

Such statistics are an impressive demonstration that different rates of illness and premature death are but part of a much bigger pattern of inequality, despite the fact that for each particular disease there are complex and specific factors determining its incidence. To use Emile Durkheim's term (Durkheim, trans., 1952) these statistics measure 'social facts' which demand a sociological explanation. At this point the reader is invited to make a catalogue of differences between social classes which might be relevant to the differential incidence of disease and disability.

It is often claimed that we live today in a more equal society than in the past. This is not borne out by the statistics for premature mortality. Differences in premature mortality for men of different classes have *widened* over the years. To a lesser extent the same pattern shows for women. The figures do not so much show that the working class has got sicker, but that the middle and upper classes have reduced the risk of premature death more rapidly than have the working class. Why and how this should be so is an interesting sociological question, but one which it is by no means easy to answer. There are two possibilities: Either (i) modern medicine has served the rich better than the poor; or (ii) modern medicine is not such an important factor as other life circumstances which affect the mortality rates of different classes.

EQUITY AND THE HEALTH SERVICES

The theme that 'the middle class have benefited most from the welfare state' is one which is well worked in the literature of social policy on various state services and benefits, including the health service. There are great difficulties in establishing this claim with regard to health, for in order to estimate which social groups have benefited most from the health service one needs some measurement of which social group is most at risk of ill-health (hence most in need of health services) and this has to be independent of the diagnoses made within the health service itself. Thus, while various studies show that working class patients consult their doctors more frequently than middle class patients, or that working class children are more frequently hospitalised and for longer periods, this alone tells us nothing about treatment in *relation to need*, or indeed about any differences in the quality of treatment experienced by patients of different social classes. (For details of the use of the health services by different classes see Carstairs, 1966; Cartwright, 1967, pp. 10–38.) Unfortunately, independent measurements of the need for health care are very difficult to come by for, in the usual course of events, levels of sickness are measured by doctors' diagnoses, and the question of whether doctors give the same diagnoses and recommend the same treatments to different social categories is part of the question being asked.

The article by Howlett and Ashley which follows this paper attempts to avoid this problem by careful choice of disease for study and their findings do seem to indicate that factors other than need for treatment (here age and class) help to determine what resources are used in treatment. However, while differences in treatment by social class were clearly shown in this study, there is no clear evidence that the services offered by well-equipped, well-staffed hospitals are actually more effective in promoting cures than the services offered by other hospitals.

This study illustrates a very important concern within the sociology of medicine and social policy studies of health care; that of monitoring the delivery of health care in relation to need and in relation to equality of treatment. Those who would like to follow the debates about equality of care in the N.H.S. are directed to Rein (1969) who considers that the N.H.S. offers an equal service to all, and Townsend (1974) who does not.

The question of the 'best way' to provide health services has produced a large literature. This includes empirical studies of service, hospital, ward and general practice organisation (Sudnow, 1963; Strauss et al., 1963; Goffman, 1969; Barnard and Lee, 1976); of medical, nursing and para-medical education (Becker et al., 1968; Psathas, 1968; Dingwall, 1977;

Atkinson, 1976; Pomeranz, 1973); doctor-patient interaction (Mauksh, 1973; Horobin and Bloor, 1974; Stimson and Webb, 1975), all of which might form the basis for positive recommendations for change. While some of this literature will be commented upon below, space forbids an extensive review here. However, one issue which seems to have generated more literature than any other is the debate about the relative merits of private versus nationalised medicine or various mixtures of the two.

Advocates of private medicine (B.M.A., 1967; Harris and Seldon, 1965) argue that people are willing to pay more for medical services when they are allowed a choice of services and that private medical care results in a higher inflow of money into medicine than is the case with a nationalised service. There is an underlying acceptance here that more money actually means a better service. Those who oppose any extension or seek to reduce the extent of private medicine in Britain (Titmuss, 1972; Townsend, 1974; Abel-Smith, 1976) argue that allowing people to purchase health care according to their means greatly disadvantages those with least income because available health care resources would tend to flow towards those who have most money. It is argued that this would be so even where the state provided a 'safety net' health service for those unable to purchase health care because such state services would have to offer a poor quality service to make private medicine a commercial proposition. Naturally this interest has led to comparative studies of health care, particularly those comparing the delivery of health care under the English National Health Service, with the American system, dominated as it is by private practice. It is fair to say that most of such studies produce a picture favourable to the N.H.S. (Lindsay, 1962; Titmus, 1970; Hurley, 1971; Abel-Smith, 1976; Nicoll, 1977) although whether this remains true after recent cuts in N.H.S. expenditure is debatable.

DEMOGRAPHIC CHANGE AND CHANGES IN THE DEMAND FOR HEALTH CARE

Changes in the structure of the population inevitably alter demands for health care. One of the major changes in modern industrial societies has been an increasing percentage of elderly people due to the survival of those born during a period of high birth rates into a period of low birth rates. Of all age groups the elderly are most vulnerable to disease and disability and at present about one third of the N.H.S. hospital budget is spent on the elderly, to which we must add general practice care and expenditure by local authority social service departments. A large percentage of the elderly who are in hospital are there not so much because they require hospital treatment, but because there is nowhere else suitable for them to go. This state of affairs has often been attributed to changes in family structure which lessen the likelihood of younger people looking after their ageing relatives. Too much should not be made of the 'decline of the extended family' argument, however, for although each elderly person today is likely to have fewer younger relatives than in the past, approximately the same percentage of elderly persons ended their days in residential care (in the workhouses mainly) at the end of the nineteenth century as do today. In commenting on the large percentage of elderly persons in hospitals it is perhaps more pertinent to point to the way in which the health and welfare services have developed to provide high status careers for doctors and social workers, rather than to provide basic needs for convenient housing, sheltered accommodation, home helps and reasonable incomes for elderly people. (On old-age health see Klein, 1972; Isaacs, 1972.)

The falling birth rate has greatly reduced the demand for maternity services and, since the hospitals until recently have been able to resist any reductions in maternity beds or staffs, this has had the effect of reducing the numbers of babies born at home. As we shall see below this has not been an undisputed advantage.

Another demographic change concerns the movement of population out of inner city areas which, for historical reasons, have been better provided with hospitals than other areas. At present the government is attempting to reduce the scale of hospital provision in these areas against intense medical opposition.

Inner city areas also contain the highest concentrations of working class immigrants from the 'new commonwealth'. These people have health problems which are particularly common in their communities. For instance, tuberculosis, rickets, and sickle cell anaemia are largely confined to new commonwealth immigrants. Such groups present particular problems of language and culture for English health services which require urgent sociological research. (On the epidemiology of new commonwealth immigrants see Carne et al., 1976.)

HEALTH CARE SYSTEMS IN THE THIRD WORLD

Until recently it was assumed that the only possible model for Third World health services was some version of the systems which characterise industrialised nations. The result has been an investment in large hospitals, usually built by multinational building contractors, staffed by highly paid doctors trained in curative medicine using the most elaborate equipment and drugs available. What this has meant in practice is a health service which is available to only a tiny percentage of the urban population, leaving the majority with almost no modern health care at all. At the same time the most pressing of the health problems of Third World populations are diseases which, although they attack large numbers of people, are easy to diagnose and treat and which are preventable by providing pure water, sewage control and dietary supplements. Thus, the concentration of resources on showy hospitals and highly paid consultants is very largely irrelevant to the real health problems of such countries.

From the outset, the revolutionary regime of the Peoples' Republic of China developed a health service tailored to treat the most prevalent diseases using minimally trained 'barefoot doctors', providing health and hygiene education to enable people to look after their own health. This type of health service has been remarkably successful in dealing with the health problems of the under-developed countries and similar versions have adopted in Cuba, Tanzania, Vietnam, Cambodia and Mozambique (Djukanovic and Mach, 1975; China Health Care Study Group, 1974; McMichael, 1976).

Modern Medicine, Life and Death

The issues involved in debates about equity and efficiency in the delivery of modern medical services are interesting but it remains a possibility that modern curative medicine is far less relevant to health than doctors and drug companies would have us believe, and indeed this is suggested strongly by the success of Third World health systems which place the emphasis on simple preventative measures rather than on elaborate medical technology. Evidence collected by medical historians and demographers suggest that medical intervention has been far less important in promoting health than have other social and economic changes.

Improvements in life expectancy for people over forty-five years of age have not been very impressive and recently life expectancy for middle-aged, working-class men has gone into reverse (Powells, 1973). Moreover most of the improvement in middle-aged life expectancy occurred before the advent of modern medical treatments. The improvement in life-expectancy at birth over the last hundred years has been dramatic because of falls in infant and child mortality rates with the reduction of mortality from major epidemic diseases. However, the major child-killing diseases of the nineteenth century were all but conquered before the development of modern prophylactic and curative medicine.

Looked at in this perspective, it seems that the contribution of modern medicine in life and death matters has been far less important than changes in diet, water supply, sewage disposal, housing and general knowledge about health and hygiene. This at least is the conclusion of most medical historians (McKeown, 1962; Howe, 1976).

IATRAGENIC DISEASES

Doubts about the relevance of modern medicine to the promotion of health arise very sharply when we consider 'iatragenic' disease – diseases and disabilities which are caused by medical intervention.

Ivan Illich has written:

> The impact of medicine constitutes one of the most rapidly expanding epidemics of our time. The pain, dysfunction, disability, and even anguish which result from technical medical intervention now rival the morbidity due to traffic, work and even war-related activities. (Illich, 1975, p. 21–2)

Shocking though Illich's indictment of modern medicine is, it is based on well authenticated data on the dangerous nature of medical intervention. While few would go so far as Illich and suggest that modern medical services should be dismantled, many are very seriously concerned that in many types of treatment the risks outweigh the advantages. We are all well aware of newsworthy tragedies such as the cases of the drugs, Thalidomide (Sjöström and Nilsson, 1972), Eraldin or Enterovioform and of the risks associated with injections against measles or whooping cough. In the case of Thalidomide there is no doubt that the adverse effects of the drug on the unborn greatly outweighed the advantages to pregnant women, but matters are rarely as clear cut as this. For instance some contraceptive pills appear to carry a risk of thrombosis for some users, but the mortality from thrombosis is lower than would have been the risk of mortality from pregnancy. Thus the question of risks and benefits is a matter of fierce contention. For instance, it has been claimed that the increasing tendency for babies to be born in hospital has increased the risk of infant mortality and malformation and the greater risk of cross-infection. The greater use of forceps delivery and induction in hospital have been specifically cited as causes. Certainly it is true that other European countries where babies are more frequently born at home have lower peri-natal mortality rates (Tew, 1977).

In addition to the question of risks there is considerable evidence that many widely practised medical treatments are ineffective. A well-known work is Cochran's 1972 monograph which details the results of many painstaking studies of the effectiveness of medical interventions. His findings, subsequently supported by other workers, suggest, among other things, that intensive care units for coronary cases marginally reduce the chances of a patient's survival, yet in the U.S.A. 10 per cent of all nurses are employed in such units and the N.H.S. has invested heavily in them. He finds also that insulin (or tolbutamide or pheniform) treatment is ineffective with those who become diabetics later in life, yet this is the standard treatment, nor does he find that iron prescriptions remove the symptoms of anaemia from non-pregnant women. Other investigators find that long hospital stays for coronary disease (Harpur, 1971), or tuberculosis (Dawson, 1966) or hernia (Morris et al., 1968) have no appreciable effect, yet they are widely practised. Professor Bunker (1974) claims that many surgical interventions are at best ineffective, while the Sainsbury Committee in the U.K. (H.M.S.O., 1967, pp. 208–9) and a government inquiry in the U.S.A. (Food and Drugs Administration, 1971) both found that over 30 per cent of drugs were ineffective or dangerous for the purposes for which they were prescribed. A recent survey of admissions to Withington Hospital showed that 62 out of 100 elderly people admitted they had been prescribed drugs in dangerously high quantitites.

These examples are given for two reasons. Firstly they suggest that we cannot understand the activities of doctors as a rational application of knowledge to the treatment of disease, but must consider also the career interests of doctors and the commercial interests of drug companies. The former point is particularly apparent with regard to the falling birth rate and the increasing percentage of hospital confinements. Secondly such findings go some way towards explaining the growing disenchantment with modern medicine shown by those who are interested in self-health (Levin et al., 1976), or who turn to Christian Science, faith healing (Skultans, 1976), homeopathy or chiropractice. It should be said that the most vigorous self-health movements are those associated with women's groups where it is claimed that pregnancy, a normal healthy activity, has come to be treated as a kind of disease by the (male dominated) medical establishment (Oakley, 1975; MacKeith, 1976).

DIET, HEALTH AND CLASS

If drug therapy, advanced surgery and electronic gadgetry of modern medicine do not account for improvements in life expectancy, then it seems most unlikely that differences in medical treatment for different social classes accounts for much of the observed class differences in illness or premature death. For an explanation of these we should look rather to social and economic factors. Just as improvements in health during the nineteenth century can be ascribed to changes in diet so it may be that some of the class differences in disease and mortality today can be ascribed to nutritional factors. Reporting on an extensive research project at Nottingham University, Richard Wilkinson writes:

> The poor eat 56 per cent less fruit per head than the rich, 19 per cent less fresh green vegetables, 28 per cent less milk, 31 per cent less carcass meat, 8 per cent less fat. To make up for this the poor eat 57 per cent more potatoes, 33 per cent more cereal products (mainly bread), 32 per cent more sugar. 'The rich' covers people who were earning £5,000 a year or more. 'The poor' . . . covers those earning £1,200 or less in 1974, but excludes old-age pensioners and households without income earners. . . . Looking at the differences in diet between income groups, it is not surprising that they have a dramatic effect on death rates. (Wilkinson, 1976, p. 567)

AN ECOLOGICAL PERSPECTIVE

An ecological perspective is becoming increasingly influential in the study of health. At this point the interests of medical sociologists mesh with those of physical anthropologists and human ecologists who are interested in the changing relationships between the human species and its environment. In this perspective 'disease' is indicative of a relationship with the environment for which mankind is poorly adapted.

It can be argued that for most of their evolutionary history human beings have been hunters and gatherers and that therefore it is likely that the human species is best adapted for the circumstances of a hunting and gathering way of life. The probable circumstances of early hunting and gathering man (small mobile bands, abundant and varied food supply) provided only poor opportunities for epidemic diseases to spread, so that early human evolution did not provide mankind with an opportunity to develop a natural immunity to those diseases which became the scourge of humanity when human beings settled down to an agricultural existence or came to live in large urban settlements. The adoption of agriculture placed human beings at risk of seasonal shortages and crop failures, while the development of unequal social systems left the poor with inadequate food supplies. Thus mankind has almost always lived in circumstances to which he is ill-adapted and one index of this maladaptation has been the history of epidemics which has marked the history of Asia and Europe.

This maladaptation was, to some extent, solved as a problem in the West by technological changes leading to better diets and sanitary engineering which ended the danger of major epidemics but which left us with other diseases of maladaptation such as heart diseases and cancers which are major killers in modern industrial societies. Thus it can be argued that the same technological developments which make modern medicine possible also bring human beings into contact with high levels of dangerous chemicals (lead, mercury, asbestos, radio active materials and various carcinogenic agents) which emanate from modern industrial processes and transportation systems (Cole, 1971; W.H.O., 1976). Again the association between bowel cancer and low roughage diets, and the suggested associations between heart diseases and either high animal fats, or diets rich in refined sugar suggest that human health may depend on adhering to a dietary regime to which the human species became adapted in the hunter-gatherer phase (Powels, 1973; Dubois, 1965; Boyden, 1973).

The ecological perspective helps us to understand how 'progress' in the form of rapid transit systems, urbanisation and irrigation works in the Third World, generates disease on a large scale (Hughes and Hunter, 1971; Doyal and Pennell, 1976). It also makes us think of disease, not as something which is caused by a germ that 'comes out of the blue', but as indicative of an individual's relationship with his/her total environment, natural and social. In this context it is tempting to quote the many studies which suggest that happy people are less likely to become ill; for instance the common correlation between high job satisfaction and low absenteeism (Hinkle, 1952) or Matsumoto's study of social stress and coronary disease in Japan (1971). Other relevant studies are summarised by Brown (1976). The idea that 'disease' emanates from an individual's relationship with his environment was part of Greek medical orthodoxy and, as anthropologists have discovered, is a quite common concept in other cultures (cf., for instance, Turner, 1964). However, in Euro-American medicine, the orthodox view is that illness is a state of mechanical breakdown in the human brain or body (McKeown, 1971).

The Relativity of Health and Illness

So far in this paper I have written as if there were no problem in defining a state of sickness or a state of health. Nothing could be further from the truth. Such definitions are not given by nature but are cultural artefacts.

In our society the medical profession claims a monopoly of knowledge and practice over what *they* define as 'medical matters', but their knowledge coexists with lay notions about the same subjects, including both the knowledge of 'the man in the street' (whatever that is) and organised bodies of knowledge such as Christian Science or homeopathy or of other groups who claim a particular insight into those conditions labelled illness. The distinction between medical and other notions of sickness is something expressed in sociology by using the term 'disease' to refer to medical diagnosis, and 'illness' to refer to subjective feelings of being unwell. While it may be difficult to sustain this distinction, it is at least useful in reminding us that patients have ideas about sickness too. In fact we know relatively little about the medical ideas of the laity (but see Krischt et al., 1966; Boyle, 1975).

Deviations from normal functioning are not necessarily defined as diseases. Thus in the sixteenth century many behavioural oddities were regarded as evidence of witchcraft or spirit possession which were theological matters. By the eighteenth century, there were well-developed ideas of 'mental illness' and the same and other behavioural oddities came to be regarded as medical matters (Rosen, 1968). This is just one index of the expansion of the medical profession into areas which were once the monopoly of other professional groups, or were private matters; thus 'obesity', 'alcoholism', 'smoking', 'sexual incompatibility', 'impotence' and 'frigidity', fear of strangers, and classroom indiscipline have become medical matters. Reading difficulties have become a neurological disease called 'dyslexia'. Homosexuality, which was defined as a disease in America, suddenly ceased to be one through a vote of the American Psychiatric Association. Pregnancy and menopause have come to be regarded as dangerous medical conditions while increasingly painters, artists and musicians find they have to take employment as art, drama or music *therapists*.

The high prestige of modern medicine is a major difficulty in seeing medical knowledge today as socially organised and socially relative knowledge rather than as a corpus of truth which is true for all men at all times. It is much easier to see medical knowledge as relative in other cultures or historical periods. For instance in 1851 Samuel Cartwright M.D., one-time chairman of the Louisiana Medical Association, published a paper in which he described a disease called 'Drapetomania'. It was a disease which only afflicted Negro slaves and its main symptom was running away. The proper medical treatment of slaves to prevent the onset of this disease is described thus:

> If one or more of them are inclined to raise their heads to a level with their master or overseers, humanity and their own good requires that they should be punished until they fall into that submissive state which it was intended for them to occupy when their progenitor received the name Canaan or 'submissive knee-bender'. They have only to be kept in this state, and treated like children with care, kindness, attention and humanity to prevent and cure them from running away. (Quoted Szasz, 1971, p. 231)

Note here how a particular type of behaviour is defined as 'natural' and 'healthy' and that what is defined as 'healthy' is actually highly convenient to the slave-owning establishment. What is inconvenient to the powerful – slaves running away – then becomes a 'disease'. The result of defining slave indiscipline as 'disease' neatly banishes any idea that slaves might not like being slaves and might run away for rational reasons.

This formula which turns a conflict of interests into a disease seems to be applicable to many conditions – for instance; aspiring or sexually enthusiastic women in the nineteenth century (Ehrenreich and English, 1974), women who fail to conform to a stereotyped female role in the twentieth century (Mitchell, 1975; Chesler, 1974), dissenters in the Soviet Union (Medvedv, 1969), draft dodgers in the U.S.A., student radicals in English universities (Maddison, 1973) have all been regarded as suffering from diseases. On any one day in America thousands of children are absent from school because they have been suspended, many for taking psycho-active drugs (Cottle, 1976), but at the same time somewhere between 300,000 and a million children are in school each day only on condition that they take psycho-active drugs such as Ritalin. These drugs are prescribed on the diagnosis of 'hyperactivity' or 'hyperkinesis' which is seen to be the cause of misbehaviour in class. 'Hyperactivity' used to be diagnosed on the basis of abnormalities in brain wave patterns, but most of these children do not show this abnormality. They are diagnosed as 'sub-clinically hyperactive', i.e. as hyperactive without the symptoms of hyperactivity (Walker, 1974; Rose, 1976; *New Society*, 7 October 1976, p. 4). For a further discussion of the medical model of deviance, see Pearson, 1976.

These examples are given here to suggest that definitions of disease frequently follow from the social and political presuppositions of doctors. As Dreitzel says:

> From a sociological point of view, there is no 'objective' definition of illness; instead it is necessary to ask in whose interest, and with what purpose in mind, illness is socially defined by different people. (Dreitzel, 1971, p. vi)

This is not to say that there are no bacteria or viruses which cause people to feel pain and discomfort. It is to say that for pain or discomfort to count as a disease it is necessary for someone to define it as such. We tend to take it for granted that certain stimuli will cause us unpleasant pain, and that certain pains are indubitable evidence of illness or injury. This is not inevitably so:

> One of the most impressive examples of the impact of cultural values on pain is the hook-hanging ritual still in practice in parts of India. . . . What is remarkable . . . is that steel hooks, which are attached by strong ropes to the top of a special cart, are shoved under the skin and muscles on both sides of the back . . . at the climax of the ceremony in each village, he swings free, hanging only from the hooks embedded in his back, to bless the children and crops. Astonishingly, there is no evidence that the man is in pain during the ritual, rather he appears to be in a 'state of exaltation'. When the hooks are later removed, the wounds heal rapidly, without any medical treatment other than an application of wood ash. Two weeks later the marks on his back are scarcely visible. (Melzack, 1973, p. 24)

Mass screening of populations, whenever they have been conducted, have found that up to 90 per cent of people screened have diseases or disorders judged by medical criteria and that only a minority are receiving medical treatment. Nor does the seriousness of conditions as judged by doctors differentiate those who feel ill from those who do not (Last, 1963; Epson, 1969; Wadsworth et al., 1971). Apparently, like the man on the cart, who in medical terms is suffering from a serious injury, many people do not define themselves as ill even though doctors would declare them to be so. The results of mass screenings suggest that, given sufficient time and equipment, doctors will diagnose most people as sick. This has the practical implication that most people who approach the doctor can obtain his or her agreement that they are indeed 'ill'. As with other kinds of deviance, the incidence of 'disease' and the types of 'diseases' and 'injuries' which exist are the product of the procedures which are available for detecting and describing 'diseases' and 'injuries'.

THE PROCESS OF BECOMING ILL

The process of becoming ill is an extremely complicated one. For all but the most disabling conditions it is evident that people have a considerable choice as to whether to define themselves as sick (say by seeking medical help), to ignore what would otherwise be 'symptoms', or to find alternative, non-medical or less serious explanations for them; for instance, 'smoker's cough' rather than bronchitis, or 'indigestion' instead of early coronary pains. The individual's area of choice may be severely restricted by others, especially by relatives or other co-residents who may place pressure on him to adopt the sick-role. Indeed forcing someone into the sick-role is often a phase in a family dynamic game where all kinds of family conflicts can be dealt with by defining one member of the family as 'sick' (Laing and Esterson, 1969).

We are used to the idea of doctors making diagnoses. We know far less about the diagnoses which people make about their own health.

It is obviously important to know what ideas people themselves have of illness. It is not surprising to learn that there are great differences between English speaking and Spanish-speaking Americans in their concepts of disease. Spanish-speakers recognise 'evil eye', 'susto' (a state of shock) and sorcery as illnesses which afflict their group alone. Thus it is believed that Anglo doctors cannot treat such conditions successfully. When a Spanish-speaking American family diagnoses one of these conditions they approach a traditional healer. Here local folk knowledge determines whether the afflicted person plays the sick role of modern America or the sick role Chicano style (Saunders, 1954).

To take a less exotic example, pain in the lower back seems to experienced frequently by lower-class, middle-aged women in America, England and Europe. The pain seems to be regarded as unpleasant, but 'normal'; not as an 'illness' but as a state of affairs to be expected. Women in other classes seem much more likely to interpret these as 'symptoms' of an 'illness' and to consult a doctor. For further differences in the interpretation of experience as 'symptoms' see Frankenberg and Leeson, 1976; Zola, 1966.

Apart from culturally and sub-culturally given knowledge about disease, all individuals and their families have some personal experience and knowledge of illness on which to base their assessments. Knowing someone who had a pain in the chest on Monday and dropped dead on Tuesday is likely to have a very important effect on the way in which I regard a pain in my own chest, or upon what advice I give to a friend.

A second important set of factors may be regarded as part of a 'cost-benefit analysis', setting the advantages of being sick (notably the advantage of getting treatment) against the disadvantages. At this point it is necessary to look more closely at the notion of the sick role; an idea which owes much to the American sociologist, Talcott Parsons (Parsons, 1951).

1 The person who is sick is exempted from normal social responsibilities. Such an exemption usually has to be legitimated by a doctor diagnosing the person as 'really ill'.
2 The patient is morally obliged to seek technically competent help and to co-operate in the process of trying to get well. Thus he should do what the doctor tells him. (This clause does not apply to people who are diagnosed as 'mentally ill'. It is part of their condition that they are unable to behave in such a rational way.)
3 There is an institutionalised definition of the situation that the patient cannot of his own will or effort get better. Moreover, his condition is regarded as involuntary. No blame attaches to the person who is sick. Here it becomes unsurprising that attempted suicides, abortion cases and

drunks are patients who are unpopular with medical personnel and tend to be treated rather worse than other patients for, unless they are defined as 'mentally ill', they cannot be seen as involuntarily ill (Bagley, 1971).

Parsons speaks of the sick role almost exclusively in terms of doctor-patient relationships. In fact, as we all know from our own experience, we can identify a 'sub-clinical' sick role in which people who claim that they 'feel under the weather' are exempted from normal obligations, allowed to stay in bed, permitted to be more than usually bad tempered and so on. Even here sickness has to be legitimated by others and the sick person is likely to be obliged to 'behave sensibly'; not to get out of bed, to keep warm, etc.

Sometimes illness may be a strategy for avoiding unpleasant situations, reneging on previous agreements, or avoiding embarrassment. The adoption of the sick role may be a move towards a very strong bargaining position within the family; from the position of an invalid it may be possible to bargain for far more care and attention. On the other hand, entering the sick role may mean loss of earnings or opportunities, or bring one into contact with medical procedures which are frightening or stigmatising. The reader can no doubt supply many examples from personal experience, but is also recommended to the case studies in Robinson's book, *The Process of Becoming Ill* (1971), and those for cancer patients presented by Salzberger (1976).

The strategies adopted in order to occupy the sick role may be quite extreme. The Braginskis study (1969) of patient behaviour in an American mental hospital suggests that patients learn to manipulate symptoms of mental illness so as to appear well enough to obtain maximum privileges within the hospital, but too sick to be discharged. Attempted suicide gives us another example (Stengel, 1964). It is, of course, a moot point as to how far such bargaining is conscious and how far it might be accounted for in terms of 'psycho-somatic' illness.

In order to be given the advantages of being ill, it is necessary to be defined as 'really ill', as 'ill enough' and as 'not pretending' or 'malingering'. The medical profession have a very important role to play in authenticating sickness. Several studies suggest that doctors sometimes approach diagnosis with the suspicion that the patient is 'malingering'. Letters by G.P.s to the medical press, complaining that patients abuse their services, are fairly common, even suggesting that patients should be fined for so doing. English G.P.s seem rarely to refuse to sign medical certificates but such behaviour is much more common among company doctors (Mohl, 1969) and military doctors. The latter seem to be more willing to diagnose sickness when the unit is on active service (Daniels, 1971). This is, of course, the theme of Heller's novel, *Catch 22* (1964).

Doctors sometimes adopt measures to cope with what they consider to be 'abuse'. Many hospital out-patient departments keep unofficial 'black-lists' of suspect patients, while G.P.s may shelter behind a fierce receptionist, refuse home visits, or adopt a cold attitude to suspect patients. As Christopher Bagley points out, such deterrent strategies are most likely to deter those patients who are already inhibited about 'bothering the doctor unnecessarily' (Bagley, 1971). Deterrent strategies are of course another important factor determining whether or not people choose to enter the sick role.

> In the Soviet Union . . . many persons who had difficulty in meeting the strenuous industrial demands or who were unmotivated towards work came to seek help from doctors and a legitimate excuse for failing to appear at work. To protect economic production the government restricted the number of sick-role clearances that doctors could grant during a certain period of time.
> (*Mechanic*, 1968, p. 80)

Here we can see that the definition of ill-health was ultimately a political one made by the Soviet government, and one designed to maximise production. Marxist writers in the West have tended to see our medical certificate system in the same light, as a device to control absenteeism and maximise the exploitation of the workforce. However, the evidence shows that since the advent of the National Health Service absenteeism from work, legitimated by doctors' certificates, has increased markedly (Teeling-Smith, 1969).

Having decided to consult a doctor, the patient has the problem of explaining to him what is wrong. Moreover the patient probably has very distinct ideas as to what should be done to put it right. Thus doctor-patient interchanges can be regarded as a type of 'strategic interaction' in which both parties have projects they wish to achieve. This is described in detail by Gerry Stimson and Barbara Webb, who also describe how patients rehearse for the coming encounter and attempt to make sense of what the doctor has said afterwards. Language and information are extremely important in doctor-patient communication. The doctor is (apparently) the master of a special language which can be used to communicate with other medical personnel without the patient comprehending, and the doctor has access to information about the patient, which the patient has not. All studies of doctor-patient communication show how little meaningful information doctors give to patients. Byrne and Long (1976) quote almost incomprehensible instructions given by doctors to patients, and Glazer and Strauss (1965) describe how patients engage in an elaborate detective game in order to discover if they are dying.

However, patients do have some opportunities for influencing the doctor's diagnosis. Roth, in his study of a tuberculosis sanatorium, details how patients are able to bargain with doctors for their treatment to be advanced from stage to stage (Roth, 1963).

Sociological studies of how doctors reach diagnoses do not inspire a great deal of confidence in the medical profession. This has been especially so where 'mental illness' diagnoses are concerned. Rosenhan's classic 'pseudopatient' experiment involved fake patients gaining admission to mental hospitals in America where they were universally diagnosed as 'schizophrenics'. Despite the fact that they behaved as normally as possible in such abnormal circumstances they were only detected as 'sane' by the other patients. Similar doubts have been thrown on diagnosis in general medicine. A study which was conducted in America before the war involved 1,000 New York school children. Sixty-one per cent of these children had already lost their tonsils and the remaining 39 per cent were assessed by a group of doctors who recommended that 45 per cent should undergo adenotonsillectomy. The rejected children were then sent to a second group of doctors who recommended surgery for 66 per cent of them. Those children twice rejected were sent to a third group of doctors who recommended surgery for 44 per cent of them. At this point only 65 of the original group had not either been operated upon or had the operation recommended for them. A recent study by Wood showed nine colour slides of children's tonsils to a group of 41 ear, nose and throat specialists, G.P.s and paediatricians. Two slides, unbeknown to the audience, were shown twice and it was found that the ability of the audience to arrive at the same assessment of the twice shown slides was only slightly better than chance. Michael Bloor provides a detailed study of the way in which different ear, nose and throat specialists reach their diagnoses (Bloor, 1976).

Similarly, other studies have shown that different doctors may diagnose the same condition differently – see for instance Cochrane, 1951; Yerushalmy, 1951; Fletcher, 1960. In cases of industrial injury claims, claims against insurance companies, cases of medical negligence, criminal trials and courts martial, where a great deal hinges on the doctor's diagnosis, we can imagine that factors other than strictly 'medical' ones affect the doctors' diagnosis. This is demonstrated for military psychiatric diagnoses by Daniels (1976).

A fascinating question for the sociologist is that of how far the social characteristics of patients affect the diagnoses doctors make. While not established by any detailed research one can speculate that the conditions of 'autism' and 'dyslexia' were initially much more frequently diagnosed for middle class children and that doctors are inclined to ascribe many conditions of women in late middle age to 'the menopause' which would be differently diagnosed for men of the same age. A more unusual example is drawn from the experience of an acquaintance of mine. A doctor herself, she was admitted to a London hospital suffering from the acute pain of gall stones. She was very coldly dealt with, given a pethidine injection and discharged. It was only after an operation to remove her gall bladder at another hospital that she realised that she had been treated as a pethidine addict in withdrawal. The critical feature of her diagnosis was the fact that she was a doctor. Almost all pethidine addicts are doctors.

Even the diagnosis of death is not straightforward. There is, of course, the problem that life persists even after the brain is irreparably damaged, creating enormous dilemmas for doctors concerning whether to discontinue life-support. David Sudnow's study of American hospitals and death shows that in two other respects the diagnosis of death is problematic. Studying the admissions procedure at a private hospital, he discovered that cases near to death where the person was obviously too poor to pay the hospital bill were docketed 'dead on arrival'. In another hospital he found that the timing of death was correlated with the shifts worked by nursing staffs. Since nurses were forced to remain on duty to lay out the body of a patient who died during their shift, patients almost never 'died' towards the end of a shift (Sudnow, 1967). (For further information on the topics raised in this section see Tuckett, 1976.)

Medicine Economy and Society

Thus far I have argued that the viruses, bacteria, cancers and accidents, miseries, confusions, anger and pain which might come to be defined as 'disease' and thus become the responsibility of the medical profession, occur in patterns which are best understood sociologically, and that the actual labelling of such conditions as 'diseases' occurs through a very complicated social process. It should be clear then that the organisation of medicine is not to be understood as any simple response to the 'problem of illness'.

Describing and accounting for the way in which medicine is organised has attracted a considerable amount of sociological and other attention. We might distinguish two sorts of approach.

1 'Middle range' theories which account for aspects of medical organisation rather than the organisation of medicine as a whole. For instance, much attention has been paid to the decision-making processes, at parliamentary and other levels, through which decisions concerning health-care are made (Hall et al., 1976; Owen, 1976; Barnard and Lee, 1976) and even more attention has been paid to the organisation of medicine in relation to the career interests of doctors (Forsyth, 1973; Freidson, 1972).

2 Attempts to relate the organisation of medicine to the social structure as a whole (Navarro, 1976). To review these explanations adequately would require an extensive review of the sociological and political economic theories of modern societies which space forbids. Instead I will indicate the role of medicine in modern societies by looking at three functions of medicine.

MEDICINE AND THE CONTROL OF SICKNESS AND DEATH

High levels of illness and disability are a threat to the operation of any society. Functionalist writers such as Talcott Parsons have tended to view medicine as a device to ensure the adequate performance of social roles.

However, the many doubts which exist concerning the effectiveness of medicine make it difficult to accept this view without qualification. After all, one of the major effects of the increasing scale of medical organisation has been an increase in the numbers of people diagnosed as sick.

In a similar way Marxist sociologists have tended to regard 'the reproduction of labour power' as an important function of medicine, seeing doctors as essential agents in a capitalist society ensuring that there are enough workers of sufficient fitness to be exploited by the ruling class. However, in the sort of society in which we live, economic productivity relies less on a supply of healthy manpower and more and more on the replacement and renewal of capital equipment. To find a situation in which medicine is clearly related to the reproduction of labour power we have to go back in history to a time when the economy did rely on sheer numbers of 'hands' and when imperial might relied on abundant cannon fodder. Thus we might regard the 'Maternal and Infant Welfare Movement' of the period 1900 to 1930 as a response to recurrent establishment panics about the falling birth rates of the time (McLeary, 1935).

Again in qualification we can point to the fact that the major health expenditures in Britain and European countries are not on workers or workers-to-be but on those who have retired.

MEDICINE AND SOCIAL CONTROL

We have already seen that, in some cases, medical diagnoses bear a very convenient relationship to the interests of dominant groups in society. Also, although sickness from work legitimated by medical certificate has increased in Britain, it is probably correct to place an emphasis on the role of doctors in guarding access to the sick role, to legitimate absenteeism from work and to the various benefits which sickness brings. More important than this, however, it can be claimed that medicine constitutes a set of ideas which mystify the effects of social inequality and alienating work by representing them as caused by germs or mechanical breakdowns of the body (Rose, 1976).

For instance, one of the characteristics of capitalist societies is the way in which unemployment is constantly generated through the replacement of manpower with machine power. Such unemployment does not appear clearly in the politically sensitive 'unemployment' figures, but tends to be hidden by the tendency to define ever more people as 'mentally ill' or 'chronically sick' or 'disabled' – indeed such diagnoses are frequently made by company doctors to reduce 'over-manning' by what is called 'natural-wastage'.

As Irving Zola comments, the definition of what are essentially 'social ills' as 'diseases' not only displaces the blame to germs, but re-focuses the blame on the individual who is deemed 'not to have looked after his health' (Zola, 1975).

MEDICINE AND THE ACCUMULATION OF CAPITAL

Analysing a capitalist society demands that we relate social formations to the central process of private capital accumulation. In Britain the bulk of medical expenditure is made through the N.H.S., one of the most expensive arms of the state. One of the long-term trends in all capitalist societies is that towards an ever-increasing scale of state activities which complements the trend towards an ever-increasing concentration of control of private enterprise into fewer and fewer huge corporations. While it is popularly thought that the growth of state activities is adverse to the efficient operation of private enterprise and the accumulation of private profit, something like the opposite is true. National governments are committed to economic growth and to political and economic stability which tends to lead them to act in a way which is broadly in line with the interests of large private corporations. The most obvious way in which this can be seen is by considering the state as a customer for private enterprise. It is almost inconceivable, for instance, that the vast armaments industry of the West would be at all profitable if it were not for government purchases. Again an important part of the profits of financial organisations comes from the interest and dividends they receive on loans made to governments, including, of course, loans which enable governments to finance health services. The state then is said to 'organise collective consumption', collecting taxes and spending them on the commodities and services provided by private enterprise, on grants and loans to private industry, on interest repayments and on infra-structural works such as road and electricity supply which are essential for the operation of industry.

Governments also nationalise or buy into enterprises which are unprofitable, but which are major customers or important services to private enterprise. Nationalised health services can be regarded as one example of this, being important customers for buildings, drugs, electronic equipment, stationery, etc., generating a need for government borrowing from financial organisations, and providing a service to private enterprise in maintaining the health of the workforce, if indeed they do.

It is worth raising two specific issues here, to pin-point the role of organised medicine in the political economy of the modern state. Firstly we will look at the way in which the interests of the drug companies help to shape the pattern of medicine. The large multinational drug companies are among the most profitable organisations in the world and geared to high pressure salesmanship. Drugs are produced to make profits and this explains the large number of ineffective drugs on the market and the enormous duplication of preparations. In England the drug companies spend more on each doctor in promoting their drugs than it costs to train a doctor. The drug is the ultimate in capitalist commodities. It has built in obsolescence, it is supplied to doctors in such a way that they find it difficult to make rational prescribing decisions, and when doctors are prescribing for national health services or insurance companies cost is a minor consideration. When one looks at the relationship between doctors and drug companies one can believe that general practice, with its standard three-minute consultations, is designed specifically to maximise the sale of drugs. The relationship between doctors and drug companies has been the subject of considerable research (Sjöström and Nilsson, 1972; Klass, 1975; Heller, 1977) and government enquiries (H.M.S.O., 1967) including enquiries into profiteering in the drugs business (H.M.S.O., 1973).

Secondly, in Britain at the present time there is intense political pressure to increase the role of private medical insurance and private medical treatment as against state medicine and at the same time the Labour Government is attempting to detach private practice from the N.H.S. The lobby for more private practice includes a large section of the medical profession who expect thereby to make larger incomes, and the insurance companies for whom more private practice would mean higher incomes from medical insurance premiums. It is sometimes forgotten that insurance companies are not philanthropic organisations, but invest premium income in stocks and shares, office blocks, shopping precincts and agricultural land. Since insurance companies account for about 20 per cent of all private investment, and a larger percentage of that which is loaned to the government, they are an interest group who have to be taken seriously (C.I.S., 1974).

The pressure to increase the role of private practice illustrates the way in which private capital attempts to shape the pattern of health and welfare services. Private practice, through medical insurance, generates profits in a way that nationalised health services do not. From a commercial point of view the American (60 : 40) mix of private and public medicine would be attractive. There, those who can afford commercially profitable premiums buy medical services according to their means, thus generating funds for investment. At the same time the state provides a deliberately less attractive medical service for those too poor to be of interest to medical insurance companies. State intervention here ensures that expenditure which would not otherwise have been made on drugs and medical equipment is made, as well as providing lucrative employment for doctors who would not otherwise have been employed (Hurley, 1971; Nicoll, 1977). In this example you will see how closely doctors' interests conform with those of private capital.

In conclusion to this section let us say that it is no accident that health services in modern capitalist societies have developed to emphasise expensive, in-patient, high-technology, curative medicine at the expense of preventive medicine, health education and social legislation which would reduce the inequalities that underlie the pattern of ill-health. Its development thus is simply in line with the overall development of capitalist economies.

Case Study

As C. Wright Mills claimed (1970, pp. 9–13) the power of sociology lies in its capacity to make connections between phenomena and events which people in society regard as unconnected. The following case study is given with this end in view.

Nurses are valuable members of the community and deserve to be well provided for in their retirement. To this end they are able to contribute to the Royal National Pension Fund for Nurses which, like most other occupational pension funds, is managed by trustees who have considerable expertise in investment and who are thus able to ensure that reasonable pensions can be paid to contributors.

In 1970, Cape Asbestos closed its Acre Mill processing plant at Hebden Bridge. The operations at this plant are reckoned to have caused 40 people to die a lingering death from asbestos dust and to have maimed permanently several hundred others. The mass media coverage of this plant closure stressed the lax application of safety precautions and pilloried the company doctor for his apparent collusion, but at the same time represented the closure as a step forward. No longer would British workers be faced with this sort of hazard.

The mill was actually closed by its owners as part of a programme of expanding their asbestos processing capacity in the Transvaal where black workers earn £9.50 a month, work with no safety precautions, no trade union representation and a lump sum compensation payment on death of £460. The ability to operate without safety regulations and the low wages of South African blacks makes good commercial sense to Charter Consolidated, the parent company of Cape Asbestos and part of the gigantic Anglo-American Corporation. Thus what is an advantage for white workers turns out to be a disadvantage to black workers. In a very tangible way the compensation payments being made to the workers from Hebden mill are paid for by the hazards suffered by black workers in the Transvaal.

Cape Asbestos is a highly profitable company. In the year it closed Acre Mill it increased its profits from £3,095,000 to £4,141,000. As a profitable company it was a good investment prospect for investors looking for safe, high yield investments. The Royal National Pension Fund for Nurses held 25,000 shares in Cape Asbestos in 1972. Thus do the low wages and high health hazards of black asbestos workers provide for reasonable pensions for British nurses (C.I.S., 1974; H.M.S.O., 1976b).

Selective Care
by Ann Howlett and John Ashley

Debate continues on whether the N.H.S. benefits the middle or working class more. This new study tends to support the view that it favours the middle class

Almost since the beginning of the N.H.S. there has been a debate as to whether the middle or the working classes have got the most out of the service. Some, like Richard Titmuss and Michael Alderson, have argued that the middle classes have had better access to, and made more sophisticated use of, the available services. There have also been those, like Martin Rein, who have claimed that the working classes not only make more use of the N.H.S., but get equally good care. But do they? Given the fragmentary evidence available, it is difficult to answer this question. It is quite clear that the working classes receive proportionately more of the essential services, as measured for example, by the number of admissions to hospital. Equally, the evidence suggests that the middle classes make better use of the preventive services, like cervical smears and conservative dentistry. It is therefore quite possible that while the working classes get more out of the N.H.S. quantitatively, they get less out of it qualitatively.

The difficulty about discussing the quality of care is that it is so many-sided: there is very little agreement about its various facets, far less on how to measure it. However, a study carried out by our unit – examining the reasons why teaching hospitals have lower mortality rates for many common conditions than do regional board hospitals – has provided some enlightening evidence.

While we cannot assume that teaching hospitals provide a higher standard of medical care, we do know that they have far superior resources: for instance, in 1969, during the study, they had 28 consultants and 18 senior registrars – the key young doctors – for every 1,000 'surgical' beds, as against 21 and 4, respectively, in the regional board hospitals. There is also evidence that similar discrepancies could be found in the nursing establishments. At that time, the London teaching hospitals spent £72 per in-patient per week; the provincial teaching hospitals, £64; and the large, acute regional board hospitals, £50. So the pattern of admissions to these hospitals offers some guide on who gets the most out of the N.H.S.

Ideally, of course, one would like to examine the class composition of all admissions. But this data, even if readily available in a more complete form than is now the case, would not be all that revealing without information about the severity of the patients' conditions. Our survey of 932 patients admitted for treatment of benign enlargement of the prostrate gland to two teaching and three regional board hospitals, while not covering the whole spectrum of medical care, at least provides more detail about severity, and social and other factors, than previous inquiries of this nature. Enlargement of the prostrate gland is a fairly common male condition: it usually leads to difficulty when passing water, and can produce very serious trouble indeed. Approximately one in ten of men over 40 can expect to be treated for it, and even more are afflicted. It is no respecter of persons (Harold Macmillan, de Gaulle and Pope John were among famous sufferers) but there is no known link, as far as incidence is concerned, with social class. It usually involves hospital treatment and operation.

If the N.H.S. services were being distributed fairly, and there were no class bias in accessibility (i.e. if resources were accurately matched to need), one would expect to find the illest, oldest, frailest, socially most deprived patients being treated in teaching hospitals – though, of course, these hospitals also require a cross-section of all sorts of cases for their teaching role. In practice, our study showed, precisely the reverse is happening.

Out of all the admissions to the two teaching hospitals, 78 per cent were 'planned', from the waiting list: that is, both the patient and the hospital were prepared. In contrast, of all admissions to the regional board hospitals, 62 per cent were emergency, 'unplanned' admissions: that is, there was a sudden flare-up of symptoms, generally acute retention (inability to pass urine altogether), and a disruption of the hospital routine – as well as a personal crisis – was involved. Amongst these emergency admissions were the older men with more incidental heart and mental disease, who also tended to be widowed and of lower social class. Consequently, it was found that only 1 per cent of those admitted from the waiting list died in hospital, whereas 9 per cent of those admitted as emergencies died. When the emergency admissions were examined in rather more detail, it was found that the highest mortality – 40 per cent – was occurring amongst those who were not operated on – as opposed to 3 per cent when an operation was performed. The majority of cases not operated on were in two of the three regional board hospitals.

Some of the differences in selection might, of course, be explained by the differences in the populations served by the hospitals. So we looked in detail at 212 men who came from a single catchment area that was served both by one of our teaching, and one of our regional board hospitals. Both hospitals were sited inside the catchment area and they were equally accessible. The regional board hospital being, as it were, a neighbourhood hospital, took 89 per cent of all its prostate patients from this area; the teaching hospital, serving a much wider population, took only 39 per cent.

However, this exercise only confirmed the previous indication of an imbalance in the intake of the teaching and regional board hospitals. To start with (see Table 1), the 212 men showed the same asymmetrical split between planned and emergency admissions: three-quarters of the emergency admissions went into the regional board hospital. Of those in

Table 1 : Type of admission to hospital

Hospital	Planned %	Emergency %
Teaching	72	23
Regional board	18	77
No. of cases	89	123

social classes one and two (Table 2) in the Registrar General's definition, 70 per cent went into the teaching hospital; while, of those in social classes four and five, 40 per cent went into the teaching hospital. With those

Table 2 : Social class of local patients

Hospital	I, II %	III %	IV, V %
Teaching	70	50	40
Regional board	30	50	60
No. of cases	20	102	90

under 65 years of age (Table 3), 59 per cent were admitted to the teaching hospital against 29 per cent of those of 75 and above.

Table 3 : Age of patients

Hospital	Up to 64 %	65–74 %	75 + %
Teaching	59	48	28
Regional board	41	52	71
No. of cases	74	89	49

Finally, we looked at some indicators of the general state of health of those going into hospital: here we examined some high risk factors, like the presence of heart failure and mental confusion, and also included those men who had no important additional condition. Here the figures (Table 4) are even more striking. Of those with no additional condition, two thirds entered the teaching hospital, while almost all of those with

Table 4 : Additional medical conditions on admission

Hospital	None %	Congestive heart failure and/or confusion %
Teaching	66	12
Regional board	34	88
No. of cases	89	43

heart failure and/or mental confusion – 88 per cent – were admitted into the regional board hospital. When we looked at the emergency admissions on their own – remembering that the regional board hospital carried far more than its share of these – we found that, even here, the patients entering the teaching hospital were fitter and tended to be younger and of a higher social class. Only in the case of marital status was little difference found between the two hospitals.

So it seems, to judge from this area at any rate, that admission to teaching hospitals may – rather like selective schools – be subject to a kind of 'creaming process'. They appear to be receiving, from a given population, the patients who present the least problems. They may, of course, compensate – such as by taking more ill patients with rarer conditions for which only they have the facilities.

But what explains this creaming process? Was the younger, fitter, middle class man selecting himself, or being selected by his general practitioner, or by the teaching hospital? Do middle class patients consult their G.P.'s earlier, while working class ones wait for trouble to blow up – either because they are more fatalistic or because they do not recognise warning symptoms? Here our own evidence did not provide any answers. However, to supplement the information available, we turned to the Emergency Bed Service for London: this finds beds for patients referred to it by doctors, usually general practitioners. With the help of the E.B.S. staff, we collected information about all the male patients with a diagnosis of an acute retention of urine – the most common symptom leading to emergency admission for an enlargement of the prostrate – referred to the service in alternate months in a recent year: 483 men altogether.

One of the most interesting things to come out of this study was that, overall, less than one in six approaches by the E.B.S. to a hospital for admission were made to a teaching hospital, including its subsidiaries; and only one in six of all the patients were eventually admitted to a teaching hospital. Yet these hospitals have one in three of the appropriate surgical and urological beds available. Age was again a crucial factor affecting admission. Not only were the older men significantly less likely to get into the teaching hospitals than the younger, but, with advancing age, there was increasing difficulty in obtaining a bed at all. It could, of course, be that the refusing hospitals have no beds to spare; however, the E.B.S. approaches only those which it believes have spare capacity (though its information may not reflect hour-to-hour changes within the hospital). It has been claimed, too, that general practitioners try to offload sick, elderly patients and use an 'acute' diagnosis as an inducement. However, a study by G. F. Abercrombie showed 'a remarkable confirmation of the clinical judgement of general practitioners'; in any event, the diagnosis in our study could hardly have been in doubt. Probably – though this can only be supported by anecdotal evidence – hospitals are simply reluctant to accommodate elderly patients for fear of 'blocking' beds.

If we could have established that teaching hospitals were less willing to accept E.B.S. patients than regional board hospitals, this would have been clinching evidence. In fact, though, this was not the case. Teaching hospitals appear to accept a slightly higher proportion of those referred to them. However, as we have shown, they were not being approached nearly as often by the E.B.S. as the regional board ones.

An interesting difference between teaching and regional board hospitals did emerge, though, when we looked at the use of the 'medical referee' system. The E.B.S. invokes this when it is faced either with a particularly urgent case, or with a series of refusals; an independent doctor is then asked to decide which hospital should take the patient. In only one case out of the 483 in our survey was this procedure used because of the urgency of the patient's condition. In 43 cases, however, it was invoked because of repeated refusals by hospitals.

What were the characteristics of these 43 men? On average, they were six years older than the rest and at least six approaches per person were needed before a bed was found for them. Most relevant of all for our inquiry, 39 out of the 43 finally landed up in a regional board hospital. So it is a vulnerable group of elderly men who suffer from the delay in obtaining treatment, with the attendant increase in pain and distress, and who ultimately find a place in the hospitals with less resources. In turn, these hospitals have to take the extra strain on the medical nursing and other staff involved in such emergency admissions – thus compounding their problems.

All this information suggests that the health service resources are not being accurately matched to medical needs. Equally, they support the view that the middle classes are better able to get the most out of the services available.

V GENDER

Sex and Gender
by Tony Marks
Polytechnic of North London

'Sex' and 'Gender' are terms which are often confused. I shall follow the distinction made by Ann Oakley (1972). She says, 'Sex is a word that refers to the biological differences between male and female: the visible difference in genitals, the related difference in procreative function. "Gender", however, is a matter of culture: it refers to the social classification into "masculine" and "feminine".' To put it another way 'sex' is a biological concept and 'gender' may be understood as a sociological concept.

A fundamental problem for sociologists is determining the social causes of human action, distinguishing between the social and non-social influences. This can be seen in several areas of social life. The 'culture of poverty' debate is one such area, so is the debate about educability and the 'intelligence' of different 'races' or different social classes. Whether criminals are inherently wicked or whether their wickedness is socially induced (let alone if they are 'wicked' at all) is another such debate with which you may well be familiar. Roger Gomm, in the previous paper, suggests that the state of being ill is, to put it most conservatively, not *just* a product of physical malfunction.

This problem of conceptualising and perhaps measuring in some way the relative importance of 'nature' and 'nurture' is especially sharp in considering the questions of sex and gender. This is partly because of the substantial lack, until very recently, of sociological material which examined the issues now being confronted and also because of conceptions about the 'rightness' and 'wrongness' of particular forms of behaviour for the sexes. Such views are at the heart of our self-conceptions, of our identities and, in particular, an important part of our moralities as can be illustrated by reference to statuses such as 'homosexual' and 'virgin'. We are not in a position accurately to evaluate the relative importance of inherited and acquired characteristics in any of these areas. But we do know that there is sufficient variation in the human experience for 'nurture' to play a considerable part in deciding how we behave in all of these matters. This fact alone justifies sociologists exploring the issues surrounding the distribution of various behaviour patterns linked to sex differences.

One problem presented to us by these considerations is that while there are two sexes there can be any number of genders. Or, to put it another way, societies generate gender roles which can be divided into a number of significant sub-categories. For example, although 'girl', 'pregnant woman', 'married woman' and 'widow' are all female roles they are not the same female role. In our society the role of 'old man' may have more in common with the role of 'woman' than 'young man' in some respects. Childless, virgin and prepubescent women (and men) frequently have different sex related roles.

So far I have implied that although gender roles vary both culturally and over time there is no problem in determining sex. This is true for nearly all of us nearly all the time. We do fail sometimes to distinguish a person's sex. This may not be important. With the very young we may sometimes wrongly identify sex especially when clothing is very similar. Parents do not necessarily feel offended. The same error at a dance may well provoke stronger reactions. Yet sex, too, is not a self-evident category at all. That there are clear physical differences between most men and most women is, justly, accepted. Nonetheless there are cases of sex indeterminacy and of people 'changing sex'. Similarly in the Olympic games there have been celebrated incidents where 'winners' of events have been disqualified subsequent to chromosome tests. Depending on the tests of hormone production or chromosomes or whatever, it appears that not only do all people not fit neatly into male and female sexes but that the degree of 'maleness' and 'femaleness' within the two categories varies.

It is most certainly clear that, whatever the biological basis of sex, the cultural definitions of gender are not a simple reflection of the biology but that differences between genders attract diverse definition within and between cultures. The biology is, presumably, more uniform. To put it another way, being 'male' or 'female' are inherited and genetic characteristics. Being 'masculine' or 'feminine' are socially generated and learnt as a central part of the socialisation process. The most commonly asked question about a newly born child may well be, 'Is it a boy or a girl?' There is no doubt that the answer to that question is a major influence on the subsequent biography of the infant in all cultures.

Life Chances

There are some activities that we see as typically or exclusively the province of one sex. Being a 'clergyperson' is typically a male preserve in our society, though less so than in the recent past. 'Having a baby' is a female preserve in our, and in any, society. This latter is rooted in biology and seems unchangeable. On the other hand, religious functionaries are sometimes female in our society and in some societies typically so. It is clear then, that the predominance of men in the clergy needs some other explanation. Women are less likely, in contemporary Britain, to become doctors, go to university, own motorcycles, smoke tobacco or gain an apprenticeship. They are more likely to pass their 'A' level sociology examinations, spend a high proportion of their life caring for children, teach in an infant school and they are likely to live longer. These differences in the life styles of men and women range from the trivial to the deeply significant. It is not important if one has a marginally higher chance of getting a seat on a crowded bus – at least not usually. If one's average weekly earnings are only just half those in fulltime equivalent employment, as was the case for female manual workers in the U.K. in 1970, it is very likely to be highly significant.

In a number of important respects the typical lives of women in our society differ from the lives of men. Most of us would agree that these patterned differences seem to leave many of the advantages with men. In large part the picture here is one of inequality, with men generally receiving the largest share of commonly desired statuses.

Subordinate groups frequently have some advantages to their position. The solidaristic tendencies of some working class, male work groups or the 'friendliness' of some working class communities are cited as possibly desirable compensations for an overall experience of underprivilege. Despite some of these claims being bogus and often romantic it is, nevertheless, the case that some elements of subordinate statuses may be subjectively experienced as preferable to aspects of higher status roles. The whole package, may, in some cases, be preferred.

It is the case that in many instances women experience a lack of privilege. It is unclear to what extent this is seen as a grievance by women in our, or any other, society. What is quite clear, as far as modern Britain is concerned, is that in many, but not all, respects, discrimination against women has diminished in recent years and that, as measured by the growth in that diverse collection of activities and groups which are often referred to as the Women's Liberation movement, the consciousness of women has increased. The patterns in other Western industrialised societies are, broadly, the same. The tendencies elsewhere are, for the most part, in the same direction but for many men and women in Third World countries, very little has changed in this century.

There are a number of basic demographic differences between the two sexes. The most obviously important is life expectancy itself. Men and women in our society today live longer than they did in the past. If we compare the years 1840 and 1960 we find that in England and Wales the average life expectations at birth are those shown in Table 1.

Table 1: Life expectancy at birth

	1840	1960
Men	40	68
Women	42	74

Although the most startling aspect of the figures in Table 1 is the greatly increased life expectancy for people as a whole in our society, it is also noteworthy that women have had a longer life expectancy at birth throughout the recent past and, moreoever, that the gap is widening. Another aspect of this difference is that there are nearly twice as many women over the age of sixty-five as there are men. Retirement ages vary between occupations and between the sexes and this fact further complicates the matter. Whatever social processes produce different retirement ages (or different conceptions of retirement) it is a significant fact that the old are disproportionately female. In fact the surplus of females to males in the population as a whole is accounted for by this gross disproportion among the elderly. Elsewhere the balance is much more even and, at crucial points in the life cycle such as typical age of marriage, there are more men than women. The causes of mortality have also altered. For both sexes there has been a decline in deaths as a result of epidemics or fatalities caused directly or indirectly by malnutrition and an increase in the proportion of deaths caused by degenerative diseases. Among the many causes of mortality which effect the sexes differently are the dramatic decline in deaths during childbirth and the sharply reducing difference in the rates of death from lung cancer as women's tobacco smoking habits more closely match those of men, especially since the Second World War.

Among the other major events in the life of many people is whether they are labelled criminals at any point. Crime rates have risen in the recent past. In spite of the reservations we may have about these and other statistical sources (Cicourel, 1964; Hindess, 1973) it is clear that women either are 'catching up with men' in the amount and type of criminal offence or that the statistics erroneously show this to be the case. If either is true it suggests that the differences between the sexes are diminishing in actual behaviour or in official attitudes towards them. It is probable that both are true.

While changes in dress are not themselves simple mirrors of social attitudes they do have some relationship. In Britain, since the Second World War, the clothes worn by the two sexes have become increasingly similar.

Men and Women in Families

The family, although its form varies widely between societies, is a ubiquitous human institution. People are members of families, typically, from birth to death. The roles of men and women in families differ but again these differences between the sexes are not constant between or even within societies. Furthermore the gender roles within families change over time. There are examples of human societies where the type of arrangements in relation to such central family functions as child care are primarily a female activity, primarily a male activity, primarily shared within the family or shared within a wider, non-family unit. In our own society child care, though still primarily a female task, is less exclusively so than formerly. The work of Mead (1935) illustrates the less common but clearly viable arrangements where the Tchambuli reverse the pattern many of us consider normal. Here men stay at home, gossip, wear decorative clothing and make up and look after the children. The Arapesh have more joint arrangements. Some kibbutzim provide the best known example of shared socialisation patterns often largely outside the family. It should be noted, however, that kibbutzim vary a great deal themselves and it is only a minority that significantly de-emphasize the role of the family in this respect. Elsewhere, institutional care or voluntary communes are very much a minority phenomenon although there is some evidence that communes of various kinds are becoming somewhat more popular in advanced industrialised societies (Abrams and McCulloch, 1976). They also make the point that communes do not necessarily produce child care patterns which significantly alter the division of labour between the sexes.

In Britain there have been several changes in social arrangements within the family in the last century. Perhaps the single most important change in the family in this period is the very sharp decline in the number of children. From a mean of above six for the marriages of 1860, mean completed family size is now less than three and has been so for a considerable period. This is both a cause and an effect of the changed status of women and has had a profound influence on the lives of adults in general as well as children. Most important has been the impact of fewer pregnancies, children and fewer years spent in primary child care. Richard Titmuss (in an essay, *The position of women*, Titmuss, 1958), expressed this change as follows: 'it would seem that the typical working mother of the 1890's married in her teens or early twenties and, experiencing ten pregnancies, spent about fifteen years in a state of pregnancy and in nursing a child for the first year of its life. She was tied, for this period of time, to the wheel of childbearing. Today, for the typical mother, the time spent would be about four years.'

Titmuss begins the same seminal article thus: 'In a period when the possibilities of social progress and the practicability of applied social science are being questioned, it is a source of satisfaction to recall some of the achievements of the Women's Suffrage Movement in Britain. The development of the personal, legal and political liberties of half the population of the country within the span of less than eighty years stands as one of the supreme examples of consciously directed social change.' We do not have to share his enthusiasm for the suffragettes (nor to accept that the social change he refers to is as consciously directed as he supposes) to agree that the changes are massive and nowhere as massively significant as in the drop in family size. The pattern of fertility is broadly in the same direction for non-working class women. It is also important for these women but perhaps less so.

Fertility changes, though very influential in altering the status of women, have done so in the context of other changes within the family which are, in their turn, related to each other. The traditional working class family described by Young and Willmott in their highly influential study (1957) remains one of the family types current in Britain. It is almost certainly less common than when *Family and Kinship in East London* was written. The matrilocal family is giving way to the neolocal but the process is less complete and less smooth than might be supposed. Similarly there is evidence of a continuing development of joint as opposed to segregated conjugal roles within the family (Bott, 1957). This process too is incomplete. The democratic or symmetrical (Young, M. and Willmott, P., 1973) family is more common than formerly in British society though few if any can claim total democracy or symmetry. It is clear that, within the family, the patterns of authority are substantially less one sided than was the case, say, between the two world wars. This has been in part a cause of (and caused by) various pieces of legislation which have extended the rights of women. For instance the Employment Protection Act requires employers to grant maternity (but not paternity) leave of up to twenty-nine weeks and up to eighteen weeks' pay. This act neatly illustrates a recurrent dilemma in this field. Is it desirable to manipulate society in order that women should be able to work and perform other functions in relation to childbearing and child rearing more easily? To follow the general pattern of proposals promoted by, for example, Hannah Gavron (1966) makes traditional role performances by women simpler and thus, perhaps, likely to inhibit any change in the distribution of tasks between the sexes. There is clearly no simple answer to this dilemma either for sociologists or for feminists or, for that matter, for anti-feminists.

Boys and Girls in Education

There is a substantial literature which demonstrates that intelligence, however measured, is not the sole determinant of educational achievement. Such literature frequently proceeds to illustrate this with reference to social class or ethnic differences in the population. It is also the case that the educational profiles of males and females typically differ and, as normally measured, differ to the detriment of females. Some features of this process are discussed in the article by Pauline Marks which follows this paper. We should be aware that Douglas, Ross and Simpson (1968) show that, in spite of some discrepancies, it is the *similarities* of the intelligence scores which are remarkable.

Nonetheless, the educational experiences of boys and girls do vary substantially in our and in other cultures. Rather more girls pass 'O' level G.C.E. examinations than boys (in 1973 the respective numbers of passes were 712,000 for boys and 715,000 for girls). At 'A' level this approximate equality had disappeared, boys achieved 189,000 passes compared to girls 139,000. The discrepancy in favour of males increases higher up the academic ladder, to degree and postgraduate levels. There are two other characteristics of the patterns which require some attention. First, the gap is in the main, closing, albeit slowly. For example, the percentage of

Table 2: Test scores of boys and girls

Population estimates
Mean scores

	Picture intelligence	*Vocabulary*	*Reading*	*Sentence completion*	*Aggregate*
8 years					
Boys	50.2	50·7	48·7	49·8	49·7
Girls	50·3	49·8	50·9	50·9	50·1

| | *Intelligence* | | | | | |
	Non-verbal	*Verbal*	*Vocabulary*	*Reading*	*Arithmetic*	*Aggregate*
11 years						
Boys	49·9	49·0	50·6	49·9	50·0	49·8
Girls	50·2	51·3	49·5	50·4	50·5	50·2

| | *Intelligence* | | | | |
	Non-verbal	*Verbal*	*Reading*	*Mathematics*	*Aggregate*
15 years					
Boys	51·5	49·7	51·0	51·6	50·6
Girls	49·8	50·7	50·3	48·6	49·3

female candidates for admission to University through U.C.C.A has risen from 31·3 per cent in 1970 to 35·2 per cent by 1974. Second, the extent to which women have entered higher education is very uneven. In some areas, such as first degrees in education, women are actually in a majority. In others, such as mathematics and engineering, women remain in a tiny minority. A minor irony of the current cutbacks in higher education is that they may fall primarily on those areas (Arts, Social Science, Education) where women have been most successful. The reasons for this distribution are numerous. In part a product of the varying self-conceptions of boys and girls, it is also the result of formal and informal processes within educational institutions. Not least the pattern is sustained by alternative conceptions of future (post formal education) lives held by boys and girls. There is no doubt that 'career' or at any rate 'work' features more prominently in the plans of adolescent boys and that girls will lay more stress on marriage, procreation and the family in our society than boys. Even those women who stress work more than most, frequently do so in areas supposedly compatible with these other roles (marriage and family). This point is illustrated by the Table 3 (which was produced by the Open University in 1976).

Table 3: Women in selected professions in Britain

	Total		Number	Women % Total
Architects (1973)	24,000	(approx.)	1,400	5·8
Chartered Accountants (1976)	61,737		1,413	2·3
Solicitors (1975)	29,850		1,563	5·2
Professional engineers (1973)	64,310		320	0·5
University professors (1972)	3,737		64	1·7
School teachers (1973)	383,542		227,147	59·2

It is clear that, before discussing the proportion of women in the professions, it is first necessary to establish whether the 'semi-profession' of school teaching is to be included. It is also clear that, in this list at any rate, the only group where women are not grossly under-represented (school teachers) has the lowest status. Further, although it does not appear on the table, it is the case that within the category 'school teacher' women are over-represented at the lower levels. This imbalance is not confined to middle class occupations but is also reflected with the working class. For instance, whereas nearly half of the male school leavers entered apprenticeships in 1974 only 6·5 per cent of females were similarly employed. There are, of course, a small and growing band of women who achieve the highest occupational attainment. We are a long way from the situation in 1931 when very nearly a quarter of all employed women were employed as indoor domestic servants, and this so shortly after the supposedly liberating effects of the Great War! We are also different in some respects from other advanced industrial societies. In the U.S.S.R., for example, medicine is an overwhelmingly female profession.

The general pattern both between and within societies is one of persistent discrimination against women. Indeed the recent spate of legislation (for example, the Sex Discrimination Act of 1975 or the Equal Opportunities Commission), whatever their long term utility, serve, in the short run, to highlight the existing patterns of inequality at work and elsewhere. The Employment Protection Act, where employers are required to grant maternity leave with pay, goes further than the others. Here the principle is one of positive discrimination not just equal reward for equal effort. A major reason for the failure of many professional women to reach the tops of their profession is the 'years out' to look after young children. A parallel process occurs with other types of employment. As society is currently structured there can be little doubt that much of this inequality will persist given the unequal demands of childbearing (which we can't fundamentally alter) and child rearing (which is both more susceptible to change and more time consuming).

Sex and Citizenship

The legislation referred to in respect of employment can be seen as a logical extension to the legislation of the nineteenth and twentieth centuries which has increasingly removed women from the legal category of children and lunatics with respect to the ownership of property, or voting, or serving on a jury. Although the changes in our and in other societies have been extensive, they are by no means complete. It is more difficult for women to obtain a mortgage, in spite of the law. The current controversy over abortion amply demonstrates that the war continues even if the boundary has shifted. It is not intended to suggest that in *all* respects women receive less than men. With pensions, for example, women tend to receive them for a much longer time than men. Even here, the position is not entirely clear and pensions for men are often very much better than for women, following their very different employment patterns.

Social Fact to Social Problem

Most, if not all, advanced industrialised societies, especially those of the west, have experienced some kind of 'women's movement' in the last two decades. These have ranged from groups of a very 'respectable' kind to the overtly revolutionary – a striking parallel to the various black groups in the United States for example. They are diverse also in regard to closeness of relationships with other reformist or revolutionary groups and in the degree to which women's problems are seen as simply that or as a manifestation of some wider malaise often as a feature of capitalism. The media treatment of these issues has followed the well-worn mix of ridicule and patronage in many cases. The 'problem' is now institutionalised in academic courses with the attendant characteristics which frequently follow such incorporation. In spite of this, at least part of the changing status of women has been a function of feminist education (consciousness raising) and agitation. It is too early to make any judgement about the long-term effect of such movements for the women involved or for women in general or society as a whole. It would also be too easy to see the women's movement as simply a product of post war Anglo-Saxon affluence. It is nevertheless the case that the movement is disproportionately well-educated and middle class, rather like Frank Parkin's (1968) description of middle class radicals.

In particular, the way in which the women's movement has demonstrated the role of ideology in sustaining the structured inequalities is significant for sociologists. A clear example of this kind is Lee Comer's pamphlet (1972). Here she draws attention to the highly influential writings of John Bowlby and produces a convincing critique of the thesis that child rearing as well as childbearing is 'best' pursued by a mother or permanent mother substitute, for example, 'What is believed to be essential for mental health is that the infant and young child should experience a warm intimate and continuous relationship with his mother or permanent mother substitute in which both find satisfaction and enjoyment' (Bowlby, 1952). The debate about the rightness or naturalness of women's role in this and other respects is certainly on the academic agenda in a way that was formerly not the case. Juliet Mitchell's work (1974) offers a rare defence of Freud in the feminist literature. Certainly medical and psychological assumption by academics and practitioners have been challenged by numerous writers.

Sex to Gender

Cultures impose gender differences on sex differences of a biological nature, actual or assumed. This does not mean that everyone in all cultures invariably acts in an appropriate way in terms of a gender specific script written by some group or other. What it does mean, however, is that various social institutions promote gender related views of the world. Thus a baby will be treated differently in the family and elsewhere according to its designated sex. The family is without doubt a primary source of initial gender identification by new human beings. It is perhaps surprisingly effective early in a child's life. Choice of toys is one such area where research has shown that children's preferences are strong. The following is quoted by Ann Oakley (1972):

Sex preferences in toys

Toy	Rating
Wheelbarrow	3·2
Cleaning set	8·4
Plane	1·7
Sports car	3·6
Teddy bear	5·8
Rocking horse	4·6
Skipping rope	7·0
Blackboard	5·3
Dish cabinet	8·3
Football	1·5
Construction set	2·7

Tool set	2·0
Sewing machine	8·2
Dumpertruck	2·5
Banjo	4·5
Cosmetics	8·8
Doll's pram	8·5
Telephone	5·6
Racing car	2·2
Alphabet ball	4·9
Roller skates	5·3
Paddling pool	5·0
Tractor	3·0
Doll wardrobe	8·7

The ratings run from 1 (strongly masculine) to 5 (appropriate for both sexes) to 9 (strongly feminine). These ratings were made by a group of twenty-year-old psychology students and proved in practice to be highly predictive of the choices made by children of each sex.

Formal and informal practices in schools tend to reinforce this division, partly by organisation of the curriculum and partly by teachers' assumptions, by reading material, etc. Reading schemes like *Janet and John* and *Ladybird* have become the target of criticism by many feminists. Girls tend to be represented as passive, caring and dependent, boys as aggressive, adventurous and independent. Adult roles are less extensive for girls. This process is paralleled by the messages given by the mass media (Millum, 1975). Sexism is a most noticeable feature of nearly all the output of the mass media. On this subject, two main questions interest sociologists.

First, are these cultural prescriptions causal in themselves or reflective of some other more fundamental characteristic of society such as capitalism, or of innate biological or psychological mechanisms? Second, given that patterns of gender roles vary, what are the likely parameters of change in our own or in any human society? It is unlikely that definitive answers will be forthcoming to either of these questions in the immediate future. It is even more unlikely that they will not be pursued.

Femininity in the Classroom: An Account of the Changing Attitudes
by Pauline Marks[1]

In *Purity and Danger* Mary Douglas wrote that '. . . it is only by exaggerating the difference between within and without, above and below, male and female, with and against, that a semblance of order is created' (p. 4). There may be those who would reject her reasoning, but there are few who would deny that the practice exists. Teachers and others involved in education are no exception. They will exaggerate concepts of femininity in the light of which they will decide what they should teach to whom, and how the behaviour and treatment of boys and girls should differ. Unlike, for example, the distinction between 'able' and 'educationally subnormal' children, this sexual division is rarely clearly expressed in educational ideology despite marked differences in the treatment, performance and expectations of boys and girls at school.

The differences in treatment vary. They were easy to see in the early nineteenth century when what was provided for middle- and upper-class girls was very much more limited in scope than the educational provision for their brothers. Now we have to look a little closer. In a modern, sexually mixed, comprehensive school which offers a wide range of subjects to everyone, girls and boys still choose to follow those which are traditionally expected of them. This is hardly surprising – because girls are expected to behave thus and so, because teachers' responses will be based on that general expectation, then, of course, girls will conform to the roles they are assigned.

These sex differences in education have been accompanied by a relative unawareness on the part of educational planners and writers about education. This discrepancy poses a problem. In the early nineteenth century, few people doubted the correctness of the division, so that educational writers, when they dealt with the matter at all, produced straightforward sexist accounts of the theory behind it. Nowadays, just as the practice is relatively hidden, little or nothing is said about it by educational writers. Girls, like the working classes, are tacitly excluded from most discussions on education. The differences in treatment and the problems they cause exist – but in the official collective consciousness they do not. Thus, when educational theorists talk of the education of children or pupils, usually they are effectively talking of the education of boys (and middle-class boys at that).

When people do think about the discernible differences in educational

---

[1] Pauline Marks was tragically killed in a traffic accident before she could finally revise this paper, which was part of a larger piece of research on the process of sex-typing in girls' education. I hope that my revisions do not falsify her intentions (Susan Budd).

practice, they customarily rely on two well-worn accounts with which to explain them. The first is that girls and boys differ physiologically and that the differing levels of achievement and the differing styles of education provided for them derive from this. This view varies from seeing biological factors as absolutely determining the way women should be educated to seeing them simply as constraints. It is worth noting that even the most liberal proponents of this view never see boys as the more physiologically limited group. Those who give the second account see it as important to educate girls differently from boys because they will be treated differently in later life. So long as we know how girls will be treated during their adult lives, we are able to provide them with the education they will need to cope with this. This account leaves aside the question as to why people define femininity in the way they do.

It is easier to understand how ideas about the education of girls vary, or have varied, as soon as we see that femininity is itself a problematic notion. What is meant by it changes both over time and within different social groups. These changes in the understanding and use of the notion are reflected, of course, in the work of educational theorists. How they use it or are influenced by it will depend on when they were working and on their social background. The Bishop of Oxford made the point well in 1923 when he wrote: '. . . [the question of girls' education] is determined by the current opinion of the status of women in the society of the time'.[1]

In order to trace, however sketchily, the relationship between ideology and social experience, a historical perspective is necessary. The research for this perspective is difficult because of the paucity of information about actual practice. Educational ideology and philosophy can be studied through the work of influential writers like Thomas Arnold or Jean-Jacques Rousseau or in the pages of government reports. The latter are important because they reveal the ideological basis on which educational legislation is made. In them we can see why institutions, the selection of pupils, curricula, etc., are as they are. But while the well-known writers and the government reports will tell us about belief and practice, and will incorporate a view of 'human nature', they will not tell us much about what actually happened in the classroom. For this information we have to turn to contemporary letters, pamphlets, autobiographies, newspaper articles and so on; the reliability of these sources is sometimes difficult to gauge. However, I will try to examine the relationship between the various definitions of femininity underlying, or incorporated into, educational philosophies, ideologies and models and the educational 'solutions' which were thought of as appropriate to the 'needs' of girls.

There are three major ways in which educators have approached the teaching of girls, and each of them has depended on differing accounts of femininity. The first way we might call 'assimilation', and it depends either on the educator seeing no difference between boys and girls, or on

[1] 'Why are We Educating Our Boys and Girls?', *Parent's Review*, vol. XXXIV, no. 8, August 1923.

the decision that any such difference is irrelevant in education. The second approach sees girls either as handicapped when compared with boys, or sees them as somewhat deficient boys. Either boys are placed in a higher cultural order than girls or girls are thought to need special help to 'catch up' with boys – because of deficiencies in their biology, socialization or environment. The first form of the distinction is likely to lead to an educational solution of pluralism. Different answers will be given to the question of the aims of educating each sex, and the content and structure of educational institutions and curricula will be different for the two sexes. If girls are thought to need special help to catch up with boys, then they will be given 'compensatory' education. Proponents of this view may say that sex differences are ultimately irrelevant in the context of education and compensatory education for girls is only needed as a short-term measure. The third approach depends on seeing boys and girls as completely different and in need of completely different kinds of education with a concentration on very different subjects. This results, once again, in a pluralist solution.

It is easy to see that not only can femininity be defined in relation to the ruling standard in this way, but so too can the working class or the racially or culturally underprivileged. As the Authoritarian Personality studies suggested, a society that organises its thinking in terms of a hierarchy for the sexes will probably do so for class and ethnicity as well.

Another difficulty is created by the fact that different people think differently about the objects of education. Some see it as necessarily geared to the 'needs' of the pupils, as something which is to prepare them for their future roles in society. In this case definitions of femininity or masculinity will loom large. Others may believe that education should not be specifically vocational, or should not be designed to produce particular kinds of people, but should be seen as a 'good-in-itself' with universally applicable objectives.[1] People who think thus are less likely to stress views about intellectual differences between the sexes, although they may feel that girls need help to catch up with boys. Yet others believe that education should be vocational, but they may differ among themselves about how far vocations, and thus education, should be sex-specific. They may see both sexes as having a heterogeneous set of possible vocations, some more or less exclusively for boys (for example, engineering) and some for girls (for example, nursing) and some as open to both (for example, teaching). It is quite common, of course, for such mixed, or open, vocations to be seen as available for the less successful boys and for the more successful girls. Those who think more or less exclusively of education as vocational are quite likely to think of boys as having a number of choices while girls are really only faced with one, i.e. marriage and motherhood.

[1] Such an education is supposed to develop a rational mind, critical faculties and an ability to grasp concepts. See, for instance, Paul Hirst in *Journal of Curriculum Studies*, vol. 1, no. 2, 1968 and 1969.

Schoolchildren are divided up not only by their sex; their 'intelligence', social class or race may also be seen as limiting them to certain sorts of education. The judgements made about what a girl is able to learn, or about what she ought to learn, are qualified, to some extent, by how intelligent she is thought to be or by the social standing of her parents. For example, it has been very widely assumed in Britain that the able child of either sex can benefit from an education which is 'good-in-itself', whereas the 'less able' can only benefit from an education which is largely vocational.

At one time it was thought that the children of the gentry would benefit from a good-in-itself education, regardless of intelligence, while the children of the poor should be taught a trade. The history of educational reform in Britain can be charted in terms of the transition between different approaches. First of all, intelligence was thought irrelevant to the kind of education provided; then education was regarded as a reward for intelligence, a ladder for the able poor to climb. Next came the view that types of education should be distributed according to ability, and the final approach has been one that attempts to abandon hierarchy altogether. Girls have been slotted into these systems in different ways and at different points, but it is fascinating to discover that their 'femininity', that supposedly biological and absolute characteristic, is dependent on the viewpoint of the observer; different social origins and intellectual abilities alter the meaning of 'femininity' which is thus not a fixed concept in educational thinking.

An educational model is a complex thing whose parts may be inconsistent with one another. For example, femininity may be used at one point in the model to explain why the daughters of gentlemen cannot be educated with their brothers; but that same femininity may be ignored when it comes to the question of the daughters of artisans. Educational provision for girls during the first half of the nineteenth century was justified in terms of an ideology of pluralism – girls and boys were thought to need different kinds of education. But this applied to upper- and middle-class girls only, and working-class girls were provided with an education similar to that for working-class boys. As always, most discussion and thought was devoted to the education of the rich, especially their sons. 'Femininity' was and is a problematic category in the field of education in a way that 'masculinity' is not, and the 'needs' of girls, though explained in terms of their sex, have varied subtly according to their social background.

The way in which 'femininity' varies according to its social context raises an important question which is difficult to answer. Did the prevailing notion of femininity in the nineteenth century control educational patterns available to girls, or were these rather an outcome and reflection of economic and organisational factors already deeply embedded in all levels of society? It may well be that educational ideology and practice for girls simply reflected the existing social and economic situation, rather than educational theory expressing an *a priori* argument about the way in which girls should be educated. A legitimising, as opposed to an *a priori*, argument has, of course, no role to play in bringing about educational change.

I want now to consider the educational provision for girls from the beginning of the nineteenth century. To some extent the choice of date is arbitrary, but not altogether, for the theoretical foundations on which twentieth-century education is built were laid during this period.

Young upper-class girls and the girls of socially aspiring families were generally taught at home by their parents (usually by their mothers) and by governesses or, less frequently by private tutors. At some time between the ages of twelve and fifteen, they might be sent to school. The majority attended private schools, although exactly how many did so is difficult if not impossible to establish, for adequate statistics are not available.[1] The few such schools prior to 1850 which were not run for profit can be divided into three classes: the denominational schools like those run by the Quakers; those established for particular sections of society like the schools for the children of clergymen, or military or naval officers; and a small number of charitable foundations like Christ's Hospital. The use of charitable funds for education, as in the case of Christ's Hospital, demonstrates very well the bias towards the education of boys. Whereas the founder of Christ's Hospital School mentioned both boys and girls in the original document, in practice most of the resources were made available to boys. In 1865 there were 1,192 pupils in the boys' school, with twenty-seven masters, and there were eighteen girls in part of the junior boys' building with one mistress.

The conditions of the private, profit-making girls' boarding schools have been well documented.[2] The school would normally be run by a lady principal with one or two governesses to help her, but it was rare for any of them to be trained professionally, particularly as girls were excluded from the universities of the time. There were many more fashionable schools for girls than for boys, but they were much smaller – the average number attending such an establishment was in the region of twenty-five. R. L. Archer has described the aims of these schools in terms of their inculcation of femininity.

> . . . to produce a robust physique is thought undesirable, rude health and abundant vigour are considered somewhat plebeian . . . a

[1] The earliest I have been able to find, date from 1865 and are not very satisfactory. In 1898 the *Return of the Pupils in Public and Private Secondary and Other Schools in England* published by the Stationery Office, simply said that the figures did not exist.

[2] See for example V. W. Hughes, *A London Family 1870–1900*, Oxford University Press, 1953; 'A Ladies' School Seventy Years Ago' by an octogenarian in *Treasury*, February 1905; 'An Enquiry into the State of Girls' Fashionable Schools', *Frazer's Magazine,* June 1945.

certain delicacy, a strength not competent to walk more than a mile, an appetite fastidious and easily satisfied joined with that timidity which commonly accompanies feebleness . . . all are held more ladylike.[1]

Girls were expected to be obsessed with fashion, to develop delicate complexions aided by starvation diets, to improve their posture with aids like straight laces, back boards, iron collars, and wooden stocks, and to keep their feet firmly in position while repeating information learned by rote. Rote-learning was the norm and the greatest emphasis was laid on gaining the 'accomplishments' – painting, singing, dancing, playing the piano, how best to enter a drawing room and so on. Visiting masters were often employed by the schools to teach these 'accomplishments'. J. Fitch, reporting to the Taunton Commission in 1864, after visiting many such schools, said that

. . . above the age of twelve the difference [between education provided for boys and girls] is most striking. Girls are told that Latin is not a feminine requirement, mathematics is only fit for boys and she must devote herself to ladylike accomplishments . . . nothing is more common than to hear the difference in the future destiny of boys and girls assigned as a reason for a difference in the character and extent of their education, but I cannot find that any part of the training given in ladies' schools educates them for a domestic life or prepares them for duties which are supposed to be especially womanly. The reason why modern languages which are especially useful in business, should be considered particularly appropriate for women, who spend most of their time in the home, is still one of the unsolved mysteries of the English educational system.[2]

The educational experiences of middle- and upper-class girls were qualitatively different from those of boys. Secondary schools for the latter were usually very much larger, staffed by professionally trained masters, and they had curricula which were dominated by the classics. Because middle-class parents were primarily concerned with their daughters' eligibility for marriage, they educated them to this end. The classical-liberal education received by their sons approximated much more closely to the idea of an education which was good-in-itself. One of the most interesting implications of this division is the idea that femininity had to be achieved, cultivated and preserved, while masculinity could be left to look after itself. Some 'masculine' traits, e.g. bravery and vigour might be in need of encouragement, but the learning of masculinity, unlike femininity, was not thought of as the central task of the school.

[1] *Secondary Education in the Nineteenth Century*, Cambridge University Press, 1921.
[2] Quoted in Dorothea Beale's edition of the *Schools' Enquiry Commission*, 1869, p. 31.

The situation, in which the learning of femininity was stressed, reflected the obsessive concern of many Victorian thinkers and moralists with the 'home'. The rapid growth of industrialism, the increase in the size of cities and of business concerns, had led to a separation of the home and the place of work among the middle classes as well as among the poor. Capitalism demanded assertive and competitive behaviour from men at work, so increasingly the middle-class home became a refuge, a retreat which had to be preserved.[1] Women thus had a special importance: they were dependent on their ascribed status, that is on being female, and the most important goal for that status, towards which education was directed, was marriage. However, this was denied to a substantial number of women for a variety of demographic and social reasons. Among these were differing rates of infant mortality – infant girls were more likely to survive than boys – the high cost of marriage and male migration.[2] These middle- and lower-middle-class spinsters were in a socially anomalous position and could, if their fathers did not support them, be in severe financial difficulties. Their only chance of socially acceptable paid employment was teaching, which did not need specialised knowledge or experience. It involved either becoming a governess and living with a family, or working in a girls' school and teaching a restricted range of subjects.[3]

Middle-class women were excluded from the educational opportunities made available to their brothers because their future roles were set out for them and they were thought to need preparation for those roles. Girls would become wives and mothers, only the deficient woman, the spinster, had to seek a career. Hence proposals that education for girls should be extended were rejected by conservatives because they thought that such proposals, if put into practice, would rob girls of their femininity, make them more masculine, reduce their chances of marriage and thus make them deficient as women.

The situation for working-class girls was very different. There were few schools for either working-class girls or boys and those which did exist were elementary. Their curricula were designed without reference to needs and abilities thought to belong to either sex.[4] Girls may well have been taught needlework, but that apart their experience would have been

[1] See 'Landscape with Figures: Home and Community in English Society', pp. 139–75, *The Rights and Wrongs of Women*, Ed. by J. Mitchell and A. Oakley, Penguin, 1976.

[2] Figures are hard to come by, but the census of 1861 shows that of nearly six million adult English women, there were 3,488,952 wives, 756,717 widows and 1,537,314 spinsters.

[3] J. and O. Banks in *Feminism and Family Planning in Victorian England* (Liverpool University Press, 1964), estimated that in 1851 there were 25,000 governesses in England.

[4] For details of provision of schools for the working classes, see H. Silver, *The Concept of Popular Education: A Study of Ideas and Social Movements in the Early Nineteenth Century*, MacGibbon and Kee, 1965.

much the same as that of the boys. In the early part of the nineteenth century there was no specific ideology of education for the poor which could counteract the model of 'minimal' education provided for them by the upper class. The poor had to be civilised; in the words of Gladstone, what this meant was '. . . sound religious instruction, correct moral training, and a sufficient extent of secular knowledge suited to their station in life . . .'[1] Even so, those who reported to the Select Committee on the Education of the Poorer Classes in 1838, concluded that the kind of education given to children of the working class was 'lamentably deficient' and only extended to a small proportion of those who ought to receive it.

During the second half of the nineteenth century various groups challenged the structure and content of the education given to middle-class girls. In doing so they called into question the class-specific notions of femininity which underlay the existing educational model. The majority of the active members of these groups were middle class, and either had been, were related to, or had narrowly avoided becoming governesses. They can be divided into three groups in terms of the assumptions they made about 'femininity' and the educational solutions that they saw as appropriate for the needs of girls.

1. *The Instrumentalists* were committed to the position that whatever the biological and social differences between the sexes, in the context of decisions about educational provision these were of very limited importance. They advocated educational assimilation as the solution to the inadequacy of middle-class girls' education. Both sexes ideally should have equal educational employment opportunities. This group included Frances Buss and Emily Davies.[2]

2. *The Liberal Humanists* were concerned to offer girls an education which would result in their becoming 'better' wives, mothers and companions than the educational opportunities of the first half of the nineteenth century allowed. They were not redefining current notions of *femininity*; rather opting for a 'solution' which would widen the intellectual interests of girls and women generally and prepare them more adequately for their traditional role. This group included Anne Clough and F. D. Maurice.[3]

3. *The Moralists* were concerned with the duties of women as Christians. The education received by girls in the private boarding schools was, of

---

[1] *Report from the Select Committee on the Education of the Poorer Classes*, 1838, p. 13.

[2] Frances Buss, who had been a governess, founded the North London Collegiate School in Camden Town in 1850, where she introduced a 'Boys' curriculum and a system of external examination for girls. Emily Davies, daughter of an evangelical family, became Principal of Girton College, Cambridge, in the 1870's.

[3] Anne Clough became Principal of Newnham College, Cambridge. F. D. Maurice was a member of the Christian Socialists. His sister was a governess. In 1848 he founded Queen's College for women and girls in Harley Street.

course, the antithesis of an education aimed at producing dutiful and piously religious women. Dorothea Beale, a significant member of this group, sought a 'solution' in the form of a 'demanding curriculum' including subjects such as mathematics, logic and classics interspersed with the teaching of religion – this she believed would be conducive to the notion of dutiful womanhood.[1]

The instrumentalists questioned most of the underlying assumptions of the educational models and philosophies in the first half of the century, whereas the other two groups took the current definition of femininity for granted and believed that the future roles of boys and girls would be quite different. The second half of the nineteenth century saw educational changes which pleased members of all three groups, and which resulted in a new dominant ideology justifying an assimilation of the educational experiences of girls to those of boys. Obviously the education received by boys in the public schools and universities had not remained static throughout this period. Many reforms were achieved – for example, the content of the curriculum was widened to include subjects such as physics and history, and the idea for an education oriented towards a vocation (that is, a profession) began to dominate the educational model for middle-class boys.[2]

Part of the explanation for the changes in girls' education was due to unease about some aspects of the social position of middle-class women in the mid nineteenth century. It was in response to the financial plight of governesses and as an attempt to improve their social status that the Governesses Benevolent Institution was set up in 1843, followed five years later by Queen's College in Harley Street, which became a school for girls and women offering an academic 'compensatory education'. The opening of the G.B.I. seemed to mark the opening of the floodgates: letters, articles, protest meetings, theories, committees and so on began to debate about the state of middle-class girls' education. A Royal Commission on Education, the Taunton Commission of 1864, devoted one section of its findings to the education of girls, the first occasion on which a government report explicitly distinguished between boys' and girls' education. The commissioners sent inspectors to girls' private secondary schools, and received evidence about conditions in them.

Dorothea Beale, summarising the evidence, argued that 'nothing can well be more extravagant than the waste of money and educational

[1] Dorothea Beale taught at Queen's College, and became Headmistress of Cheltenham Ladies College in 1858. She was supposed to have little understanding of the problems of unsupported spinsters as she was 'comfortably off'.

[2] For interesting discussions of changes in the education of boys see D. V. Glass, 'Education and Social Change in Modern England', in Halsey, Floud and Anderson (eds.), *Education, Economy and Society*, (Free Press, U.S., 1965), and R. Williams, *The Long Revolution* (Penguin, 1965), chapter, 'Education and British Society'.

resources in these schools'. There was ample evidence in the Commission's report to support her views. The inspectors found that few teachers and governesses had been professionally trained, and in some cases were barely educated themselves. The girls were reported to be absorbed in the minutiae of dance steps and etiquette. In one school, an inspector reported, he had questioned an eighteen-year-old girl as to what she remembered of a recent visit to Paris, and she answered that she recalled two things – that she had seen the Empress and she had been very plainly dressed; and that she had seen some priests in a church, and they had been magnificently dressed.

The substantive changes in girls' secondary schools during the latter part of the century meant that the new ideology advocating educational 'assimilation' became more acceptable. Girls schools were founded with curricula approximating to those in equivalent boys' schools; girls were successful in external examinations which had previously been restricted to boys, and a very small number of women students were admitted to university in the 1870's. Although girls were admitted to the Cambridge Local Examinations in 1865, and Oxford's in 1870, unlike boys they were not placed in order of merit but were given a *pass* or a *fail*. It was argued that girls were unable to deal with competition and would be likely to respond badly to it. London University opened its examinations to women students in 1878, apart from the medical schools which remained barred to females. Colleges for women were opened at Cambridge in 1870 (Girton), and 1871 (Newnham). Girls were not given the class of their degree but were officially informed that they had either passed or failed. At Girton, where Emily Davies was Principal, women were encouraged to compete with men on an equal basis; a position which was consistent with her membership of the instrumentalist group. At Newnham however, it was originally intended that *if* the girls wanted to take examinations, these should be different from those taken by men students so as to avoid the 'unpleasantness' of outright competition; Anne Clough's sympathies were with both the liberal humanists and the moralists. Newnham, however, eventually followed Girton's lead.

The reaction to these innovations was fierce. The fears which were expressed as to the effects of education on women and the way in which this would reverberate through society demonstrated the relationship between 'femininity' and key social institutions such as the home, female chastity, and the separation of women from any active role in the social domain. The main fear was that educating women would lead to a decline in the importance of the home, and hence to a decline in morality generally. Just as the Victorians maintained a double standard of morality between the sexes, so did they maintain a double standard of morality between the private and public domains. Trollope, Dickens and other Victorian novelists often depicted the contrast between the ruthless entrepreneur or financier at work, and his sentimental but authoritarian attitude to his family. The importance of the idealised 'home' as refuge and safety-valve was very great, apart from the Veblenesque desire to demonstrate financial prosperity by maintaining one's women in conspicuous and decorative idleness.

The tension and antagonism produced by changes in girls' education is hard to understand unless we see that an elaborate system of symbolic boundaries was being broken down. Male fears of competition from women in jobs, examinations and so on were all the greater in that symbolically women were stepping from a different and non-competitive world, and thus were polluting the values of both the world they left – 'the home' – and the world that they entered. The reluctance to allow them to compete, the fear that this experience might irrevocably contaminate them, demonstrated the importance of the symbolic separation between men's and women's worlds.

> ... boys are sent out into the world to buffet with its temptations, to mingle with bad and good, to govern and direct . . . girls are to dwell in quiet homes, amongst a few friends, to exercise a noiseless influence, to be submissive and retiring . . . to educate girls in crowds is wrong.[1]

Other anxieties and rationalisations about 'femininity' were also aroused. The educated woman, the bluestocking, then as now, was thought to be at once over-sexed and not sensual enough, both masculine and neuter. The general concern with eugenics and the breeding capacities of the race which had resulted from the Darwinian revolution extended to the effects of educating girls

> ... in regard to the possible effect on health and physical vigour of women students. It was feared that the opening of new facilities for study and intellectual improvement would result in the creation of a new race of puny, sedentary and unfeminine students, and would destroy the grace and charm of social life, and would disqualify women for their true vocation, the nurture of the coming race and the governance of well-ordered, healthy and happy homes.[2]

Evidence from the medical profession was brought forward by those who subscribed to the ideology of educational pluralism: the development of nervous troubles and the harming of the reproductive organs were said to be likely consequences of a 'boy's education'. Medical men repeatedly argued that it was of the utmost necessity to rest during menstruation. Dr Matthew Duncan claimed that a boy's education would result in women's reproductive organs being harmed. He suggested to the B.M.A. that such an education would produce amenorrhoea and

---

[1] E. M. Sewell, *Principles of Education Drawn from Nature and Revelation and Applied to Female Education in the Upper Classes*, Longman, Roberts and Green, 1865, vol. II, p. 219.

[2] J. Fitch, 'Women and the Universities', *Contemporary Review*, August 1890, p. 252.

chlorosis, and destroy sensuality 'of a proper and commendable kind'. H. Spencer thought that flat-chested girls, after a period of higher education, would be unable to suckle infants.[1] It is a striking demonstration of the class-related nature of the debate that no one appeared to derive from these logicists any concern about the working conditions of girls and women who were servants or factory-hands.

In spite of the substantive changes which took place in education for some girls, the pluralist ideology remained dominant. It has been said[2] that of all girls receiving secondary education in England in 1898, 70 per cent were being educated in private boarding schools, often in towns where grammar and high schools had empty places. The chief advantage of boarding schools was that they were socially homogeneous: eligibility for marriage and not the content of their daughter's education remained the dominant concern of middle-class parents. However, the ideology advocating 'assimilation' seems to have had some impact on these private schools; hence the following advertisement for,

> *Ellerslie High School and College, Blackheath*
> *Boarding* School – but otherwise conducted similarly to the high *Day* schools . . . but without the indiscriminate mixture of all grades as the Public High Day Schools.[3]

During the latter half of the nineteenth century working-class girls benefited together with boys from the improvements introduced by the 1870 Education Act, when for the first time children were legally entitled to public primary education (although attendance was still voluntary).[4] Those advocating improvement in the quality of 'mass' education tended to be members of the middle classes, who ironically were arguing the need for increased differentiation in the content of the education offered to working-class boys and girls, no doubt prompted partly by their dependence on the domestic services of working-class girls. It was argued that the type of educational provision made for the poor should be determined by their need for vocational training – for instance, as domestic servants.

James Booth, writing about the education of the working-class girl in 1835, asked '. . . why should she not be taught to light a fire, sweep a room, wash crockery and glass without breaking them, wash clothes and bake bread?'[5] The philanthropic members of the middle classes also believed that if working-class women could be educated to run their home 'well', they would re-create the sacred middle-class resting place, and would thus discourage men from visiting public houses, and thus

---

[1] H. Spencer, 'Principles of Biology', *Lancet*, no. 2, 1886, p. 315.

[2] Alice Zimmern, *Renaissance of Girls' Education in England*, Longman, 1898.

[3] ibid. Advertisement inside the back cover.

[4] In 1880 attendance at the elementary school was made compulsory up to the age of ten, and in 1893 it was raised to eleven and in 1918 to fourteen.

[5] James Booth, *Female Education of the Industrial Classes*, Bell and Daldy, 1855.

drunkenness, poverty and wife-beating would be stamped out. As a result, there were many schemes to include the domestic arts in the curricula of elementary schools. Those who provided a vocational education for working-class girls worked on the assumption that girls would become first servants and then housewives. Much of the treatment of domestic servants was equally based on the supposition that they would eventually become housewives.

In the twentieth century, the recipients of the vocational education were redefined as the 'less able'. The able daughter of poor parents who climbed the ladder of educational opportunity was rewarded with an academic education on the 'assimilation' model. Her brothers and sisters who remained to receive a vocational education in the junior technical schools, which were started in the first decade of the twentieth century, found that vocations were defined in a sex-specific way, and that notions of 'femininity' were here mediated less by psychological assumptions than by the nature of the women's employment market.

During the twentieth century we have seen a growing commitment to the educational ideology of equality of opportunity for all children, a commitment which has included assimilating the educational experiences of girls to boys. This commitment was neither immediate in its appearance nor uniform in its manner amongst those involved in the process of education. For example many educationalists in the Conservative Party remain committed to the continuing existence of a private section in education. The commitment to the ideology of equality of opportunity derives partially from the necessity for the 'ruling class' to choose more 'universal' grounds for selection and privilege in education. With the founding of the mass party and a universal franchise, combined with the trade union movement's commitment to a universal system of secondary education from the 1890's on, those in power were obliged to think in terms of the expansion and improvement of educational facilities for the whole population. In reality, as has often been shown, a very great gulf has existed between this ideology and actual practice.

With the 1902 Education Act the government officially recognised that secondary education was a fit object for public expenditure and should eventually be extended to all children. The majority of the working class were using the elementary schools for their formal education, in which little differentiation was made between boys and girls in terms of the selection of the content of curricula, etc. This was so in spite of protests from middle-class people woried about the 'servant problem'. For instance, in 1916 Edith Sellers asked over 1,000 working-class girls about their career aspirations. Finding that most answered in terms of factory work or typing, and that only fifty wanted to become servants, she wrote,

. . . surely their choice of calling in life is proof that there is something wrong somewhere in our system of elementary education?[1]

The history of girls' education in the twentieth century reveals significant class differences; as I have implied, these differences are often officially legitimated in terms of the 'needs' of the 'less able' and the 'academically able' child. These labels can often be taken as euphemisms for 'lower-working' and 'lower-middle to middle-class' respectively; the upper classes escape such labelling by being educated in the private sector.

Many upper- and upper-middle-class girls during the first few decades of the twentieth century continued to experience the type of education which had been deemed appropriate for 'young ladies' in the nineteenth century. But middle-class girls were much more likely to receive an education which would offer them many of the same opportunities as their brothers, i.e. a public day school with an academic curriculum; possibly followed by university. However, this did not lead to the position held by the nineteenth-century instrumentalists. Instead the experience gained in the education of girls was increasingly used to differentiate between the supposed intellectual capacities of the sexes, and thus to rationalise the different choice of subjects. In a series of papers written by members of the Association of Headmistresses (voicing the opinion of the most influential group of middle-class female educators) we find that the majority of contributors emphasised those differences between the sexes which pointed to the necessity of differential treatment within the same general kind of education. Girls were said to 'lack reasoning power, were unable to give a lucid direction, an accurate description or a clear and logical explanation'.[2]

The conclusion drawn from these assumptions was that girls were innately predisposed towards certain subjects. It was believed that girls found mathematics and science difficult to grasp and that few would want to specialise in them. It was argued regularly that it would be conducive to the cultivation of 'good health' and prevention of 'overstrain' if science (particularly physics and chemistry) and mathematics (not arithmetic) were eliminated from the curriculum of girls' secondary schools, or at the very least these subjects should be given a subordinate place. The assumption that girls dislike and are bad at science and mathematics has been consistently held throughout the twentieth century. It is interesting to speculate how this notion was originally conceived, as its influence on the shape of girls' secondary education has been considerable. Girls' schools found great difficulty right from the beginning in obtaining qualified science teachers, reasonable laboratory space and resources,

[1] Edith Sellers, *An Antediluvian on the Education of Working-Class Girls: Nineteenth Century and After*, August 1916, p. 337.

[2] S. A. Burstall and M. A. Douglas (eds.), *Public School for Girls*, Longmans, Green and Co., 1911, quote from p. 26.

etc.[1] In many ways, therefore, middle-class girls' education tended to be a compromise between the 'solutions' of *assimilation* and *pluralism*.

The majority of working-class girls did not have access to secondary education as free scholarship places were scarce. Some were able to afford a two- or three-year course at the Junior Technical Schools, which provided vocational training of a sex-specific nature. Others, whose parents could not afford further education beyond the age of thirteen, could attend 'continuance' classes. Their aim, according to the Board of Education, was to '. . . train girls to become efficient workers and the mothers of healthy children', though they found that the long hours worked by girls meant that few attended.

By the first decades of the twentieth century, a pattern was seen to be emerging in a girl's education similar to that for boys; a small, highly able élite was identified and given an academic education which led on to university. The number of girls so identified, however, was always very much smaller, and many observers considered that, unlike boys, by becoming highly educated they were forfeiting their chances of gaining the goals natural to their sex. Several 'emancipated' women appeared to be regretting it: Alice Ikin, for example, an ex-Newnham scholar, thought that 'the next stage of woman's emancipation must allow of the combination of intellectual development and motherhood', and an old pupil of Francis Buss, from the North London Collegiate felt that

> . . . instead of facing squarely the real needs of future wives and mothers, as the vast majority of girls were to be, Miss Buss seized the tempting instrument at her hand . . . the stimulus to mental ambition afforded by outside exams.[2]

These views no doubt reflected the social position of the few highly educated women of the period. Until the First World War, women's employment opportunities were severely restricted and they were often required to relinquish their jobs on marriage. The view that they would have to choose between a career (usually teaching) and marriage was thus socially created but perfectly real; graduate women at this period in fact were less likely to marry than their non-graduate sisters. Various biological bogies continued to be raised. Havelock Ellis thought that the active and athletic life of some contemporary women made their confinements so difficult as to endanger their babies; another commentator feared that the present-day methods of educating girls had made them less capable of bearing and nursing their children. Things had

[1] See for instance in the *Journal of Education – a Monthly Review and Record*, vol. XXXII, 'Science Teaching in Girls' Schools', by four Girton and Newnham tutors, January 1910, pp. 36–8.

[2] Alice Ikin, 'Education for Womanhood', in *Education – Primary, Secondary and Technical*, vol. XLVII, April 1926, p. 358; V. M. Hughes, *A London Family 1870–1900*, Oxford University Press, 1954, p. 179.

got even worse in America, apparently – one doctor could only find 4 per cent of his countrywomen physiologically fitted to become wives and mothers.[1]

The impression that one is left with after reading educationalists and doctors of the period discussing topics such as the impact of education on childbirth or menstruation is that women and girls have a fixed store of energy, a little bit of which is used up every month. If 'education' or physical exercise uses up too much of this irreplaceable store, then girls' health will be damaged with unpleasant consequences for future generations. It is fascinating to note that the best way to prevent 'overstrain' was to eliminate science from the curriculum of girls secondary schools, or at least considerably to reduce its importance.[2]

In 1922, these problems were confronted directly by the Hadow Report on the differences of curriculum appropriate to the 'needs' of boys and girls. For the first time, 'male' and 'female' were treated as problematic categories in educational research commissioned by a government body. Academic experts – principally Cyril Burt and R. L. Thorndike – were asked to provide evidence concerning the innate differences between the sexes in mental capacity and educability. They concluded that the most important characteristic of such differences was their small amount. But the teachers who gave evidence to the Committee accepted the current notions of femininity and masculinity and reported that they found boys more original, constructive and self-assertive; girls on the other hand were seen to be persevering, industrious, passive, imitative, emotional and intuitive. Girls were reported to be more lethargic in secondary school, and naturally more prone to opt for arts subjects.

The committee seemed on the whole to accept the non-expert evidence, and thought that since girls were less capable of prolonged mental effort and more prone to neurotic disturbance than boys, it would on the whole be desirable to educate them differently. But they were not prepared to suggest an alternative model for their education, and felt that the solution should be found by teachers themselves. We can only speculate as to the extent to which women teachers in the twenties and thirties were able to transcend the boundaries of their own experience and of the conventional wisdom. Overall, the assumptions about 'femininity' and the effect that they had on the provision of educational facilities for girls of different social classes changed very little between the latter part of the nineteenth century and the first few decades of the twentieth century, despite the general improvement in both the quality and quantity of education available.

The publication of the Norwood Report in 1943 and the subsequent 1944 Education Act heralded a new era in secondary education. For the

[1] Meyrick Booth, 'The Present Day Education of Girls – an Indictment', in *Nineteenth Century and After*, August 1927, pp. 259–69.

[2] See for instance W. Felter, 'The Education of Women', *Educational Review*, vol. XXXI, 1906, pp. 351–63.

first time LEAs were required to provide secondary education for all children up the minimum age of fifteen. Fees were abolished in maintained secondary schools from 1945. The marked gulf between the ideology of equality of educational opportunity for all children of both sexes and actual educational practice promised to be diminished as a result of this Act – at least in the public sector of the educational system. However, educational selection as a principle continued to operate – although the criterion for selection became 'innate ability' (measured IQ) rather than 'social class' (as in the Taunton Commission, for instance). As I have suggested this resulted in general use being made of the labels 'academically able' as referring to those children who were believed capable of benefiting from a grammar school education which was defined as 'good-in-itself', and a large residual category of 'less able' were believed to be suited to a more practical and 'relevant' education defined as being oriented towards a *vocation*. Together with the belief in the different 'innate abilities' of children went an assumption of their 'natural interests', which the Norwood Committee considered varied between the sexes. For girls these were still defined as marriage and motherhood, and for boys, a concern with a job or career. This assumption represented the official legitimation of actual differences in the content of the curriculum for boys and girls, particularly in the case of the 'less able'. Like the Hadow Committee, the Norwood Committee subscribed to the belief that there were innate differences between the sexes, but did not recommend the construction of alternative sex-based models of education. Flexibility of curricula and autonomy for teachers were again though to be adequate solutions. Teacher autonomy would be necessarily somewhat curtailed in those schools catering for the 'able' child, i.e. in grammar, direct-grant and private-sector secondary schools, where the structure of curricula and subject choice was constrained by the external demands made by examining bodies and universities.

In spite of the existence of universal secondary education offering equal opportunities for those of equal measured ability, within each category of ability marked differences in the performance, aspirations and expectations of the sexes have continued to exist. These differences have not been defined as a problem either by official Government bodies, by whom they have been generally taken for granted, or by researchers. In those schools catering for middle-class and/or 'able' children these differences manifest themselves in terms of subject choice, numbers of public examinations taken and passed, age of leaving school, destination after leaving, career aspirations, and so on. Documentation describing the differences between the sexes is available in the annual volumes of the *Statistics of Education*. In schools catering for the 'less able' or working-class child, differences of the same sort are found, and in addition there is even more marked sex-differentiation in the provision of 'vocational' courses such as engineering or typing, metalwork or needlework, which are usually only available for those of the appropriate sex.

The Crowther Report, 1959, noted that the less able the girl, the more sex-based her school curriculum was likely to be.

> (of the 'far more able' girls) . . . there is not much scope in school hours for giving them any education which is specifically related to their special needs as women.
> With the less-able girls, however, we think schools can and should make adjustments to the fact that marriage now looms much larger and nearer in the pupils' eyes than ever before.[1]

It is difficult to see why, if interest in marriage and one's personal appearance is seen as 'natural' and a dominating interest for all girls, it is necessary for this interest to be incorporated into the educational experience of the 'less able' girls only. Currently, many educationalists are committed to an educational 'solution' of assimilation – at least in theory – for the 25 per cent of 'able' girls in the public sector of education, and to educational pluralism for the 'less able' remainder. Substantive differences between the sexes still exist at both levels, however much they have been reduced.

Several possible explanations exist for the differences in subject-choice, etc., between boys and girls. Part of the difference may be due to the differential allocation of resources to boys' and girls' schools. Girls' schools have found it more difficult to employ qualified science and mathematics teachers, and have in the past been allocated less laboratory space. The introduction of comprehensive coeducational schools should remove this sort of difficulty. In addition, different opportunities after school may affect the choices made by boys and girls. The quotas and barriers which limit the number of girls at medical schools, at Oxbridge, in some of the professions and apprenticeship schemes have not always been abolished and often continue to exist informally. Above all, teachers, parents and pupils themselves have notions of 'femininity' which affect the treatment and expectations of girl pupils.

Conclusion

Throughout this paper, it has been necessary largely to ignore the variations between schools in terms of their size, source of finance, traditions and whether they are single-sex or coeducational. These are important considerations, but for the purposes of this paper I wanted to make very general preliminary statements about the relationships between ideology and practice in the history of girls' education.

In my opening paragraphs I suggested that 'male' and 'female' have not been prominent explanatory categories in educational models and philosophies in the way that the categories 'able' and 'less able' have been. I have tried to show that notions concerning 'femininity' have been

---

[1] Report of the Central Advisory Council for Education '15–18', Ministry of Education 1959, The Crowther Report, Para 51.

shown to vary both historically and between the social classes; and to be dialectically related to the changing roles of women in the society. Many questions remain unanswered which seem to be important and interesting. For example: why have science and mathematics been defined as subjects which girls were predisposed to find difficult? Why have differences in performance between girls and boys been seen as unproblematic? How do teachers in schools define 'femininity' today, and does this affect the treatment and expectations of female pupils *vis-à-vis* male pupils?

This paper is a first step towards raising some of the problems associated with sex-typing in schools – I hope that there will be others.

Bibliography

Abbott, S., and Love, B., *Sappho was a Right-on Woman* (Stein and Day), 1972

Abel-Smith, B., *Value for Money in Health Services* (Heinemann), 1976

Aberle D. F. et al., 'Functional Prerequisites of Society', *Ethics*, 60, 1950

Abrams, P., 'The Conflict of Generations in Industrial Society' (*Journal of Contemporary History*, vol. 5, no. 1, 1970)

Abrams, P., and McCulloch, A., *Communes, Sociology and Society* (Cambridge University Press), 1976

Adorno, T. W. et al., *The Authoritarian Personality* (Harper), 1950

Allen, S., Sanders, L., and Wallis, J., *Condition of Illusion* (Feminist Books), 1974

Althusser, L., 'Ideology and Ideological State Apparatuses (Notes towards an Investigation)' (1970), in *Lenin and Philosophy and Other Essays*, trans. Brewster, B. (New Left Books), 1971

Ambrose, P., and Colenutt, B., *The Property Machine* (Penguin), 1975

Ashton, T. S., 'The Treatment of Capitalism by the Historians', in Hayek, F. A. von (ed.), *Capitalism and the Historians* (Routledge and Kegan Paul), 1954

Atkinson, J. M., 'Societal Reactions to Suicide: the role of the Coroner', Cohen, S. (ed.), *Images of Deviance* (Penguin), 1971

Atkinson, P., 'Reproduction of Medical Knowledge', Dingwall et al., *Health Care and Health Knowledge* (Croom Helm), 1975

Austin, J. L., *Performative Utterances in Philosophical Papers* (Blackwell), pp. 233–52, 1970

Bagley, C., 'Sick Role, Deviance and Medical Care', *Journal of Social and Economic Administration*, 5:3, pp. 42–57, 1971

Banton, M., *Racial Minorities* (Fontana), 1972

Baratz, J., and Baratz, S., 'Early Childhood Intervention; the Social Science Basis of Institutionalised Racism', *Harvard Educational Review 20 (1)*, Winter 1970, 29–50, abstracted in Open University Educational Studies: second level course E282, units 9 and 10. Open University, 1970

Barker, E., *The Politics of Aristotle* (Oxford University Press), 1947

Barnard, K., and Lee, K., *Conflicts in the Health Service* (Croom Helm), 1976

Barnes, D. et al., *Language, the Learner and the School* (Penguin), 1969

Bauer, P., *Dissent on Development* (Weidenfeld and Nicolson), 1971

Beauvoir, Simone de, *The Second Sex* (Penguin), 1976

Becker, H., 'Problems of Inference and Proof in Participant Observation', 1958, in Becker, H., *Sociological Work* (Allen Lane), 1971, 'The Career of the Chicago Public School Teacher', *American Journal of Sociology*, vol. 57, 1952

Becker, H., Geer, B., and Hughes, E., *Making the Grade* (Wiley), 1968

Becker, H., Geer, B., Hughes, E., and Strauss, A., *Boys in White* (Chicago Press), 1961

Becker, H. S., *Outsiders: Studies in Sociology of Deviance* (Free Press), 1963; *Making the Grade* (John Wiley), 1968; 'Whose Side Are We On?', Douglas, J. D. (ed.), *The Relevance of Sociology* (Appleton-Century-Crofts), 1970

Bell, D., *The End of Ideology: on the exhaustion of political ideas in the Fifties* (Collier Books), 1961; *The Coming of Post Industrial Society* (Heinemann), 1975

Benney, M., Gray, A. P., and Pear, R. H., *How People Vote* (Routledge and Kegan Paul), 1956

Benston, Margaret, 'The Political Economy of Women's Liberation', *Monthly Review XXI*, 1969

Berelson, B., Lazarsfeld, P., and McPhee, W., *Voting* (University of Chicago Press), 1954

Berg, I., *Education and Jobs: The Great Training Robbery* (Penguin), 1973

Berger, Bennett, 'On the Youthfulness of Youth Cultures', *Social Research*, vol. 30, 1963, pp. 319–42

Berger, P., and Kellner, H., 'Marriage and the Construction of Reality', Cosin, B. (ed.), *School and Society: A Sociological Reader* (Routledge and Kegan Paul), 1971

Berger, P., and Luckmann, T., *The Social Construction of Reality* (Allen Lane), 1967

Berger, P. L., *Invitation to Sociology, A Humanistic Perspective* (Penguin), 1966

Bernstein, B., 'The Sociology of Education: A Brief Account', Bernstein, B. (ed.), *Class, Codes and Control*, vol. 111 (Routledge and Kegan Paul), 1975

Bernstein, B. B., and Henderson, D., 'Social Class Differences in the Relevance of Language to Socialization; *Sociology*, 3, 1–20, 1969

Beynon, H., *Working for Ford* (EP), 1975

Bittner, E., *Police Discretion in the Emergency Apprehension of Mentally Ill Persons, Social Problems*, vol. 14, 1967

Blackburn, R., 'Inequality and Exploitation', *New Left Review*, 1967: also to be found as 'The Unequal Society' Urry. J. and Wakeford, J. (eds), 1973, *Power in Britain* (Heinemann Educational Books)

Blake, J., *Family Structure in Jamaica* (Free Press), 1961

Blishen, E., *The School that I'd Like* (Penguin), 1969; 'Why Some Secondary Teachers are Disliked', *Where?* September 1973; 'Your Children on Their Teacher', *Where?* September 1973

Bloor, M., 'Bishop Berkeley and the Adenotonsillectomy Enigma', *Sociology*, 1976

Blumer, H., 'Society as Symbolic Interaction', in Rose, A., *Human Behaviour and Social Processes* (Routledge and Kegan Paul), 1962

Bogdan, R., and Taylor, J. S., *Introduction to Qualitative Research Methods* (John Wiley), 1975

Bott, E., *Family and Social Network* (Tavistock), 1957

Bowlby, J., *Maternal Care and Mental Health* (WHO Monograph), 1952

Bowles, S., and Gintis, H., *Schooling in Capitalist America: Educational Reform and the Contradictions of Economic Life* (Routledge and Kegan Paul), 1976

Boyden, S., 'Evolution and Health', *Ecologist*, vol. 3, no. 8, August 1973, pp. 304–9

Boyle, C., 'Differences between Patients and Doctors, Interpretations of some Common Medical Terms', in Cox, op. cit., 1975

Braginski, B. and D., and King, R., *Method in Madness: the mental hospital as the last resort* (Holt, Rinehart and Winston), 1969

Braverman, H., *Labor and Monopoly Capital. The Degradation of Work in the Twentieth Century*, Monthly Review Press, 1974

British Humanist Association, *Objective, Fair and Balanced – a new law for religion in education* (BHA publication), 1975

British Medical Association, *Health Service Financing* (BMA), 1967

Brown, G. W., *The Social Causes of Disease*, in Tuckett, op. cit., 1976

Bruyn, S. T., *The Human Perspective* (Prentice-Hall), 1966

Bunker, J., 'Risks and Benefits of Surgery', Taylor, D. (ed.), *Benefits and Risks in Medical Care* (OHE), 1974, pp. 85–92

Butler, D., and Stokes, D. E., *Political Change in Britain* (Macmillan), 1969

Byrne, P., and Long, B., *Doctors Talking to Patients* (DHSS/HMSO), 1976

CIS, *Your Money and Your Life* (CIS), 1974

Campbell, A. et al., *The American Voter* (Wiley), 1965

Carne, R. et al., 'Problems of an Immigrant Population', *Proc. Roy. Soc. Med.*, vol. 63, pp. 629–36, 1976

Carstairs, A., 'Distribution of Hospital Patients by Social Class', *Health Bulletin*, July 1966

Carter, M. P., Jephcott, A. P., and Sprott, W. J. H., *The Social Background of Delinquency* (University of Nottingham Typograph), 1954

Cartwright, A., *Patients and Their Doctors* (Routledge and Kegan Paul), 1967

Catton, W. R. and Smircich, R. J., 'A Comparison of Mathematical Models for the Effect of Residential Propinquity on Mate Selection', *American Sociological Review*, 29, 522–9; also in Anderson, M. (ed.), *Sociology of the Family* (Penguin Education), 1964

Chambers, W., and R. (eds), *Chambers' Information for the People, Volume 11*, (Chambers), 1857

Chapman, D., *Sociology and the Stereotype of the Criminal* (Tavistock), 1968

Chater, A., *Race Relations In Britain* (Lawrence and Wishart), 1966

Cheetham, J., and Hill, M. J., 'Community Work: Social Realities and Ethical Dilemmas', *British Journal of Social Work*, vol. 3, no. 3, Autumn 1973

Chesler, P., *Women and Madness* (Avon), 1972

China Health Care Study Group, *Health Care in China*, Christian Medical Commission, Geneva, 1974

Cicourel, A., *Method and Measurement in Sociology* (Free Press), 1964

Cicourel, A. V., and Kitsuse, J., *The Educational Decision Makers* (Bobbs-Merrill), 1963

Clark, D., 'The Concept of Community: A re-examination', *The Sociological Review*, vol. 21 (3), August 1973

Cochrane, A. L., *Effectiveness and Efficiency; Random Reflections on the Health Service*, Rock Carding Lecture, 1971, Nuffield Provincial Hospitals Trust, 1972

Cochrane, A. L., Chapman, P. J., and Oldham, P. D., 'Observer Errors in taking Medical Histories', *Lancet*, i, pp. 1007–9, 1951

Cole, L., 'Playing Russian Roulette with Biochemical Cycles', in Dreitzel, op. cit., 1971

Coleman, D. A., 'Marriage Movement in British Cities', Roberts, D. F. and Sunderland, E. (eds), *Genetic Variation in Britain* (Taylor and Francis), 1973; 'Assortative Mating in Britain', Chester, R. and Peel, J. (eds), *Equalities and Inequalities in Family Life* (Academic Press), 1977

Coleman, J., *Community Conflict* (Collier-Macmillan), 1957

Coleman, J. S., *The Adolescent Society* (Free Press), 1957

Colfax, J. D., and Roach, J. L., *Radical Sociology* (Basic Books), 1971

Comer, L., *Wedlocked Women* (Feminist Books), 1974; 'The Myth of Motherhood', *Spokesman Pamphlet*, no. 21, 1972

Community Relations Council, *Summary of the PEP report on Racial Discrimination*, Community Relations Council, 1972

Cornford, F. M. (trans.), *The Republic of Plato* (Oxford University Press), 1941

Coser, L. A., *The Functions of Social Conflict* (Free Press), 1954; *Continuities in the Study of Social Conflict* (Free Press), 1967

Cotgrove, S., *The Science of Society* (George Allen and Unwin), 1967

Cottle, T., 'School Suspension in America', *New Society*, 30 September 1976

Coulson, M. A., and Riddell, C., *Approaching Sociology* (Routledge and Kegan Paul), 1970

Cox, C., and Mead, A. (eds), *A Sociology of Medical Practice* (Collier-Macmillan), 1975

Cross, C., 'Masons', *Observer Supplement* (18 June 1967), 1967

Crossland, C. A. R., 'The Future of the Left', *Encounter*, March 1960, 1960

Daniel, W., *Racial Discrimination in England* (Penguin), 1968

Daniels, A., 'The Social Construction of Military Psychiatric Diagnoses', in Dreitzel, H., *Recent Sociology 2* (Collier-Macmillan), 1978

Davies, B., *Social Control and Education* (Methuen), 1976

Davies, L., and Meighan, R., 'A Review of Schooling and Sex Roles', *Educational Review*, vol. 27, no. 3, 1975

Davis, F., 'Deviance Disavowal: the Management of Strained Interaction by the Visibly Handicapped', *Social Problems*, 9, 120–32, 1961

Davis, K. and Moore W. E., 'The Functionalist Theory of Stratification', Bendix and Lipset (eds), *Class, Status and Power* (Routledge and Kegan Paul), 1953

Davison, R., *Black British* (Oxford University Press/IRR), 1962

Dawe, A., 'The Two Sociologies', *British Journal of Sociology*, vol. 21, 1970, pp. 207–18

Dawson, J. et al., 'A Four Years Study of Patients with Pulmonary Tuberculosis', Bulletin World Health Organisation, 1960

Dearlove, J., 'The Control of Change and the Regulation of Community Action', Jones, D., and Mayo, M. (eds), *Community Work One* (Routledge and Kegan Paul), 1974

Defoe, D., *Robinson Crusoe*, 1719

Dingwall, R., *The Social Organisation of Health Visitor Training* (Croom Helm), 1976

Djukanovic, V., and Mach, E., *Alternative Approaches to Meeting Basic Health Care Needs in Developing Countries* (WHO), 1975

Douglas, J., *The Social Meanings of Suicide* (Princeton University Press), 1967

Doyal, L., and Pennell, I., 'Pox Britannica; Health Medicine and Underdevelopment', *Race and Class*, vol. XVIII, no. 2, 1976

Dreitzel, H., 'The Social Organisation of Health', *Recent Sociology*, no. 3 (Collier-Macmillan), 1971

Dubois, *Man Adapting* (Yale University Press), 1965

Durkheim, E., *Suicide*, trans. Spaulding and Simpson (Routledge and Kegan Paul), 1952; *Rules of Sociological Method* (Free Press), 1950; *Elementary Forms of Religious Life* (Collier N.Y.), 1961

Easton, D., and Hess, R. D., 'The Child's Political World', *Midwest Journal of Political Science*, 6: 229–46, 1962

Easthope, G. *A History of Social Research Methods* (Longman), 1974

Edgerton, R., *Behavioural Research in Mental Retardation*, Prehm, H. J., Hamerlynck, L. A., and Crosson, J. E. (eds) (University of Oregon), 1968

Ehrenreich, B., and English,, D., *Complaints and Disorders; the Sexual Politics of Sickness* (Compendium Books), 1974

Eisenstadt, S. N., *From Generation to Generation* (Routledge and Kegan Paul), 1956; 'Archetypal Patterns of Youth', *Daedalus*, vol. 91, no. 1, 1962, pp. 28–46

Eliot, T. S., 'The Hollow Men', 'A Penny for the Old Guy', in *Collected Poems 1909–1962* (Faber and Faber), 1963

Engels, F., *The Origins of the Family, Private Property, and the State* (Charles H. Kerr and Co.), 1902

Engels, F., and Marx, K., *The German Ideology*, 1846. The version used for this paper is that edited by Arthur, C. J. (students' edition) (Lawrence and Wishart), 1974

Epson, P., *The Mobile Health Clinic* (London Borough of Southwark), 1969

Erikston, E., *Identity: Youth and Crisis* (Faber), 1968

Eysenck, H. J., *Race, Intelligence and Education* (Temple Smith/New Society), 1971

Fanon, F., *Black Skins, White Masks* (Paladin), 1970

Festinger, L., Riecken, H. W., and Schachter, S., *When Prophecy Fails* (University of Minnesota Press), 1954

Feuer, Lewis S., *The Conflict of Generations* (Basic Books Inc.), 1969

Filmer, P. Phillipson, M., Silverman, D., and Walsh, D., *New Directions in Sociological Theory* (Collier Macmillan), 1972

Fitton, B., 'Behaviour Ratings of Criteria for Behaviour Modification', *Journal of Association of Educational Psychologists*, 1972

Flacks, Richard, 'The Liberated Generation: An exploration of the roots of student protest', *Journal of Social Issues*, vol. 23, 1967, pp. 52–75

Fletcher, C., *Beneath the Surface* (Routledge and Kegan Paul), 1974

Fletcher, C. M., 'Criteria for Diagnosis and Assessment in Clinical Trials', in Hill, A. B., *Controlled Clinical Trials* (Blackwell), 1960

Food and Drugs Administration, Survey on behalf of FDA by National Academy of Science and National Research Council 1967–69, FDA, 1971

Foot, P., *Immigration and Race in British Politics* (Penguin), 1965

Forsyth, K., *Doctors and State Medicine* (Pitman), 1973

Foster, P., *Education and Social Change in Ghana* (Routledge and Kegan Paul), 1967

Foster-Carter, A., 'Neo-Marxist Approaches to Development and Underdevelopment', Kadt, E. de, and Williams, C. (eds), *Sociology and Development* (Tavistock), 1974

Frank, A. G., *Latin America, Underdevelopment or Revolution* (Monthly Review Press), 1970

Frankenberg, R., *Village on the Border* (Cohen and West), 1957; *Communities in Britain* (Penguin) 1966

Frankenberg, R., and Leeson, 'Disease, Illness and Sickness', in Loudon, J., *Social Anthropology and Medicine* (Academic), 1976

Freidson, E., *The Profession of Medicine* (Dodd Mead), 1972

Friedan, B., *The Feminine Mystique* (Penguin), 1968

Fromm, E., *The Fear of Freedom* (Routledge and Kegan Paul), 1968

Galbraith, J. K., *The Affluent Society* (Penguin), 1958

Gamson, W., 'Rancorous Conflict in Community Politics', *American Sociological Review*, vol. 31, 1966

Garfinkel, H., *Studies in Ethnomethodology* (Prentice Hall), 1967

Gavron, H., *The Captive Wife* (Routledge and Kegan Paul), 1966

Gerth, H. H., and Mills, C. W., *From Max Weber* (Routledge and Kegan Paul), 1970

Glaser, N., and Strauss, A., *Awareness of Dying* (Aldine), 1965

Gluckman, M., *Custom and Conflict in Africa* (Oxford), 1955

Goffman, E., *Encounters* (Bobbs-Merrill), 1951 (Allen Lane), 1962; *Asylums* (Doubleday Anchor), 1961 (Penguin), 1968; *Stigma: Notes on the Management of Spoiled Identity* (Prentice-Hall), 1963; 'The Inmate World', Cressey, D. (ed.) *The Prison, Studies in Institutional Organisation and Change*, New York, 1961; *The Presentation of Self in Everyday Life* (Doubleday Anchor), 1959 (Allen Lane), 1969 (Penguin), 1971; *Behaviour in Public Places* (Allen Lane), 1963; *Strategic Interaction* (Allen Lane), 1970

Gold, R., 'Roles in Sociological Field Observation', 1958, in Denzin, N. K., *Sociological Methods* (Aldine), 1970

Golding, W., *Lord of the Flies* (Faber), 1954

Goldthorpe, J., and Lockwood, D., *The Affluent Worker: Industrial Attitudes and Behaviour* (Cambridge University Press), 1968

Goldthorpe, J. H., Lockwood, D., Bechhofer, F., and Platt, J., *The Affluent Worker: Political Attitudes and Behaviour* (Cambridge University Press), 1968a; *The Affluent Worker: Industrial Attitudes and Behaviour* (Cambridge University Press), 1968b; *The Affluent Worker in the Class Structure* (Cambridge University Press), 1969

Goodacre, E., 'Teachers and Their Pupils' Home Background', Open University Course Team, *School and Society* (Routledge and Kegan Paul), 1971

Goode, W. J., and Hatt, P. K., *Methods in Social Research* (McGraw-Hill), 1952

Goodson, I., 'Illusion and Reality', *New Era*, August 1976, 1976

Gorer, G., *Sex and Marriage in England Today* (Nelson), 1971

Gouldner, A., *For Sociology* (Penguin), 1973

Gouldner, A., *The Coming Crisis of Western Sociology* (Heinemann), 1971

Gough, K., 'The Origin of the Family', *Journal of Marriage and the Family*, November 1971

Greer, G., *The Female Eunuch* (Paladin), 1971

HMSO, *Report of the Committee of Enquiry into the Relationship of the Pharmaceutical Industry with the National Health Service, 1965–67*, Cmnd 4310; *Chlordiazepoxide and Diazepam*, The Monopolies Commission, 1973; *Fit for the Future: Report of the Committee on Child Health Services*, Cmnd 6684, 1976; *Report of the Parliamentary Commissioner on Acre Mill, 1976*, Social Trends, 1976, no. 7

Hall, P., Lend, H., Parker, R., and Webb, A., *Change, Choice and Conflict in Social Policy* (Heinemann), 1976

Hall, S., and Jefferson, T. (eds), *Resistance Through Rituals* (Hutchinson), 1976

Halmos, P., *The Personal Service Society* (Constable), 1970

Hampden-Turner, C., *Radical Man* (Duckworth), 1970

Hargreaves, D., *Social Relations in a Secondary School* (Routledge and Kegan Paul), 1967

Hargreaves, D., Heston, S., and Miller, F., *Deviance in Classrooms* (Routledge and Kegan Paul)

Harpur, J. et al., 'Controlled Study of Early Mobilization and Discharge from Hospital', *Lancet*, ii, pp. 1331–4

Harre, H. R., and Secord, P. F., *The Explanation of Social Behaviour* (Blackwell), 1972

Harris, R., and Seldon, A., *Choice in Welfare* (IEA), 1965

Hazelmere Group, *Who Needs Drug Companies?*, Hazelmere/War on Want/Third World First, pub. nel.

Heller, J., *Catch 22* (Corgi), 1964

Heller, T., *Poor Health, Rich Profits: multinational drug companies in the Third World* (Spokesman Books), 1977

Hindess, B., *The Use of Official Statistics in Sociology* (Macmillan), 1973

Hinkle, L., and Pluman, N., 'Life Stress and Individual Absenteeism', *Medicine and Surgery*, vol. 21, pp. 365–75, 1952

Hoare, Q., and Nowell-Smith, G. (ed. and trans.), *Selections from the Prison Notebooks of Antonio Gramsci* (Lawrence and Wishart), 1971

Hobsbawm, E., *Industry and Empire* (Penguin), 1968

Hodgkinson, R., *Science and Public Health*, AST 281, Block 5, Unit 10, Open University, 1973

Hoffman et al., *Woman-identified-woman*, paper for Second Congress to Unite Women, 1970

Holt, J., *How Children Fail* (Penguin), 1970

Horobin, G., and Bloor, M., 'Conflict and Conflict Resolution in Doctor/Patient Interactions', in Cox, op. cit.

Horowitz, I., 'Establishment Sociology: the Value of Going Value Free', *Inquiry*, Spring 1963

Horowitz, M. (ed.), *Peoples and Cultures of the Caribbean* (Natural History Press), 1971

Howe, G., *A Geography of Life and Death: Man, Environment and Disease in Britain* (Penguin), 1976

Hughes, C., and Hunter, J., 'Disease and Development in Africa', in Dreitzel, op. cit., 1971

Hughes, J. A., *Sociological Analysis* (Nelson), 1976

Hurley, R., 'Health Crisis of the Poor', in Dreitzel, op. cit., 1971

Hyman, H., *Interviewing in Social Research* (University of Chicago Press), 1954

Illich, I., *Medical Nemesis* (Marion Boyars), 1975

Institute for Research into Mental Retardation, *Sixth Annual Report*, 1 April 1971–31 March 1972, London 1972.

Isaacs, B., *Survival of the Unfittest* (Routledge and Kegan Paul), 1972

Israel, J., and Eliasson, R., 'Consumption, Society, Sex Roles, and Sexual Behaviour', Dreitzel, H. P. (ed.), *Family, Marriage and the Struggle of the Sexes*, 1972

Jackson, B., and Marsden, D., *Education and the Working Class* (Routledge and Kegan Paul), 1962

Jackson, P., 'The Student's Work', in Silverman, M. L., *The Experience of Schooling* (Holt, Rinehart, Winston), 1971

Jefferson, G., 'Side Sequences', Sudnow, D. (ed), *Studies in Social Interaction* (Free Press), pp. 294–338, 1972

Jencks, Christopher, and Riesman, David, 'The War between the Generations', *The Record*, vol. 69, 1967, pp. 1–21

Jones, K., 'Immigrants and the Social Services', *National Institute Economic Review*, no. 41, August 1967

Katz, D., 'Do Interviewers Bias Polls?', *Public Opinion Quarterly*, vol. 6, pp. 248–68, 1942

Keddie, N., *Tinker Tailor . . . , the Myth of Cultural Deprivation* (Penguin), 1973

Kerr, C., *Industrialism and Industrial Man* (Heinemann), 1962

Klass, A., *There's Gold in them there Pills* (Penguin), 1975

Klein, J., *Samples from English Culture*, vol. 1 (Routledge and Kegan Paul), 1965

Klein, R., and Ashley, J., 'Old Age Health', *New Society*, 6 January 1972

Kluckhohn, F., 'The Participant Observer Technique in Small Communities', *American Journal of Sociology*, 1940. Also quoted in Carter, M. P. (1954, p. 82), Bruyn, S. T. (1966, p. 14), and Parker, H. (1974, p. 222)

Kohl, H., *The Open Classroom* (Methuen), 1969

Krischt, J. P. et al., 'A National Study of Health Beliefs', *Journal of Health and Human Behaviour*, Winter, pp. 248–54, 1966

Labov, W., 'The Logic of Non Standard English', *Georgetown Monographs on*

Language and Linguistics, vol 22, pp. 1–31. Reprinted in Giglioli, P. P. (ed.), *Language and Social Context* (Penguin), 1972, pp. 179–216

Laing, R., and Esterson, A., *Sanity, Madness and the Family* (Penguin), 1969

Lane, T., and Roberts, K., *Strike at Pilkingtons* (Fontana), 1971

Lasch, C., 'The Narcissist Society', *New York Review of Books*, 30 September 1976

Last, G., 'The Iceberg: Completing the Clinical Picture in General Practice', *Lancet*, ii, 1963

Lenski, Gerhard, *Power and Privilege: A theory of social stratification* (McGraw-Hill), 1969

Lewis, J., *Max Weber and Value Free Sociology* (Lawrence and Wishart), 1975

Levi, E., *The History of Magic* (Rider), 1969

Levin, L., Katz, A., and Holst, E., *Self-Care: Lay initiatives in health* (Croom Helm), 1976

Liebow, E., *Tally's Corner* (Little, Brown and Co.), 1967

Lindsay, A., *Socialised Medicine in England and Wales* (North Carolina Press), 1962

Lipset, S. M., and Ladd, E. C., 'College Generations and their Politics', *New Society*, 1971

Lockwood, D., *The Black Coated Worker* (Allen and Unwin), 1958

Lomas, G. B., The Census of 1971: *The Coloured Population of Great Britain, Preliminary Report* (Runnymede Trust), 1974; *Census of Population of Great Britain*, 1971; *Colour and Citizenship*, 1966; *New Community*, vol. 3, 1976; *Ethnic Minorities in Britain: Statistical Data*, Community Relations Commission; *Race Relations Bulletin*, no. 29, 1972

Lundberg, G. A., Schrag, C. C., and Larsen, O. N., *Sociology* (Harper Bros.), 1958

Lupton, T., *On the Shop Floor* (Pergamon), 1963; *Management and the Social Sciences* (Penguin), 1971

MacKeith, N., *Womans' Health Handbook* (P. S. King and Son), 1976

McClain, E., *The Relationship Between Student Teacher Self Perception and Pupil Education*, unpublished doctoral thesis (University of Texas), 1961

McCleary, G., *The Maternal and Infant Welfare Movement* (George Allen and Unwin), 1935

McGinley, P., Mid Century Love Letter quoted in Poppenheim, F., 'The Alienation of Modern Man: an Interpretation based on Marx and Tonnies', *Monthly Review Press*, 1967

McKeown, T., 'A Sociological Approach to the History of Medicine', in McLachlan, G., and McKeown, T., *Medical History and Medical Cares* (Oxford University Press), 1971

McKeown, T., and Record, R., 'Reasons for the Decline of Mortality in England and Wales, during the Nineteenth Century', *Population Studies*, 16, pp. 94–122, 1962

McMichael, J., *Health in the Third World: studies from Vietnam* (Spokesman Books), 1976

McMurty, J., 'Monogamy: A Critique', *The Monist*, vol. 56, 1972

McRobbie, A., and Brooke, E., 'A Girl's Best Friend', *Spare Rib*, no. 35, May 1977

Maddison, S., in Taylor, L., and Taylor, I., *Politics and Deviance* (Penguin), 1973

Maizels, J., 'How Leavers Rate Teachers', *New Society*, 24 September 1970, 1970

Makins, V., 'Child's Eye View of Teacher', *Times Educational Supplement*, 19 and 26 September 1969, 1969

Mannheim, K., *Essays in the Sociology of Knowledge* (Routledge and Kegan Paul), 1956

Marx, K., *Capital, Volume 1* (Lawrence and Wishart), 1961; *The Economic and Philosophic Manuscripts of 1844*, 1964, quoted in J. Mitchell, *Women's Estate*

Marx, K., and Engels, F., *The German Ideology* (Progress Publishers – Moscow), 1964 (Lawrence and Wishart), 1973; Feuerback, 'Opposition of the Materialist and Idealist Outlooks', in the first part of *The German Ideology*; *Manifesto of the Communist Party*, Cohen, C. (ed.), *Communism, Fascism and Democracy* (Random House), 1972; *School and Society: A Sociological Reader* (Routledge and Kegan Paul/Open University), 1971

Matsumoto, Y., 'Social Stress and Coronary Heart Disease in Japan', in Dreitzel, op. cit., 1971

Mauksh, J., 'Ideology, Interactions and Patient Care in Hospitals', *Social Science and Medicine*, vol. 7, no. 10, 1973

Mead, M., *Sex and Temperament in Three Primitive Societies* (William Morrow), 1935

Mechanic, D., *Medical Sociology: a selective overview* (Free Press), 1966

Medvedev, R., *A Question of Madness* (Penguin), 1969

Meighan, R., 'Pupils' Perceptions of the Classroom Techniques of Postgraduate Student Teachers', *British Journal of Teacher Education*, vol. 3, no. 2, 1977a; 'The Concepts of Authoritarian and Democratic Regimes and Classroom Discipline', *Dudley Educational Journal*, Spring 1974a; 'Children's Judgements of the Teaching Performance of Student Teachers', *Educational Review*, vol. 27, no. 1, 1974b; 'The Pupil as Client: The Learner's Experience of Schooling', *Educational Review*, vol. 29, no. 2, 1977b

Melzack, R., *The Puzzle of Pain* (Penguin), 1973

Merton, R. K., *Social Theory and Social Structure* (Free Press), 1957

Miliband, R., *The State in Capitalist Society* (Weidenfeld and Nicolson), 1969

Mills, C. W., 'The Professional Ideology of Social Pathologists', Horowitz, J. L. (ed.), *Power, Politics and People* (Oxford University Press), 1967

Mills, C. Wright, *The Sociological Imagination* (Penguin), 1969

Millum, T., *Images of Women* (Chatto and Windus), 1975

Mitchell, J., *Women's Estate* (Pelican), 1971; *Psychoanalysis and Feminism* (Allen Lane), 1974 (Penguin), 1975

Mohl, H., 'Das Image des Arztes. Ergebnisse eine reprasentative Betragung', *Deutsches Arzteblatt*, no. 25, 1969

Morris, D. et al., 'Early Discharge after Hernia Repair', *Lancet*, pp. 681–3, 1968; *An Introduction to Epidemiology* (Livingstone), 1964

Moser, C. A., *Survey Methods in Social Investigation* (Heinemann), 1958

Musgrave, P. W., *The Sociology of Education* (Methuen), 1965

Musgrove, F., *Youth and the Social Order* (Routledge and Kegan Paul), 1964

Nash, R., *Classrooms Observed* (Routledge and Kegan Paul), 1973

National Children's Bureau, *Born to Fail* (NCB), 1975

Navarro, V., *Medicine under Capitalism* (Croom Helm), 1976

Nicoll, A., 'American Health Care in Expansion and Crisis', *Medicine in Society*, vol. 3, no. 2, 1977

Oakley, A., *Sex, Gender and Society* (Temple Smith), 1972; 'The Trap of Medicalised Motherhood', *New Society*, 18 December 1975, pp. 639–41; *Housewife* (Pelican), 1976

Open University, D 101 Summer School Material, 1976

Orwell, G., *Animal Farm* (Penguin), 1951

Owen, D., *In Sickness and in Health: the politics of medicine* (Quartet), 1976

Parker, H. J., *View from the Boys* (David and Charles), 1974

Parkin, F., *Middle Class Radicalism* (Manchester University Press), 1968; *Class, Inequality and the Political Order* (Paladin), 1970 (Granada Paladin), 1972

Parsons, T., *The Social System* (Routledge and Kegan Paul), 1951; 'The School Class as a Social System: Some of its Functions in American Society', *Social Structure and Personality* (Free Press/Macmillan), 1964

Patrick, J., *A Glasgow Gang Observed* (Eyre Methuen), 1973

Pearson, G., *The Deviant Imagination* (Heinemann), 1976

Pierce, R. M., 'Marriage in the 50's', *Sociological Review*, II, 2, 215–40, 1963

Pinker, R., *Social Theory and Social Policy* (Heinemann), 1971

Platt, A., 'The Rise of the Child-Saving Movement', Cosin, B. et al. (eds), op. cit.

Platt, J., *Social Research in Bethnal Green* (Macmillan), 1971

Plowden Report, *Report of the Central Advisory Council (England), Children and their Primary Schools, vol. 1 Report, vol. 2 Research and Surveys* (HMSO), 1967

Polsky, N., private correspondence reported in Becker, H. (1963, p. 171), *Outsiders* (Free Press), 1963

Pomeranz, R., *The Lady Apprentices*, Occasional Papers in Social Administration, no. 51, LSE, 1973

Pons, V., 'The Community in Modern Society', Worsley, P. (ed.), *Introducing Sociology* (Penguin), 1970

Postman, N., and Weingartner, G., *Teaching as a Subversive Activity* (Penguin)

Powles, J., 'On the Limitations of Modern Medicine', *Science, Medicine and Man*, 1, pp. 31–48, 1973

Pring, R., *Knowledge and Schooling* (Open Books), 1976

Psathas, G., *The Student Nurse in the Diploma School of Nursing* (Springer), 1968

Radcliffe-Brown, A. R., *Structure and Function in Primitive Societies* (Free Press), 1952

Redfield, R., 'The Folk Society', *American Journal of Sociology*, 1947; *The Little Community* (University of Chicago Press), 1955

Rein, M., *Social Science and Public Policy* (Penguin), 1976; 'Social Class and the Health Services', *New Society*, 20 November 1969

Rex, J., 'The Sociology of a Zone of Transition', Pahl, R. E. (ed.), *Readings in Urban Sociology* (Pergamon), 1968

Rex, J., and Moore, R., *Race, Community, and Conflict: A Study of Sparkbrook* (Oxford University Press/IRR), 1976

Roberts, D. F., and Sunderland, E. (eds), *Genetic Variation in Britain* (Taylor and Francis), 1963

Robinson, D., *The Process of Becoming Ill* (Routledge and Kegan Paul), 1971

Roger, C. R., *Client-centred Therapy* (Houghton Mifflin), 1951

Rose, E. J. B. et al., *Colour and Citizenship* (Oxford University Press/IRR), 1967

Rose, M., and Rose, S., *The Political Economy of Science* (Macmillan), 1976

Rose, S., and H., 'The Politics of Neurobiology: Biologism in the Services of the State', in Rose, H., and Rose, S., *The Political Economy of Science* (Macmillan), 1976

Rosen, G., *A History of Mental Illness* (Routledge and Kegan Paul), 1968

Rosenham, D., 'Sane in Insane Places', *Science*, 179, pp. 250–8, 1973

Rosenthal, R., and Jacobson, L., *Pygmalion in the Classroom* (Holt, Rinehart, Winston), 1968

Rosser and Harris, C. C., *The Family and Social Change* (Routledge and Kegan Paul), 1964

Roth, J., *Timetables* (Bobbs-Merrill), 1963

Rowntree, J. S., *Poverty: a study of town life* (Nelson), 1910

Rowntree, John and Margaret, 'Youth as a Class' *International Socialist Journal*, No. 25, pp. 22–58, Feb. 1968

Rutter, M., Tizard, J., and Whitmore, K. (eds), *Education Health and Behaviour* (Longmans), 1970

Sacks, H., 'On the Analysability of Stories by Children', Gumperz, J. J. and Hymes, D. (eds), *Directions in Socio-linguistics* (Holt, Reinhardt and Winston), pp. 239–45, 1972

Sacks, H., and Schegloff, E., *Two Preferences in the Sequential Organisation of Reference to Persons*, unpublished manuscript, no date

Sacks, H., Schegloff, E., and Jefferson, J., 'A Simplest Systematics for the Organisation of Turn Taking for Conversation', *Language*, vol. 50, no. 4, part 1, pp. 696–735, 1974

Salzberger, R., 'Cancer Assumptions and Reality concerning Delay, Ignorance and Fear', in Loudon, J., *Social Anthropology and Medicine* (Academic), 1976

Sanders, W. B., *The Sociologist as Detective* (Praeger), 1974

Saunders, L., *Cultural Differences and Medical Care* (Russell Sage), 1954

Scanzoni, J., *Sexual Bargaining* (Prentice-Hall), 1972

Schegloff, E., 'Sequencing in Conversational Openings', *American Anthropologist*, vol. 70, pp. 1075–95, 1968

Schegloff, E., and Sacks, H., 'Opening up Closings', *Semiotica*, vol. 8, no. 3, pp. 289–332, 1973. Reprinted in Turner, R. (ed.), *Ethnomethodology* (Penguin), 1974, pp. 233–64, 1973

Schenkein, J., 'Towards an Analysis of Natural Conversation and the Sense of Heheh', *Semiotica*, vol. 6, pp. 344–73, 1972

Schenkein, J., and Ryave, A., 'Notes on the Art of Walking', Turner, R. (ed.), *Ethnomethodology* (Penguin), 1974

Schur, E., 'Reactions to Deviance: a Critical Assessment', *American Journal of Sociology*, 75, 305–22, 1969

Schutz, A., *Reflections on the Problems of Relevance* (Yale University Press), 1970; 'The Problem of Rationality in the Social World', in Emmet, D., and Macintyre, A., *Sociological Theory and Philosophical Analysis* (Macmillan), 1970, pp. 89–114; 'The Stranger: an Essay in Social Psychology', *School and Society, a Sociological Reader*, p. 32 (Routledge and Kegan Paul/Open University Press), 1971

Sergeant, G., *A Textbook of Sociology* (Macmillan), 1971

Sharma, U., *Rampal and his Family* (Collins), 1971

Sharpe, P., and Green, A., *Education and Social Control: a study in progressive primary education* (Routledge and Kegan Paul), 1975

Shaw, M., *Marxism and Social Science* (Pluto Press), 1975

Shelton, D. I., unpublished data, 1977

Shils, E. and Young, M., 'The Meaning of the Coronation', *Sociological Review*, 1, 1953

Silberman, M. (ed.), *The Experience of Schooling* (Holt, Rinehart, Winston), 1971

Simey, T. S., quoted in Sprott, W. J. H., *Human Groups*, p. 39 (Penguin), 1958

Simmel, G., Fashion, *American Journal of Sociology*, 1957, pp. 541–58

Simpson, G., and Yinger, J., *Racial and Cultural Minorities: an analysis of prejudice and discrimination* (Harper and Row), 1965

Sjostrom, H., and Nilsson, R., *Thalidomide and the Power of the Drugs Companies* (Penguin), 1972

Skultans, V., 'Empathy and Healing: Aspects of Spiritualist Ritual', in Loudon, J., *Social Anthropology and Medicine*, 1976

Smith, D. J., *The Facts of Racial Disadvantage* (PEP), 1975, Fact Sheet, Immigration, Community Relations Commission

Smith, R., 'Why the East Needs Cash', *The Guardian*, 23 November 1976

Social Science Research Council, *Health and Health Policy: priorities for research* (SSRC), 1977

Sommer, R., *Personal Space. The Behavioural Basis of Design* (Prentice Hall), 1969

Spencer, P., 'Towards a Measure of Social Investment in Communities', *Architectural Research and Teaching*, 1, 3, 32–8, 1971

Spinley, B. M., *The Deprived and the Privileged; Personality Development in English Society* (Routledge and Kegan Paul), 1952

Stark, R., and Glock, C. Y., 'Dimensions of Religious Commitment', Robertson, R. (ed.), *Sociology and Religion* (Penguin), 1963

Stengel, G., *Suicide and Attempted Suicide* (Penguin), 1964

Stimson, G., and Webb, B., *Going to See the Doctor* (Routledge and Kegan Paul), 1975

Stone, J., and Taylor, F., 'The Sad Tale of Pupils' Rights', *Where?*, 122, 1976

Strauss, A., Schatzman, M. et al., *Psychiatric Ideologies and Institutions* (Free Press), 1964

Strauss, A., Schatzman, L., Ehrlick, P., Bucher, R., and Sabshin, M., 'The Hospital and its Negotiated Order', Freidson, E. (ed.), *The Hospital in Modern Society* (Macmillan), 1963

Sudnow, D., *Passing On* (Prentice Hall), 1967; 'Dead on Arrival', in *Society Today* (no. 4, 1976)

Sutherland, E., 'White Collar Criminality', *American Sociological Review*, vol. 5, no. 1, 1940

Szasz, T. S., *The Manufacture of Madness* (Routledge and Kegan Paul), 1971; 'The Sane Slave: A Historical Note on the Use of Medical Diagnosis as a Justificatory Rhetoric', *American Journal of Psychotherapy*, 25. 2, pp. 228–39, 1971

Teeling-Smith, G., 'Off Ill Again', *New Society*, 6 November 1969, p. 731

Tew, M., 'The Children Hospitals Kill', *New Society*, 20 January 1977, pp. 120–1

Titmuss, R., *The Gift Relationship* (George Allen and Unwin), 1972

Townsend, P., 'Inequality and the Health Service', *Lancet*, 15 June 1974, pp.1179 ff

Tuckett, D., *An Introduction to Medical Sociology* (Tavistock), 1976

Turner, Ralph, 'The Theme of Contemporary Social Movements', *British Journal of Sociology*, vol. 1, XX, no. 4, December 1969

Turner, V., 'An Ndembu Doctor in Practice', Kiev, A., *Magic, Faith and Healing* (ed.) (Free Press), 1964

Vadja, M., and Heller, A., 'Family Structure', *Telos no. 1*, Spring 1971

Veldman, D. J. and Peck, R. F. 'Student Teacher Characteristics from the Pupils' Viewpoint', *J. Educ. Psych.*, 54

Wadsworth, M., Butterfield, W., and Blany, R., *Health and Sickness: the choice of treatment* (Tavistock), 1971

Walker, R., Goodson, I., and Adelman, C., *Teaching, that's a joke*, CARE, mimeo, University of East Anglia, 1973

Walker, S., 'Drugging the American Child', *Psychology Today*, vol. 8, no. 7, 1974

Wall, W. D., and Williams, H. L., *Longitudinal Studies and the Social Sciences* (Heinemann Educational), 1970

Waller, W., *The Sociology of Teaching* (John Wiley and Sons), 1932

Wander, M., 'The Conditions of Illusion', 1972, in Allen, S., op. cit.

Warren, N. D., 'Who are the Backward?', *New Society*, 361, 321–2, 1969

Wates, N., *The Battle for Tolmers Square* (Routledge and Kegan Paul), 1976

Webber, M. M., 'Towards a Definition of the Interest Community', Worsley, P. (ed.), *Modern Sociology Introductory Reading* (Penguin), 1970

Weber, M., *The Protestant Ethic and the Spirit of Capitalism* (Allen and Unwin), 1930; *The Methodology of the Social Sciences*, Shils and Finch (Glencoe Free Press), 1949; *Economy and Society* (Bedminster), 1968

Werthman, C., 'Delinquents in School', Cosin, B. (ed.), *School and Society* Routledge and Kegan Paul), 1971

Wilkins, E., *An Introduction to Sociology* (MacDonald and Evans), 1970

Wilkinson, R., 'Dear David Ennals . . .', *New Society*, 16 December 1976, pp. 567–8

Wilson, G., and Nias, D., *Love's Mysteries: the psychology of sexual attraction* (Open Books), 1976

Wolverhampton Council for Community Relations, *Commonwealth Immigration; The Economic Effects* (Runnymede Trust), 1970; *How Black?* (A book of essays by Wolverhampton School Children), Wolverhampton Council for Community Relations, 1972

Woods, P., 'Pupils' View of School', *Ed. Review*, 28, 2 (1976)

Wootton, B., *Social Science and Social Pathology* (Allen and Unwin), 1959

Worsley, P., 'The Distribution of Power in Industrial Societies', Halmos, P. (ed.), *The Sociological Review Monograph No. 8*, October 1964: also to be found in Urry and Wakeford, op. cit.

Yerushalmy, J., Markness, J., Cope, J., and Kennedy, B., 'The Role of Oral Reading in Mass Radiography', *American Review of Tuberculosis*, 61, 1950, pp. 443–64

Young, M., and Willmott, P., *Family and Kinship in East London* (Penguin), 1957

Young, M. F. D., *Knowledge and Control* (Collier-Macmillan), 1971

Zipf, G. K., *Human Behaviour and the Principle of Least Effort* (Addison-Wesley Press), 1949

Zola, I., 'Culture and Symptoms: an Analysis of Patients presenting Complaints', *American Sociological Review*, 31, pp. 615–29, 1966; 'Medicine as an Institution of Social Control', in Cox, op. cit., 1975

Subject Index

Name Index